JUST THEORY

For Art,
    my lifetime mentor.
I know that you have
always been there for me.
This book has roots that
go all the way back to
our time together in
Buffalo.

      always, David.

Just Theory

An Alternative History of the Western Tradition

293 I MAGINING III

DAVID B. DOWNING

Indiana University of Pennsylvania

NCTE

National Council of Teachers of English
1111 W. Kenyon Road, Urbana, Illinois 61801-1096

Publication acknowledgment: Chapter 8, "The Struggle between Communality and Hierarchy: Lessons of the Paris Commune for the Twenty-First Century," is derived in part from an article published in *Socialism and Democracy*, available online: http://www.tandfonline.com/10.1080/08854300.2018.1513757.

Staff Editor: Bonny Graham
Manuscript Editor: Lee Erwin
Interior Design: Jenny Jensen Greenleaf
Cover Design: Pat Mayer
Cover Images: iStock.com/serts; Wellcome Images; Wikimedia Commons

NCTE Stock Number: 25304; eStock Number: 25328
ISBN 978-0-8141-2530-4; eISBN 978-0-8141-2532-8

Library of Congress Cataloging-in-Publication Data

Names: Downing, David B., 1947- author.
Title: Just theory : an alternative history of the western tradition / David B. Downing, Indiana University of Pennsylvania.
Description: Urbana, Illinois : National Council of Teachers of English, [2019] | Includes bibliographical references and index.
Identifiers: LCCN 2018053942 (print) | LCCN 2019002400 (ebook) | ISBN 9780814125328 (ebook) | ISBN 9780814125304 ((pbk))
Subjects: LCSH: Justice (Philosophy) | Knowledge, Theory of. | Metaphysics.
Classification: LCC B105.J87 (ebook) | LCC B105.J87 D68 2019 (print) | DDC 190--dc23
LC record available at https://lccn.loc.gov/2018053942

For Joan

Contents

CONTENTS

Cultural Turn 3. Surviving the Sixth Extinction and Resolving the Crisis of Care

ACKNOWLEDGMENTS

I have written this book for my graduate students. Twice a year for thirty years in our Literature and Criticism doctoral program, I taught various iterations of a course called "The History of Criticism and Theory." Students brought different perspectives and challenging questions to the course, and this engagement with so many important issues greatly enriched my writing of this book. By my calculation I have now had nearly nine hundred students pass through this seminar. Unfortunately, there's simply no way to thank each by name, so I apologize for this generic note of gratitude.

I want to thank my colleagues who serve or have served in the IUP Literature and Criticism Program: Gail Berlin, James Cahalan, Susan Comfort, Ron Emerick, Tanya Heflin, Melanie Holm, Maurice Kilwein Guevara, Chris Kuipers, Chris Orchard, Mike Sell, Ken Sherwood, Tom Slater, Veronica Watson, Michael T. Williamson, and Lingyan Yang. They have provided a remarkably supportive environment, and it has been my pleasure to work with them. The friendship and commitment to high standards and fair working conditions of Gian Pagnucci, chair of the IUP English department, means a great deal to me; assistant chair Todd Thompson (also an L&C colleague) has also been a wonderful friend who has made all of our lives at IUP better since he arrived in 2008. The former directors of the Composition and TESOL Program, Sharon Deckert and Ben Rafoth, were a pleasure to work with during the nine years when I served as director of L&C. Together with the other members of the English department, they made it possible for me to teach and write about things that matter to me. Finally, my dean, Yaw Asamoah, exemplifies a progressive administrator dedicated to the faculty he serves. IUP also granted me both a sabbatical leave and a research award that have helped me complete this book.

This is a long book that has taken me a long time to write, so I really have a lifetime of gratitude for the many colleagues whose conversations and work influenced me in ways that I cannot easily enumerate but that deserve my thanks: Abdullah Al-Dagamseh, Jonathan Arac, Susan Bazargan, Jim Berlin, Don Bialostosky, David Bleich, Michael Blitz, Paul Bové, Kay Boyle, William Cain, Sean Carswell, Ed Carvalho, Leonard Cassuto, Tom Caulfield, Cathy Chaput, Ward Churchill, Ralph Cintrón, Deborah Clarke, Victor Cohen, Teresa Derrickson, Jeffrey DiLeo, Edem Dzregah, Leslie Fiedler, Kevin Floyd, Barbara Foley, Grover Furr, Henry Giroux, Susan Searls Giroux, Robin Truth Goodman, Gerald Graff, Giles Gunn, John Herold, Ruth Hoberman, Patrick Hogan, Claude Mark Hurlbert, Tracy Lassiter, Vincent Leitch, Melissa Lingle-Martin, Steven Mailloux, Jeffrey Markovitz, Paula Mathieu, Sophia McClennen, Eric Meljac, Ellen Messer-Davidow, John Mowitt, Greg Myerson, David Raybin, Joe Ramsey, Ken Saltman, Jeffrey Schragel, John Schilb, Leroy Searle, Cynthia Selfe, David Shumway, Heather Steffen, Ron Strickland, Richard Sylvia, Alan Trachtenberg, Harold Veeser, Victor Vitanza, Evan Watkins, and Martha Woodmansee.

My career-long friend and mentor Arthur Efron first showed me what radical critique and anarchism were all about. Since graduate school, Brian Caraher has been a great friend, intellectual comrade, and one of the original founders of *Works and Days*. I am also very grateful for James Sosnoski and Patricia Harkin, with whom I collaborated for many years; Richard Ohmann represents for me what it means to be a committed intellectual; Marc Bousquet's friendship combined with his stunning analysis of the contemporary university always leads me in new directions; and Jeff Williams, a wonderful friend in the neighborhood, read long sections of this manuscript and offered invaluable advice.

I had the good fortune, once again, to work with exemplary editors and readers at NCTE. A special note of thanks to Kurt Austin, who patiently helped me work through the editorial stages from the proposal, through the readers' reports, to all stages of the editing and publication process. His advice has always been spot on. I have also benefited from having extremely careful readers of the manuscript, so I thank them all for improving the book. I especially want to thank Bonny Graham, who was my production editor at NCTE, and the copyeditors who did an outstanding job with the entire manuscript and saved me from more mistakes of my own than I would like to admit. Any remaining mistakes are, of course, of my own making.

My extended family may not always know exactly what I am up to in my writing, but I am always grateful for their unending support, so I thank John and Sue Clippinger, Rena and Alon Mei-Tal, and Mike and Rosemary Whitney. No words can express my gratitude for my children and grandchildren: Peter, Katie, Nico, and Elliot; Jordan, Kurt, Simone, and Julian. And, of course, my lifetime partner and spouse, Joan, to whom this book is dedicated.

PREFACE: WHAT IS *JUST THEORY*?

Just Theory offers an alternative history of critical theory in the context of the birth and transformation of the Western philosophical tradition. But rather than a summary survey, it situates the production of theoretical texts within the geopolitical economy of just two pivotal cultural turns. Especially in the fifth to fourth centuries BCE, Socrates, Plato, Aristotle, and their cohorts in Athens brought into being a whole new discourse called philosophy. From this bustling southern Mediterranean city, population nearly 300,000 at the time (although only about 40,000 males had the status of citizens), we can now trace forward a 2,500-year history of the aftereffects of what has been called Western metaphysics or European universalism as it migrated around the world. A new vocabulary of reason, logic, and dialectic came into being as a powerful cultural narrative. Twenty-two hundred years later, the founding discourse was significantly reworked so that in different manifestations it could serve both conservative and revolutionary agendas. What happened in the eighteenth and nineteenth centuries in northwestern Europe, particularly in France, Germany, and England, would transform the literary, social, cultural, political, and geophysical landscapes that emerged in the modern world. I refer to these two major cultural revolutions as "cultural turns."[1]

The other key feature of this book is that it focuses on the desire for universalism and the quest for social justice. Whereas most histories of criticism and theory focus on a survey of the history of ideas relatively independent of the geopolitical economy, *Just Theory* situates theoretical texts within their complex social histories. For that reason, I have completely abandoned the coverage model of trying to survey in chronological order the "hit parade" of canonized theorists over the entire history of Western theory.[2] In contrast, I offer close readings of a smaller, select group of texts and authors, always situating the local details within the broader geopolitical economy. There are some obvious risks in this plan to combine the principles of close reading with the sweeping historical narrative. As Anna Tsing puts it, "big histories are always best told through insistent, if humble, details" (111). The real advantage of the framing structure is that it allows me to tell a story that leaves out so much. One of the advantages of theorizing is that by gaining some distance from the particulars, it generalizes, and in our complex worlds we need simplified frames with which to orient ourselves. On those grounds, I hope that my concentration on a few exemplary figures and events will compensate for my otherwise ruthless omission of so many other important writers and movements.

Finally, my focus on these two brief cultural turns situates them within deep time primarily because we are all caught within the transition to an entirely new geological epoch: we are bearing witness to the end of the 11,700-year-old Holocene epoch and the beginning of what many have been calling the Anthropocene. Cultural Turn 1 gave birth to the Western philosophical tradition during the Holocene; Cultural Turn 2 witnessed the beginnings of the shift to the Anthropocene when the Industrial Revolution and the fossil fuel age began to alter our complex biospheres and geospheres.

With increasing persistence, my graduate students in Literature and Criticism have been telling me that we should all be concerned about climate change. They have also repeatedly told me that what they most need to understand the ongoing impact of the Western tradition of philosophy and critical theory are, first, some long-term historical frames to contextualize their encounters with specific theoretical and literary texts; and, second, some detailed close readings linking the frames to the texts. In answer to their requests, I have tried to tell the story I have been teaching. Given my own professional interests in the connections between literature and composition, I also hope that many compositionists, rhetoricians, and linguists will be interested in this book.

I have also tried to interest teachers of graduate courses (and upper-division undergraduate courses) in the history of criticism; and beyond that, faculty in English studies and comparative literature who seek a general overview of the history of the Western tradition. And beyond that, students and faculty in related humanities and social science fields: everything I argue for in this book about the concern for social justice addresses widely shared commitments. I have been aware during the writing process of tensions among these expanding audiences, but I think the overlaps are far greater than the distances. For all these reasons, I have made sure to use ordinary language throughout, translating any specialized terms accordingly. I have also tried to include sufficient detail from the texts I address so that a general reader can make sense of the story without necessarily having read all those sources. We only have so much time, and we inhabit a vulnerable world.

In the early twenty-first century, everyone on the planet is confronted with increasing socioeconomic inequality tied to life-threatening forms of climate change as democratic governments around the world sacrifice public responsibility for human resources to the economic logic of a private market economy. Because of these dramatic ecological changes, the "Anthropocene sweeps humankind into the turbulent flow of geohistory" (Davies 11) so that we are now "being plunged into deep time" (15), like it or not. We, therefore, need accessible historical overviews of the powerful Western justifications for the current global economy, especially as these forces have so altered the geohistory of the planet that they affect all human beings, although in dramatically different ways. In our age, geological history, political history, philosophical history, and literary history are all conjoined. Of course, they always have been, although for the past two hundred years the voices of dissent in the countermovements that objected to the exploitation of the natural world were often ignored or suppressed by the dominant powers. No longer is such suppression possible: the signs are all around us, and scientific knowledge of the history of the planet through carbon dating provides the comparative data. *Just Theory* contributes to this much bigger project through its selective attention to both the dominant cultural narratives in the West and the alternatives opened up by a few of the key countermovements. Although interdisciplinarity has now become a normal practice in most academic fields, my strategy in this book still leads me into many social, political, and geophysical analyses ignored by most comprehensive surveys of literary and cultural theory.[3]

My general thesis is that the two cultural turns are not un-related periods, but deeply interwoven sociohistorical contexts. Despite the historical mutations, Western metaphysics remains (too often in banefully reductive ways) a powerful discourse in our world because its binary hierarchies have become deeply enmeshed in the language, culture, and history of the West, which means it has now taken on global dimensions in our postcolonial geographies. Plato's fear of the world of appearances reappears in the fear (or love) of simulacra and spectacle everywhere in our seemingly postmetaphysical world.

The two main sections of the book correspond to these two cultural turns: Cultural Turn 1 (roughly 450–350 BCE) focuses on the Platonic revolution whereby a new philosophic, universal-ist, and literate discourse emerged from what had long been an oral culture; Cultural Turn 2 (roughly 1770–1870) investigates the Romantic revolution and its nineteenth-century aftermath up to the remarkable two months of the Paris Commune. The Renaissance was certainly the rebirth of interest in the classical Greek writers; and the Enlightenment reinforced the Western philosophical investment in reason and science; but it was the ensuing Romantic period that altered the discourse irrevocably for modernity and altered the political economy by extracting energy sources from beneath the earth's surface. Indeed, ethno-centric versions of Western metaphysics justified human mastery of nature as an objectified "resource" to be endlessly consumed by the wealthy European nations, regardless of the environmental consequences. Nonetheless some strains of what I have called radical Romanticism resisted identifying modernity with capital-ism to the exclusion of alternative possibilities. So it is important in the twenty-first century to recover the origins of these coun-tertraditions. The late-eighteenth- and early-nineteenth-century concerns for alternative geopolitical economies, for mutuality, reciprocity, and social justice rather than endless competition, may now seem naïve or merely wishful thinking, yet they were occurring at the very historical juncture when the fossil fuel age began. As Jeremy Davies argues, "the best conceptual repertoire

Preface: What Is Just Theory?

for ecology at the birth of the Anthropocene might overlap a good deal with the vocabulary of democracy, devolution, and egalitarianism" (200). Much of that vocabulary was rewritten into the discourse of modernity during Cultural Turn 2. So if we are to "guard against philosophically clumsy dualism" (204), we have to understand where the history of those dualisms began in Cultural Turn 1, and how they were rewritten in various ways to both accommodate and resist the capitalist world system.

Indeed, a huge change has taken place in our assessment of Romanticism, particularly after World War II. In the first half of the twentieth century, the work of the Romantic writers was often devalued as a kind of unruly excess, an emotional chaos devoid of rational planning. Jacques Barzun argues that before 1943, when he wrote *Romanticism and the Modern Ego,* the entire Romantic period "was held in particular detestation and contempt: it was naïve, silly, wrongheaded, stupidly passionate, criminally hopeful, and intolerably rhetorical" (*Classic* ix).[4] The origins of this contempt for the Romantics go at least as far back as Matthew Arnold, who explicitly argued that the Romantics lacked intellectual rigor and thoughtfulness, especially in their support of the French Revolution.[5] Ironically, Arnold adopted some of the key doctrines of Romantic idealism, such as the high valuation of art and literature, even while rejecting the more radical strains of Romanticism tied to direct political engagement. Arnold's view of the separation of high culture from the contaminations of "philistine" culture resonated deeply into the twentieth century.[6]

More than ever, we may now need to reconsider these fundamental transformations in our cultural and political histories, especially as they are so deeply affected by our collective responses to the epochal changes in planetary history to which we are now bearing witness. As Terry Eagleton explains, "[W]e ourselves are post-Romantics, in the sense of being products of the epoch rather than confidently posterior to it" (*Literary Theory* 18). Some of the Romantic writers offered powerful ways of integrating art, imagination, nature, culture, and politics. They participated in the rebirth of democratic governments and the creation of the distinctions between public and private domains as they struggled for the revolutionary values of liberty, equality, and justice—vital political concepts that exceed any form of strictly economic language. Yet we live in an age when these crucial distinctions have virtually collapsed, as the private economy infiltrates all social spheres. In the twenty-first century, questions about social justice rarely intrude in the calculations of profit and loss, economic growth, and return on investment (ROI). Such neoliberal economic rationality only intensifies social inequalities and environmental damage, both of which are accompanied by the disturbing worldwide increase in authoritarian political regimes.

When in 1961 Barzun published a revised version of his book, now called *Classic, Romantic, and Modern*, he could argue even more insistently that "the tendency of historic Romanticism was away from authority and toward . . . the sovereignty of the people" (xv), or at least those people who previously had had no voice in social and political decisions affecting their lives. Among many other sociopolitical changes, the newly invigorated category of aesthetics sustained powerful but contentious relationships with the social, political, and economic forces. As we will see in Chapter 6, it was in 1790, at the beginning of Cultural Turn 2, that in *Critique of Judgment* Kant developed some of the most sophisticated philosophical arguments for the autonomy of literary art just as the French Revolution was in its early stages. Some of the nineteenth century's most ardent advocates of political revolution were equally ardent about the need for aesthetic autonomy: they modified Kant's influential ideas as they cheered the revolutionary ideals of freedom and equality even though Kant himself opposed revolution. So it was not always an easy compact: autonomy from sociohistorical contexts could disable the very political agendas being championed by the Romantic revolutionaries. The Romantic tendency to idealize the natural world in contradistinction from the human world of politics and economics could therefore defeat the critique of an economic system that we now know was contributing to massive ecological changes. Like many other critics, Barzun did not really see this two-sided tear in the fabric of Romantic discourse. The conflicts between the idealist and materialist visions have historically varied depending on the circumstances, but the tensions have not disappeared.

Any account of the history of theory will inevitably grapple with the struggle for the big picture, but global perspectives based on deep time are hard to come by, particularly in the atomistic, fragmented, and specialized domains of academic and professional life. Critical theories can be packaged as isolated schools and methods relatively decontextualized from the geopolitical economy in which they were produced. Indeed, in the early twenty-first century, the powerfully marketed common sense of our age is that anything that does not improve an individual's or firm's competitive advantage in the marketplace is just theory, as in useless verbiage cluttering up the real business of being in the world. But there is no such thing as just theory—that is, so long as you understand the word *just* as a synonym for *only,* as in the belief that some set of ideas can be *only* theory, and have nothing to do with practice, the physical world, the political economy, or everyday living. The title of this book thus plays off a pun resonating both an ironic and a literal meaning of the word *just:* just meaning "only," and just meaning "fair." In the first sense, the book title is ironic because it is a distinctly false theory that the essence of pure theory can be divorced from history, politics, economics, and ecology; as if theory could be *only* itself, just *theory.*[7] Indeed, such a metatheory of theories has been the goal for many who seek to "depoliticize" theory—as well as literature, art, economics, education, and, most important, climate change.

In contrast, what I have been calling *just theory* is a literal, non-ironic, evaluative term naming the good kind of theory that contributes to making the world a more just place. Just theory includes both the negative critique of oppressive hierarchies and the positive affirmation of life-sustaining possibilities. The twentieth-century philosopher Paul Ricoeur famously coined the phrase "hermeneutics of suspicion" to describe the kinds of interpretive work that could uncover the complicities of political oppression in virtually any discourse. But he also spoke about the dialectical necessity of its theoretical opposite, what he called the "hermeneutics of recovery," and what Eve Kosofsky Sedgwick called "reparative criticism."[8] Such theory often arrives as a reflective response to a problem or painful situation, with the aim of providing ideas about how to relieve unnecessary suffering and repair the damages wrought by historical cruelties. Especially since the global economic crisis of 2008, many people around the world have returned to basic questions about equality and justice.

In this second, literal sense, we need more just theory.[9] But the truth is, I don't know exactly what this is—in short, I don't really know what "just theory" means. Fortunately, I'm not alone, because no one else does either, so the situation invites openness to multiple possibilities through dialogue and discussion.

Despite all the vast literature in philosophy, art, and theory trying to articulate justice in concrete representations, the desire for universal human justice exceeds all its particular renderings. As Curtis White puts it, "When we speak of justice, freedom, or creativity, we do not know entirely what we mean. These are not calculable concepts, and yet they are the entire force behind what we claim we want in the world" (*Middle* 188). For many people, justice is a deep, human *desire* for a different future. But however incalculable by economic or statistical metrics, what we can do is situate the desire for justice in the contexts of social injustice, and those can, indeed, be represented in many different media. Critical theory often begins with the effort to name and describe those contradictions and injustices from which so many suffer. Most forms of human suffering have something to do with the geopolitical economy.

Political economy is, of course, the term made most famous by Karl Marx, but the term itself actually emerged in the eighteenth century. It was then adopted by the nineteenth-century political economists such as Adam Smith, David Ricardo, Jeremy Bentham, and others, although the shared aim of most of these classical economists was to remove (or reduce) the political from the economic. The fulfillment of their aim was only recently realized; as Timothy Mitchell points out, "the economy," as a noun naming a separate domain, rather than a process of efficiency, saving money by choosing wisely, only emerged in the 1940s and 1950s.[10] Nevertheless, this desire for separating market economics from state politics began a long historical evolution even as state and capital became deeply enmeshed in Cultural Turn 2. Today, Western metaphysical dualism enables neoliberal economists to separate market analysis from the contested arenas of sociopolitical values so that government can now be organized exclusively by supposedly "universal," scientific, and apolitical economic metrics. It becomes very difficult to find a contemporary public figure who would deny that, like any corporate firm, all government policies should be orchestrated to serve the engines of economic growth through capital appreciation. From this perspective, global warming must be resolved by more free-market deregulation, even though it was the market system that accelerated the production of greenhouse gases.

Despite these ideological mystifications, healing these rifts in our critical histories calls for recovery as well as suspicion. Indeed, there can be no ultimate "material" history that has successfully avoided metaphysics. As David Harvey points out, Marx's materialism is haunted throughout by the desires of metaphysics and the phantoms of objectivity. But as Harvey also reminds us: "If you think you can solve a serious environmental question like global warming without actually confronting the question of by whom and how the foundational value structure of our society is being determined, then you are kidding yourself" (*Companion* 21). Any effort to construct a just history of theory should therefore attempt to address the question of the "foundational value structure" of the Western tradition as it was produced and disseminated in the political economy of diverse geographical regions with a focus not just on epistemological problems, but also on how such knowledge pertains to questions of social justice and the possibilities for human flourishing even as we confront a warmer planet.

Of course, whatever people call "theory" tends to run in the direction of the thin, the abstract, and the general. After all, the etymological roots of the word *theory* are the Greek words *theorein*, which means "to look at," which in turn comes from *theoros*, which means "spectator," or one viewing the action from outside the field where the game is being played. But that is only part of the story of theory, since you can't ever quite get out of the mode of production if you are going to produce theory. Any general theory that does not pay respectful attention to both the local and the nonlocal realities of any given context tends not to be very accurate, and thus not very useful, unless, that is, you are using the theory to deceive some other people, and that happens quite often. Indeed, these dialectical tensions between the general and the particular, the universal and the specific, objectivity and subjectivity, sameness and difference, text and context, the thin and the thick, theory and data, depth and surface, distant and close reading, and suspicion and recovery characterize the modern version of the discourse that many people have called "Western metaphysics" or "European universalism." We can get trapped in those binary discourses in some pretty troubling ways when "transcending history" or "attaining the universal" neglects the lives of those who don't get to do the transcending.

Living in the twenty-first century, the question of what's left for theory and the humanities that don't operate according to the quantifiable logic of cost-effectiveness ratios becomes a real question. Why should we pay attention to a rhetoric and tradition that arose in ancient Greece out of a very different political economy? There are no easy answers here. But my premise is that the Western traditions have filtered down to us in so many powerful variations that some versions of the discourse live encoded within our own culturally produced identities, affecting our bodily, physical, and ecological realities such as global warming. In short, these "powerful cultural narratives" (Klein, *This Changes* 159) are deeply in us; or, perhaps more accurately, when speaking of "the founding myths of modern Western culture" (74), there are no clear boundaries between inside and outside.

As I often put it, humorously, to my students, we are still "sick" with Western metaphysics. But the diagnostic implication of that expression has a serious ring because it names a kind of ideological illness that often prevents us from seeing a different history or a different future than the one our dominant culture has cast for us. The influential twentieth-century critical theorist Theodor Adorno configured this condition in a slightly different register: normative social life in the twentieth century had for him precluded the possibility of human happiness because we all now lived "damaged life"—that's from the subtitle of his book, *Minima Moralia*. Adorno argued that any hope for healing meant that philosophy had to become historical, attuned to a self-reflective analysis of the political economy and responsive to both the constructive and the destructive forces of the modern world. Despite the difficulty of his distinctive style, which might suggest a writer who has completely abstracted himself from real-world struggles, Adorno spent much of his life in exile from the horrors of the Holocaust arguing that critical theory could avoid the debilitating effects of a false belief in total independence from the social domain, but only through a recognition that theory was immanent, emerging from within sociohistorical struggles, tainted and complicit with what it hoped to critique.[11] His "negative dialectics" can seem rather grim, a kind of ultimate "hermeneutics of suspicion," and his aesthetic theories have often been seen as a high-modernist retreat from the political world, but as Eagleton argues, there is another side of Adorno, deeply concerned with the hermeneutics of recovery and "the creation of a just life" (quoted in Eagleton, *Ideology* 350) because he is "implicated enough in the political struggles of his time to be able to see more than metaphysical delusion in such fundamental human values as solidarity, mutual affinity, peaceableness, fruitful communication, loving kindness—values without which not even the most exploitative social order would succeed in reproducing itself" (354). "A just life" requires the dialectical processes of healing and affirmation besides critique and negation.

The problem is that our times and spaces have become so big, international perspectives and interdisciplinary knowledge so complex, as to defeat our understanding of the forces that affect our lives. Before I begin the story itself, I, therefore, first need to elaborate two key assumptions organizing this two-part history of theory: first, the divergent social consequences of materialist and idealist strains of theory as they pertain to the struggle for a genuinely universalist discourse that also respects our vast ethnic and sociocultural differences; and second, the dialectical tensions between communality and hierarchy as they affect the possibilities for social justice. Finally, I will speak to the central issue raised by both the geographical and ideological meanings of "Western" theory.

Cultural Turn 1

INVENTING WESTERN METAPHYSICS

CHAPTER ONE

Introduction:
Framing the Common Good

The Social Consequences of Universalism

Most versions of universalism aim to provide a metalanguage: a stable, foundational discourse in the face of the uncertainties of life and the instabilities of language.[1] Emerging from the violent and materialistic world of ancient Greece, the discourse of reason and knowledge offered a powerful critique of myth and ignorance. The transcendent logic of reason rose above the local cultural stories in favor of the general, universal truth, or *aletheia,* a term that, ironically, came out of the mythical traditions. According to Georg Wilhelm Friedrich Hegel (1770–1831), it took many historical stages over two thousand years for the universalist discourse to reach its fulfillment in the Christian era of the Enlightenment. Even though many reject Hegel's narrative, most critics accept that prior to Cultural Turn 2, God or the Divine served as the uncontested anchor for any version of sovereignty based on the Universal or the Absolute. But the advent of secular humanism revised the ancient discourse so as to modernize the new foundational terms such as *Man, Nature, Freedom, Reason, Science,* or the *Imagination* (among a much longer list)—in short, human rights rather than divine rights—and we are left with contention all around. Such foundational disagreements have been at the root of most political revolutions, religious intolerances, or international wars. As a young man deeply influenced by Hegel's historical version of philosophy, Karl Marx developed his key concept of ideology from the class struggle, whereby the ruling political powers of any society also become the ruling intellectual force by falsely representing their ideas as universal, or common to all people. Indeed, there are just too many such "spurious formulations" (Butler, Laclau, and Žižek 264) of the universal that are oppressively ethnocentric and racist—which is exactly what happened to most of the migrations of Western metaphysics, as Edward Said made apparent in his classic study, *Orientalism.*[2] Can we invoke a nonspurious formulation or way of thinking about universals?

There is a good reason Plato begins his most famous book, *The Republic,* by talking about justice as the universal goal of philosophy. It is an old but persistent theme for anyone exploring the possibilities for "the good life." And it stretches back over the past 2,500 years, since what has been called the Axial Age. This term was coined in the 1940s by the philosopher Karl Jaspers, who recognized that the "axis" of civilization for both the East and the West happened in a period from roughly 800 BCE to 200 CE, and that both traditions have tried to achieve such transcendence of the particular in the name of the universal. Discourses of transcendence also developed in the East, mainly China (Confucius being the most notable example) and India (for example, in the *Mahabharata,* which is about ten times the length of the *Iliad* and the *Odyssey* combined; or in the life of Siddhartha Guatama, the Buddha). Rather remarkably, these discourses in the East and the West developed in their vastly different geographical regions in about the same period, the Axial Age, even though they did so relatively independently of each other. The differences between Eastern and Western transcendence are significant. However, this book focuses on the West.[3]

One enduringly positive legacy from the tradition of Western philosophy is the understanding that one of the universal features of human life is the historical processes of working out the dialectical tensions between general and particular, appearance and reality, negation and affirmation (see Harvey, *Seventeen* 4).[4] These and other well-framed binaries may be metaphysical and ontological in scope, but if they have any claim to universality they cannot just be "Western."

But too often what happened was some form of "epistemic violence." Rather than the imaginative understanding of the complex interconnectedness of local and nonlocal phenomena, what we most frequently got was a less radical, more convenient way of abstracting theory from its sociohistorical contexts as if, for example, democracy or freedom explained themselves, so we could escape altogether the dialectical tension between our views and those of others. Instead of the back-and-forth movement of the dialectical process, we get a rigid, hierarchical binary—self/other, us/them, good/bad, universal/particular, master/slave—and the fixed poles all line up reproducing familiar racist, sexist, classist oppositions when the dialectical oscillation comes to an end in the white, male, privileged "Truth." In some ways, the tendency to dehistoricize and decontextualize seems understandable. No matter what the specific content, theories are always struggling toward general concepts and away from particular circumstances. Yet as the well-known postcolonial critic Gayatri Spivak argued in her famous essay "Can the Subaltern Speak?," blindness to those circumstances typically means blindness to one's privilege. Such blindness produces what Spivak called "epistemic violence" (284) that perpetuates unjust forms of cultural superiority and environmental degradation.[5] The hermeneutics of suspicion is crucial in these circumstances.

Indeed, whatever we have called "theory" has too often been the abstract register by which the material circumstances of production and exchange slipped out of view. But such slippage is not a necessity. Rather, just theory can be "immanent" and dialectically dynamic, deeply engaged within the struggles of social life in any political economy and for people of any race, gender, class, or ethnicity: a struggle not just to critique all the oppressive distortions of domination, but to recover and articulate what is common as well as what is different among all peoples, not just privileged individuals or cultures. There are, of course, risks in this process of what is called "scaling," moving from the particular and concrete to the general and abstract. Yet as Caroline Levine argues, "generalizing will be essential to the work of a just collective life, however imperfect and difficult" ("Model" 636). However, it is not an easy route, and there are no quick fixes.

These distinctions between immanence and transcendence can seem highly abstract, which they are, but they also have real sociopolitical consequences.[6] Some versions of pseudotranscendence can work so powerfully that they enable state and corporate rulers to offer public rationales for what would otherwise be seen

SCAL-ING

as bald-faced lies: as when powerful political leaders authorize the invasion of other countries in the name of supposedly transcendent (or universal) commitments to freedom and democracy; or when such leaders offer only technocratic solutions to global warming; or when defunding public expenditures is carried out in the name of an unquestioned, transcendent belief that market competition and possessive individualism are the only freedoms necessary to remedy poverty. The hermeneutics of suspicion debunks such false versions of universals, but too often the tendency has been to throw the baby out with the bathwater.

From this perspective, universals of any kind are always suspect; yet ask anyone involved in political movements left or right (women's movements, civil rights movements, national liberation movements, antiabortion movements, neoliberalism, etc.) if they can completely jettison the metanarratives of truth, justice, and freedom. Even more, grand narratives about universality are closely tied to the complex issues of autonomy: the need to recover some *relative* separation from the reigning ideological discourses as a necessary condition for both critique and reconstruction.[7] As Terry Eagleton puts it in his assessment of François Lyotard's abhorrence of *grand recits,* "it is a sentimental illusion to believe that small is always beautiful" (*Ideology* 399). Also, in psychological terms, sometimes the vital emotional experience of transcendence reflects the basic human need to feel connected to something larger than oneself: human flourishing necessarily depends upon mutuality, interdependence, and compassion. In contrast to the falsely idealized belief in "individual autonomy and relentless competition," "Twenty-first-century research on organisms ranging from bacteria to insects to mammals has shown that . . . such assumptions were wrong" and "that symbiosis is a near-requirement for life—even for Homo sapiens" (Swanson et al., M5). Such powerful experiences can occur in the local context of bonding to one's intimate relationships in family, friendship, or community, but also in symbiotic relationships with all other species with whom we share life on this planet. While critique can always find in these intimate bonds the threads of complicity with unjust social hierarchies, the dialectical project also calls for the recognition and recovery of those deeply personal satisfactions when contributing to the struggles for species-sharing commonalities.

Theory's movement toward higher levels of abstraction can aid the need for detachment from national, ethnic, and other localized forms of attachment (see Robbins, *Perpetual*). But here's the catch: the higher registers of generality are sometimes called the transcendent, as if those higher levels could transcend the material world of dialectical processes altogether to attain, as in Plato's case, the ultimate Forms.

The variable uses of "transcendence" as a necessary condition for the universal can be confusing as well as troubling.[8] The persistent difficulty is that some writers have used the term *transcend* but meant by it an immanent process dialectically tied to material reality much as Adorno advocated or the kind of critical "detachment" from forms of cultural dominance that Robbins recommends.[9] In such instances, we can easily misread if we insist that the term *transcendence* always means a total break from material realities. Some writers and critics use the term *transcend* to mean the resistance to and overcoming of the officially sanctioned values tied to the dominant geopolitical economy. Other writers use *transcendence* in an almost ordinary language sense as a kind of "crossing over," as in the claim that interdisciplinary work transcends disciplinary borders. Indeed, etymologically speaking, *trans* means "across."

With those cautions in mind, a crucial distinction in my account of Cultural Turn 2 is that between immanent materialist and immaterial idealist strains of the Romantic movement. As Kojin Karatani asserts, "romanticism was ambiguous in nature; it contained two sides: a nostalgic desire for a return to the past [and Nature] and a contemporary critique of capital-state" (215).

The immanent versions of the critique of social injustice and the affirmation of human freedom exemplified by radical Romanticism stand in stark contrast to the versions of Romantic idealism based on nostalgia for a lost past or harmonious Nature. Radical Romanticism is one strain of what David Harvey calls the tradition of "radical humanism" that sustains the "vision of the uninhibited flourishing of individuals and the construction of 'the good life'" (*Seventeen* 283). Ideas of "uninhibited flourishing" can, indeed, seem overly idealistic, so they must function in dialectical tensions with the lived realities of social, political, and ecological life. In contrast, the significance of the various strains of Romantic idealism is that these ultimately antidialectical discourses, often emphasizing universal form over historical context, have had enormous impact on the institutionalized study of literature and the arts as well as on the political economy. Romantic idealism is a persistent force severing epistemology and politics, science and society, knowledge and labor, philosophy and history, the humanities and the sciences.[10] In practical terms, it justified the separation of literature as a field of study from the disciplines of history, sociology, and political science; internal to English studies, it split reading/literature from writing/composition. We are still struggling with those disciplinary divisions. Most important, they reproduce some fundamentally idealized divisions between human history and geological history. In contrast, when we look to deep time, the idea of the Anthropocene "abolishes" such falsely idealized breaks "between nature and culture, between human history and the history of life and Earth" (Bonneuil and Fressoz 19).

A fundamental division in Western philosophy is that between, on the one hand, Plato's idealism and otherworldliness, and, on the other, Aristotle's empiricism and this-worldly materialism.[11] But this typical binary division tends to diminish the extent to which both writers share different versions of Western formalism. The division between radical Romanticism and Romantic idealism cuts another way. The former tends to draw on some of the radical potential in both Plato and Aristotle: the Socratic/Platonic questioning of conventions (negation) and championing of compassion (affirmation); the powerful strains of Plato's critical utopianism; Aristotle's this-worldly materialism and his attention to biological organisms; and his political pragmatism in search of virtue and equality but not his ethnocentrism, sexism, and racism. Radical Romanticism also tries to avoid Plato's ahistorical and dreamlike cosmology as found in, among other sources, the *Timaeus,* one of the last texts he composed; or his otherworldly belief in the unchanging and absolute Forms; or his belief in the ultimate self-sufficiency of the individual; or his and Aristotle's disdain for democracy. Likewise, Aristotle's polemical formalism often imposes itself as an objective description of the fixed categories of the world (as ahistorical as Plato's more ethereal Forms), and this reductive version of Western metaphysics could be resurrected during the Enlightenment when the rapidly emerging market economy could justify the objectification of nature as a passive resource to be exploited by human mastery. Indeed, in the twenty-first century, this key ideological reduction has been raised to the pinnacle of neoliberal rationality so as to justify the relentless extraction of fossil fuels without any regard for their environmental risks. The idealized discourse could mask significant social injustices, especially when the content of what transcends has tended to be male, European, and well-heeled.

To this extent, just theory is always already engaged in the struggle to make life better for *all* human beings, not just the human beings within one nation, one race, one gender, one class. Historically speaking, the reduction of the universal to a form has been the most common pattern of decontextualizing theory (and literature and art). It is not that form, in general, isn't crucial, but that an exclusive focus on autonomous versions of formal unity can be quite disabling. Many writers in the Western tradition have had a great deal to say about the significance of form. It began in the West with Plato's universal doctrine of transcendent Forms. Some, like Hegel, say it began with Heraclitus, who may have better resisted the slide into formalism, whereby the ultimate content is a form. Others refer to the Eleatic school founded earlier in the fifth century BCE by Parmenides in southern Italy, which was at that time still a geographical part of greater Greece.

Universalism has its philosophical origins in the Axial Age, but following the Renaissance its rebirth in secular philosophy is one of the great achievements of what we call modernity, emerging with new force during the Enlightenment and taking vivid new directions in the art, literature, philosophy, and political life of the Romantic period. In the twenty-first century, we now know that all human beings share 99.9 percent of what has been called the "human genome" even though about half the cells in every human body "include about 160 different bacterial genomes" (Gilbert M75)—we all live symbiotically with the natural world. Nevertheless, genuine universality would justify opposition to all forms of oppression based on unnecessary and arbitrary hierarchies of differences. At the same time, the ecological disasters we confront in the Anthropocene have not been brought about by some idealized and falsely universalized humanity: it is simply not true "that 'we humans' are all equally at fault for environmental destruction" (Davies 195; see also Bonneuil and Fressoz). Rather, the ecological crisis has been produced by the elite and wealthy minority who have extracted labor and resources to serve their own interests, not "humanity's" interests. In short, sorting out the achievements from the disasters of modernity is actually very difficult work.[12]

There are, therefore, some high-stakes risks in this kind of theorizing: when you seek higher levels of abstraction, useful generalizations that span large time periods, vast geographical areas, and extensive geological epochs, the conceptual hierarchies can slide over into social hierarchies. Indeed, I will risk the following generalization: the dialectical unity to be found in the tensions between communality and hierarchy are always at work in any society. As we make the transition to the Anthropocene, accelerating climate change goes hand in hand with accelerating socioeconomic hierarchies. We had better then address the philosophical and social roots of these problems.

Communality and Hierarchy in the Organization of Production and Exchange

Every society must negotiate the dialectical relations between communality and hierarchy. Those relations are largely determined by the organization of production and exchange in the geopolitical economy. The two periods that I link together in this book both exemplify dramatic shifts in the way the given societies orchestrated relations between communality and hierarchy. Significantly, for our purposes, democratic social organizations purport to mitigate unfair hierarchies, although in actual practice most of these systems are quite limited in the level of participatory democracy for all citizens. Constitutional democracy had its birth in ancient Greece but collapsed for more than 1,200 years before re-emerging in eighteenth-century Europe and North America.

In a general way, communality highlights the collective, interdependent dimensions of social life as they emerge from the deep biological and geophysical commonalities shared by all life forms: basic needs for food and security. The economic model most suited to human communality is that of gift exchange (see Karatani 1–28), but all functioning economies include some dimensions of communality. Hierarchy, in contrast, refers to differences that can be both conceptual and social: conceptual hierarchies emerge as linguistic registers of increasing generality; social hierarchies emerge as increasing levels of differential power based on economic, social, and institutional differences. In this sense, communality and hierarchy dialectically resonate in all communicative contexts.[13]

I use the rather ugly term *communality* rather than any other etymologically related term mainly because I intend communality to be the more conceptually general (or hierarchically larger) category, thereby including its cognates and derivatives as more contextually focused meanings. Thus, terms such as the *commons, commonality, communal, community,* and *communism* do indeed highlight issues of communality and collectivity, and for that reason, I will occasionally use them, but these terms are often tied to particular historical circumstances.[14] For example, the social struggles over the political meaning of *communism* hinge on the degree to which the mode of production can and should exemplify principles of communality. This link is crucial. But I also think it is wise to respect the familiar uses of this term as a reference to the historical movement associated with communism since the nineteenth century.[15] Finally, I also want to conceive of the "commons" in a deep, ontological sense. Anna Tsing refers to the "latent commons" (255), and Ralph Cintrón has called it the "deep commons": "that which cannot be priced and owned" (16), as opposed to the more socialized sense of the "public commons," or the "popular commons," or the "resource commons," the latter represented by, say, the "common" sharing of an electrical grid or a local fishery in contrast to the deep commons of brute biological and geohistorical commonalities shared by all beings in our biosphere.[16] Given all these differences, trying to figure out what's common to human life on this planet is no piece of cake.

Critical theorists aligned with the hermeneutics of suspicion have been highly critical, and rightly so, of the huge injustices of hierarchy. Nevertheless, as the anthropologist David Graeber explains, to whatever extent a given social organization realizes principles of communality, social life inevitably also involves hierarchy. Even small, tribal cultures based on reciprocal gift-giving and shared social life will have some hierarchies, if only between adults and children, but also because of obvious differences that arise with respect to skills, aptitude, commitment, and interest.[17] As any organization of production becomes more complex, division of labor necessarily increases, creating inevitable kinds of social hierarchies. Political struggles are almost always over what kind and what degree of hierarchies should be preserved or destroyed. Democracy, for instance, tries in principle to idealize a kind of ultimate meritocracy where hierarchies of privilege are established according to some assessment of differing levels of individual merit. As the twenty-first-century economist Thomas Piketty puts it, "Inequality is not necessarily bad in itself: the key is to decide whether it is justified, whether there are reasons for it" (19).

As conceptual categories, then, communality and hierarchy work at a very thin, high level of abstraction; but they materialize in quite different ways for different individuals, depending upon their position within the specific class structure made possible by the socioeconomic organization of production. The conceptual hierarchies can in many cases be carried over into social hierarchies, and sometimes this crossing over can be very destructive of communality, as, for instance, when a privileged class of philosopher-kings has access to the surplus value necessary to sustain their education for fifty years. In these instances, as Timothy Morton puts it, "Going meta is a great way to sneer at someone" (*Hyperobjects* 146)—or at least all those who can't afford to reach the elite perch. In Plato's model, only after philosophers obtain a knowledge of universal truths can they become the enlightened rulers of farmers, peasants, slaves, and other manual producers who have no time for such educational pursuits. When analyzing the organization of production by attending to the play between communality and hierarchy, such an analysis highlights the question of social justice because equality tends to derive from communality and inequality from hierarchy.[18]

Hierarchy, therefore, often gets a bad rap just because it produces inequality, which indeed it does, as any critic following the hermeneutic of suspicion can tell us: hegemony, domination, and colonial superiority infiltrate our everyday practices. Any social revolution or rebellion involves an attack on the dominant forms of social and economic hierarchy. But, especially prior to the Romantic period, hierarchy was the source of justice as authorized by God, or, in a more modern idiom, as the Neoclassicist Alexander Pope put it, "Nature methodized" ("An Essay on Criticism," l. 89): we had to respect the Newtonian laws of nature and the hierarchies of the Great Chain of Being. Literature and criticism were called upon to follow those predetermined laws. So it would then be foolish to try to unjustly alter what Aristotle called the "natural hierarchies," such as between master and slave, as he argued in his *Politics*. Aristotle and Pope, of course, are not isolated figures, but they express paradigmatic ways that European universalism served to reinforce social (not natural) hierarchies. These disputes remain central debates in our age of rapidly increasing socioeconomic hierarchies.

In the face of these theoretical and practical problems, a common mistake for many liberal and left-leaning theorists is a slide into a kind of false idealism whereby all forms of hierarchy are inevitably unjust. Every trace of hierarchy becomes suspect—what Sedgwick refers to as a kind of totalizing paranoia.[19] But no such society could ever exist, or thrive, for long. We then reach the limits of the hermeneutics of suspicion, and we need alternative, reparative elements in our critical repertoire. Some forms of hierarchy actually contribute to communality, shared belonging, and public good.[20] Michael Hardt and Antonio Negri forcefully articulate the risks: "[I]t is a terrible mistake to translate valid critiques of leadership into a refusal of sustained political organization and institution, to banish verticality [hierarchy] only to make a fetish of horizontality [commonality] and ignore the need for durable social structures" (*Assembly* xiv). The division of labor that occurs in any complex organization of production will inevitably introduce conceptual, epistemological, and social hierarchies that may serve the public good (or may not). We cannot unequivocally, or hierarchically, stand outside our local contexts and pronounce the sin of hierarchy, because it is also fair to say that the search for truth should be hierarchically favored over the manipulation of falsehoods, as Socrates, Plato, and Aristotle continually argued even though in practice they sustained some pretty falsely racist and sexist hierarchies. The name "just theory" is itself intended to hierarchically valorize what we assess to be better kinds of theory in contrast to false or unjust kinds of theory.[21] Indeed, such contemporary doctrines as academic freedom have their justification in this dialectical conundrum between serving the common public good (public accountability) while at the same time hierarchically prohibiting the general public from disciplinary decision making (professional autonomy).[22]

As should be clear by now, any individual's attitudes toward communality and hierarchy will be deeply dependent on political values: those on the political right generally understand hierarchy in positive terms, as a natural consequence of inherent kinds of ability, wealth, or status. They therefore look askance at communality as threatening the hierarchical stability of the ruling classes, the inviolable rights of private property, and the virtues of cultural traditions. Conservative advocates for preserving social stability, therefore, resist any form of state-sanctioned economic redistribution as impinging on the rights of individuals. Those on the political left generally valorize communality, nonhierarchy, and equality.[23] Indeed, as we will see in Chapters 8 and 9, the major countermovements to the capitalist world-system such as anarchism, socialism, and communism can be distinguished by their differing ways of valorizing the social relations of communality and hierarchy in the organization of production and exchange. Their struggles to resolve these issues cannot simply be imported into the twenty-first century, but a historical knowledge of their efforts can be an enormous resource for their contemporary reconsideration.

But from either side of the aisle, the struggle to define and defend some version of what is common crosses through most all political ideologies and philosophical positions. In our own times, when the ruthless rush toward privatization crushes our public commons, accelerates global warming, and produces staggering economic hierarchies, the questions about what constitutes our "common wealth" may be more important than ever.

Framing the Cultural Turns: Social Development, East or West?

What, after all, is the "West"? A good question, since it serves as the basic geographical frame organizing this book. There are so many answers to this big question that I would like to avoid the many digressions by claiming (following Ian Morris) that I simply want to use the term *West* in as neutral a way as possible, simply as a geographical marker.[24] The West in this sense refers to all the core societies that emerged in and around the Middle East and the Mediterranean regions, especially since about 9,700 BCE, a date those working for the International Commission on Stratigraphy (ICS) ratified in 2008 as the beginning of the Holocene epoch following the last Ice Age. In contrast to the quite variable cycles of climate change during the 100,000-year series of Pleistocene Ice Ages, the Holocene has been a *relatively* stable period in climate variation, although those relatively small climate changes have affected the entire drama of the transformation during the Holocene of hunter-gathering tribes to settled human communities and, later, into large empires. In this geographical sense, the East refers to the regions associated with what we call Asia, with its primary core mainly in eastern China. From a long-term historical perspective, the core centers of power in the West migrated further west: beginning in Mesopotamia, then Greece (CT1), then northwestern Europe (CT2). Today, the weakening center remains the United States, but the axes of power have shifted toward the massive economic differences between the Global North and the Global South.

In contrast, the adjectival derivative "Western" is not merely geographical but deeply ideological. For instance, "Western metaphysics" refers to the many varieties of discourse that emerged primarily in Greece in the fifth to the fourth century BCE, but ever since then have been circulating all around the globe. In this sense, "Western" refers to an ideological identity that carries the strong traces of its geographical origin; but even then, as a variable identity that includes Eastern influences even in its core, it can appear anywhere in the world, often as a form of cultural hegemony or political hierarchy, a cognate of the critical term

Eurocentric.[25] Whatever we call "neoliberalism" may be the latest incarnation of this version of ethnocentrism.

From a historical perspective, it was about 11,700 years ago that hunter-gatherer tribes began to settle into domestic agricultural regions in and around what archaeologists call the "Hilly Flanks, an arc of rolling country curving around the Tigris, Euphrates, and Jordan valleys in southwest Asia . . . which saw humanity's first major movement away from hunter-gatherer lifestyles—and with it, the birth of the West" (Morris 86). This "Fertile Crescent" was unlike all other regions of the world because it offered geographical and climatic possibilities for this movement toward domestication leading to settled communities. Ever since 1865, when the International Geological Congress (ICG) met in Bologna, Italy, this long period beginning after 11,700 BCE has been called the Holocene (or "recent whole").[26] These settlements with fixed dwellings characterize what some geological stratigraphers have called the First Age of the Holocene. "Age" is the name of a smaller stratigraphic period than "epoch," and of the three ages of the Holocene, the first lasted until about 6,200 BCE, when the towns expanded and began to develop the kinds of hierarchical institutions, ruling authorities, and governing strategies that will gradually emerge in the formation of large kingdoms characteristic of the Middle Holocene Age.[27] These were major transformations in the geopolitical economy that organized production and exchange in that region of the world—a shift, as Karatani explains, from gift-giving modes of reciprocity for survival to centralized bureaucracies orchestrated by large empires. "By 7000 BCE the dynamic, expansive agricultural societies at the western end of Eurasia were unlike anything else on earth, and by this point it makes sense to distinguish 'the West' from the rest" (Morris 114). In short, what Morris calls "social development" took off in the region of the Hilly Flanks or Euphrates Valley.[28] Social development in this region emerged not from any attribute of cultural superiority, but mainly because of the good fortune of geographical advantages in the Hilly Flanks. Morris points to the remarkable biodiversity, partly due to the range of elevations, grasslands, and marshes in the region: "Of the fifty-six grasses with the biggest, most nutritious seeds, thirty-two grow wild in southwest Asia and the Mediterranean Basin. East Asia has just six" (117). Most other areas in the world had even less biodiversity than Asia. The significance of paying attention to the *geo*political economy of developing regions should be apparent from this evidence.[29]

Over the 4,000 years between 6,200 and 2,200 BCE (the date proposed for the beginning of the Late Holocene Age), both the East and the West developed, but the West's social development seems to have been about 2,000 years ahead of the East's.[30] In the Fertile Crescent, therefore, we find the growth of huge kingdoms such as the Akkadian, Babylonian, Assyrian, and Sumerian. These dynasties developed vast agricultural settlements during what is called the Bronze Age, from about 3,000 to 1,200 BCE, but orchestrated by remarkably centralized bureaucratic structures for administration and market exchanges. They competed in trade and in war with other large Mediterranean kingdoms in Egypt, Greece, and Anatolia (the Hittites). They were also quite sophisticated civilizations with religious institutions, legal systems, domesticated animals, military forces, medical training, mathematics, and literature—all facilitated by the crucial development of cuneiform writing systems starting around 3,300 BCE. Indeed, the Sumerian epic, *Gilgamesh*, compiled into clay tablets in cuneiform over about a millennium, tells the story of the king of Uruk, who reigned around 2,500 BCE in what is now Iraq.

But toward the end of the Bronze Age, around 1,200 BCE, one of the most mysterious events in world history took place. No one knows exactly what happened, or why, but Morris calls it the "paradox of development" when "[r]ising social development generates the very forces that undermine further social development" (28). The empires and dynasties disintegrated within a century, and this decline actually happened in both the East and the West. One possible explanation for the sudden decline has to do with climate change, increased temperatures, and decreased rainfall, all leading to draught, crop failures, and famine (Morris 217). But as Eric Cline points out in his vivid account of this civilizational collapse, there were so many complex forces at work that no scholarly consensus has yet been reached. In addition to climate change, there were numerous invasions by various, enigmatic "Sea Peoples," destructive wars among the competing kingdoms, significant earthquake activity, and outside invaders cutting international trade routes, as well as social uprisings. However, scholars also have generally agreed that the period just prior to and after 1,200 BCE produced huge social hierarchies, rampant economic inequalities, and unsustainable levels of debt (sound familiar?). Slavery and forced labor also led to the first recorded massive strikes in Egypt around 1,170 BCE. Shortly before the collapse accelerated, during the early twelfth century, the Biblical story of Moses and Exodus might have occurred around 1,250,[31] and Homer's *Iliad* may represent a regional war around 1,220 BCE.

In any case, one of the key events that seems to have led the Mediterranean out of this four-hundred-year period of social disintegration was the remarkable invention of the Greek alphabet shortly after 800 BCE. We will be paying close attention to this invention in Chapter 3, but, in Morris's terms, the real advantages of this "information processing" advance in the ways social and political life could be produced led to the relatively high level of development in the Greek city-states during the Axial Age. The new twenty-four-letter alphabet was instrumental also in facilitating the production of metallic coinage, the administration of larger military forces, and the increased use of slavery in the newly discovered silver mines—and it is out of these confluences of geopolitical changes that emerge the discourses of transcendence associated with the umbrella term *Western metaphysics*.

In the Mediterranean region, the Axial Age is generally subdivided into four periods, three dominated by Greece and one by Rome. The first, archaic, period begins with the Greek alphabet and continues through the formation of the first democracy in Athens around 590 BCE; the classical Greek period (often called the Golden Age; Pericles called Athens the "School of Hellas") begins around 500 BCE with the great dramatists Sophocles, Aeschylus, and Euripides and continues through the great age of philosophy during the lives of Socrates, Plato, and Aristotle; the Hellenistic period begins with the spread of Greek culture around the Mediterranean, primarily through the conquests of Alexander the Great (who died in 323 BCE) and ends with the Roman Octavian's victory in the battle of Actium in 31 BCE; and the final period is the rule of the Roman Empire beginning when Octavian became the first Roman emperor, Augustus.

Cultural Turn 1 of this study thus focuses on the classical period, when heightened social development led to the production of the philosophical discourse that emerged especially in Athens during the lifetimes of Socrates, Plato, and Aristotle. The chapters that follow have a roughly chronological order, but the sections within each chapter do not always follow a linear time progression: in many instances, a section or subsection scales back to pick up historical threads from the past necessary to understand the social, political, and intellectual context of the period under consideration.

Chapter 2 begins with a brief look at the material conditions of Plato's "workshop," outlining a few of the many circumstances that enabled him to compose his amazing dialogues and to establish his influential Academy. This chapter focuses almost exclusively on Plato's most famous text, the *Republic,* and, even then, it narrows its focus, first to a close reading of Chapters 2 and 10, where Plato develops his controversial critique of the social function of poetry, and then to Chapter 7, the "Allegory of the Cave," which may be the most widely circulated excerpt from Plato. It is in the "Allegory" that Plato provides his most compact representation of what we call Western metaphysics.

Chapter 3 reframes the interpretation of Plato's work within the sociohistorical context of the shift from orality to literacy, especially as it bears on our understanding of Plato's arguments about poetry. I begin with an overview of the remarkable scholarly work in the 1920s by Milman Parry, with a broader view of the emergence of the controversial "orality hypothesis." In order to understand the nature of this shift, I also provide a brief background in the origins of writing in the Mediterranean region and its material impact on social organization. The chapter concludes with a view of the social and political consequences of the fundamental splits made possible in literate culture between subjectivity and objectivity, the knower and the known, especially as they sustain the characteristically Western divisions (and historically variable hierarchies) between the individual and the society, the self and the other, the private and the public, and the human and the natural.

Chapter 4 turns to Plato's abrupt about-face in the *Phaedrus,* where he now criticizes writing in favor of the oral presence of

the speaker. Indeed, this text seems to reverse the previous judgments in the *Republic* where emotion, rhetoric, love, madness, and
inspiration were devalued in favor of reason, dialectic, and the
universal Forms. The second half of this chapter re-examines the
Phaedrus through the eyes of Derrida's famous essay on "Plato's
Pharmacy" (*Dissemination* 61–172). Despite Derrida's difficult
prose, his methodological procedures are relatively simple: he
notices the "traces" of other, double meanings in the word *pharmakon,* a word that appears three times in the original Greek
version of the *Phaedrus.* The history of translation has concealed
this ironic doubling so crucial to understanding Plato's growing
ambivalence regarding writing. The philosophical tracings turn
out to be grounded in quite powerful hierarchical relations between gender, logic, and the political economy.

Chapter 5 provides an overview of Aristotle's revision of
Plato, which was made possible by the former's innovative
synthesis of the key analytic categories of Western metaphysical
formalism. I begin with a brief sketch of the complex but uncertain
history of the physical travails of Aristotle's original texts before
turning to his influential articulations of the common ground or
the basic "substance" of Western metaphysics. For some writers,
these articulations became a founding model of "materialist"
criticism in contrast to Plato's idealist criticism. I also examine
Aristotle's *Logic,* where he formulated the basic binary principles
of symbolic identity with a particular focus on his doctrine of the
"excluded middle," which has proven so pervasively ethnocentric
in its situational uses throughout history. I pay special attention to
Aristotle's proclaimed distinctions between rhetoric and dialectic
in the *Rhetoric,* especially with respect to how the dialectic earns
its hierarchical power to determine the presumptive categories for
rhetoric. Then, in the *Poetics,* we are challenged to understand
how Aristotle used some of the key Platonic doctrines of formal
critical analysis, but arrived at a diametrically opposite evaluation of poetry. Finally, I examine Aristotle's controversial but
influential ideas about politics and government.

The second part of the book, Cultural Turn 2, jumps abruptly
to two simultaneous events that triggered the advent of European
modernity in the shift from the Enlightenment to the Romantic
periods in England, France, and Germany: the French Revolution

of 1789–95 and the Haitian Revolution of 1791–1804. These two events configure the challenge to hierarchies of aristocratic rule by the few and colonial control of oppressed populations. The advent of mechanized labor under industrial capitalism (especially in England), the newly emerging trinity of capital-state-nation, the beginning of the fossil-fuel age, the newfound technological power of mass warfare, the consequent global expansion of colonial empires, and the revolutionary struggle for fledgling democracies and countermovements to the dominant capitalist system—it was indeed a vast cultural turn in the geopolitical economy of human life around the world as we began the transition to the Anthropocene. This period also set the terms for the formation of our modern discourses with respect to the relations between aesthetics and politics, literature and society, knowledge and power—the tensions between hierarchy and communality were shaken to the core as the bourgeoisie took control of the capitalist world-system from the aristocrats, in a new kind of plutocracy. But the increasingly economic basis for these hierarchies was always in tension with democratic hopes for wider social distribution of political decision-making powers and with numerous critiques of the dominant capitalist exploitation of the natural world.

I begin Chapter 6 with an overview of some of the key issues in this period (the beginning of the Anthropocene or the ending of the Holocene) before turning to a close reading of William Blake's striking poem "The Marriage of Heaven and Hell." This poem serves as an early example of radical Romanticism with its concern for integrating political and aesthetic revolutions. Plato and Aristotle now appear as characters in the poem, and they are both subjected to pretty severe critique for their versions of classical idealism. I then move to William Wordsworth's influential "Preface" to the 1802 edition of *Lyrical Ballads*, which serves as a discursive explication of some of the principles of radical Romanticism (tinged with idealism, also). This discussion raises issues of textual authorship, ownership, and copyright law, so it moves from a consideration of the relationships between Wordsworth's public poetry and his sister Dorothy's private journals to a brief historical background in copyright law to demonstrate how fully these legal issues were tied to the discourse of Western metaphysics. The next section turns to the remarkable resolutions proposed by Immanuel Kant to such central issues in the binary discourse of Western philosophy as the divisions between subjectivity and objectivity, empiricism and rationalism, and particularism and universalism. Most important, Kant established the basic parameters of the emerging discourse of idealist aesthetics that will be crucial to the Romantic movement and influential for the next two centuries. Indeed, among the British Romantic authors, Samuel Taylor Coleridge offered the most sophisticated articulation of aesthetic idealism based on organic formalism, partly because of his knowledge of the German Romantic philosophers. The final section of this chapter examines Percy Bysshe Shelley's "A Defense of Poetry," where his paradigmatic version of Romantic idealism enables him to envision Plato himself as a poet despite Plato's having banished poets from his republic.

Chapter 7 first examines how the discourse of Romantic idealism shaped the emerging splits between the domains of social rhetoric and idealized aesthetics, a division that later in the century will have a great deal to do with creating and sustaining the long-standing institutional divisions between composition and literature in English departments. With this background, I turn to one of the exemplary texts of the Romantic period, torn as it is between radical and idealist versions of Romanticism. I focus on Wordsworth's aesthetic representation of the French Revolution in his canonical epic poem, *The Prelude*, especially Books 9 through 14. There is a palpable tension in this poem between his radical version of Romanticism on the one hand, with its powerful resistance to the economy of commodity exchange and a deep commitment to social justice, and, on the other, his slide, mostly in his later years, toward Romantic idealism and nostalgia for a lost Nature (a precursor to some forms of contemporary environmentalism). I then turn from the close reading of the *Prelude* to a broad-ranging interpretation of the political economy of eighteenth-century France leading up to the Revolution. My point here is to demonstrate that the binary discourse of Western metaphysics produces some remarkable parallels between, on the one hand, Wordsworth's division between idealized aesthetics and material politics, and, from a much different arena, the divisions found between economics and politics in the rising discourse of industrial capitalism.

Chapter 8 turns to countermovements beginning with the work of the great feminist writer, Mary Wollstonecraft. Besides her landmark book about the rights of women, I also look to her lesser-known history of the French Revolution to demonstrate that she offered more materialist understandings of the political economy of the Revolution than did any of her contemporary British Romantic poets. I then provide an overview of the emerging classical economists such as Adam Smith, David Ricardo, Jonathan Say, and others, since this discourse provided the theoretical justification for the expanding capitalist economy with its dramatic impact on the production of art and literature within globalized commodity markets. What follows is an overview of the countermovements of socialism, anarchism, and communism, all distinguished by their different versions of social justice based on different relations between communality and hierarchy and on alternative relationships with the natural world. This leads directly to a section scaling back to consider the influence of the historical turn in philosophy represented by G. W. F. Hegel, including his articulation of the "master-slave" dialectic. But I also consider the larger impact of Hegel's philosophical historicism and his highly influential aesthetic, as well as his unfortunate turn to conservative politics and racist attitudes later in life. These considerations lead to an overview of Karl Marx and Friedrich Engels's version of dialectical materialism and the class struggle.

Chapter 9 focuses on the bookend event for the Romantic period, the quite remarkable social transformation associated with the Paris Commune of 1871, an event that led Marx and Engels to revise their own views of the class struggle and the analysis of the mode of production. I particularly highlight the tensions between communality and hierarchy as they played themselves out in these two short months. We often forget just how progressive were many of the social transformations carried out during that fateful spring in Paris, so I highlight some of these accomplishments such as women's rights, freedom of the press, economic equality, and artistic expression. This brief event, therefore, resonates dramatically with many contemporary issues facing all liberal democracies in the world. The closing section of this chapter sketches some of the tensions in the ensuing Communist movement that emerged after the period of the Commune, and continued right into the next century.

Chapter 10 addresses the transitional figures Darwin and Nietzsche, whose profound influences have filtered down to our contemporary age in very different ways. I focus, first, on the complex ways that Darwin struggled to come to terms with the evolutionary theory that his own sociocultural background led him to doubt at every turn because of the dominance of creationism with its philosophical basis in Western metaphysical formalism. After all, in the biblical version of creation, species are like fixed Forms, so I also demonstrate that in *On the Origin of Species* Darwin himself repeatedly recognized the difficulties of defining the category of "species." This is not a minor point, because it also questions the deep philosophical presumptions based on the false binaries often used for distinguishing humanity from nature, homo sapiens from its many generic hominid ancestors. When we turn to the *Descent of Man,* I locate the unfortunate expressions of Darwin's racism, not to point a finger at Darwin but to see his beliefs as a representative sign of the dominant discourse of his age. I close this account of Cultural Turn 2 with a brief look at one of the nineteenth-century writers who most challenged all the presuppositions of Western philosophy. Friedrich Nietzsche was a complex and contradictory figure, and I have chosen to selectively focus on his revolutionary brand of radical Romanticism and its emphasis on pessimism concerning the limits of reason to solve the world's problems, but always in conjunction with his version of what he called "affirmative philosophy," whereby music, art, and literature were deeply enmeshed in social and political values. Toward the end of his life, Nietzsche reevaluated his earlier attack on what he had felt to be the blind Enlightenment hopes for reason and science, and he offered a less reactionary and more radical version of scientific inquiry grounded in hypotheses and what he called "regulative fictions."

In the concluding section, I can only suggest how this book's account of the rise (CT1) and transformation (CT2) of powerful Western narratives affect our understanding of what I have called Cultural Turn 3, a period beginning after the Second World War, after the invention of the microchip, after the beginning of the Nuclear Age, and after the Bretton Woods agreements that shaped the global economy of "Three Worlds." Any effort to frame the past century must recognize the sheer historical complexity of the task: as Chris Harman explains, "There was more change to the lives of the great majority of the world's population in the twentieth century than in the whole preceding 5,000 years" (619). Yet historical understanding requires some form of periodizing. Any possible "sense of our age" has been irrevocably affected by the newly emerging geological epoch of the Anthropocene, when carbon dioxide levels in the atmosphere have risen to a level (400 ppm) not seen for three million years. That fact, among many other geophysical changes, means that any version of just theory shares social and political responsibilities to situate life on this planet in the twenty-first century within this huge frame: as Jeremy Davies puts it, "deep time has become politicized" (196). In the precincts of English departments, how can we struggle to maintain the virtues of close reading without losing the deep-time perspective?

Letting the big picture recede a bit, we can also briefly frame the episode of Cultural Turn 3 in two phases. The remarkable period of economic expansion (the "Great Acceleration") between 1945 and 1980 has been followed by the equally remarkable period of contraction. In the last forty years, innumerable policy changes favoring privatization, deregulation of financial institutions, and corporate tax breaks have led to massive socioeconomic inequalities and deadly forms of global climate change. Many paleontologists have called the Anthropocene epoch the beginning of the "Sixth Extinction." As Nancy Fraser has argued, we are suffering from a prolonged "crisis of care" that has affected all living species on earth. She outlines three stages of this crisis, beginning with the simple neglect of human resources characteristic of industrial capitalism in Cultural Turn 2, followed by the limited ameliorations of the twentieth-century welfare state, and leading up to our contemporary moment, wherein for the last forty years this crisis has been on a rampage of epoch-making climate change ("Contradictions"). I offer in this section a very simplified overview of how these global effects have played out within the narrower confines of English departments even while revealing deep aftereffects of the long history traced in this book. I conclude with a general assessment of the need to reconsider the historical roots of the culture of care advocated by many writers in the Western tradition. The radical Romantics opened the possibilities for a vigorous public realm preserved by political democracies and aimed at building viable communities where *all* citizens, not just the wealthy,[32] could contribute to significant social decision making. In an age of ruthless competition for profit, we are more than ever in need of recovering these lessons from the past that gave shape to the modern struggles for a more humane culture of care, compassion, and reciprocity.

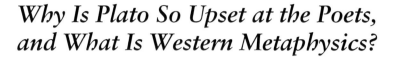

CHAPTER TWO

Why Is Plato So Upset at the Poets, and What Is Western Metaphysics?

Our story shall be the education of our heroes.
—PLATO, *Republic*

Plato's Workshop

Imagine all the materials that must have been produced in order for Plato to write his dialogues. Certainly there were blank scrolls of papyrus around, made from a tedious process whereby the outer rind of the papyrus plant is stripped and the sticky inner pith is cut into strips, flattened, and pressed into overlapping layers to form a writing surface once it dries. The papyrus itself would have been rolled around wooden spindles. Plato must also have had some kind of writing instrument, a stylus, with some kind of fluid ink, both also prepared from natural resources such as feathers, reeds, and possibly carbon extracts for black ink. In addition to these immediate writing instruments, of course, he had other necessities of his craft such as benches and writing surfaces (although scribes often squatted with the papyrus rolls in their laps) arranged in a room, presumably in his Academy, although we don't know where he composed; some of his students might have been assisting him.

There were probably several slaves involved with housekeeping and food preparation, both at the Academy and at Plato's home nearby, as slaves typically worked as household servants or in the mines rather than in the fields where peasants and farmers produced the crops. Plato is said to have freed one slave, and he left four others when he died, a small number for a moderately wealthy Athenian. Aristotle, for instance, appears to have had about fifteen slaves (Wood, *Peasant-Citizen* 44). It is difficult to tell Plato's attitude toward slavery since he rarely mentions it in his dialogues, although in the *Laws* he argues that medical care by freemen would be superior to that of medical care by slaves. Aristotle was more explicit in justifying slavery, especially in Book 1, chapters 4–7 of the *Politics*, where he argues that slavery is natural because "some men are by nature free, and others slaves, and that for these latter slavery is both expedient and right" (Aristotle, *Basic Works* 1133). Aristotle may be more of the empiricist than Plato, but his justifications for slavery are based on his claims to knowledge of universals whereby the binary division between freedom and slavery "originates in the constitution of the universe" (1132). These fundamental divisions follow from Aristotle's basic political assumptions, because, as Ellen Meiksins Wood explains, "his political theory requires a principle of natural hierarchy between rulers and ruled" (*Citizens* 94). Of course, as for Plato, living off his inherited resources as a well-known Athenian bachelor who often strolled the city neighborhoods in conversation with friends, he also enjoyed all the other necessities of life: clothes, food, and shelter, constructed by many workers supported by the agricultural economy of the surrounding area, yet somehow paid for by money changing hands in the form of silver minted coins, or other forms of debt, rent, or less commonly by informal bartering.

Plato opened the Academy around 387 BCE, partly from funds that he had inherited at the age of thirty, ten years earlier. Many illustrious philosophers and politicians attended, including Aristotle for four years, although the school was not open to the general public. Also, Plato did not charge students fees in the Academy, and his students were mostly aristocratic landowners and their sons; although Aristotle did charge fees in his Lyceum (founded in 344 BCE), ironically his students were mostly middle-class businessmen and small landowners. Before Plato had acquired the physical site for the Academy about a mile north of Athens itself, a wall had been built enclosing a sacred grove of olive trees dedicated to the Greek goddess of wisdom, Athena. This particular landscape has passed down to us as the common reference we have inherited for the "groves of academe." The site was called Akademia in reference to a legendary Greek hero, Akademos. It was a remarkably durable beginning for academia: the Academy actually persisted in various permutations for nine hundred years, until it was shut down by Justinian I in 529 CE.

All these necessary goods and services were of course produced and made available to Plato as a result of his position as a son of relatively wealthy landowners, of his friendships and connections with many of the leading figures in fourth-century BCE Athens, and, therefore, of the social class structure of that society. His ownership of his own private property and his rights as an elite, native citizen of Athens were all granted to him according to the legal system established by the Athenian courts in the fledgling democracy. But, still, all these material details will not give us any immediate access to his subjective experience of his writing activities or his emotional relations to his peers, especially his teacher, Socrates, and his student, Aristotle; his family, especially his brothers, Adeimantus and Glaucon, who often appear as interlocutors in his dialogues; or his fellow citizens from various social and political positions, especially considering that as a young man he was asked, in 404 BCE, to serve as one of the Thirty Tyrants after the collapse of the Spartan rule over Athens. He wisely refused, although two of his relatives, Charmides and Critias, did serve among the Thirty. We can presume he must have loved wrestling as a young man because apparently he was quite good at it—his name comes from a youthful nickname, *platon,* meaning "broad shouldered." Granting the enormous gaps in our knowledge about Plato, the inferences we make when reading his texts should still take into account as many factors regarding the geopolitical economy of his day as possible, because without that knowledge, our readings can be wildly inaccurate.

Many people have inferred that one of Plato's motives for writing was that he sought ways to imagine a better life, for himself, but also as a moral commitment to the life of others who he could see were unjustly suffering. In short, he shared a commitment to what many have called a view to the common good. One of Plato's peers, Diogenes the Cynic, when asked where he came from, replied, "I am a citizen of the world," or *kosmo polites,* the etymological root for our term *cosmopolitan.* Especially following the crushing Persian devastation of Athens in 483 BCE,

"Hellenism" and Greek city-state identity had become a powerful local form of identity and attachment, but by the end of the fourth century BCE, both Diogenes and Plato aimed for something grander, more universal. Perhaps—but we'll never know for sure, especially since many others have argued that Plato was trying to ensure the class privileges of the elite members of the educated Athenian citizenry: his vision of a perfect society, based on the *Republic*, was highly stratified and hierarchical, from the rulers to public servants, to peasants, to slaves. Women stayed at home, whether occupied with aristocratic leisure for the few or domestic chores for the many.

Nevertheless, despite these disagreements about Plato, no one denies that he left us a remarkable body of influential texts. After more than two thousand years, the experience of reading his "Allegory of the Cave" in the *Republic,* or his emotionally gripping account in the *Apology* of the execution of Socrates, or many of the other Platonic dialogues continues to hold the vivid attention of many contemporary readers. The aesthetic resonance of these Platonic texts also made it easy for Percy Bysshe Shelley to say during the Romantic revolution that Plato was a poet even though, paradoxically, he banished poets from his *Republic.* We will look more carefully at Plato's assessment of the poet, and it will take some real imaginative work to reconstruct the political economy in which what he called "poetry" was produced, because otherwise we can't very well see from the texts themselves the reasons for his judgment.

Chapter 3 will address those issues, but for now, it is a good materialist starting point to see writing as a form of labor, even if it was the kind of work Plato didn't literally have to sweat over. Briefly, Plato's life was situated in a complex organization of production and exchange of goods within and between city-states that sustained the population in various states of health, disease, pleasure, and pain. Whatever we call critical theory in the West arose out of this complex political economy in ancient Greece. In many ways, Western theory and philosophy arose as a form of protest against the unjust ways of the world. In this light, Plato was protesting some social ills and perhaps reproducing some others, but it will take some further investigations to find out what the problems were that so disturbed him. We had better not just assume that he was insensitive to the virtues of poetry when he banned it from his imaginative version of an ideal republic. Let's turn then to Plato's version of the *Republic*.

Prologue to Justice

According to legend, Socrates could outdrink everyone in Athens.[1] One assumes this means that he could remain rational and alert while his companions lolled off into various irrational states of inebriation or sleep. That may be one way to win an argument, and Socrates won a lot of them if we trust the Platonic dialogues. It may also be that Socrates's skills at managing his liquor provide a good beginning for the start of Western logical, linear, analytical thinking. "Don't lose your cool" might be the best representation in ordinary language of what some people have called Western metaphysics. The men who invented this powerful discourse undoubtedly had to be cool, calm, and collected. Women, other than hetaras, or high-class call girls, didn't usually show up at these all-night drinking parties.

Getting to the calm at the heart of things is what most people have believed the *Republic* is all about: the unchanging, absolute, universal truth is the only goal. God's frame, as it were; not mere mortal meddlings with uncertainties. Given the significant increase in violence, slavery, and warfare during the Axial Age, how can we see this new philosophical emphasis on transcendence and idealism as anything other than an escape from the social realities of life during and after the Peloponnesian Wars? And what kind of cultural changes would it have taken to establish the grounds for what we call rational critique and universal knowledge?

The conversation in the *Republic* takes place in the affluent home of Cephalus, brother of Lysias and father of Polemarchus, where Socrates is greeted warmly upon his arrival for the evening. The time for this gathering appears to be in the later stages of the Peloponnesian War, which had produced poverty throughout the Peloponnesus; by its end in 404 BCE Athens had been devastated and subjected to the rule of Spartan oligarchs. Even after the war ended, for eight months in 404–403, the Thirty Tyrants engaged in a ruthless reign of terror, purging the city of many dissidents. Although Plato composed the *Republic* many years after this time of extreme violence, he had lived through this earlier period as a young man under the tutelage of Socrates. By the time of writing, moreover, he was living through the increasing decadence of the democratic polis of the city-state as new, more geographically sweeping forms of imperial power and empire would soon be taking shape under the aggressive warmaking of Phillip II of Macedon and then his son, Alexander. Given these geopolitical conditions, it might appear ironic that the evening's conversation quickly turns to the fundamental questions about the "great sense of calm and freedom" (11): the peace of mind that comes with the good life, and the way to get there through virtue and justice.[2] Twenty-four hundred years later we have not stopped asking those questions, so it is useful to return to one of the West's foundational conversations about them.[3]

What we find is that the discussion does not begin with an abstract definition of justice but with the practical, political, and economic questions concerning the unjust connections between wealth and social power: the distinctions between riches earned by human labor or acquired by inheritance and the unjust relations between the rich and the poor. Clearly, in the Axial Age, the surplus went entirely disproportionately to the oligarchs, just as it does today: communal social values of equality often vanished under the powerful hierarchies of the city-state, even under the limited kinds of formal democracy set up in ancient Athens, where the political economy still depended upon monarchical rulers and peasant producers. Even so, Athenian democracy was quite remarkable in that peasants, laborers, craftsmen, and artisans were citizens of the polis, even though they undoubtedly may have had less persuasive force in the senate and governing bodies than did the aristocratic landowners who served as rulers. Slaves, women, and metics (resident aliens) were clearly not so enfranchised, but neither were they in any other parts of the world. Socrates, Plato, and Aristotle all had deep reservations about democracy. Giving manual laborers voting rights was risky because it neglected the necessary stages leading to wisdom through education and philosophy in favor of uninformed voting rights exercised by illiterate citizens and potential mob rule. But a closer look at the geopolitical economy reveals the tensions between philosophical and political battles in the way Hellenistic democracy emerged.

Philosophically speaking, democracy reflects more horizontal and communal social organization than the hierarchical arrangement of most autocratic forms of government rule, and this challenge to hierarchical status recurs throughout the long history of interpreting Plato's and Aristotle's politics. In the twentieth century, Marxist thinkers offered the most compelling arguments criticizing Plato's elitism. For instance, Wood explains that Plato's version of the dialectic between rulers and producers meant that his "idea of social and political stability was uncompromisingly an order of motionless hierarchy, with lower elements in complete submission to the higher" (*Citizens* 112). Plato certainly believed in a hierarchy of values, with a leisured ruling class governing an impoverished producing class. But some significant qualifications of this general view are important to consider. For one thing, Plato expresses his most nearly unequivocal reservations about democracy later in his life, in the *Statesman* and the *Laws*, the last text he ever wrote, just a few years before he died. In these texts, we also find significant stylistic changes in the dialogue form of Plato's texts. In the *Laws*, Socrates is no longer a character, and the three elderly men of the dialogue, the Cretan, the Spartan, and the Athenian, address logical arguments about government formations: the text itself might as well be an expository argument without characters at all. Missing entirely is Plato's early and frequent use of irony, allegory, and myth, as well as the sometimes humorous banter of the characters themselves, who often entertain divergent, even playful differences of opinion, especially in the *Phaedrus*. The *Laws* thus represents a more hierarchical, monological discourse, as one might expect from an authoritarian lawgiver as opposed to the more dialogical play of the demos (the people). Wood never attends to this kind of unsettling stylistic play with multiple meanings.[4] Second, Plato clearly recognized the role of differences in skills, tastes, and attributes, all of which could be altered through education, so the picture of Plato as an irresolute aristocrat yearning for a rigid social order deserves at least some careful qualification, especially given that he was highly critical of injustice, cruelty, and ignorant rule by power and wealth, rather than by knowledge and wisdom. Plato's political hierarchy was based on his epistemological hierarchy of knowledge, wisdom, and the dialectic, not merely the arbitrary and unjust powers of wealth, militarism, and hereditary class privilege.

Nevertheless, we are right to see that the epistemological and political hierarchies in Plato's writings are deeply wrapped up in the social relations of production and exchange in the society itself. As Kojin Karatani argues (here following Karl Polanyi), "reliance on the market rather than officials to set prices was the source of Greek democracy" (*Structure* 101). Because of the relatively independent nature of the city-states, there was no empire, nation, or centralized bureaucracy regulating prices and exchange practices among the various poleis. Instead, "Greece entrusted the setting of prices to the market. . . . Letting the market set prices was politically equivalent to letting the masses decide public questions. It implied that judgments made by the masses were more reliable than those made by kings, officials, or a small number of wise leaders. This is why Plato and Aristotle opposed both democracy and the market economy. They thought that rule by a centralized state and an economy based on self-sufficiency were desirable" (101). From a twentieth-century perspective, it sounds as though they might have preferred some version of state-centered socialism so long as it prohibited communal governance by the population at large. But in any case, there were clear downsides to the limited forms of democracy that arose: "The move to democracy in Athens was nothing more than an attempt to preserve the existing community of rulers within the polis. This democracy led to an ever-increasing expansion of slave-system production" (102) and increasing reliance on city-state militarization: "Athenian democracy was adopted above all as a means to preserve the state. Athens enforced universal conscription for citizens" (115), at the same time that only about 12 percent (40,000 of 300,000 residents of Athens) of landowning males enjoyed the status of voting citizens. Accordingly, Plato configures the whole discussion in the *Republic* in exactly those terms: hereditary power, political realism, and militarism.[5]

Thus, significantly, the elder patriarch, Cephalus, is himself a wealthy man who has profited as a military arms manufacturer in Athens. Philosophical discussion in ancient Athens was performed primarily by the elite military rulers of the polis, not by the farmers, artisans, and others who did not have the resources or privilege to spend time in theoretical reflection, even though, it was true, they could vote and serve on the large juries formed for disputing legal issues. But Cephalus leaves the house early to attend to "sacrifices"[6] so the conversational torch is passed to his philosopher son, Polemarchus, who holds the hyperrational "payback" view of justice: an eye for an eye, a tooth for a tooth. The sophist Thrasymachus tries to argue that injustice is more practical and beneficial than justice because it produces more results favorable to those in power; Thrasymachus is a kind of updated version of the ruthless sophist, Callicles, from Plato's earlier dialogue *Gorgias*. Another interlocutor, Glaucon (as noted, one of Plato's two older brothers), is also generally described as a sophist, and he proposes another variant: that "justice is nothing else than the interest of the stronger" (21). This is a view that gained force from the historian Thucydides in his account of the bloody Peloponnesian War, and Glaucon's examples provide the proto-Machiavellian justification that might makes right, a basic view that will later serve as a model for what in the modern age we call political realism, with Thomas Hobbes capping the Enlightenment version. Socrates's role, of course, is to sort out all these arguments and provide the counterexamples that illustrate the true nature, or essence, of justice.

At least that's the expectation of most readers, but let's back up a minute. That the historical Cephalus is mentioned in the context of sacrifices resonates with the mythical figure of Cephalus, who was kidnapped by the goddess of Dawn, Eos, and taken away from his beloved wife, Procis. Cephalus and Procis were eventually reunited, but not without many trials and tribulations, and, according to the legend, in southern Greece many sacrifices had to be made to Cephalus and Procis. Now in contrast to the historical Cephalus's business acquisition of wealth, the mythical Cephalus inherited his wealth: he was the founder or "head" of a powerful family that included Odysseus. The conflict between historical reality (Cephalus of Syracuse) and mythical legend (the Cephalus of lore) is embedded in a conflict between earned wealth and aristocratically inherited wealth. But there is never any voice given to the workers, the slaves, and the disenfranchised who have really furnished the labor for that wealth, whether inherited or produced by individual effort: the maldistribution of the surplus is taken as a given, foundational to a domesticated farming economy heavily indebted to peasants who worked the land and slaves who worked primarily as domestic servants in homes or as laborers in the silver mines. Likewise, these conflicts reflect the underlying tensions represented in the *Republic* between pagan ritual sacrifices (like those the historical Cephalus goes off to participate in) and the new civilized logic of reason that takes place in his house but after he leaves.

Nevertheless, we shouldn't miss several layers of irony that resonate in this intertextual context: a founding discourse about justice and peace takes place in the home of the son of a military arms dealer that is actually located in Piraeus, the port city near Athens, right next to a building where shields are made by the labor of more than a hundred slaves. The story of justice is often framed as a rise of civilization out of paganism, yet the elder in attendance at the civilized party leaves to attend a pagan ritual carried over from actual practices we know to have occurred within the previous decades. The boundaries between the literal/ historical and the mythical/legendary seem themselves to be pretty blurred. The concept of equality never directly enters this ancient Greek discourse on justice, nor does any economic concern for equitable distribution of the resources and surplus produced by the workers and the slaves: in Plato's eyes neither of these groups should have any democratic vote in decisions about how the goods they make are produced and disseminated.

Significantly, the rise of these Axial Age philosophies of transcendence takes place at roughly the same time as the rise of coinage, slavery, and increased territorial warfare.[7] Indeed, one of the great advantages for the Athenian city-state prior to the Peloponnesian War was the 483 BCE discovery nearby of the Laurium silver mines, where up to thirty thousand slaves worked to produce wealth for what many scholars have called the Golden Age of Athenian democracy, during the time of Pericles.[8] Stamped into coins starting around 600 BCE, this new portable kind of money produced a remarkable value-measuring effect that went hand in hand with the search for the universal. As Marc Shell argues in *The Economy of Literature,* "Money is the universal equivalent par excellence. . . . [T]he mint in the ancient world shatter[ed] tradition. Coins destroyed the aura of individual objects and encouraged a sense of the universal equality of things" (86). Different objects could be given value according to a single, universal scale. But, as Shell also explains, it is, of course, "a false sense of 'universal equality'": "Money, the development of which plays a crucial role in the origin and development of inequality, is like modern commercial language; both are perversely equalizing common denominators in a one-dimensional society" (122). This perverse effect of a material leveling instrument in the form of money runs very deep, and this misleading presumption persists in the twenty-first-century pressures to reduce all value to the "universal" measures of the market economy.

What most characterizes the Axial Age, then, is the nearly simultaneous origins of money, coinage, slavery, and philosophy. The philosophical search for the ultimate Forms as a kind of abstract universal rising above particular historical contexts hauntingly mirrors the rapid rise of slavery that in material terms represents the ultimate violence of reducing humans to an economic form of exchange. Slavery violently dislocates individuals from their lives and social contexts in order to turn them into saleable commodities. As David Graeber explains, slavery "requires first of all ripping her from her context; that is, tearing her away from that web of relations that makes her the unique conflux of relations that she is" (159). The violent material decontextualizing at the heart of a slave-based economy resonates in disturbing ways with the potential violence of false universals that justify the hierarchy enjoyed by the dominant groups.[9]

Returning now to the *Republic*, to cap off all this irony, Socrates, the very man who is supposed to sort out the good from the bad, the just from the unjust, the truth from the myth, and the stable reality from the unstable world of appearances—well, this very man concludes the entire discussion with the following admission: "And the result of the whole discussion has been that I know nothing at all. For I know not what justice is, and therefore I am not likely to know whether it is or is not a virtue, nor can I say whether the just man is happy or unhappy" (40).[10] For those who see the absolutist side of Plato, here we have Socrates expressing the limits of his own knowledge. There seems to be something abnormal taking place at the very heart of the discourse designed to establish universal values as the "new normal" for knowledge in Western cultures.

What could Plato mean by all this unseemly irony and confusion when the ostensible goal is to end confusion and establish a universal foundation? Without closing off the difficult question of the interpretation of irony and uncertainty, we might best proceed by looking closely at the text itself to see what features we can identify as less ambiguous and more amenable to consensus.

Poets as Educators

Our starting point is a close reading of Books 2, 7, and 10 of the *Republic*. In Books 2 and 10, Plato develops his arguments for excluding the poet from the ideal state he is imagining.[11] Book 7, "The Allegory of the Cave," is the most widely disseminated representation of Western metaphysics that has ever been produced. Two focus questions provide useful starting points: (1) Why is Plato so upset at the poets? (in Books 2 and 10); and (2) What is Western metaphysics? (in Book 7).

The first question about Plato's banishment of the poet quite understandably triggers significant emotional reactions, especially for all of us who love literature and poetry. Many contemporary readers feel angry or annoyed with Plato for so lacking any "real" understanding of poetry. But despite this wide range of emotional reactions, close reading still works well to help us outline the three main reasons Plato offers in the text itself for his condemnation: the first is in Book 2; the other two are in Book 10.

In Book 2, Plato makes an ethical argument about the pros and cons of imitation as a practice central to the education of young children. When children hear stories of heroes, they often imitate their behavior. This is not a problem when the behaviors of the heroes are noble, pure, and good. But it certainly is a problem if a poem tells the story of dangerous or immoral deeds: who would want their children to imitate stories about Zeus going around raping women? Rape, murder, and incest are not uncommon in the Greek myths, reflecting cultural realities in the Axial Age. Since, as Plato puts it, "the poets are the authorities to whom they appeal" (48), Plato has an understandable concern. Homer may be very good, but he is a human being nevertheless, so he is inevitably fallible, whereas God as the author/creator of all true stories never tells a lie: "God is not the author of all things, but of good only" (66). Homer is off the hook because he's human.

But the decision is not so easy: many readers are still caught up when Plato (or Socrates?) speaks about censorship. "Then the first thing will be to establish a censorship of the writers of fiction, and let the censors receive any tale of fiction which is good, and reject the bad; and we will desire mothers and nurses to tell their children the authorized ones only" (62). It just rubs most of us the wrong way to think that there should be a group of people called "censors" who "authorize" what we can tell our children. But given the context in which he raises his objections, it is a reasonable question to ask: "And shall we just carelessly allow children to hear any casual tales which may be devised by casual persons" (62) even if they are untrue or inappropriate? As Socrates explains, although we are admirers of Homer, we do not admire the lying dream which Zeus sends to Agamemnon" (69). Even though such tales might have important allegorical meanings, many children cannot yet distinguish "what is allegorical and what is literal" (64).

In this discussion of censorship in Book 2, Plato's arguments are all on ethical rather than ontological grounds, which will not be the case in Book 10. In short, he is not eliminating all poems, just the bad or immoral ones. The liberals among us hate the word *censorship,* but none of us can really avoid it at some points in the practice of our everyday lives. The question is where do we draw the line? Should young children be exposed to sex, violence, sadomasochism, and pederasty, at age five? So we all inevitably end up drawing a line based on our hierarchies of value—how we socially construct and politically execute the limits of good taste is the question. In short, Plato's basic argument here resonates with some of our contemporary concerns—it might plausibly have a kind of universal resonance regarding the hierarchies of care between parents and children.

But when we get to the two arguments in Book 10, all those contemporary concerns seem to have vanished. Indeed, in the concluding chapter of the *Republic,* Plato's banishment of the poet is total, categorical, and ontological (based on the "reality" of poetry), and not judgmental, evaluative, and partial as it was in Book 2: "*all* poetical imitations are ruinous to the understanding of the hearers" (288, my italics). That is a universal claim. Nevertheless, we can provide short, literal synopses of his two main arguments against poetry. The first argument is the famous one about imitation and the "thrice-removed" bed of the artist/ poet: there's (1) God's bed; (2) the carpenter's bed; and (3) the painter/poet's bed. Since in Plato's metaphysic the ultimate Form or reality of a bed is a creation of God (and thus a bed with universal, not particular, characteristics), the actual beds made by carpenters for people to sleep in are only proximate imitations of God's ideal bed, and when the poet speaks about or the artist draws a bed these imitations of imitations are "thrice-removed" from the reality.

If you grant the premise of this three-tiered hierarchy, then: "The imitator or maker of the image knows nothing of true existence; he knows appearances only" (295). Whereas in Book 2, imitation was a fine educational practice for children so long as they were imitating virtuous practices, imitation itself is now condemned: "The imitative art is an inferior who marries an inferior, and has inferior offspring" (296–97). Bad news all around for imitation and poetry.

The second argument in Book 10 is also not hard to understand at a literal level: poetry arouses feelings, and therefore leads to the irrational, thus defeating all the benefits of philosophy and logic. As Socrates so famously puts it: "poetry feeds and waters the passions instead of drying them up; she lets them rule, although they ought to be controlled, if mankind are ever to increase in happiness and virtue" (301). Poets are thus dangerous to the well-being of the rational state because the poet "awakens and nourishes and strengthens the feelings and impairs the reason" (299).

Assuming for the moment that this is a relatively accurate summary of what Plato says about poetry in the *Republic*, the big question is: *Why* does he say that? Given that the evaluative argument in Book 2 is relatively understandable to us moderns, the two arguments in Book 10 seem ludicrous by contemporary standards. Can you imagine my saying that you can't write a poem about a bed because you have never made one as a carpenter, and you certainly aren't God, so you have no real knowledge of beds? And that if you *feel* something when you read poems, this is bad? Plato is a pretty smart man, but let's face it, these rationales about banishing poetry sound meaningless with respect to making any kind of contemporary judgments about the value of poetry.

Of course, these reactions are especially common since the secular turn beginning in the Renaissance. But for many Christian writers of the Middle Ages, Plato's judgments about poetry could be taken as quite literal, and so they sympathized with his banishment of poetry. For instance, St. Augustine (354–430) and Boethius (480–524) cite Plato's condemnation of the poet as a commendable understanding that poetry, drama, and the arts more generally gave rise to unrighteous emotions unsuitable for spiritual purity and divine law: poetry was "unclean," was associated with idolatry, and could seduce men into depravity. As M. A. R. Habib argues, "Augustine's strategy . . . [was to adapt] . . . classical thought and literature to Christian purposes" (*Literary Criticism* 54). In stark contrast, however, most modern readers who love literature find Plato's pronouncements odd and unsettling. Yet most modern, post-Enlightenment responses are actually not so idiosyncratic as they may first appear, because they tend to share certain characteristics and fall into two main groups. The first group finds ways to disparage or attack Plato's judgment: Plato just does not understand poetry; he's an ultrarationalist; he's a philosophical elitist; he has bad taste; he's narrow-minded. Plato is one of the most famous human beings who has ever lived, so it takes some gumption to make judgments of that order. The second group tends to be apologists, recognizing that Plato is, after all, a legendary figure, so he couldn't exactly mean what he says. These interpretive excuses for Plato's excesses can, however, be very shrewdly worked out. For instance, it could be that Plato is more ironic than the literal text seems to warrant, and, after all, we have seen many instances where irony does seem to be at work in the *Republic*. It could be that Plato is making a logical argument, taking it to its extreme because he's talking about an ideal state, and in the real world we know that he loves an awful lot of Homer, as he says in Book 2.

Significantly, the apologists re-create a long-standing history of what Eric Havelock called the "method of reduction," the long tradition of ways that modern readers have had to reduce Plato's pronouncements about poetry to fit modern understandings. We have to do some sociohistorical contextualizing in order to make sense out of what to contemporary readers can only appear as odd and abnormal judgments about poetry. But we will learn about that in Chapter 3. At this point, it appears that neither of these explanations, by reduction or by denigration, is exactly satisfying. Something seems to be missing (which is indeed the case, as we will see), but with the recognition of that lacuna, I suggest that we turn back to the *Republic* and look carefully at Book 7, the "Allegory of the Cave," so we can get a cultural materialist understanding of Western metaphysics as represented in this book.

Out of the Darkness and into the Light

Any discussions of this allegory ought to begin with an image, and even a brief search on the Web yields many variations of the cave with the prisoners chained, facing the back wall, the fire, and the raised walkway with people or puppeteers casting shadows against the wall of the cave (see Figure 2.1).

Despite the variations, the structural components are all the same, so that different images of the cave still accurately represent

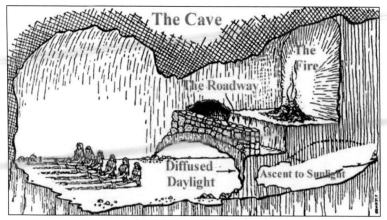

FIGURE **2.1.** *A typical depiction of Plato's "Allegory of the Cave."*

the structurally "universal" and visually significant properties of the image Plato has constructed in words.[12] Interestingly, most all of the drawings are based on the interior of the cave, and they thus leave out any image of the exterior, of the sun outside the cave, and the sun is a crucial part of the meaning of the allegory, representing the ultimate goal of all philosophy: to reach the light of the universal. In any case, consider the basic affective question: "What do you *feel*, if anything, for the prisoners?" Since the question loads the deck, the most common answer is: sympathy. Who wouldn't feel sympathy for people chained so tightly that they cannot even move their heads to look around or in back of them? Their situation appears worse than slavery. It is a sorry state indeed to be in the cave where "the truth would be literally nothing but the shadows of the images" (206). Not a nice place to be.

But no one reads it at the literal level, because we have all been trained to read it as an allegory rather than a literal description of a real cave. No one ever thinks to ask a realistic historical or political question: who imprisoned the prisoners? Who judged them guilty of a crime? What crime? Wouldn't the prisoners have known about the outside, "real" world before they were imprisoned, even as children? Or even more pedestrian questions: how do the prisoners relieve themselves without looking around their surroundings? How can chains prevent someone from turning his or her head? Who feeds the prisoners? Absurd, I know, but worth pointing out, since once you also recognize the allegorical level, a moment later (if there's a lapse at all), you realize that you can't exactly feel sympathy for the prisoners on the grounds that they have it so much worse off than you, because you, the readers, everyone—we *are* all the prisoners. The allegory universalizes the particular content of the configuration. We are all enslaved to our own ethnocentricisms.

Plato makes this allegorical doubling explicit right after his literal description of the cave: "This entire allegory . . . you may now append, dear Glaucon, to the previous argument; the prison-house is the world of sight, the light of the fire is the sun, and you will not misapprehend me if you interpret the journey upwards to be the ascent of the soul into the intellectual world" (208). The act of allegorical rereading is crucial. God becomes "the universal author of all things beautiful and right" (208). This is the key moment of allegorical doubling as a configuration of the dialectical process. Where we might have been reading the narrative of the cave at a relatively literal level, feeling sympathy for the poor prisoners, the second reading, the move to the allegorical level, is the fundamental doubling of the dialectic, and without making that allegorical move we can completely miss the depth reading. That is, in the new, second rereading, everything gets displaced from the surface to the depth: "we" (the reader) become the prisoners; the fire becomes a version of our literal sun; and the "sun" in the allegory becomes (ironically) the unseen absolute truth. The truth as light cannot be "seen"—as Derrida puts it in "White Mythology," the "heliotrope" of the sun, the alternating states of night and day, becomes foundational (a kind of master trope) for Western metaphysics, and it has been so powerfully inscribed in the West that we can't use most Indo-European languages today without to some extent being dependent upon this powerful discourse: when we say "Do you *see* what I mean?" of course nobody literally "sees" anything, and the dead metaphors have passed into the language as literal synonyms for understanding.

The ultimate irony of the allegory is that although we can see the cave in the image, the whole point of the visible image is to get past visuality and the senses to the absolute truth that we cannot see.[13] But the image and its allegorical doubling greatly aid our efforts to abstract some of the basic formalistic principles of Western metaphysics. Socrates names the basic binary relations: being vs. becoming; reality vs. appearance; universal vs. particular. As Socrates says: "the instrument of knowledge can only by the movement of the whole soul be turned from the world of becoming into that of being" (209). This vision (to use the paradoxical term) for an invisible but ultimately knowing absolute "soul" will, two millennia later, provide some degree of provocation for Immanuel Kant's tremendously influential version of what he called, in rather ungainly terms, the "transcendental unity of apperception," but that story will have to wait for Cultural Turn 2.

The allegory turns out to be a metaphor for founding the discourse of philosophy, which turns out to be the very process of moving beyond the contingent, visible details of the image to reach the unchanging, invisible, universal truth. Basically, philosophy becomes the method for getting out of the darkness of the cave into the light of the truth so long as you "see" that the sun the literal prisoner sees upon leaving the cave turns out to be the invisible Truth that you cannot see with your senses. Our literal sun that we see in the sky turns out to be only the fire inside the cave, the source of casting the misleading shadows that constitute, by analogy, our everyday sensual world of appearances. The philosophical process is indeed one of turning (from the literal to the figurative? Or vice versa?). Once you get to the truth you've passed beyond the figurative doubling to the ultimate oneness of Being: "The process . . . is . . . the turning round of a soul passing from a day which is little better than night to the true day of being, that is, the ascent from below, which we affirm to be true philosophy" (212).

Consequently, the allegory becomes a founding story of the origins of Western metaphysical dualism: "And thus arose the distinction of the visible and the intelligible" (216), And from this division follows the whole binary division of Western metaphysics: true/false, absolute/contingent, reality/appearance, light/dark, form/content, abstract/concrete, mind/body, universal/particular, etc., with the irony falling on the light/dark division: light from the sun represented in the allegory is clearly the absolute light of reason, and the fire is the allegorical representation for our sun which enables us to see with our eyes, our senses, thus locking us into the misleading (and dark) world of appearances. The true "light" of knowledge is invisible, but represented in the allegory as the sun, our literal source of light. We can list these many dualities as two columns of parallel attributes, but once they are there, side by side, another crucial feature of Western metaphysics becomes evident: the dual listings are not equivalent columns, but a hierarchy. The hierarchy appears to be a conceptual hierarchy, but Plato understood implicitly that it was also a social hierarchy: only certain individuals, philosophers, highly educated and privileged citizens who were not burdened with physical labor, could become philosopher-kings. The conceptual hierarchy was always related to a social hierarchy in Plato's vision, as Wood makes clear: Plato's "philosophical project was never divorced from Athenian political realities, and his search for absolute and universal truths was never dissociated from the mission to regenerate Athens" (*Citizens* 66). Indeed, Plato offers a "philosophical defense of inequality" (69) in both the conceptual and the political realms, because social life could be stabilized around natural hierarchies of abilities and talents. But it is especially easy to diagram the conceptual hierarchy: the good, absolute, reality side is always above (or superior to) the lower counterparts (see Figure 2.2).

The goal of Western metaphysics is pretty clear: to get out of the cave of ignorance and reach the light of the Truth. That's the object; and Plato also gives us a method for how to get ourselves out of our allegorical cave and our literal ignorance: the dialectic. As Socrates puts it: "And so, Glaucon, I said, we have at last arrived at the hymn of dialectic. This is that strain which is of the intellect only, but which the faculty of sight will nevertheless be found to imitate. . . . And so with dialectic; when a person starts on the discovery of the absolute by the light of reason only, and without any assistance of sense, and perseveres until by pure intelligence he arrives at the perceptions of the absolute good, he at last finds himself at the end of the intellectual world, as in the case of sight at the end of the visible" (224). Here's the ultimate rationalist, antiempiricist doctrine of the dialectic of reason freed from the senses, ironically expressed by "sight at the end of the visible." Of course, object and method is another characteristic dualism of Western metaphysical formalism: dialectic is the "method" (or process, or technique) to enable us to reach the "object" or true

Absolute	Contingent	Absolute True Light
True	False	Reality Form
Light	Dark	Abstract Mind Reason
Reality	Appearance	General Objective Universal
Form	Content	
Abstract	Concrete	
Mind	Body	Contingent False Dark
Reason	Emotion	Appearance Content
General	Specific	Concrete Body Emotion
Objective	Subjective	Specific Subjective
Universal	Particular	Particular

FIGURE 2.2. *Diagram of the conceptual hierarchy of the "Allegory of the Cave."*

knowledge, a dualism that plays out in the formation of modern disciplines of knowledge based on scientific "method" demarcating the separate "objects" of knowledge.

As human beings who live in our senses, and thus in the slothful cave, the source of our redemption lies in our use of the method of dialectic. The Judeo-Christian as well as Islamic discourses about heaven and hell, a second wave Axial discourse about redemption, will develop out of this metaphysical doubling but with prayer rather than dialectic as the method. Our secular interpretation of the allegory depends greatly on whether we emphasize the "arrival" at the end point, the *product* of our investigations, when the philosopher/prisoner "arrives at the perceptions of absolute good" at "the end of the visible world" of everyday living, or whether we emphasize more the ongoing *process* of engaging the dialectical struggle with the basic contradictions between appearance and reality, including the social obligation to return to aid the other prisoners still chained in the cave. There's nothing we can do to affect the unaffected absolute reality of Being except try to use the one method available in our world of action and becoming to get out of that world of becoming and into Being. Since dialectic signals the role of philosophy, it of course makes sense that the philosopher should gain supremacy over the poet, which supplies at least a logically consistent reason for condemning the poet, as he is inevitably subordinated within this value structure: "Dialectic, then, as you will agree, is the coping-stone of the sciences, and is set over them; no other science can be placed higher—the nature of knowledge can go no further" (227). Philosophy via metaphysics provides the absolute grounds for the practical work of the sciences to produce truth; poetry is pretty irrelevant in this epistemology.

The dialectical process is perhaps the most dynamic legacy to emerge out of ancient Greece. As David Harvey argues, the fundamental contradiction "between reality and appearance in the world in which we live" still appears to be "perhaps the most important contradiction of all" (*Seventeen* 4). Viewed in this way as unavoidable dialectical unities consisting of tactical contradictions whereby you can't occupy one pole without the presence of the other, what appears to be universal is not one pole of the dialectic (say, reality) but the dialectical process itself when engaged in the ongoing human struggle to negotiate between false appearances and true realities, or between general theories and specific cases. Epistemic violence always occurs when any group of people say they have reached the endpoint, the *Truth*, and that, therefore, others have not—the claim to possess the absolute reality is always spuriously ethnocentric, as it was for Plato.

The best way to think of dialectic in ordinary terms is to think of it as a conceptual doubling: you say something, a thesis, and then you say it again (perhaps its opposite, or perhaps a more general but related claim), an antithesis, and bring these two concepts together to get a synthesis, which then becomes a new thesis.[14] Using this process of dialectical doubling, human beings can rise toward the absolute Truth. The new dialectical rhetoric of philosophy provides a progressive plan for gradually working our way out of the cave of ignorance by proceeding from our specific circumstances to higher and higher levels of generality until we reach the universal Forms that transcend all particular instances. This otherworldly emphasis seems so extreme that it will come under fire by Aristotle and many other philosophers. Plato himself questioned the difficult logical problem of insisting that universal Forms from an unchanging world can somehow come down to cause the particular forms of objects in our everyday world.

For instance, late in his life, in the *Parmenides,* he raises doubts about this crucial theory. The problem is that the *Parmenides* is such a difficult text to decipher (and many have even suggested that it is incoherent), because of its progressively more intricate linguistic analyses. The characters in the dialogue are familiar since Cephalus, who owned the house where everyone met for the discussion in the *Republic,* now meets Adeimantus and Glaucon, Plato's brothers, in the marketplace. Cephalus seeks to recover a conversation between Socrates and Parmenides, and for that they have to walk to Antiphon's house because the latter had memorized that conversation "by heart" (*Collected* 921). At this third remove, we thus get a rendering of the conversation between Socrates and Parmenides, and Socrates tries to resist the difficult questions from his interlocutors, who argue that "perplexities are everywhere involved in the forms themselves" (924). Yet for some time Socrates persists in his explanations, even using the example of the "master or slave of another" (928), but his analysis becomes so convoluted it is difficult to follow. It becomes increasingly abstract, especially when the terms under discussion move from visible objects to "those objects which are specially apprehended by discourse and can be regarded as forms" (930), such as the "'beautiful,' 'just,' 'good,' and other particular forms" (930). Such nonvisible abstractions have a kind of built-in double remove when trying to discover the ultimate Forms of such already abstract concepts. Socrates and Parmenides head right into these multiple levels of abstractions, and it is not easy going. Although Hegel praised the *Parmenides* as the greatest of the Platonic dialogues, few people have agreed with him because it remains difficult to appreciate sentences like the following: "If, then, the one and its being are each different from the other, it is not in virtue of being one that the one is different from the being, nor is it in virtue of being 'being' that the being is other than the one" (936). Clearly, they are raising doubts about the likelihood that universal Forms can be the causes of particular forms in the world of appearances. Finally, at the very end of the dialogue, Socrates reverses the doubts with another assertion of the inevitability of the ultimate Forms, here articulated as the "one."[15]

Returning to the everyday world represented by the "Allegory," we can choose to emphasize the ongoing process of dialectical engagement in determining what should count for knowledge. In other words, the dialectic is like rereading: you read it once (literally), then read it again (figuratively) to get another, better (more general, more abstract) reading, and so on. Or you can read it, as Plato would have it, as an allegorical reading of human beings leaving the dark on the journey to the light of the absolute truth, or universal Form.

In this sense, to engage in dialectics as the method of choice is to participate in a powerful kind of translation beginning with the low and dark and ascending to the high and light: "But the release of the prisoners from chains, and their translation from the shadows to the images and to the light," represents an "*ascent* from the underground den to the sun" (224, my italics). The entire discourse of images pertinent to the foundations of Western metaphysics seems to be based on metaphors of rising: "*elevating* the highest principle in the soul" (224); "*raising* of that faculty" (224); "the eye of the soul . . . is . . . *lifted* upwards" (225, my italics). All this business of "raising" consciousness is central to the hierarchical set of values antithetical to democratic rights for all, but another powerful feature of the discourse is that you can reverse directions and get much the same effect.

To shift directions 180 degrees works fine: Western metaphysics can be rendered as a movement from surface to depth, a digging beneath the particular surface appearances to the hidden, deeper, universal structures of meaning. Indeed, this model of depth interpretation supplies the basic structural model for most modern Western versions of "deep" reading called the hermeneutics of suspicion. For instance, Marx sought to move from the cultural superstructure to the underlying economic base, or from ideological false consciousness to true historical understanding; Freud's model of interpretation moves from the conscious mind to the unconscious depths and back again; Saussure's structural linguistics sought to move beneath the individual speech acts, parole, to the underlying linguistic features, the langue.[16] As we will also see in Cultural Turn 2, the eighteenth-century Scottish rhetoricians could use this model to seek the underlying universal laws of fine writing, and it could be further employed to reduce language to grammatical forms as the primary causes of meaning. Twentieth-century New Critics imagined the ultimate aesthetic accomplishments of the finest canonized poems as "verbal icons" and "well wrought urns," vessels of universal, formal unities in the texts themselves. In these instances, again, the emphasis is on the fixed goal more than on the ongoing process of interpretation. But, in general terms, we speak of Western metaphysics as "foundational" according to this depth model: the technical term, *hermeneutics*, even takes its basic sense from Hermes, the messenger god, who carries meaning from the superficial surfaces we encounter on a first reading to a deeper level of understanding based on the foundation, the grounds, the deeper truth that we cannot see on first glance. The reverse direction, elevating meaning toward universal, transcendent truths, gets rewritten in the aesthetic discourse about poetic beauty that will emerge in CT2, often called "Romantic idealism." But whether we go up or down, translation serves Plato as a metaphor for rereading, a moving from one (inferior) level to another (superior) level, and regardless of whether you imagine it as going up or down, the vertical dimension visualizes hierarchy; the binary elements of opposition never bear equal value.

This strenuous educational process takes time: as Plato outlines it, there are stages to be reached at the ages of twenty and at thirty, but full education is not achieved until the age of fifty! The conceptual hierarchy thus becomes de facto an antidemocratic kind of intellectual aristocracy where only a privileged few, free of manual labor, have the time to become the highly educated rulers. As Wood argues, "the realization of the philosophic nature depends on the life conditions of a leisured aristocracy, able to appropriate the labour of others and free from the need to engage in productive work" (*Citizens* 71). Nevertheless, Plato was unique in his inclusion of women: "for you must not suppose that what I have been saying applies to men only and not to women as far as their natures can go . . . since we have made them to share in all things like the men" (233). Acknowledging that the qualification of women going only so far as "their natures" allow, this remark, and others regarding the education of women, strike many as astounding given the widely shared belief in the patriarchal nature of knowledge in the Western metaphysical tradition.[17] There is, however, no inclusion in Plato's version of the education of the material producers of goods (the farmers, slaves, laborers, artisans) because only the philosopher-kings and other rulers will have time for such extended educational pursuits. There are real limits to these educational freedoms.[18]

But to return to our overview of the "Allegory of the Cave," we can now list three basic structural properties of Western metaphysics:

1. It is binary (a dialectical process, at best).

2. It is hierarchical.

3. It is based on ideal, absolute Forms that are unchanging, ahistorical, universal, and potentially communal, at least to the extent that they are the same for everyone.

Knowledge produced through the dialectic is ultimately stable, unified, and predictable, so that to this extent the dialectic aspires to exemplify a basic property of our communality. That is, Western metaphysics seems to have it both ways: hierarchy and communality are combined, but at the expense of leaving the material level of social organization altogether in order to arrive at the universal level. At the social level, the hierarchy of the philosopher-king establishes the leadership of the wise, not the democratic will of the Athenian citizens, nor the unruly fluctuations of an unregulated market that was too often manipulated for private gain by the unscrupulous. Given these assumptions, it makes sense that Plato can then demarcate the various domains of knowledge beginning with the most abstract (mathematics, geometry, and astronomy), each field or discipline standing on its own eternal terrain, the stable foundations based on objective properties of the different objects themselves, and, of course, hierarchically arranged. Now, it is fair to say that none of the leading sophists of his day such as Isocrates, Protagoras, or Gorgias would be very accepting of this ultimately fixed metaphysics, and thus for these reasons Plato is also positioned as an antisophistic absolutist. The historical Socrates, even as represented by Aristophanes and Xenophon, held strong in the belief that virtue had to be based on universal knowledge, not relative beliefs and opinions, but it is certainly fair to say that with this radical break, and the doctrine of Forms as absolutes, Plato created the opportunity for a chasm to open between the contingent/historical and the universal/timeless, and the history of how that chasm has played out over two thousand years is one key element in the story of Western metaphysics. The supposedly universal conceptual hierarchy could only too easily be converted into an anti-universal social hierarchy devaluing non-Western cultures, indigenous societies, people of color, and women, partly because Plato himself believed in a hierarchical organization of production.

The greatest irony is that these founders of Western metaphysics often professed nonhierarchical universals but used those concepts to produce inequality in the social order. As Wood explains, "The political relations among citizens was a relationship among equals, but there remained a fundamental inequality between the civic community and those outside it" (*Citizens* 100)—a sharp division, that is, between rulers and producers. Nevertheless, it is also fair to say that we have in Plato's plan for organizing knowledge in his Academy the prototype of the first university of the West, insofar as it set up epistemological distinctions between related branches of knowledge produced by experts trained in these specific fields. In short, our modern formation of separate disciplines of knowledge produced under conditions of academic freedom has its roots in this discourse: the basic conundrum of academic freedom as we know it is that disciplinary knowledge produced in specific disciplines serves the communal life of public good by paradoxically establishing a hierarchy that excludes the public from the decisions about what counts as knowledge, as established by the self-governing body of experts trained in those very disciplines. There is both joy and fear in the autonomy and self-determination required of disciplinary knowledge. Indeed, we will return often to this conundrum between communality and hierarchy.

Recapping the Origins

Given this general overview of the basic structural features of Western metaphysics, we can at least see now that Plato's interpretation of the poet makes sense within this framework. The philosopher, not the poet, is the one who is going to have success with the dialectic. Nevertheless, to determine the banishing of poetry from the state on the basis of such strictly formal logic seems unreasonably restrictive. Something is indeed missing, but the real questions are how and why it so often happens that the absent sociohistorical contexts vacated the scene of reading.

Let's begin by asking the *how*: how have we been trying to answer the two basic questions about Plato's banishment of the poet and the meaning of Western metaphysics? We have been reading the text, but we remain in the dark, perplexed that claims about poetry seem so wrong in fundamental ways for our own modern tastes. A contemporary critique of these reading practices is familiar and easy to articulate: we have been interpreting a text as if the meaning were in the text itself even though we know we shouldn't be doing it that way. We have been trying to read a text that is more than 2,300 years old, in translation, and to determine what it means, as if the meaning were contained in the isolated text. In the twenty-first century, few readers believe in the New Critical view of self-contained textual meanings, yet in some key instances it persists as an unconscious normal disciplinary practice to assign a text that is perhaps hundreds, or even thousands, of years old, in translation, and to then discuss or write about that text. That is a common experience in a truly transnational sense: teachers, students, and readers from all over the world have shared this experience.

Plato himself acknowledges the ethical consequences of historical misreading: "because we do not know the truth about ancient times, we make falsehood as much like truth as we can" (68). That is, he acknowledges that some of our ahistorical predispositions lead us into many historical misunderstandings. Even in the twenty-first century, when contextual and historical readings have gained disciplinary ascendance in English studies, we still have to ask ourselves how some of our familiar teaching and reading habits may still be informed by Western metaphysical assumptions: the assumption that we can read ancient texts without distorting the historical archive leaves us especially vulnerable to the very ways that we unconsciously shape that archive according to our own values and needs. Such ethnocentrism is always our starting place, as most scholars would agree, but it need not have final say in our translations of cultural and historical differences.

With this invocation of the historical, let me summarize what I hope will be a more ethical reading of the past, a reframing more responsive to the social conditions in the geopolitical economy of ancient Greece. What Plato means by the word *poetry* is very different from what we mean by the word *poetry,* and there is no way to know this unless we investigate the culture in which he was living. We may then begin to understand that what he means by poetry is a reference to an oral tradition in the context of a culture that is making the transition from orality to literacy. The performance of poetry was fundamental to an oral culture in the sense that it provided a way for the society to preserve some sense of its historical background: its important stories and myths, which embody fundamental cultural values. As Havelock puts it, poetry was a kind of "technology for the preservation of culture," a social practice for re-creating and preserving traditions that would otherwise be lost forever since there was no mechanism for writing things down or recording the stories. Oral forms of poetic memorization provide aid in the organization and production of a meaningful tradition for social bonding, and oral cultures tend to deeply invest time and energy into those oral modes for that reason. In short, poetic imitation in an oral culture is more a form of necessary memorization to preserve the cultural past than a product of a singular creative genius who transcends the culture.

We have inherited a definition of poetry that was transformed more exclusively into its modern meaning within the last 250 years: we think of poetry as literal written poems that are creative, imaginative, and unique. But for Plato, poetry was to a large extent exactly the opposite: it was repetitious, formulaic, and stereotypical. To this extent, then, instead of being seen as a conservative foundationalist setting the terms for the status quo in an antidemocratic elitism, Plato can be reread as a more radical cultural critic, attacking the dominant modes by which traditional oral culture reproduced itself. This counterintuitive rereading contradicts the common view whereby for Plato, poetry is the chaotic, disorganized, "subversive" emotional force that unsettles the rational, rigid, unified, stable version of the hierarchical republic that he advocates. For example, M. A. R. Habib exemplifies this view when he explains that, for Plato, poetry "must be subjected to constant vigilance lest it unleash forces which undermine the political, economic, and legal structure," and this view "suggests that Plato accredited it with an inherent subversiveness" whereby poetic performance is "an ideologically destabilizing force" (*History* 27–28). In short, Habib (both summarizing and exemplifying the most highly sophisticated of critical readings) contrasts what is presumed by modern standards to be the subversive, destabilizing poetic tradition with what's to come in Plato's teleology, the rigidly prescribed, universal routines of the ideal future republic governed by philosophy. That wished-for ideal is, indeed, represented in the text by Plato, so Habib defines poetry within the argumentative dialogue of the *Republic* rather than locating it more directly in the social and political context of the oral tradition of poetry, which as we have seen served as a necessary historical archive for preserving the traditions of the preliterate society preceding Plato's day. With that perspective in mind, Plato appears then to offer a critique of the oppressive features of that tradition: philosophy, rather than the conservative function of poetry, is the subversive force. Likewise, Habib sees Plato as engaged in the debate between aesthetics and politics: but aesthetics is *our* term, modernized out of the Greek term *esthetics* (sense perception) during the Romantic revolution (CT 2). Aesthetics, per se, as primarily formalist theories about art and literature, seems irrelevant to Plato's argument, as Havelock will make clear.

No doubt, Plato's ideal state is based on a hierarchical elite that rigidly enforces obedience to its philosophical values. Nevertheless, taking fuller account of the role of poetry in an oral culture, the opposite may be the case: poetic performance itself blindingly re-creates, stabilizes, and preserves through memorization of verse the traditional social and moral order. According to Habib, poetry, like democracy, "fosters genuine individuals" (33) who, therefore, threaten the unified order of the aristocratic state ruled by a philosopher-king. But if poetry in an oral tradition is based on memorization and meticulous repetition of the same, it yields not radical, wayward individuals, but blindly conservative subjects repeating and adhering to the memorized social order exemplified in the poetic myths. If that is the case, as we will see in the next chapter, Plato now appears somewhat more like Socrates as "gadfly," the bug that stings the dimwitted horse, irritating the ruling powers that held sway in the Athenian democracy when citizens could be miseducated to support oppressive but popular views. And he irritated both the oligarchs and the democrats.

This play on Western metaphysical dualism intentionally reframes the question of poetic performance and value: we must now try to reread the text in the social, cultural, and political context with respect to the geopolitical economy in which it was produced. Not an easy task, but made much easier by the work of Milman Parry, Havelock, and Walter J. Ong. These critics allow us to see that Plato's representation of the poet may have a much more empirical basis in the actual habits of poetic performance in an oral culture than do all the modern views that see him constructing not a historical but an idealized "a priori definition" of poetry as an imaginative art.[19] So now we have to slow things down a bit and begin again with a kind of foray into the cultural context of ancient Greece to get some sense of what was going on back then. Much of the material we now have available to us for this purpose has emerged from research done within the last one hundred years, and it has opened entirely new ways of rereading the Platonic canon. That's what we will take up in the next chapter, where our inquiry takes us well beyond the text itself.

CHAPTER THREE

Reframing the Republic: From the Homeric to the Platonic Paideia

> Poetry was not "literature" but a political and social
> necessity. It was not an art form, nor a creation of the
> private imagination, but an encyclopedia maintained
> by co-operative effort on the part of the "best Greek
> polities."
>
> —ERIC HAVELOCK, *Preface to Plato*

The Orality Hypothesis

In 1935, when Milman Parry was accidentally shot and killed in
Los Angeles, he was only thirty-three years old, but the scholarly
work he had already completed changed the way many of us now
read ancient Greek texts, especially those of Homer. Between 1924
and 1928, as a student of the famous French linguist Antoine
Meillet at the Sorbonne, Parry made some remarkable discoveries
about the Homeric poems.[1] In thoroughly convincing fashion, he
demonstrated the truth of Meillet's basic hypothesis that, contrary
to most received interpretations of these texts, the *Iliad* and the
Odyssey were constructed out of formulas, stereotypes, clichés,
if you will, rather than unique, innovative, creative language.

Given our modern frames of viewing poetry and literature
as those kinds of writing that create new, beautiful, and original
kinds of language, Parry's hypothesis was nothing less than astounding. Indeed, he reframed the entire way of interpreting these
ancient texts by embedding them in the sociocultural conditions of
an oral culture. If you have ever read the *Iliad* and enjoyed what
you experienced as the beautiful uniqueness of imagery such as

"rosy-fingered dawn," it can be unsettling to learn that such expressions were not original expressions of a single, creative author at all but epithets, customary uses of language, part of a series of set formulae composed for oral memorization and performance in strict hexameter verse to augment ease of memorization. Walter Ong succinctly summarizes Parry's discovery: "virtually every distinctive feature of Homeric poetry is due to the economy forced upon it by oral methods of composition" (*Orality* 21).

Living as we do in a literate culture that conceives of poetry in the aesthetic terms developed in the Romantic period, it can be disconcerting to learn that our very enjoyment of Homer has been dependent on an ahistorical disembedding of the written text from the oral culture from which it emerged. That ancient culture organized a great deal of its citizens' time around the production of oral performances designed to ensure the preservation of important social narratives. Even more, our notion of authorship attributes specific texts to individual authors, but Parry demonstrated that much more likely the Homeric poems emerged from hundreds of years of transmission through oral cultures until they could be, perhaps collaboratively, transcribed into textual forms shortly after the invention of the Greek alphabet in the eighth century BCE. He therefore casts doubt on our very belief in Homer as an individual writer of poetic texts.[2]

Parry served as one of the founders of the orality/literacy debates that have become increasingly important over the past hundred years, especially with respect to the study of various "oral literatures," an oxymoron crucial to all ethnographers who have transcribed oral performances in cultures where literacy has been much less pronounced than the oral tradition. About forty years after Parry's work, Eric Havelock extended the oral hypothesis to his reframing of the Platonic dialogues. In his equally groundbreaking study, *Preface to Plato* (1963), Havelock offered stunning new ways to understand Plato's arguments against the poets in the *Republic*. As a classical scholar responding to the newly emerging orality/literacy theories, Havelock adapted Parry's theses to demonstrate that three hundred years after Homer, Plato was writing at a time when literacy was becoming more widespread, transforming some of the basic ways the culture of the Greek city-states of that time organized social life. Or, as Havelock puts it, poetry was (or had been) a useful technology for the preservation of oral culture, but it was no longer serving the same purposes in the newly emerging literate culture between the eighth and fourth centuries BCE in Athens. In fact, what Havelock suggests is that the *Republic* should be viewed not as a political treatise on ideal forms of government, but rather as an attack on the existing educational system of Greece. The sociopolitical impact of such an attack arises from the sense that Plato was inaugurating a cultural revolution in the whole way the society organized its knowledge, power, pedagogy, and technology, a revolution that signified a broad-based shift from oral to literate culture.[3]

Gradual, rising rates of literacy would also make possible the newly emerging forms of democracy that began to form in Athens with the written constitution adopted in the age of Solon (638–558 BCE) that would usher in the classical age of Greece. The Homeric poems refer to a combination of both real and mythical events in what is called the archaic age of Greece, when, as Ellen Meiksins Wood explains, the "Homeric property regime" was based on "hereditary nobility" (*Peasant-Citizen* 91). Solon is given credit for establishing the basic principles of a democratic polis in the shift from the archaic to the classical age of ancient Greece. Basically, in the archaic period, a group of nine archons administered the city-state, and they were selected on the basis of their inherited noble status and their wealth. Prior to Solon, tribal feuds and informal oral laws became increasingly ineffective, and so in the seventh century BCE Draco was appointed to establish a harsh set of written codes (hence, the origin of our term "draconian" measures). But the key transition was Solon's establishment of the Athenian Constitution around 593 BCE, which gave rights as citizens to common people, peasant farmers, and artisans, who could elect representatives to the high courts, although scholars dispute the exact nature of these rights because there are so few clear records from this period. Solon's reforms enabled a domestic agrarian society where most people lived on small farms to expand and enter more commercial markets over greater distances. Later, these market exchanges were orchestrated by political and military alliances (primarily arranged by Pericles in the mid-fifth century BCE) into the loosely affiliated Delian League of more than one hundred otherwise independent Greek city-states, a move also facilitated by the invention in Lydia of the first minted coins, combined with the more widespread use of Greek literacy, which could facilitate contractual agreements, recordkeeping, and reliable communication.[4] The Delian League was often challenged by and in conflict with the opposing Peloponnesian League centered in Sparta. Democracy in ancient Athens enabled some citizens with voting rights to participate in market pricing and social welfare, but internal modes of redistribution of resources came about by "money acquired from other poleis through the Delian league. Imperialism and exploitation for the exterior, democracy and social welfare policies for the interior: that was Athenian democracy, making it a prototype for today's states" (Karatani, *Structure* 118). Oral modes of cultural reproduction were much less important during the periods of transition into these prototypical democracies, and Havelock situates Plato's fourth century argument against the poets in the *Republic* within the larger frame of the gradually emerging forms of literacy in the four-hundred-year shift from the archaic to the classical periods in ancient Greece.

The gist of Havelock's argument can be summarized quite succinctly: what Plato means by poetry and what we mean by poetry no doubt share a great deal, but in most respects they refer to entirely different objects or processes. Most of what Plato says about poetry now makes much more sense when we realize that Plato is not referring to unique, textual poems such as we admire as moderns, but to the oral tradition wherein poetry was the performance of repeated, memorized, formulaic verse. The latter qualities may be the greatest vices we can imagine for what *we* call poetry, but in an oral culture they are all virtues because they assist anyone trying to learn long but important stories about their culture.

We can now, therefore, reframe Plato's attack on poetry as an attack on the oral tradition, blind memorization, and the archaic-age organization of production in an agrarian society where literate forms of knowledge, education, and understanding played no part other than through the enormous energy and time spent on the recitation and memorization of poetry. Ancient poetry was dominated by performers, poets, singers, primarily in the service of the tyrannical hereditary rulers and ruling classes.

Havelock provided the evidence to suggest that poetry and poetic images were central to the ancient Greek educational apparatus and, furthermore, central to the maintenance of the land-tenure system whereby wealthy landowners used and appropriated the agricultural surplus produced by landless serfs, the latter having no say in the established patterns of dominance and social hierarchy. In this light, Plato's attack on the poet begins to make sense. In its oral performance, poetry is an entire technology for the preservation of useful knowledge, cultural history, and traditional practices and values as conveyed by the examples, stories, and images memorized and recited by not only the poets and rhetors but also the fathers, archons, rulers, and military leaders—virtually all significant land-owning male members of the society. Fundamental to the geopolitical economy of an oral culture, the poet/rhetor often reinforced the hierarchies of power, typically those upheld by the oligarchs ruling various Mycenaean regions as they gradually began to organize into specific city-states.

Plato's attack now takes on a more radical ideological force lost in the assumption of his reactionary and repressive doctrines of censorship as gleaned from the formalist unity of the text "itself." In general, we are forced to realize that Plato assumes among his contemporaries a view of the poet wholly unfamiliar to our post-Romantic ways of thinking. As Havelock explains:

> In fact, it is not too much to say that the notion of the aesthetic as a system of values which might apply to artistic composition never once enters the argument. Plato writes as though he had never heard of aesthetics or even of art. Instead he insists on discussing the poets as though their job was to supply metrical encyclopedias. The poet is a source on the one hand of essential information and on the other of essential moral training. (*Preface* 29)

Thus the actual performance of poetry was far more central to the Greek cultural pattern prior to and even in the early stages of the Axial Age, beginning around 800 BCE, than we can easily conceive to be the case. A new dimension of Plato's attack on the poet now opens up to us: to attack mimesis and imitation can be seen as an attack on blind memorization and identification with dominant cultural images.

As a way of illustrating the ideological consequences for Greek culture of this mnemonic rhetoric, Hesiod (who came slightly after Homer) provides an example of the early signs of a shift from concrete oral images to abstract, literate categories. Whereas the Homeric narratives provided no abstract system of meanings apart from the particular images and examples of the good ways and acceptable customs of the traditional culture, Hesiod in his introductory "Hymn to the Muses" in the *Theogony* begins to identify the source and justification for such memorization. As Havelock explains: "Homer simply invoked the Muse who is figuratively responsible for anything he says. Hesiod in effect asks, Who is the Muse? What precisely does she do? What am I doing, and how do I do it? As he asks and answers this question he begins himself to transcend the epic purpose and conception" (*Preface* 99).

As Hesiod hymns his invocation to the muses, he "commemorates their birth and identifies them as the daughters of *Mnemosune*" (Havelock, *Preface* 100), or memory. The Greek notion of memory suggests as well "the notions of recall and of record and of memorization. Through this allegorical parentage Hesiod identifies the technological reasons for poetry's existence: it describes the muses' function" (100). And they are not the daughters of Romantic inspiration and creative invention (our romanticized version of the Muses), but rather the offspring of a far more traditional and static process of memorization of the cultural record: "their central task is not to create but to preserve" (100). Since their other parent is Zeus, their songs memorize and commemorate the power of Zeus, the father as patriarchal origin of the social and political order. To this extent, poetry aids the traditional phallocratic order. And Hesiod's allegory in turn suggests "for poetry precisely that central role in the maintenance of Greek culture which Plato would reject" (102). Indeed, in his earlier poem, *Works and Days,* the speaker of the poem, Hesiod, is describing to his younger brother, Perses, the operations and practices best suited for successful farming for a relatively small-scale landowning aristocracy, the central mode of food production in the domestic economies of ancient Greece. Hesiod champions hard work and labor, and he offers a mild critique of the unjust powers of the greedy basilees, or lords, who oppress the hard-working farmers who produce the crops while the landowners reap the surplus.

The contrast with Homer is subtle but significant and thus worth being precise about. Whereas the Homeric epics display very little self-reflexive verse, very little interest in examining the sociocultural role of the narrator, the poet, and the rhetor, Hesiod's allegory begins at least a quest to name the sources, reasons, and roles of the poet and the Muse. In other words, in Homer's case, the presentation of the culturally acceptable "custom ways" (ethos) and laws (nomos) always proceeds by way of specific, concrete examples of such behavior. The narrative therefore serves as a model for specific practices and behaviors. Rarely does Homer reflect in more general or abstract terms upon the poet's relationship to the dominant laws and customs. In contrast, Hesiod begins just such a reflection, but of course he does not challenge the order and source that he identifies (other than through his relatively mild but specific complaints about the basilees); that role falls to Plato. And since Plato is now so generally credited as the father of the dominant Western metaphysic called "phallogocentrism," it is a necessary corrective to see Plato within the newly emerging discursive formations of ancient Greece as playing a critical, anticanonical, and less repressive function with respect to the poet than the more ahistorical generalizations may suggest. Plato sought, in this view, to replace the repressions of a tyranny and the blindness of an uneducated democracy with a highly educated elite of philosophers—to put this in a more contemporary idiom, we might say that he was trying to create an alternative counterhegemony to the dominant oral tradition of authoritarian rule.

Imitation, or mimesis, was, indeed, central to oral culture. But the process of mimesis was not, as it generally is in modern discourse, placed within the problems associated with accurate or mimetic representation (think of imitation in the discourse of realism, or the doctrine of verisimilitude), but rather within the dynamics of accurate repetition or blind memorization.[5] The hexameter dithyrambs Parry analyzed were actually repetitious and didactic clichés and common stereotypical images or epithets. They had to be: otherwise it would be extremely difficult, if not impossible, to memorize such lengthy narratives. As opposed to our notions of poetic images as unique creations, Homer's verse was primarily constituted by the formulas which would later be seen as defeating the originality and creativity valued by Romantic aesthetics as it later emerged in the nineteenth century and subsequently set the terms for our modern understanding of poetry as an art.

Memory is indeed the key: if the poet or singer fails to remember the myths, stories, and set of cultural values transmitted through the epic poems, the society risks losing its own cultural history—there are no tape recorders or camcorders around, nor texts, for that matter, in a primary oral culture.[6] Whereas in the dialectic, the force of repetition is on rereading, or saying it differently, in the oral tradition poetry relies on the force of repetition, which, in turn, depends largely on immense powers of human memory. Indeed, oral cultures devote enormous social energy and time to such memorization: think what it would mean to have memorized all of the *Iliad* or the *Odyssey*. Amazing accomplishments looked at in that context, but that appears to be exactly what was happening.[7]

Everything about the verse we have inherited by way of textual transcription from the oral was then actually composed to aid oral transmission through memorization. Repetition of stereotypes, clichés, formulas—these features all function as positive strategies serving very practical mnemonic uses since they make it easier to remember so much material. Emotional identification on the part of the poets also plays a key role: ask any actor and they will tell you what the ancient Greek poets knew, that emotionally identifying with the character whose lines you must remember is an aid to successful learning of the lines. Plato's critique of emotional identification on the part of poetic performances was therefore based on his efforts to break with the dominant cultural tradition of emotional identification and blind memorization (mimesis) of poetic verse in an oral culture.

In this context, it is no wonder, then, that Plato so critically characterizes "the effect of poetry as 'a crippling of the mind' . . . [as] a kind of disease" (Havelock, *Preface* 4), or a cultural illness from which the citizens of ancient Greece need to be cured. The

poet, like the actors, dramatists, and singers, was given to rhap-
sody because, as Ong explains, "The meaning of the Greek term
'rhapsodize,' *rhapsōidein*, [is] 'to stitch song together' (*rhaptein*,
to stitch; *ōide*, song)," but this patchwork process of memorization and performance "became ominous: Homer stitched together
prefabricated parts. Instead of a creator, you had an assembly-line
worker" (Ong 22). In these circumstances, the urgency of Plato's
critique now becomes understandable also: "Plato speaks passionately in the tones of a man who feels he is taking on a most
formidable opponent who can muster the total forces of tradition
and contemporary opinion against him. He pleads, he argues, he
denounces, he cajoles. He is a David confronting some Goliath.
And he speaks as though he had no choice but to fight the battle
to a finish" (Havelock, *Preface* 9).

In a literate culture, texts provide a repository that frees labor
(and thus time) formerly spent in the tasks of memorization to do
other things. Contrary to the oral procedures of the poets, what
Plato is asking his readers to do is look again, correct things as
much as possible, and say them in a new and better way. Plato
appears in this role more as the radical reformer, not the prig; his
concluding argument against emotion in Book 10 is not against
feeling *per se,* but against its use as a technology of identification
for the speaker to better memorize very long poetic narratives.
Rather than more memorization, Plato is arguing for change and
alteration, and to this extent (contrary to much received opinion),
he is much more aligned with the sophists and the rhetors, against
the oral tradition of the poets.[8]

Whereas in our modern discourse mimesis is associated with
the problem of accurate representation, Plato saw that blind
memorization used in oral mimesis often ineffectively repeated
inaccurate kinds of cultural knowledge. Homeric verse was being used as a didactic instrument so that the poetic and rhetorical performance sustained the culture through memorization of
orally transmitted information. One aspect of the cultural crisis
of Plato's day was that the content of the knowledge "reposited"
in the Homeric poems was no longer very useful; basically, it
was outdated.

To use a simple example, consider the famous catalog of
ships in Book 2 of the *Iliad:* like all of the Homeric epics, this

section was well-memorized and repeated by the poets because it provided useful knowledge for commanders of ships in battle. The epic poem served partly, that is, as a kind of archive whose oral repetition passed along to other generations important knowledge about how to conduct naval battles. But as ship technology had changed (the three rows of oars in the triremes were being replaced by quadriremes and quinqueremes during the fourth century BCE), and as the demographics of Mediterranean culture had changed, the oral knowledge was no longer so useful to the users of the new kinds of ships. Plato's argument, in this context, is to free a culture from such blind memorization to produce new, more useable knowledge. Moreover, even the social function of the poet in the era immediately preceding Plato's day was primarily to serve as an instrument of the tyrannical state, the official discourse whereby the poet (as, for example, Pindar) wrote odes to commemorate athletic and military heroes by ascribing to their feats the images of a heroic and godly genealogy characteristic of the wealthy rulers of the state. As Havelock explains, poetry "provided a massive repository of useful knowledge, a sort of encyclopedia of ethics, politics, history and technology which the effective citizen was required to learn as the core of his educational equipment. Poetry represented not something we call by that name," but rather served educational and social functions that today would be much more akin to "a shelf of text books and works of reference" (27) or even digital archives on the Internet.

In contrast, the emerging discourse of philosophy as the preeminent form of literacy did offer the potential for an analytic language through its ability to generate a new dialectical syntax of being and becoming, thus separating the knower from the known, the subject from the object, the self from the other. These new technologies of literacy affected social relations in both positive and negative ways. But before we get to the details of those linguistic transformations and their social consequences, it can be helpful to see the broader historical frame for the shift from orality to literacy at the very time when coinage and new forms of warfare were emerging in this geographical region of the Mediterranean.

Shifting the Tense in an Emerging Literacy:
What's So Popular about the Copula?

In *Orality and Literacy* (1982), Walter J. Ong offers a comprehensive timeframe that provides approximate dates for the emergence of literacy in ancient Greece. The background story of writing is that it emerged out of various versions of scripts that developed in many places around the world, typically in isolation from one another, which accounts for their dramatic variations. There have been many different kinds of scripts (Mesopotamian cuneiform, Egyptian hieroglyphics, Minoan "Linear B," Chinese script, Mayan script, etc.), but as Ong puts it, there are "many scripts but only one alphabet" (85). The tactical problem with the basic graphic nature of all scripts is that they require an enormous number of signs, so, as Ong explains, these script precursors to alphabetic writing tended to be cumbersome, learned as a skill by only a very few members of the society, and better for static recordkeeping than dynamic storytelling.

Ong adopts Havelock's description of a four-stage historical process beginning with primary orality, and proceeding through the stages of craft literacy and semiliteracy before reaching more widespread conditions of literacy. The prototypical beginnings of lexigraphic writing (visual writing codes based on speech) occurred between 3400 and 3300 BCE with the invention of the oldest known script, the Sumerian cuneiform.[9] Prior to that date, at the beginning of the Bronze Age, all cultures in the world were maintained on an exclusively oral basis. By about 2700 BCE, the rudimentary phonetic characters of cuneiform could now be combined into what we would call grammatical and syntactic units. As Barry Powell explains, "Old World lexigraphic writing was invented only once, in Mesopotamia, and perhaps a second time, much later, in China. But even in China the idea of 'writing' must have come from Mesopotamia over the Gansu corridor north of the Himalayas, where caravan traffic was constant. China was never wholly separated from cultural developments in Mesopotamia" (4). Cuneiform went through numerous permutations, variations, and geographical differences in uses. Nevertheless, these were relatively minor differences compared to the varieties of spoken languages. As Powell argues, "Writing's overarching power stabilizes speech, represses local differences, and fashions standards for thought and expression" (7).

The real turning point came around 1500 BCE in Egypt, when Semitic Phoenician cultures developed the original alphabet. But a more direct precursor to the Greek alphabet, called Linear B, evolved as a syllabary (based on syllables rather than phonetic letters) out of what was called Linear A in Mycenae and Minoan Crete from around 1400 to 1200 BCE. Of the nearly three thousand Linear B tablets that have been recovered, what is noticeable about most of them is that they are more like inventories and records than stories or myths. Significantly, these early alphabets were constructed almost exclusively out of consonants, so they had quite limited phonetic equivalence in the relation between the spoken word and the written text. Nevertheless, during the long first stage of craft literacy (3300–800 BCE), the skills of the scribes were typically acquired by servants, sometimes slaves, and the writing itself was most often in the form of recordkeeping for illiterate but powerful landowners: in short, writing was class-based, but in an inverse way with respect to the contemporary status of writing. It was a craft, on the order, say, of blacksmithing, and, that being the case, social or political leaders did not need to stoop to do it themselves because the work could be done for them by their servants, tenants, peasants, or casual laborers.

Paradoxically, however, within a few hundred years of the invention of the alphabet the entire regions of Mycenaean, Macedonian, Mesopotamian, Egyptian, and Phoenician cultures generally went into a period of decline sometimes referred to as the Dark Age, between about 1200 and 800 BCE. Events narrated in the Homeric poems are assumed to have occurred during (or just prior to) this period, when regional and institutional unity seems to have disintegrated into smaller, decentralized farming communities. What appears to have been happening was a breakdown in the large, palace-based kingdoms of the Bronze Age in some kind of mysterious cultural cataclysm. Ian Morris offers a more naturalistic explanation by calling it the "paradox of development," whereby the rise of social development in a region produces new problems that cannot be resolved by the then-current system of production and distribution. But Morris also offers geographical and climatic reasons: "some archeologists point to signs of higher temperatures and lower rainfall in every part of the Western core after 1300 BCE" (217). Climate change also led to "famine, state failure, and migration" (224) so that the social disruption escalated into a kind of collapse—a fear not all that dissimilar to contemporary fears about global warming. The kingdoms of the Bronze Age had established huge bureaucratic structures designed to move agricultural products to the palace centers, redistributing the surplus to the already wealthy rulers.[10] Beginning around 1200 BCE with the breakdown of these massive redistributive kingdoms, what gradually emerged by around 800 BCE was the Axial Age orientation toward smaller, more localized city-states. As Wood argues, the amazing thing "is the apparent disappearance of writing in Greece for several centuries. . . . Once the need for compulsive record-keeping so characteristic of the palace-economy had evaporated, it was to be a long time before new social needs and possibilities created new literary and intellectual forms, together with a new and more versatile system of writing, the Greek alphabet" (*Peasant-Citizen* 85). Significant also is that early forms of script were composed on clay tablets so it really was a time-consuming task, but the kingdoms around Mesopotamia and Mycenae had deeply invested in these activities, and by the time of the Phoenician alphabet more convenient and portable forms of writing surface such as papyrus, wax tablets, and leather had come into use. As Ian Morris explains, by 1250 BCE "There were thousands of literate scribes and burgeoning libraries" (215). Nevertheless, many of these artisanal tasks associated with the production of writing tablets seem to have withered away during the ensuing Dark Age with a corresponding rise in aristocratic and tribal factionalism and discontent among the serfs and peasants.

Although it was not really until Solon's reformation that dramatic social and political changes began to take place, especially in Attica, the key precursor to a dramatic rise in social development seems to have come with the invention of the Greek alphabet during the early phase of the Axial Age around 800 BCE. As Havelock demonstrated in *The Origins of Western Literacy*, what was remarkable was the invention of a vowel-based phonetic alphabet of about twenty-four characters.[11] The social effects of the phonetic alphabet were game-changing since, for one thing, it became unnecessary to support a class of specialist scribes. As Powell explains, "In a stroke the need for a special class of men who mastered the system and served the state, and its religion, by the manipulation of graphically encoded information was disabled. . . . In Greece there was no scribal class" (251). What may be most remarkable of all is that this invention (setting aside one or two other scripts that have not survived or are rarely used) has happened only once in the history of the world.[12] All existing phonetic alphabets are derivatives in one way or another of this fundamental invention in ancient Greece. One of the most dramatic effects this invention had was, as Ong points out, a dramatic increase in the potential for democratizing literacy: that is, many people can memorize and internalize twenty-four characters, but in scripts and syllabaries and pictographic writing there were often thousands of characters that had to be memorized. With the invention of the phonetic alphabet, many more citizens, mostly aristocrats and leaders to begin with, did have enough time to learn the alphabet, and so literacy gradually became an important vehicle with which to administer their own authority in this period of semiliteracy, which ran from roughly 775 BCE to 450 BCE. Significantly for the historical relation to Plato's life, the Greek alphabet was finally standardized in 403–402 BCE by the archon Eukleides upon the return of democracy in Athens following the Peloponnesian War, and immediately following the short-lived but brutal reign of the Thirty Tyrants. From a materialist perspective what may be even more significant is that, as Wood explains, "Greek became the main commercial language from Massalia (modern Marseilles) to the borders of India" (*Peasant-Citizen* 101). In short, linguistic invention triggered an expansion of social development, military operations, and political and economic growth throughout the regions of the West.

Even given this brief overview, it is significant that most scholars agree that the Homeric epics were composed in textual form in the period from 750–700 BCE, an obviously transitional time shortly after the invention of the Greek alphabet. Even more dramatically, the shift from semiliteracy to a more broad-based social literacy seems to have happened in relatively short order, roughly corresponding to the birth and death of Plato, 427–347

BCE, although such dates are much more approximate and the transitions ongoing and geographically uneven.[13] In short, this timeline supports Havelock's basic contention that Plato himself was among the leaders of the shift away from the Homeric paideia, or acculturation, to the newly emerging literate culture in Attica.

Even with this brief summary, it should be clear that several enormously significant changes occurred quite rapidly because they were made available via the potential of writing to alter the technologies by which a culture reproduced itself. For one thing, the possibilities of generating an expanded vocabulary increased exponentially. The easiest way to think about this is to consider how many words there are in the English language in the early twenty-first century. Now, it is notoriously difficult to determine such a number, primarily because it depends in part on how you define what counts as a word. But the gist of it can be gleaned when you check the online edition of the *Oxford English Dictionary,* where the homepage asserts that there have been more than 600,000 words; and the Global Language Monitor claims that in June, 2009, "the English language had crossed the 1,000,000-word threshold." The point is that a literate vocabulary can quickly exceed any individual's ability to memorize and internalize it. Whereas oral cultures can work just fine with vocabularies of about 5,000 words, suddenly the sheer number of words a culture could store in textual form far exceeds any individual's ability to memorize them. This is not generally the case with oral cultures, in which most children grow up to acquire as adults the vocabulary shared by the given society.

The historical frame can be paired with an individual developmental frame: the size of our vocabulary is a common way of thinking about our cognitive development, even though, again, professional estimates vary widely. For instance, linguists tell us that three- to five-year-old children have learned several hundred words; by the age of puberty a child might have a vocabulary of 5,000 words and by the age of eighteen 20,000; the upper edge for most highly educated people is around 40,000 to 50,000. Depending on what you think constitutes a word, the entire Shakespearean canon has between 18,000 and 25,000 different words (*World Wide Words*). In short, even the most sophisticated literary genius has internalized to personal memory a mere fraction of the entire language into which he or she was born. Yet it is important to also note that of the thousands of languages that have existed in the course of human history, most of them never made this transition to literacy. As Ong explains, "Of the some 3000 languages spoken that exist today only some 78 have a literature" (7).

The growth of a literate vocabulary is notable in another significant way: most of the new words tend to emerge in the form of abstractions rather than concrete nouns (you don't get a whole lot of new words for *bed*). Oral cultures clearly had abstract concepts, but they also had limits on how many could be memorized and how many were necessary for daily activities in small communities. But in a literate culture, you can write things down, and then begin to make definitions of new words using the old ones, and this is an infinitely expansive process, as witnessed today when neologisms and new terms are constantly being invented and put into use around the globe. Where you once had stories about an eye for an eye as a just act, you can now invent the abstraction *justice*, take the word out of the narrative and define it in literate space, and do so in a lot of different ways. The same is true of other abstractions such as *truth, absolute, dialectic, freedom, democracy, universal, masculine, feminine, race*, etc.

The change in vocabulary also involved the emergence of a new syntax and grammar suitable for a literate culture. Perhaps most notably a new kind of verb becomes dominant: the copula. The transformations toward literacy take place with the growing predominance of the state-of-being verbs: this [definition] *is* democracy; this *is* love; this *is* courage; this *is* virtue; this *is* justice. In other words, definition emerges as a state of being using the copula that so conveniently facilitated the naming of concepts and abstractions as fixed essences (or so it might seem). Nouns can be isolated from the flow of narrative time so that, fixed in literate space, they can then be conceived of as having essences, or Forms, that transcend their fleeting aural designations in narrative accounts. Indeed, in the newly literate culture, statements about the abstracted objects of knowledge take place in a syntax that appears universal because it "excludes tenses of the verb 'to be', Principles and properties and categories and topics just 'are'" (Havelock, *Preface* 226).

Understandably, then, Plato's entire discourse deploys the language of being, and, consequently, the copula proliferates everywhere in this new discourse. For evidence one can turn to any of Plato's texts such as the *Republic*. Here's an example: "he who is of a certain nature, is like those who are of a certain nature; he who is not, not" (33). So far as we know, no oral culture has ever spoken sentences like this. Oral language is performative, creative, and imaginative, to be sure, but it takes place in the present, in the *agon* (a contest, the root of *agonistics*), and in the presence of the speakers, with mostly active verbs and concrete nouns. One did not ask "What *is* courage?" One asked "How was Achilles courageous?" And the stories of Achilles came back as a narrative answer with lots of action verbs, and very little conceptual abstraction or use of the copula.

The origins of Western metaphysics, in short, depend on this shift to a literate culture as the copula takes over the syntax. With the powers of a new literate syntax featuring "being" and "to be," the society could easily generate a lot of abstract essences. These abstracting powers have both positive and negative effects. On the downside, the persistence of such essentialisms became a catch-all complaint during the age of high theory in the 1970s and 1980s, when the most potent charge you could level against fellow critics was that they were "essentializing," that is, un-self-consciously holding onto some fixed essences as grounds for interpretation but slipping them in the back door unacknowledged. To claim someone was an essentialist was a bit like claiming the emperor had no clothes: it was always a moment of embarrassment, like being exposed. The problem, however, is that you can't just announce that you will henceforth avoid all essentialisms and end up accomplishing the housecleaning of your language and ideology, at least not without great effort. And even then, if you want to take up some forms of social action, you will likely end up with what Gayatri Spivak famously called "strategic essentialism."[14] Our foundational terms are strategic because they provide us with the historical and theoretical framings by which we make sense of the world in order to change it.

But to return to ancient Greece: in a literate syntax, visual space predominates over narrative time, so narrative modes of discourse diminish as exposition moves center stage, and, indeed, the whole period of Greek drama and poetry goes into a period of decline following Plato and Aristotle. Form is a spatial metaphor at root anyway, and it begins to serve as the conceptual foundation for ways of knowing. In a literate culture, you can lay a text out in space, like a physical graph or map, and then examine where the parts go, and even generalize about the different parts. The etymological root of analysis means to break down, and one can break down a speech as a text into its parts because one can see the parts on the page and leave off viewing one section but come back to it later without its having changed (an impossibility in an oral narrative). The craft of composing a text was somewhat like a carpenter building a bed, working on one section at a time. Thus visuality dominates in a literate culture, and this change provides the underlying premises, at least, for the five-paragraph essay: you have to see the indents marked by the paragraphs; it is hard to hear paragraph indentations (even though you can usually hear periods as pauses). Western metaphysics is thus tremendously slanted toward formalism as in laying out the structural parts of objects in spatial configurations.[15]

One of the important things we can do, however, is break down the founding terms of this formalist discourse so we can begin to trace out the impact they have had on our own lives, having been for so long inscribed in our inherited cultural discourses. Two of the foundational binary pairs that continue to challenge us are the separation of the knower from the known, and of the subject from the object. In the previous chapter, I discussed a number of the basic binary terms as they emerged from the "Allegory of the Cave," but here we can reframe these dualities in the oral/literate historical transformation. In short, you can't have a Delphic oracle saying "know thyself" and a gadfly like Socrates advocating that kind of self-knowledge until you had a self separate from the rest of the society. As we will see in the next section, this key separation is profoundly at the root of all our theories of individualism since they are based on the conceptual separation of the individual from the society. No oral culture ever seems to have rendered such a binary split between individual members and the society in which they were deeply entwined. Individual differences can justify new forms of hierarchy and new ways to enslave others whose different status means they fall below the limited forms of communality granted to legitimate citizens. Only we moderns can be truly alienated, as in alien, strangers to our own social world, and we have to thank the ancient Greeks for making that kind of distress conceivable.

Knowing Thyself: Separating the Knower from the Known, the Subject from the Object

One of the basic problems for Plato was that, especially early in his life, there was no fully developed system of abstractions, and thus a much more minimalist vocabulary or syntax with which to begin the process of criticism.[16] So Plato's attack on traditional poetic images can be seen as an effort to bolster the creation of a grammar and syntax of abstract terms with which to break from the mnemonic, mimetic, imagistic mode of learning. The newly emerging "philosophical rhetoric" based on the dialectic could, in principle, criticize the political hierarchies of the dominant order by contrasting it with the supposed truth of the transcendent hierarchy based on a universal order. As Havelock explains, in Plato's move from concrete images and examples to abstract ones, Plato understood that there was a kind of necessary emotional intensity enacted by didactic forms of mimesis since the best method for memorization was identification with a character in an oral story: to "become" Achilles in the heat of battle. In order to memorize vast amounts of verse, it was best if the poems were rhythmic and repetitious and the images were stereotypical clichés so as to be easily memorized. Under these conditions, there was, of course, less time or energy to stand back, to think about, to distance oneself from and criticize that which one was memorizing. In order to abstract, one must refrain from such immediacy of identification: one must separate the knower from the known, the self from the received images of the self (Havelock, *Preface* 197-233).

In the specific context of the *Republic*, then, one of Plato's first tasks was to create a sense of the self or subject independent of the object. Because the language that he had historically available to him was that of the psyche and the soul, as Havelock explains, Plato's dialogues are instrumental in redefining the term *psyche* and moving it away from concrete images of "breath," "life-cloud," and "ghosts" toward a notion for signifying the autonomous self or soul, a personality separate from the social arena of customs and habits, "the seat of moral responsibility, something infinitely precious, an essence unique in the whole realm of nature" (Havelock, *Preface* 197). The psyche/soul had to separate itself from immersion in the poetized statement, and even personal and reflective pronouns could now emerge in new syntactic contexts such as "I am," "I think," "I know," with the newly independent seat of knowing in the soul in antithesis to the body or "corpse" in which the soul rested. Newly abstracted terms like justice now become concepts that can be internalized within the psyche/soul of the learner rather than narrative actions of observable behavior. Thinking, calculating, knowing can now all be hierarchically valued above seeing, hearing, feeling. Thus, this separation had to take place in opposition to the oral tradition. Havelock describes this emergence of the self or ego:

> It must separate itself out and by an effort of sheer will must rally itself to the point where it can say "I am I, an autonomous little universe of my own, able to speak, think and act in independence of what I happen to remember." This amounts to accepting the premise that there is a "me," a "self," a "soul," a consciousness which is self-governing and which discovers the reason for action in itself rather than in imitation of the poetic experience. The doctrine of the autonomous psyche is the counterpart of the rejection of the oral culture. (*Preface* 200)

In Plato's words: "our argument shows that the power and capacity of learning exists in the soul already" (Book 7, 209). Such radical autonomy requires a transcendental (not just local and idiosyncratic) soul. In Part 2 we will see this basic notion of a kind of (oxymoronic) universal subjectivity transcending our limited, historical, contingent sense of self being reworked by Enlightenment and Romantic thinkers. But in ancient Greece, the linguistic shifts enable a whole system of terms seeking abstraction and the divestment of particular images in a turn toward, ultimately, universal essence, Being, and so forth. This assertion of the thoughtful, critical psyche had to be theoretical because one had to stand back from action and doing and become a "spectator"; indeed, one of the root words of *theory* is *theoros*, which literally means "spectator."

Shifting to more modern terms, the separation of the knower from the known meant that "it now became possible to identify the 'subject' in relation to that 'object' which the 'subject' knows" (Havelock, *Preface* 201). The subject can think and know about the objects of knowledge external to the knower. The objects, ultimately the Forms, could be realized through the method of dialectic used by the self. Universality, rather than relativism, was the key to genuine knowing in the hierarchical binary. But, to be counterfactual for a moment and conjecture, the model could conceivably have gone the other way: the Greeks could have emphasized self/subjectivity so much in these formulations that the philosophy would have turned into some variants of subjectivism,[17] or they could have emphasized the dialectical process more than the absolute goal of ending the dialectic in the universal Forms, but they did neither. They went the other way, toward objectivity of the Forms.

Under the conditions fostered by such theoretical distance, one could disengage the sheer activity of thinking in order to break the habit of self-identification with the memorized images of the oral tradition. This break or rupture from patterns of memorization and identification takes place through the fundamental act of isolation, the separation of the general laws from any particular story, history, or event. Knowledge must be isolated and "set 'itself by itself' and identified 'per se'. It must be 'abstracted' in the literal sense of that word. The Greek for this object, thus achieved by an effort of isolation, is 'the "thing" in itself', precisely the equivalent of the Latin *per se*" (Havelock, *Preface* 217). Thus, in Book 10 of the *Republic*, Plato wants not the flawed, temporal bed that he sleeps on but the bed *per se*—the ultimately essential and universal Form underlying any particular bed. These are profound transformations in that this separation of universal knowledge from the act and event of narrative takes place in the effort to dispel mere opinion by resting knowledge on the truth of the "thing itself." In Part 2, we will see the pre-Romantic philosophers such as Kant and Hegel struggling with these same binary difficulties. In less abstract and more emotional terms, the search for objective knowledge and universal truth can be seen as a search for a bedrock of secure foundations resistant to the insecurity and unpredictability of mortal life. The dialogues of the *Republic* take place in intensely violent times, the waning years of the brutal Peloponnesian Wars, not long before the eight months in 403 BCE when the Thirty Tyrants executed their own reign of terror on Athens. No wonder some form of transcendence might seem powerfully appealing. Indeed, once produced in ancient Athens, this new dialectical discourse acquired many enduring powers as it was translated into different historical times and geographical locations. All of our modern terms registering such Western ideals for pure knowledge transcending history, such as knowledge for knowledge's sake, disinterestedness, and objectivity, have their roots in this ancient Greek discourse.

An ideological contradiction is that in his effort to break with the conservative oral tradition and the dominance of poetic images, Plato deployed images of his own. Paradoxically speaking, the figurative allegory of the cave must become an image of the transcendence of imagery: the literal light that the freed prisoners perceive is not the truth but merely an allegorical image of the invisible light of Being. Thus, at the very heart of Plato's doctrine of forms is a central contradiction: the forms are invisible, but the very term "form" derives from idea, *eidos* (pl. *eidei),* which in turn derives from the Proto-Indo-European *weid*. The participial form of *weid* became *videre* in Latin, which meant to see, to look. Yet when you use your sense to look for the invisible Forms, you can't see them. Thus, the etymology of Plato's own term, Forms, registers the return to the visual that Plato seeks to escape. In the context of the orality/literacy issues, the irony of the light/dark binary in the Allegory of the Cave repeats itself in a slightly different register. It all may thus seem like a zero-sum game. But, for Plato, the gains far overshadowed these contradictions.

When Havelock reframes the context of Plato's *Republic,* he ends up describing the cultural formation of a whole new grammar, syntax, and philosophical rhetoric of abstractions suitable for critical distance, analysis, and critique—all of which were to a large extent not even possible in oral performance. The desire for universalism finds a grammar for its possibility, just as Judith Butler explains: "The claim to universality always takes place in a given syntax, through a certain set of cultural conventions in a recognizable venue" ("Restaging" 35). But the quick insistence upon any group's specific claims for universality provides the basis for most forms of fundamentalism that close off any alternative other than those proffered by the fundamentalist group itself, whether religious or secular.

Given these cautions, consider the ethnocentric risk of framing the social changes in ancient Greece as a conflict between orality and literacy: they so clearly reflect the linguistic, cognitive, and geopolitical frames of our own historical context. Again, to a large extent, this is simply impossible to avoid, and ethnocentrism is everyone's starting point for framing: you see things in terms of the lenses you bring to the objects of attention. The issue before us, and one that has deeply concerned the orality/literacy debates over recent decades, is the effort to describe the alteration from primary orality to literacy without, even unconsciously, invoking the superiority of our literate cultures over the "vulgar," less educated, illiterate, oral culture. How can we avoid replaying the nineteenth-century civilized/primitive dualism? For one thing, even the words *orality* and *literacy* are our inventions. Neither Plato, nor Aristotle, nor any of the other ancient Greeks used these terms: they are ours, and we use them to frame cultural change according to our concepts and interests. And some of the terms that have gone along with these changes have indeed invoked cultural superiority, especially when we speak of consciousness and cognition. If we, as Ong often did in his initial formulations, claim that "Writing restructures consciousness" (*Orality* 78), it can be difficult to avoid not seeing this restructuring as a clearly implied improvement in the mental capacity or consciousness of human beings, as if people in oral cultures were cognitively inferior sorts of beings.[18]

But we can at least try to minimize these forms of ethnocentrism by attending carefully to the way we translate between our differences. As Butler puts it, "Without translation, the very concept of universality cannot cross the linguistic borders it claims, in principle, to be able to cross" (35). Indeed, under pressure from his critics, Ong himself qualified and revised some of his formulations, and, in the effort to avoid ethnocentric condescension, I have chosen throughout this book to frame the cultural turn within the geopolitical economy, rather than in terms of cognition or consciousness. In a sociohistorical frame, whatever happened, it seems descriptively fair to say that the new technologies of literacy enabled human beings who had access to it to do different kinds of things, in the same way that the microchip allows us to work on digital word processors rather than cumbersome typewriters, or the way the invention of the cotton gin and the steam engine transformed the manufacturing of clothing. I make no claims about cognitive, mental states of consciousness in the brain: indeed, as I have told it, the idea that many individuals in an oral culture could actually memorize and perform, say, the entire length of the *Iliad* and *Odyssey*—these are remarkable achievements. But it is also true that you cannot have something called objectivity in an oral culture, and that is, indeed, a foundational distinction in the social discourse and technologies available to those who have access to literacy.

Given these qualifications, it seems fair to say that in the cultural revolution framed by the shift from orality to literacy, Platonic critique had a potentially more radical orientation, a perspective often lost from the familiar view of the traditional Platonic formalism that we have sustained in contemporary cultural receptions of Plato. Even though Plato was deeply skeptical of democracy as a kind of mob rule akin to letting the market have its way, his version of an educated citizenry and its philosopher-king was also equally critical of the terribly oppressive reign of terror exorcised when the oligarchs took over from the democratic constitution of Athens. Plato's attack on the poet now takes on a new significance as an attack on the whole way oral cultures organized social life.

Plato adopted the Greek term *philosophy* as an effort to name the new discourse that he had authorized, and that he hoped would gain power in the new social order. In our day, philosophy often seems otherworldly, a kind of retreat from the world, at least in the eyes of many. But as Havelock points out, for Plato, philosophy was "that capacity which turns a man into a student by defying the pressure of his environment" (282). In other words, philosophy for Plato, even in its manifestation as an otherworldly Doctrine of Forms, was also, for him, a discourse of resistance, of dissent from the doxa or orthodoxy of the day, the reigning powers of blindly hereditary rule and unscrupulous market pricing in the agrarian economy. There is a deeply ethical and political charge to those motives—a dimension that often gets lost in the more typical focus on logos and form. Orality is much more the root of the cultural orthodoxy than were the sophists who, while resisting the timeless, universal properties of Plato's philosophy, were deeply concerned with argumentative persuasion. Besides, as history tells us, the sophists often served the repressive aims of the oligarchs—they weren't all radical political libertarians by nature, even though some of them clearly were advocates of equality and justice, as were some of the philosophers. As Havelock points out, philosophy and sophistry have more common etymological roots than one might assume:

> In the *philo-sophos*, meaning a man who is instinctively drawn to intellectualism and had an aptitude for it, Plato thought he saw a fresh human type emerging from the society he knew. As a type, it was symbolized effectively in the conjunction of the verb "to like" or "love" with the adjective *sophos* which more than any other had stamped a man as "intelligent." *Sophos* and its noun *sophia*, the "intelligent" person and his "intelligence," had been traditional terms, and as such we would not have expected them to denote the new "intellectualist" form of intelligence. Yet it was indeed precisely for this meaning that they became adapted. (*Preface* 286–87)

These new kinds of philosophers, sophists, and rhetors all engaged in dialogue over these ideas, even as they differed vastly in their conclusions, such as we witness in the Platonic dialogues themselves. But there is no evidence that any of them spent any time memorizing epithets from the oral tradition. Thus, whereas most contemporary readers have had to make excuses for why Plato so centrally positioned his arguments against the poet in the *Republic*, it now makes sense that Plato places his analysis of the poet at the beginning and the conclusion of his book because the poet served as the primary educational medium for the transmission of the oral culture that Plato seeks to transform using the new literate technologies. Indeed, the root of our common synonym for *education, pedagogy,* comes from a combination of its root words, *paidos,* meaning child, and ágō, meaning to lead, so pedagogy is the basic process of "leading the child" through the processes of acculturation necessary for social life. Similarly, the term also comes from the root word *paedeia,* or learning the cultural heritage which for the ancient Greeks meant learning *arête,* or virtue, or learning excellence in all areas of endeavor by imitating the actions of the heroes in the mythical poems. In this sense we now refer to the notion of the Homeric "paideia," the cultural pedagogy by which the young were acculturated to the ways and values (virtues) of the oral culture in archaic Greece when the only characters in the epic poems were the leaders and heroes drawn from the wealthy few, who had no direct role in agricultural production other than as landowners. These basic educational tasks of acculturation had to change for any kind of significant social change to take place.[19] To this extent, Plato is inaugurating what we now call a Platonic paideia, new processes of acculturation by literate means, and it is fair to say that what he accomplished spread around the world from its origin in the city state of Athens, although the way it got rewritten and transformed in new and different cultural contexts is the basis for the story of this book. Whatever Plato was like in real life, he does not at all seem like what we have come to call Platonism.

In Plato's most famous text, cultural education in the broadest sense of how one becomes acculturated to the ways and habits of social life, shaped by the geopolitical economy of domestication in the Axial Age, is primary to, and precedes, his analysis of the political state of the republic. Economic, political, and social values are all learned and acquired through the material processes of production and exchange, the specific ways that a society produces subjects or citizens, bonded serfs or slaves, and distributes (or maldistributes) the surplus value they produce. Even though the *Republic* has usually been read as the creation of an ideal state, and thus subject matter for political science, its organization in these frames has always seemed odd because "That part of the argument which deals directly with political theory occupies only about a third of the nine books" (Havelock, *Preface* 13). We can now reread the *Republic* as a primarily educational argument about how ancient Greeks should, according to Plato, alter their entire educational practice to create a new kind of society. Despite all the reservations, in the *Republic* at least, Plato explicitly gives voice to some of the virtues of the emerging forms of Athenian democracy: "This, then, seems likely to be the fairest of States, being like an embroidered robe which is spangled with every sort of flower" (249). Or: "in a democracy alone will the freeman of nature deign to dwell" (255). But he offered us the idea of a republic led by philosophers, or lovers of wisdom, because he was wary of democracy when large numbers of uninformed citizens could vote against rational political decisions and slip into a form of tyranny. Even with these qualifications, he voices clear objections to the more obviously unjust, totalitarian, and hierarchical forms of civil society such as tyranny and plutocracy: wisdom and justice, not power and wealth, should be the guiding principles in his ideal world if it had any hope of honoring the truly universal.

The remarkable thing is the history that followed: these new sociolinguistic formations of literacy spread about the world, whether through military conquest and colonization or through less directly violent forms of influence and assimilation. As Ong puts it, literacy has an imperialistic dimension as it tends to rapidly conquer the now more vulnerable, time-consuming forms of oral social organization. Many people around the world have internalized these transformations as if they were natural to the way we feel and think and behave, but rather than nature or the universal what we then get is the more geographically local, the European, version. But toward the end of his life, Plato recognized some of the limitations of the very literate discourse he had so depended on during his career, and that's the story in the *Phaedrus*, to which we turn in the next chapter.

Finding Love (and Writing) in All the Wrong Places: Plato's Pharmacy and the Double-Edged Sword of Literacy in the Phaedrus

Having a Good Time with Speech

By the time we get to the *Phaedrus*, everything Plato had evicted from the *Republic* comes rushing back in: love, emotion, rhetoric, madness, divine inspiration. Whereas the *Republic* seems to have been the great analytic text, distinguishing rational modes of literacy from the mimetic modes of the oral tradition, the *Phaedrus* seems to reverse directions and be the great synthetic text, closing the chasms between abstract and concrete, mental and sensual, that he had sought so hard to open in the *Republic*. If this text was composed later in Plato's life, as most critics now agree, it may be that the whole argument concerning mimetic modes of social reproduction has simply evaporated because the long, slow process of literacy has accelerated during his lifetime. He now seems to cast doubt on the very medium of his literate revolution: writing.

Clearly, Plato's entire philosophical project has been dependent on the texts he has been composing, but now he hesitates, giving space to his own ambivalence about the new technology. Every idea he has articulated has been based on his concern for the nonlinguistic truths behind the words: not the empty, dead letters and rapidly fading marks of ink on parchment, but the true, universal meanings that must be animated by a living, breathing soul. And the living truth corresponds with what the author/god/ authority meant, or intended, not what the listener or reader can just invent, or misinterpret, once the text gets out of the presence of the author/speaker. We will elaborate on these features later, but let's begin, as with the *Republic,* by first reading the text itself, although the historical context will also readily come into play even as we focus on the translated words on the page.

One thing about this text seems immediately striking: anyone who reads the *Phaedrus* without laughing ought to loosen up and read it again. Plato can be a wise guy, just as cheeky as his hero, Socrates, who seems to delight in playing with Phaedrus. There are just so many examples of this irony and humor, as when Phaedrus threatens to speak without reading the text of Lysias's speech, which he has hidden under his cloak, and when he seeks to compel the attention of Socrates with an oath and has a bit of trouble locating the seat of authority: "It's an oath. 'I swear to you by'. . . but by whom? By what god? Perhaps this plane tree? 'I swear by this plane tree . . . '" (15).[1] And Socrates is overcome: "Woe! Alas! Wretch: How well you've discovered how to compel a lover of words to carry out your commands" (15). Or is Socrates in love with the spirit behind the words, not the dead letters? Well, that's central to the interpretation of this text, but it's hard to tell where the irony begins and ends, and that is no joking matter.

Indeed, the question of irony is profound in the sense that irony is always the most socially activated of all the tropes because you can be duped as an outsider, shamed as the naïve fool, if you do not get the insider irony intended by the speaker. Irony happens when you say one thing but mean something else, and one must depend on context to detect when that ironic shift should be brought into play. If someone says, "Nice day" when it's cold and rainy, most people will get the ironic reversal because they too have immediate knowledge that the weather outside is pretty awful. Tone of voice can, of course, also make a difference, but again that's not signaled by the words themselves. For a text composed in ancient Greece, detecting when the irony is in place and when not can be a daunting interpretive task. And Socrates basically makes this point to Phaedrus: "Do you really think I'm joking? Don't I seem serious?" (12). Well, really, Socrates (or Plato?), it's tough to tell. Our only option is to make the best guesses we can, modestly trying to take into account the long historical and geographical shifting of contexts that separates our lives in the Anthropocene from these late Holocene contexts when the arguments were composed. Jacques Derrida is even more insistent: "Always with irony" (*Dissemination* 67).

With that caveat in mind, we can see some signs of the transformation from orality to literacy as oral speech plays out in tension with written texts, except now the hierarchies have been exactly reversed, with speech/orality seeming to be the favored mode. Nevertheless, there is at least one moment when it appears that the emotional conditions of oral culture itself are not so great for clear thinking, when Socrates's first speech is briefly interrupted with an apology for the inferior quality of what he's saying: "I often seem to be in a frenzy, don't be surprised. Already my words are almost dithyrambic" (18). It appears that such a reference to dithyrambic frenzy is a recognition of a throwback to the oral tradition of mimesis as blind memorization through emotional ("frenzied") identification with the speaker, as a technique for repeating without knowing.

Of course, we have no need to memorize the three main speeches because the text of the *Phaedrus* provides for us a literate version of them, the first by Lysias as read by Phaedrus, and then the two subsequent speeches by Socrates. Lysias's speech and Socrates's first speech seem to have the same basic thesis: that relationships with a nonlover are superior to relationships with a lover because the latter involve all kinds of complications such as jealousies, possessiveness, and emotional pains, whereas the former are free of these kinds of difficulties. In a modern idiom, it's like saying that casual sex is better than sex between people deeply committed to each other in a love relationship: rational encounters between nonlovers for their mutual satisfaction are preferable to the irrational emotional entanglements of love relationships. The reference also seems to be to relationships between teachers and students, and between two males, an older one and a younger one, but, at least, from what we can see, neither Socrates nor Phaedrus seems much concerned about these issues.[2]

Socrates's second speech, however, reverses the basic premise and conclusion of the two earlier speeches: Socrates now champions the love relationship in complete contradiction to his first speech. Ask almost any reader of these three speeches which is the "best" one, and the answer is almost always the same: Socrates's second speech. The reasons for this judgment are also easy to articulate: in general, it has by far the best form and the best content. It is clearly organized from beginning, to middle, to end, and it has by far the most convincing details and examples. In short, Western metaphysical categories of form and content end up valuing just what the theoretical frame says they *should* value.

In fact, we can use the division between form and content to map the three speeches: Lysias's speech begins at the end, and thus messes up completely the principles of formal organization based on a sequence of beginning, middle, and end; Socrates's first speech maintains the same basic content, but does begin with an introduction, proceed through the examples, and end with the same conclusion with which Lysias began his speech; and in his second speech Socrates corrects both the form and the content in his exemplary model of a good speech. We could map this out in a visual chart with "X" meaning bad, and "✓" meaning good (see Figure 4.1).

This schematic visualizing of judgments about proper form and content in the three speeches has the advantage of illuminating a particular feature. The sequence of speeches proceeds in dialectical fashion: the first speech (or thesis) is bad in both form and content; the second (Socrates's first) speech is the antithesis, with good form and bad content; and the third speech (Socrates's second) is the synthesis of good form and good content. As we have seen in the Allegory of the Cave, it is always a vertical progression toward the higher levels of truth or, the other alternative, toward the rooted depth concealed beneath the surface appearance.

Of course, Socrates himself agrees with exactly this assessment of the virtues of the three speeches, and he is particularly adamant about the distinctions between good and bad writing/

	Form	Content
Lysias's speech	X	X
Socrates's first speech	✓	X
Socrates's second speech	✓	✓

FIGURE **4.1.** *Visual representation of speeches from* Phaedrus.

speech. Indeed, after his first speech, Socrates tells Phaedrus that "it was a dreadful, dreadful speech, both the one you brought and the one you forced me to deliver" (23). His point is that you cannot just correct form alone: you have to get the content of the speech to be truthful as well, and the truth is that "Love is a god, the son of Aphrodite." And so by humorous invocation of bewitchment, Socrates blames Phaedrus for compelling the bad first speech in which, following Lysias's example, he condemned the god of love. Was the truth spoken in these instances? "[N]ot by Lysias and not by that speech of yours which was spoken by you through my bewitched mouth. If Love is, as he certainly is, a god, or something divine, he cannot be anything evil. This, then, is their sin against Love" (23).

The whole text of the *Phaedrus* seems intent on rescuing love and emotion from their banishment in the *Republic,* yet Socrates's arguments follow a binary logic based on what Aristotle will later call the universal law of noncontradiction (something not even conceivable in the concrete narratives of an oral culture): if love is good, then it cannot be bad—case closed by the strict, hierarchical categories of logic (see Chapter 5). Socrates proceeds to atone for his sins and his shame regarding his first speech by performing one of the exemplary speeches in Western discourse, using the analogy of the chariot with a black and a white horse, where the goal of the charioteer, like that of the philosopher-king ruling both good and bad citizens as well as the emotional versus rational sides of his own psyche, is to rein in the emotional dark horse to make it work with the rational, pure white horse in a synthetic integration evoking the universal balance.[3]

Several features of this final speech should be noted. First, the speech begins by redefining the terms of the discussion in a process that could be called etymological tracing. Socrates claims that the term for madness and mania has positive meanings when he exhumes its historical roots, even though those precedents have been lost in the ordinary speaking conventions of fourth-century BCE Greek culture. He gathers evidence for that claim by tracing the way the word was actually used by his ancestors: "our ancestors who invented our vocabulary thought there was no shame or reproach in madness. . . . But nowadays people have inserted T, a tasteless modern addition, and changed *manic* to *mantic*" (25). In short, the dynamics of the way the word was employed in a former history parallels our examination in the previous chapter of how the word *poetry* was used quite differently in a primarily oral culture than it is in our modern literate culture. As we will soon see, Derrida will also trace a significant etymological blindness in the widespread practice of translating the word *pharmakon* in ancient Greek into current English as "remedy" or "recipe."

The remarkable synthesis in the *Phaedrus* involves the integration of love and philosophy, emotion and reason, rhetoric and dialectic—precisely the opposite of the arguments aimed at separating them in the *Republic*. Significantly, in the extended discussion (it takes up the next twenty-five pages [42–67]) that follows the speech, Socrates elaborates the many criteria that distinguish good from bad writing, and this analysis constitutes one of the first major acts of formal, textual criticism to be found in the West. As Socrates summarizes his case: "Can you explain his arrangement of the topics in the order he has adopted as the result of some principle of composition?" (53). And, yes, indeed, Socrates can, and he proceeds to do so by developing the first set of formal rules of composition in Western philosophy, upon which Aristotle will later build his system of rhetoric. Basically, the *Phaedrus* offers us a primary text, Socrates's second speech, to serve as the basis on which secondary reflection, criticism, can subsequently perform its analysis. In our age, we have inherited this hierarchy as the one between secondary literary criticism and the primary literary texts on which it is performed.

What Socrates claims to end up with is enormously significant and influential: "The power to organize into a single comprehensive system the unarranged characteristics of a subject" (54–55). Only a literate culture can accomplish that kind of systematic unifying of the discrete forms of knowledge, and the entire basis of that system depends on the confidence with which one can identify those preexisting forms, or species of objects, texts, and ideas. The system can be visualized to the extent that the text can be laid out in space, removed from the flux of narrative time. The truthfulness of the analytic system thus relies on our humanly unique powers to engage the dialectic as an "ability to divide into species according to natural articulations" (55). These powers of a literate system of classification demonstrate the founding moments in the Western origins of the species (and genre) distinctions that will be challenged by Darwin and Nietzsche in the nineteenth century and by Dewey, Derrida, and many other theorists in the twentieth century.

The problem of linguistic reference can complicate the process of making absolute distinctions, and Plato raises exactly this issue as it pertains to what he must have been struggling with: the enormous proliferation of abstractions. Recall from the last chapter that this remarkable growth in the number of new abstract words had much to do with the shift from orality to literacy. These cultural changes created for Plato, Socrates, and their cohort worries about seemingly arbitrary differences in the meanings we ascribe to single words. It is primarily a worry about texts and words going "astray," suggesting meanings that might not have been part of the author/speaker's intention. As Socrates explains there powers: "a man who knows the truth may play with words and lead his audience astray" (50). And such risks are deeply magnified when it comes to abstract terms:

> SOCR. If one uses a word like "iron" or "silver," all of us understand the same meaning, don't we?
>
> PHAEDR. Of course.
>
> SOCR. But when one mentions "just" or "good," what happens? Don't we all veer off in different directions and dispute the meaning, not only with others, but with ourselves as well?
>
> PHAEDR. We certainly do. . . .
>
> SOCR. Then in which of these two cases are we more readily deceived; in which has rhetoric greater power?
>
> PHAEDR. Obviously in cases where our interpretation of a term varies.
>
> SOCR. So, then, a man who is going to develop an art of rhetoric must first make methodical distinctions and grasp the distinguishing mark, as it were, of each class, of both the class of terms whose meanings must generally be interpreted variously and of that in which they generally are not. (51)

Socrates certainly acknowledges the gap between a word and its meaning, but his answer to this problem is what today we call the theory of linguistic transparency or the correspondence theory of truth. According to this theory, language is merely a transparent vehicle for carrying (but not modifying) the meaning of a word, which must correspond in a one-to-one way with its single true meaning. Of course, such a theory then places a burdensome responsibility on the shoulders of a philosopher or anyone else: for Plato, "A man must first know the truth about every single subject on which he speaks or writes. He must be able to define each in terms of a universal class that stands by itself" (72). Today, most of us are skeptical, to say the least, of any such fixed attributions of meaning, and only the extreme fundamentalists would ever put faith in the idea that a text, one of the most unstable of objects, could contain only one authorized meaning. But we should also be skeptical of the opposite: that a word can mean anything we want it to. Social history and physical reality are both far too powerful arbiters of linguistic differences to uphold any such disembedding of words from context. The birth of Western forms of dialectical reason now infiltrates most all questions of communication and interpretation with respect to the tensions between local, particular speech uses and more widespread, generally shared meanings. These problems with respect to the instability of meaning are the ones with which Derrida begins his own interpretation of the model of interpretation offered by the play between speech and writing in the *Phaedrus*.

The Revenge of the Pharmakon: Writing as a Crime

We can translate some of the key ideas of Derrida's complex text into simpler terms. In some passages, Derrida is quite concise when it comes to articulating the reasons for our uncertainties in reading almost any kind of text. As he puts it: "A text is not a text unless it hides from the first comer, from the first glance, the law of its composition and the rules of its game" (63). The basic point is that any text hides from an initial reading of the "text itself" the social context of its origins of composition, its particular way of being produced within the political economy of its day, and that context provides the preliminary rules and laws necessary to compose any kind of text. These conventions can be as basic as the semantic and grammatical rules that govern any language, but they also include the underlying sets of socially constructed values and assumptions orchestrating the economic production of everyday social life. On first glance, texts can seem divorced from their contexts of origin: since we may know very little about those contexts, especially the organization of the political economy, the "hermeneutics of suspicion" calls for a healthy dose of modesty when making initial inferences.

Readers bring to any text some knowledge of the codes by which it operates; texts must be supplemented by the reader's knowledge of historically constructed codes that necessarily antedate the text itself. As I tried to dramatize in our initial, decontextualized reading of Plato's *Republic,* nothing in the text itself points to our extended discussion of orality and literacy. It was hidden from our first glance, or at least from our discussion of Plato in most of Chapter 2 of this book.[4] So we still need to be wary of our built-in habits to disembed texts by reading them out of context. And context, in turn, cannot be simply asserted as some kind of alternative bedrock of meanings and assumptions upon which solid and uncontested meanings can be determined (that's an "old" positivist version of history, rather than a more contemporary "New Historicist" version of historical context). As Ellen Meiksins Wood puts it so elegantly: "for the truly great and creative theorists, historical context and political commitments present themselves not as ready-made answers but as complex questions" (*Citizens* 83).

The context of any text's production does not generally show up in the text itself. Some strenuous attention to the historical context, however we reconstruct it, serves as an aid to create a more just and less ethnocentric reframing of the key issues as they emerge out of our interpretive translations. Social history, political economy, and cultural discourse provide the implicit and explicit rules by which writers compose texts; however, we must always keep in mind that those histories and discourses are themselves also texts. We are wise, therefore, to be wary, especially when writing/textuality itself seems to be the source of these decontextualizing problems.

We can take this point a step further by now taking on a somewhat more opaque passage that follows in Derrida's two-page introduction to his section on "Plato's Pharmacy" in *Dissemination:*

> There is always a surprise in store for the anatomy or physiology of any criticism that might think it had mastered the game, surveyed all the threads at once, deluding itself, too, in wanting to look at the text without touching it, without laying a hand on the "object," without risking—which is the only chance of entering into the game, by getting a few fingers caught—the addition of some new thread. (63)

One can reasonably ask how a nonperson like "anatomy or physiology" can be "surprised," but if we grant these terms as metaphors representing reading as a kind of medical diagnosis, an openness to being surprised by the unexpected can be a virtue for both a doctor and a reader. "Mastering the game" is the belief in closure, and that one can end the play of different meanings and the dialectical struggle between self and other, subject and object, with an authoritative, determinative reading or diagnosis. In this light, then, the irony is that Western metaphysics poses as the very foundational discourse that establishes the formal rules of this linguistic game, and one of those rules is that the play of interpretation must come to an end in the Truth: as Derrida puts it, "It is part of the rules of the game that the game should *seem to stop*" (*Dissemination* 128).

Derrida's reading practices deconstruct the pretense of mastering and offer instead a willingness to play with the language of a text while recognizing that this takes risk: when you read you "touch" texts in the sense of modifying them by your own presuppositions; your metaphorical reading fingers get caught when you embarrass yourself by proposing unusual interpretations of the reading that no one around you is willing to share, or any time you take a strong, different reading in opposition to others, including the author(s). In short, strong reading is thus an ethical act with political consequences because it takes some courage to risk venturing down dead ends and going around blind corners, making mistakes, reversing directions, and trying again. Playing, in this sense, takes work and labor if only because it takes time away from doing other things. These links between the economy of writing and the politics of reading in the *Phaedrus* may seem far-fetched because this is in a context long before the economics of a capitalist system had developed. But it was a market-based economy in ancient Greece, and the implications for later economies are real. Derrida himself sketches them out, even if he does not pursue such links in a social/political context. In his analysis of Socrates' myth about the young son Theuth's invention of writing, Derrida clearly emphasizes both the political and the economic ties when the illiterate father, Ammon-Ra, becomes the sole authority to determine the meaning of literacy. In this instance, he links the *Phaedrus* back to the *Republic*. As he puts it: "The meaning of *pater* is sometimes even inflected in the exclusive sense of financial capital. In the *Republic* itself, and not far from the passage we have just quoted. One of the drawbacks of democracy lies in the role that capital is often allowed to play in it" (*Dissemination* 82).

The questions I initially posed in Chapter 2 with respect to our reading of Plato's *Republic* deliberately tapped into the historically dominant tendency of many teachers and students to read a text from more than two thousand years ago, in translation, and believe that we could somehow learn to "master" particular meanings in the process. The lesson is that we can learn, instead, to pay attention to textual threads that lead away from the text at hand, and recognize the risks we inevitably take in reading texts divorced from the various social, economic, political, and discursive contexts in which any act of reading and writing is situated. Even more, reading and writing can be seen as a dialectical unity where, to use the cliché, "you can't have one without the other." And it is always already on ethical (not strictly logical) grounds, and thus in turn, political grounds, that we risk taking up the time with others to discuss the threads we have been tracing in a text, especially in a consumerist culture where there is no immediate payoff for engaging those threads.

Derrida risks an even stronger claim: "Reciprocally, he who through 'methodological prudence,' 'norms of objectivity,' or 'safe-guards of knowledge' would refrain from committing anything of himself, would not read at all" (64). Western metaphysics itself offers the method of dialectic, the standard of objectivity, and the safe foundations for knowledge, all in the name of removing the commitment of our selves and our subjectivities from the

— 95 —

knowing. Derrida's claim thus seems to be a strong critique that blind adherence to those basic tenets of Western metaphysics prevents us from being able to "read at all." The question for us all is: can the rhetoric of objectivity, dialectic, and universalism sometimes serve us well, rather than blindly? No matter how desirable such universals might be, we don't really know what they are, and when we start to specify them, the particulars can slide away from the universal toward the ethnocentric. The desire to articulate universals then has to engage with very careful acts of cross-cultural translation.[5]

Such careful acts of translation can help us to see that Plato and Platonism are not the same things. Indeed, Western metaphysics as a discourse often called Platonism is a historically evolved discourse not identical with the texts of Plato himself: *Western* metaphysics bears the deadly opposite of its ostensible claim: anti-universalism and ethnocentrism dominate to the extent that it is a discourse particular to the West. In contrast to such betrayals of Plato's universal hopes, Derrida's reading of the *Phaedrus* demonstrates that Plato himself keeps alive the deep play of irony throughout this text: like Derrida, Plato himself seems skeptical, via irony, of the very possibilities of ethnocentric mastery called for by Platonism as a form of interpretive closure. In Derrida's reading, it is as if Plato himself brings irony and critique to the discourse of Platonism that later generations produced out of some of the threads (certainly not all) that evolved into the dominant rhetoric for much of the subsequent history of Europe and the Western world.

We can now turn to one of the simplest yet most profound points Derrida makes about the risks of disembedding the *Phaedrus* from its sociohistorical context. It turns out that one of the most persistent misreadings of *Phaedrus* has been perpetuated through acts of translation whereby the double meanings, both positive and negative aspects, of the root Greek word, *pharmakon*, have been lost through a common practice of translators, particularly in English, to translate this word as either "remedy" or "recipe." Given these latter translations only the more positive connotations cross over to us modern readers. As Derrida point outs, the original Greek term *pharmakon* had a more risky double meaning since it could be associated not only with such positive things as a remedy or recipe, but also with such potentially dangerous things as "'poison,' 'drug,' 'philter,' etc." (*Dissemination* 71). The word *pharmakon* appears three times in the Greek version of the *Phaedrus,* and each time it appears the ironic doubling of its meaning is significant yet impossible to detect without knowledge of those original Greek codes. In fact, as Derrida points out, some degree of reviving those source codes is crucial to gaining a sense of the deep ambivalence that Plato is registering about writing.

We can begin to sort out these meanings by looking briefly at each of the three instances where the word appears in the text. But, first, once we recognize the root word of *pharmakon,* we can also recognize an allusion or link to the mythical story of Orithyia being led away from her innocent play by Pharmacia, a story that Socrates refers to very early in the text. The shared etymological roots of Pharmacia, pharmakon, and pharmacy are simply not possible to notice in English translations when recipe and remedy have no such homologous links to Pharmacia. That is one of the casualties or risks of translation: as Derrida says, it is not that the translators tried to be tricky or imprudent "but first and foremost by the redoubtable, irreducible difficulty of translation" (72) itself. But once recovered, what Derrida points out is that the basic action of the myth and the basic point about writing as a pharmakon resonate with each other. The innocent maiden, Orithyia, was lured away by Pharmacia, and this "leading astray" ended in her rape by Boreas. Here's the parallel: Pharmacia deceptively enchants and leads an innocent, pure maiden away to a dangerous event, and it thus constitutes a kind of crime; writing can be an enchanting remedy for a lonely self, but it can also act like a drug or pharmakon and thus lead one astray to believe in meanings of words even when they were not intended by the author, a kind of criminal killing of living intentions.

Let us now look briefly at the three times the word *pharmakon* appears in the *Phaedrus:*

It first appears only moments before Phaedrus proceeds to read the speech of Lysias, when Socrates says "You, however, seem to have found the *remedy* to draw me out . . . so you brandish before me words in books and could lead me on a tour of all Attica and anywhere else you pleased" (7, my italics). Texts may indeed be remedies that cure, but once we recognize the root word of *pharmakon,* the otherwise invisible ironies emerge: texts can also function like poisons or drugs that corrupt prior meanings. They can lead astray, and this doubled irony resonates with the overall thematic ambiguity that Plato registers in weighing the risks as well as the benefits of writing.

In the second and third instances where *pharmakon* appears in the text it has been most commonly translated as "recipe." These instances occur in the same paragraph, toward the end of the book, when Socrates relates the crucial myth of the invention of writing. This famous passage deserves an extended quotation:

> Theuth said, "This discipline, my King, will make the Egyptians wiser and will improve their memories: my invention is a *recipe* for both memory and wisdom." But the King said, "Theuth, my master of arts . . . , to one man it is given to create the elements of an art, to another to judge the extent of harm and usefulness it will have for those who are going to employ it And now, since you are father of written letters, your paternal goodwill has led you to pronounce the very opposite of what is their real power. The fact is that this invention will produce forgetfulness in the souls of those who have learned it. They will not need to exercise their memories, being able to rely on what is written, calling things to mind no longer from within themselves by their own unaided powers, but under the stimulus of external marks that are alien to themselves. So it's not a *recipe* for memory, but for reminding, that you have discovered. And as for wisdom, you're equipping your pupils with only a semblance of it, not with truth." (68, my italics)

Given the oral/literate context in which we have embedded our discussion of Plato, the King Ammon-Ra's critique of his son Theuth's invention of writing takes on some striking new ironies. Theuth claims to have discovered a new recipe "for both memory and wisdom," but the King says, no: it is just a recipe for reminding, and as such it is divorced from a concern for the truth; it is just a recipe for dead, "external marks" and not the living, animate, truth of the soul. The irony, from our perspective, is that Plato's critique of poetry in the *Republic* was based on exactly the same charge: that poetic oral performance depended upon blind memorization, a mere technique for repetition without knowing.

Writing repeats without knowing for the obvious reason that it cannot talk back, at least not in any ordinary sense, like a speaker: ask a text to say it again, and all you can do is read the same words again—just blind repetition. As Socrates explains: "So, too, with written words: you might think they spoke as though they made sense, but if you ask them anything about what they are saying, if you wish an explanation, they go on telling you the same thing, over and over forever" (69). And then, on top of this is another irony: if Socrates's claims represent the truth about writing, that it blindly repeats itself without knowing, Socrates tells us this story by repeating the myth, or fable, he has heard even though he does not know whether it is true or not.

As Derrida argues, "The link between writing and myth becomes clearer, as does its opposition to knowledge" (74). Writing is the technology Plato used to construct a version of Western metaphysics that moved the culture out of the false myths of an oral culture toward the truths of a philosophical culture, from supposedly blindly repeated, particular stories, to universal truths. Yet here, in the *Phaedrus*, writing appears as just another myth: "writing will later be accused of . . . repeating without knowing. . . . One thus begins by repeating without knowing—through a myth—the definition of writing, which is to repeat without knowing" (74–75). One simple explanation is to say that we moderns cannot so easily escape myth (or at least the dialectical tension between myth/appearance and reality/truth): indeed, one of the potentially enabling myths of a genuine universalist discourse is our belief that reason and science can help us to escape myth. In many instances, the desire for the universal motivates us to keep ...ng toward clarification and further inquiry, pursuing the ...tical process, and thus leading to more accurate kinds of evidence-based knowledge that can ameliorate social injustices even if such understandings fall far short of any ultimate ending in the Absolute. Respect for universals will surely aim to expose blatant lies, especially those that are self-serving rather than serving the common good, and that remains a basic ethical virtue that resonates in the founding moments of Western metaphysics. In our "post-truth" era of fake news we may need these ethical reminders.

As Derrida suggests, all these questions about what is "proper" (questions of "seemliness and unseemliness") are deeply engaged in questions about "political and social proprieties" (74), which are in turn produced by the dialectical relations between hierarchical and communal ways of organizing the particular geopolitical economy. Questions about political power emerge in consideration of questions of who has the authority to make these judgments. In the myth about the status of writing, the illiterate father has the power to enforce his judgment regarding the invention by his literate son: "The value of writing will not be itself, writing will have no value, unless and to the extent that god-the-king approves of it. . . . God the king does not know how to write, but that ignorance or incapacity only testifies to his sovereign independence. He has no need to write. He speaks, he says, he dictates, and his word suffices" (76).

We should, indeed, "pay systematic attention . . . to the permanence of a Platonic schema that assigns the origin and power of speech, precisely of logos, to the paternal position" (76). Patriarchy is powerfully embedded as an anti-universalist dictum in the very discourse that supposedly transcends all particular distinctions between gender. These "phallogocentric" traces embedded in the discourse cannot just be attributed to Plato himself: "Not that this happens especially and exclusively to Plato. Everyone knows this or can easily imagine it. But the fact that 'Platonism,' which sets up the whole of Western metaphysics in its conceptuality, should not escape the generality of this structural constraint" (76)—that's the key point. All of which confirms the common complaint we have heard in recent decades that this search for universals has tended to have its origin in a male discourse where only fathers, not mothers, make the authoritative pronouncements. What Derrida calls a universalism "which wouldn't destroy the idioms" (*Ethics* 44) would not make such particular kinds of ethnocentric assumptions and claims.

The judgment of this father/king is that the son, Theuth, is, through his invention of writing, toying with two main crimes: patricide and illegitimacy. The upstart son seeks to subvert the authority of the father; writing seeks to kill the power of orality. "Isn't this pharmakon then a criminal thing, a poisoned present?" (Derrida, *Dissemination* 77). As Socrates laments, "Once a thing is put in writing, it rolls about all over the place, falling into the hands of those who have no concern with it. . . . And when it is ill-treated or abused as illegitimate, it always needs its father to help it, being quite unable to protect or help itself" (*Phaedrus* 69–70). So Theuth's invention calls for the overthrow of the father: "The specificity of writing would thus be intimately bound to the absence of the father" (*Dissemination* 77). The presence and voice of the father is lost. With respect to writing, the presence and voice of the author is mediated if not lost.

For Plato such a loss could be devastating because, again, his entire theory of meaning and truth is that it rests ultimately in the presence of the soul, not the ghostly, absent marks of writing: "A discourse which is inscribed with genuine knowledge in the soul of the learner . . . . Do you mean the living, animate discourse of a man who really knows? Would it be fair to call the written discourse only a kind of ghost . . . of it?" (*Phaedrus* 70). What Socrates wants to call "true inscription" is the only kind of good writing, and so he must indulge in the oxymoron: the "lessons in justice and beauty and goodness . . . are delivered for the sake of true instruction and are, in fact, inscribed in the soul; such discourses as these should be counted as his own legitimate children" (73). Inscribed in the soul? Soul writing? The good, true, lucid kind of writing/inscription that is visible occurs in the invisible soul? And we are supposed to deduce the value of any concrete piece of writing by comparing it to this invisible, ideal soul writing? How could we ever know the universal if we can never see it, feel it, touch it? Indeed, it appears beyond the senses, beyond the world of appearances, in the metaphorical light of the truth, not of the visible sun. The whole discourse calls for this animate, living kind of soul-writing, or what Derrida calls "arche-writing." Plato cannot avoid the metaphor even when he wants to get past metaphor to the literal, absolute truth that would bring the dialectical process to a close, a lesson replayed from the irony of the Allegory of the Cave, and the ironic play between light and dark.

Perhaps the final irony here is that while Plato seems intent on registering his ambivalence about the positive and negative effects of writing, and thus distinguishing between the virtues of speech and the risks of writing, he actually ends up having to distinguish two different kinds of writing, good from bad writing: natural, true, soul writing versus bad, false, artificial writing; writing engaged with universal truth versus false, criminal, and manipulative forms of anti-universal writing. As Derrida puts it, this is "a pattern that will dominate all of Western philosophy. . . . And if the network of opposing predicates that link one type of writing to the other contains in its meshes all the conceptual oppositions of 'Platonism'—here considered the dominant structure of the history of metaphysics—then it can be said that philosophy is played out in the play between two kinds of writing. Whereas all it wanted to do was to distinguish between writing and speech" (*Dissemination* 149).[6] And, of course, we have inherited those practical effects: no one speaks of the soul as the seat of authenticity, but we are all concerned about what should count as good writing. That is a hierarchical (and dialectical, good vs. bad) value we all struggle to translate in our lives as teachers of writing and literature.

As we will see in the next chapter, Aristotle just did not seem to anguish about all these difficulties in the status of writing: he simply ignored the deductive problem of determining the ideal Forms. He did not abandon the idea of a universal, but he thought the way to proceed was through descriptions of the best instances of what he could see in the world around him. Those descriptions would then stand in place as the best prescriptions available for universal standards. In short, he proceeded more inductively and empirically: he just went to work with the tools at hand and laid out the system that has served as a foundational discourse for the rest of the West. And one of the most noticeable differences is that all the humor and irony that Plato invoked to navigate the difficulties of the universal Forms simply evaporates. For Aristotle, deadly serious exposition is almost always the way to proceed with the natural classification of things.

Aristotle's Natural Classification of Things: When Dialectic Trumps Rhetoric and Poetry Gets Rescued

Some Scroll Stories

The travails of the many papyrus scrolls that Aristotle and his students left us have provided the basis for many entertaining stories. Upon Aristotle's death in 322 BCE, Theophrastus, his student, apparently took most of them on horseback to Rome. Legend has it that many of these scrolls were later taken by ship to Skepsis in Asia Minor, what is now the northwestern tip of Turkey, where they were hidden for years in a cave and supposedly suffered from rot and mold. Papyrus is not a very stable medium, much less so than parchment, which, although sometimes available in Aristotle's time, did not become the primary writing surface until the second century BCE. In 87 BCE, the Roman general and dictator Sulla captured Athens with a brutal slaughter of many of its citizens, but while ransacking most of the city and burning to the ground the entire Athenian seaport of Piraeus managed to recover a list of some of Aristotle's papers (though most of them were lost) and brought those that survived back to Rome. While it was still difficult to determine the authenticity of many of them, it was in 30 BCE that, as C. D. C. Reeve explains, Andronicus of Rhodes arranged the papers in a "logical sequence" (xv), one that became so influential that it has been preserved into the modern age. Best of all, however, may be the story of Julius Caesar and the fire at the great library in Alexandria that supposedly destroyed many of the written masterpieces of the Western world, including many of Aristotle's writings. As the story goes, in 48 BCE Caesar had occupied the city of Alexandria and taken up residence in the Royal Palace, but the Egyptian fleet managed to hem him in by surrounding the harbor. Caesar ordered his men to set fire to the Egyptian ships, but the ensuing conflagration got out of hand, spread ashore, and consumed nearby warehouses and supposedly the library. The only problem with this story is that the library or museum was not located near the harbor, and most of what was stored as papyrus scrolls in the warehouses appear to be only records of various kinds. Over the coming decades, there were several other significant fires involving the Alexandrian library, so there were other opportunities for the destruction of important texts, but in each instance the historical record varies and inconsistencies appear.[1]

One of the most persistent debates has been whether or not there was a second book to Aristotle's *Poetics:* the one we have focuses on tragedy, so perhaps the missing volume dealt with comedy, and perhaps it was one of those crucial texts destroyed in one of the Alexandrian fires. In Umberto Eco's famous 1980 novel, *The Name of the Rose,* the entire mystery revolves around the various characters' reactions to Aristotle's book on comedy, although no such book exists in historical fact. Eco's interpretive point appears quite insistent throughout his novel: the basic Western metaphysical assumptions about being able to distinguish fact from fiction, history from imagination, the universal from the anti-universal, is itself an inadequate theory about how we come to know things. Aristotle, however, did not appear to suffer from this postmodern anxiety.

The only thing we know with certainty is that we have lost many of his original writings, whether by carelessness, rot, mold, fire, inaccurate copying, careless translation, or "collateral damage" in war it is hard to say.[2] But all these possibilities should certainly make us wary of how true the texts we now have in translation are to the original sources.[3] Recall Socrates's warning that an orphan text, once outside the presence of its father/author, "rolls about all over the place" (Plato, *Phaedrus,* 69–70), and scrolls could, indeed, roll: they were stored on top of one another in libraries, like rolls of wallpaper, so you had to move them about to retrieve what you wanted.

Now those are all stories about what happened to the manuscripts *after* they were produced, but there are further uncertainties regarding the process of their composition. Authorship as an individual act of composition is taken for granted in our modern world, yet of the many texts that have his name attached as author, it appears to be more accurate to say that Aristotle talked and his students wrote. Or, better yet, he walked and talked (or lectured), and his students listened and composed, although many assert that Aristotle himself took on the tasks of writing later in his life when he settled in Athens and ran the Lyceum.[4]

Actually, Aristotle did write some texts, but scholars tell us that what he initially wrote would have looked a great deal like what Plato wrote: dialogues. According to the records, Aristotle apparently wrote twenty-seven of them, but they have all been lost. The texts that have been preserved were written primarily toward the end of his life, during his time at the Lyceum. Whether students or slaves actually did the labor of handwriting the texts on papyrus manuscripts remains unclear but, in addition to all their physical translocations, we can be sure that what survived through history has been copied, recopied, modified, translated, and typeset as it has been disseminated around the world.

I begin with these stories of textual uncertainties because they provide a note of caution when we start to make claims about the texts themselves, especially their formal properties. Those cautions are especially important in this chapter because I will be paying particularly close attention to several of Aristotle's texts, especially the *Organon,* the *Metaphysics,* the *Rhetoric,* the *Poetics,* and the *Politics,* and I will be doing so without constant reminders of the variable sociohistorical contexts of their production and reception. Aristotle actually makes reference to some of the issues we have discussed regarding orality (as I will point out, below), but the texts that have survived almost always exhibit a kind of expository authority that suggests more stability of meaning than may be warranted.

The Arrival of Substance and the Mystery of the Excluded Middle

The pervasive influence of Aristotle's rewriting of Platonic idealism and his practical applications of Western metaphysics have provided the templates for just about everything that has subsequently passed down to us in the various guises of formalism, positivism, rationalism, scientific empiricism, European universalism, and inductive methodologies. But when one shifts from reading Plato to reading Aristotle, an immediate impression is the stylistic differences: Plato's complex, playful, metaphoric, and allegorical dialogues contrast sharply with Aristotle's more deliberate and less playful assertion of knowledge about the natural classification of things. Plato inaugurated the discourse of Western metaphysical formalism, but his texts consistently resonate with destabilizing kinds of myth, metaphor, allegory, and irony (at least until the end of his life, when his texts become less like dialogues and more like expositions). Not so with Aristotle. All his texts are serious business: they are humorless, literal, and expository. Dialogue, irony, and playfulness such as we found in Plato have left the scene of writing.[5] This absence can resonate as a moment of startling recognition. The power of these texts has seeped into every phase of education in the West, from textbook exposition; to the five-paragraph essay; to the formal analysis of plot, character, point of view, tone, and style in literary texts; to the inductively descriptive procedures of science. It can be a scary sense of encountering a foundational text that is not just "out there" in the world, but incorporated into many of the normal practices in our personal as well as our professional lives as students and teachers. Aristotle's adaptation of Plato appears to positively identify the "natural hierarchies," that is, hierarchies that are a natural endpoint or telos in the development of the fixed, unchanged categories, genres, and objects to be found both in the natural world and in human social organization. Since he finds the forms, or species (the secondary substances), embedded in the primary substance of every object he observes, Aristotle is sometimes referred to as an "immanent formalist."

In contrast, Plato's standard of the idealized Forms, external to particular objects, has been called "transcendent formalism," registering the notion that the form transcends the particular object itself, the latter derived more deductively from the governing form. Rather than Plato's more idealized formalism, Aristotle's more tactical version has provided much more of the practical, material basis for our inherited version of Western metaphysics. Plato seems the idealist to Aristotle as empiricist: Aristotle rejected

Plato's otherworldly doctrine of Forms but the former still sought permanence and stable knowledge about the natural world.

Over the twenty-five-hundred year history of Western metaphysics, these conflicts between Plato's idealist focus on reason and the more this-worldly empiricism of Aristotle have not just had an impact on the history of ideas, but have also had tremendous impact on the material foundations of the geopolitical economy. However, despite all these qualifications, Aristotle remains a formalist in quite fundamental ways, and he is deeply concerned with universal properties that he says must manifest themselves in particular things even as he seeks the underlying essence, or substance, of those particular objects. Aristotle's categories all have subcategories, and his metaphysics is an elaborate, formal system of distinct classifications based on logical principles at every turn. We need, therefore, to turn first to Aristotle's remarkably influential formulations of what he felt was the fundamental, material "substance" of the universe, partly because he felt that his notion of substance allowed him to develop his critique of Plato's otherworldly Forms.

This critique takes place in the collection of works called the *Organon (Basic Works* 1–212), which includes (along with four other books) the *Categories* and the *Posterior Analytics*. These two books are where Aristotle develops his most comprehensive critique of Plato's Forms. He goes on to elaborate this critique in a later work, the *Metaphysics,* and I will draw on all three of these sources in order to clarify Aristotle's fundamental distinctions between primary and secondary substance. Aristotle aims to be a materialist by claiming a more foundational status for substance than form, even though in his practical work of analysis and classification he ends up being as much a formalist as Plato.

Aristotle highlights the illogical nature of Plato's notion that there is a transcendent world of Forms existing independently of the world of appearances. As he explains in the *Metaphysics,* his foundational term is not *Form* but *Substance,* a term that rings with a much more materialist meaning. But the Greek word for substance, *ousia,* can be translated as "essence," which accurately conveys Aristotle's concern for universal essences. Indeed, he sounds much like Plato when he says that metaphysics is the systematic study of "being qua being" (*Metaphysics* 43). And, as he explains in the *Posterior Analytics,* he is still deeply con-cerned with root causes and true essences of the things in this world. Unlike Plato, Aristotle acknowledges four different types of causes: the material cause, referring to the material out of which something is composed; the formal cause, referring to the pattern, shape, or structure that gives an object an identity; the efficient cause, referring to temporal cause and effect, as when one action causes another to happen; and the final cause, referring to the telos or essential purpose of an idea or object. In Aristotle's analysis, Plato's mistake is that he allowed only for an ultimate kind of formal cause, whereas in the empirical world everything emerges out of the simultaneous operation of all four kinds of causes. In the *Categories* (the first book of the *Organon*), Aristotle also distinguishes different categories by which we can perceive the world, but substance is the underlying, universal category, and his use of this term will, indeed, become the foundation for more than two thousand years of various versions of materialism. In short, substance names the broadest category beyond which there is no other more general name for the stuff of the world. To this extent, substance is the ultimate reality of the metaphysics. All other material attributes, such as quality, quantity, relation, place, time, "affections of the soul" (*Basic Works, Categories* 25), etc., tend to be secondary categories that give particularity to the undifferentiated, primary substance. Our contemporary situation seems to be the reverse: we deny any immediate access to the undifferentiated nature of the primary substance and emphasize the many differences of the variable attributes.

Any individual subject, personal identity, or particular object can be identified as such on the basis of its secondary substances; in short, its genera and species (for example, human being, horse, butterfly); and then by the specific set of qualities and attributes that emerge in the particular arrangement and intersection of identifiable categories. For Aristotle, what we perceive is always a combination and "composite" consisting of "substance, quantity, quality, relation, place, time, position, state, action, or affection" (*Basic Works* 8). But underlying these individual attributes lies the primary substance, the essence of being as a universal substratum to all particular forms.

These elaborate theories of the categories of substance provided Aristotle his primary means of objecting to Plato's notion of a transcendent Form, outside and independent of material substance. In Parts 6 and 9 of Book A of the *Metaphysics*, Aristotle directly addresses Plato's distinctions between "sensible things" and the universal "Forms." He grants that Plato diverged from his predecessors such as Pythagoras and Heraclitus specifically in his dialectical method of addressing the dualism between appearance and reality (12–17), and Aristotle clearly adapted the dialectic from his teacher, but in such a way as to serve his own agenda for a more scientific or empirical definition of Form. Aristotle faults Plato for his analysis of first causes: for Plato, the Forms serve as the primary causes for the appearance of particular species and objects in this physical world. Yet, as Aristotle argues, this might make some degree of logical sense for natural species, such as human being or horse, since individual development after birth appears to follow a predetermined plan; "And so Plato was not far wrong when he said that there are as many Forms as there are kinds of natural object" (183). But with respect to human-made items, such as a bed (Aristotle uses the example of a house or a ring), it makes no sense, since such objects follow so obviously from the intention and design of, say, the carpenter. As Aristotle puts it, "all other things cannot come from the Forms in any of the usual senses of 'from'" (18). He also disagrees with Plato's "illogical" claim in the *Phaedo* "that the Forms are causes both of being and of becoming" (18).[6] The ultimate Heraclitan "One" cannot be the originator or cause of difference if it, as claimed, is homogeneous by definition; just as the Platonic Form cannot both determine the sameness of characteristics shared by a species while also determining their particular, identifiable differences. In contrast, Aristotle's sense of the interactions and combinations of primary substance and secondary categories better explains the dialectic between sameness and difference. He elaborates on these distinctions at great length in the rest of the *Metaphysics*, and he returns in Part 4 of Book M to again critique Plato's belief in the preexistence of the otherworldly Forms.

At the same time, Aristotle's definition of philosophy as "knowledge of the truth" (*Metaphysics* 23) and the claim that "being and unity are the substances of things" (37) can sound very much like Plato if only we substitute "Forms" for "substances." Therefore, in Part 6 of Book B, Aristotle tries to distinguish his definition from Plato's by tying the Forms to his metaphysics of substance. Accordingly, "the Forms also must therefore be held to exist," and this must be so "because each of the Forms is a substance and none is by accident" (40). These foundational principles are the basis of his philosophy, in which, very much like Plato, the "principles are universals" (41) so that there is "one science of being qua being" (43). Nevertheless, it is always the case for Aristotle that, as he points out in the *Posterior Analytics,* such a radical separation of particular and universal as Plato argues is nonsensical partly because of the fundamental subject/predicate structure of language: you can't make any common assertion, such as "A man is tall," if you absolutely severe the particular quality of "tallness" from the subject "a man." Yet, as we will see by returning to the *Organon,* Aristotle also sustained some pretty radically binary oppositions (the "excluded middle") that continue to plague the dominant traditions of Western metaphysics over the next two millennia.

Indeed, the entire *Organon* is a highly logical, technical analysis, which is why this book is rarely taught in surveys of the history of Western thought—it requires a specialist in philosophy to find this work engaging. The *Rhetoric* and the *Poetics* are much more accessible to the general reader, but the *Organon* has remained foundational to all subsequent writing about the science of logic. And for both Plato and Aristotle, it is safe to say that logical analysis and dialectical method take formal precedence over rhetoric and sophistry, even when the latter are granted significant roles within their metaphysics, as we have seen Plato do in the *Phaedrus* and as we will see Aristotle do in the *Rhetoric.*

Aristotle established the binary basis of symbolic logic in the deductive syllogism. Book 1 of the *Prior Analytics* is devoted almost exclusively to defining and describing the foundational importance for any epistemology of the four different kinds of syllogism: the "pure syllogism" (hierarchically valued over the others); the "categorical syllogism;" the "hypothetical syllogism"; and the "modal syllogism," which precisely follow the "laws of logic" (*Basic* 27–29). Indeed, many of the articulations regarding fundamental logical terms such as *refutation, induction, reduction, objection,* etc., are described in such systematic fashion that, subsequently, any sustained exposition of logic had to address the foundational discourse of Aristotle. Many of these articulations in the *Organon* recur in other books, and, as we will see in the *Rhetoric*, they are sometimes close to word-for-word transcriptions of the earlier formulations.

Most significantly, Aristotle's description of what he calls the three basic "laws of logic" established the categorically rigid binary hierarchies characteristic of most versions of Western metaphysics. On a first glance, these three laws seem rather obvious, almost trivial: the first, the law of identity, simply states that "A is A"; the second, the law of noncontradiction, asserts that A cannot be not-A at the same time; and the third, the law of the excluded middle, maintains that there is no middle ground between A and not A. In a sense, these are just three restatements of the same basic law as told from three different points of emphasis. Later, in the *Metaphysics*, Aristotle becomes quite emphatic about the binary point of his metaphysics, namely, the "impossibility of anything both being and not-being" at the same time so "that this is the most indisputable of all principles" (48). But these rigidly binary laws have had enormous social and political consequences. For instance, they can be taken to mean that an Englishman can only be an Englishman, not a Frenchman or an Iranian, and that there is no hybrid middle ground between one essential identity and the other. Ethnocentric violence is an almost surefire consequence of these Manichean opposites between East and West, or between man and woman. As M. A. R. Habib puts it, "these 'laws,' which unfortunately still largely govern our thinking today, are not only coercive but also encourage a vision of the world as divided up sharply into categories, classes, nations, races, and religions, each with its own distinctive essence or character. The elimination of the middle ground has long been an ideological, political, and economic strategy, one that removes all possibility of definitional flexibility and change according to altered circumstances" (*History* 46). Every deconstruction or postcolonial critique engages in the refutation of such binary versions of the "excluded middle," and for good reason, since in today's global diaspora we find difference and hybridity everywhere we look.

We will reconsider this opening to the political economy in the section on Aristotle's *Politics*.

But given this brief overview of Aristotle's metaphysical presuppositions, we can more easily understand the significantly different emphases between Aristotle and Plato. We can also more clearly see that, as Ellen Meiksins Wood argues, "whatever else may divide these two philosophical giants, their social values and political commitments are, for all intents and purposes, the same. They are both opposed to the Athenian democracy, from the standpoint of aristocratic values" (*Citizens* 82).[7] They are also, and this is crucial, formalists, even though Aristotle looked for form within the empirical realm of physical "substances." Plato and Aristotle have sometimes been so conjured according to their differences (see especially Herman) that we can lose the historical fact that the real intellectual differences in ancient Greece were between the philosophers, on the one hand, and the sophists and rhetors such as Isocrates, Protagoras, Gorgias, and Parmenides, on the other. The more pragmatic, contextual, and situational praxis of the latter group lost the battle as the dialectical models, whether Platonic or Aristotelian, that emphasized reason, logic, and being became the dominant version of Western metaphysics in both the idealist and empiricist strains (see Romano). Perhaps it is even more important to recall that the majority of people in ancient Greece were noncitizens, such as women, metics, slaves, and many others, and so they had no voice whatsoever in the social decision-making processes. For that reason alone, these dispossessed others clearly lost the battle even more significantly than did the privileged sophists and rhetors of the ruling classes.

Nevertheless, anybody who has ever read a textbook owes a great deal to this monumental transformation wrought by the legacy of Aristotle. The easiest way to name that transformation is, following our analysis in Chapter 3, to say that the copula takes over: the immanent possibilities of the state-of-being verb becomes dominant, and this syntactical transformation takes place about equally in Plato and Aristotle. Third-person omniscient exposition becomes a textual possibility even though no such point of view was ever possible in any oral culture. We can thus witness in these Aristotelian texts the historical origins of the mode of explication that will become the voice of virtually all textbooks ever since:

the authoritative, declarative perspective becomes naturalized in these papyrus scrolls. We are now better prepared to look more closely at our codex version of the text of the *Rhetoric* before we turn to the remarkable redefinition of poetry and drama that, as post-Romantics, we are so much more comfortable with than we are with Plato's condemnation of these genres.

How Counterparts Become Hierarchies

Just take a look at the first sentence in the *Rhetoric*, where, of course, the verb is the copula: "Rhetoric *is* the counterpart of dialectic" (19, my italics). The ostensible meaning (in our translation) of this sentence asserts an equivalency between rhetoric and dialectic, at least to the extent that "counterpart" suggests equal valences, just as the two sides of a coin are "counterparts," equal halves, and you can't have one without the other. The assertion carries no doubt, because the copula registers unquestionable confidence. Aristotle appears to speak with a literal authority that has nothing to do with irony. Nevertheless, we can recover a hidden irony in the text that follows the opening sentence: a close look at the text itself undoes, or we could say deconstructs, its own ostensible meaning. The irony can be located in the way that the text bears the traces of a meaning pretty much the opposite of the apparent meaning registered by the opening sentence: as it turns out, rhetoric is the weaker form, or dependent mode, thus subordinate to the stronger dialectic. They are not really counterparts as equal partners. This subordination is required by the dominant discourse of Western metaphysics: it is not just binary, but also hierarchical.

Again, we cannot ignore the influence of Aristotle's students in the actual composition of this perspective, but it certainly is consistent with his version of metaphysics: the classical Greek episteme, the root of the natural sciences, is fixed, static, and real, which means there is no fundamental change in the forms, species, and genres he observes around him in the natural world. Indeed, Aristotle's main project was to cut through motion, change, and flux to stable, fixed categories of natural objects: the telos of his empirical method is the goal of describing the world as a natural hierarchy of beings and things. The new point of view enabled by literate culture also provided the author a godlike perspective, or omniscience, because there is no human subjectivity that appears to intervene in the natural classification of things. Aristotle now writes (or speaks) as if attaining objectivity in the matters at hand is no longer a problem: it can be adequately accomplished by literal description of those objects. Recall from our last chapter, on the *Phaedrus,* Derrida suggested that this analytical confidence is, ironically, one of the main mythical elements of Western metaphysics: we can't become gods, but we can write as if we were. But, of course, for Aristotle it is not a myth but a positive assertion about reality and its immanent categories of primary substance, modified by secondary substances into species and genres. As Aristotle puts it, the danger is that citizens "will often have allowed themselves to be so much influenced by feelings of friendship or hatred or self-interest that they lose any clear vision of the truth" (*Rhetoric* 20–21). One can emphasize the ethical components of that last sentence: the concern for friendship, the worry about "hatred or self-interest," and the implied sense of relationships with others in the community, all reminiscent of his famous description, also in the *Rhetoric,* of ethos and pathos, in addition to logos. But Aristotle's claim has been more commonly registered in epistemological rather than moral terms. Given such a focus on knowledge (logos rather than ethos), the entire rhetorical position Aristotle takes in most of his major texts is that he, at least, has a "clear vision of the truth" so that he can speak omnisciently. So, of course, the verb in the first sentence is the copula: the state of being, "is," registers the static world of truth attained prior to the act of composition itself, in which case writing and composing takes on a fait accompli: the reporting of the finished results of dialectical inquiry. It's as if the "I," the subjectivity of the speaker per se, has indeed been successfully either (1) separated from the objective account of the truth so that it does not interfere in that objectivity, or (2) integrated with the objective outside world so that the subjectivity does not interfere in the representation of the object itself (the procedure Kant offers, as we will see in Part 2). But let's observe how this happens in the text.

In the early pages, Aristotle maintains the conceptual equivalence between rhetoric and dialectic, as when he claims "that rhetoric is not bound up with a single definite class of subjects, but is as universal as dialectic" (23). It may be as "universal," but as we will see, it will nevertheless remain subordinate to the primacy of the dialectic. Indeed, two pages later, the subordination begins, when it turns out "that rhetoric is an offshoot of dialectic" (25)—in other words, the qualification hints at the necessary subordination of the persuasive arts to the dialectical foundation: philosophy trumps rhetoric (and sophistry). And the irony is that it so clearly does so in a book called *Rhetoric*.

The key passages that follow reiterate the foundational definitions for the terms of logical analysis in Western discourse: *syllogism, deduction,* and *induction.* Deduction moves from the general to the particular, as exemplified in the thesis, antithesis, synthesis of the syllogism; induction moves from the amassing of many particulars that share the same characteristics in order to make a more general claim. And it is significant that all three of these foundational terms come from dialectic, not rhetoric, even as Aristotle deploys those definitions in the service of defining rhetoric:

> [J]ust as in dialectic there is induction on the one hand and syllogism or apparent syllogism on the other, so it is in rhetoric. The example is an induction, the enthymeme is a syllogism, and the apparent enthymeme is an apparent syllogism. I call the enthymeme a rhetorical syllogism, and the example a rhetorical induction. Every one who effects persuasion through proof does in fact use either enthymemes or examples: there is no other way . . . it must follow that enthymemes are syllogisms and examples are inductions. (26)[8]

Since Aristotle sets up these distinctions as a set of structural oppositions, it is easy to chart those formal properties:

Dialectic =	Induction +	Deduction (syllogism)
Rhetoric =	Example +	Enthymeme

In the diagram, dialectic appears on the top line because it provides the key terms for defining the subordinate term of rhetoric. Given its binary nature, the key terms also have a binary division whereby dialectic splits between induction and deduction. Rhetoric likewise follows the binary divide into examples, a weak form of induction to the extent that in writing you can only elaborate on a few examples though induction proper works best on a great number of specific instances; and enthymemes, a weaker form of a syllogism because an enthymeme is essentially a deductive claim with one of the premises missing. The conceptual subordination is complete: although Aristotle began with the claim that "rhetoric is the counterpart of the dialectic," his own analysis demonstrates that rhetoric is defined exclusively in the binary terms of the dialectic, and in both induction and deduction rhetoric is the weaker version of the basic principles of the dialectic. Later in the text he simply puts these hierarchies to work, even using Plato's language of appearance versus reality as when he says, "[T]he whole business of rhetoric being concerned with appearances, we must pay attention to the subject of delivery, unworthy though it is, because we cannot do without it" (165). As is always the case with Western metaphysics, it is not only binary, but hierarchical, and dialectic always gets the upper hand, as the philosopher triumphs over the rhetorician. This is in contrast to our own contemporary moment, when most of us think of rhetoric as the broader term, affecting all discourse insofar as it involves persuasion. Even when we grant great significance to the dialectical process, we tend to view it as a specialized discourse within the broader category of rhetoric—most of what we encounter in our daily lives is hybrid.

The analytical hierarchies Aristotle favors also elevate his own rhetorical position as an authority, and without hesitation he proceeds to lay out the foundational terms and categories for the analysis of virtually all kinds of texts. As he puts it, "Of the modes of persuasion furnished by the spoken word there are three kinds. This first kind depends on the personal character of the speaker; the second on putting the audience into a certain frame of mind; the third on the proof, or apparent proof, provided by the works of the speech itself" (24–25). So here we have the three main categories: the speaker/author, the speech/text, and the audience/reader, and it is not too much to say that these three perspectives have provided the basic ways that we categorize communicative, literary, and linguistic theories in terms of where meaning resides: in the speaker's/author's original and primary intention; in the formal properties of the speech/text itself; or in the active experience of the audience/reader.[9]

Throughout his analysis, Aristotle speaks with such assurances of his own neutrality that when he offers his system of natural classifications, such as that there are "three classes" (31) of speakers, "three divisions" of oratory (32), "three points" (164) to a good speech, or "five heads" to the characteristics of "good style" (174), it appears as simply unthinkable that there might be, say, four or six characteristics (or forty-six!). Any other system of classification would be untrue and artificial, as opposed to the "natural" classification of things offered by his own system, because the latter is presumed to be universal and foundational. And he registers a self-conscious observation about his own foundational role in offering this system: "No systematic treatise upon the rules of delivery has yet been composed" (165).

Given these claims to systemic neutrality, it then appears a bit more shocking when we see instances of his own ethnocentricity and racism emerge. For example, in his discussion of the basic principles of happiness he says the constituent parts consist of: "good birth, plenty of friends, good friends, wealth, good children, plenty of children, a happy old age, also such bodily excellences as health, beauty, strength, large stature, athletic powers, together with fame, honour, good luck, and virtue. . . . Now good birth in a race or a state means that its members are indigenous or ancient" (38). Foreigners do not seem to have a good prospect for happiness in his account, and this must have been a touchy point in his own life because he was not a native Athenian, but a Macedonian. Immigrant status with respect to birthright, citizenship, and social belonging clearly has long historical roots.

In spite of all these powerful systematic moves to decontextualize his own analysis in order to make it appear universal, on more than one occasion Aristotle does actually make reference to some historical conditions that seem to resonate quite well with Havelock's and Ong's discussion of the threads of orality and literacy, although, of course, without those terms. One specific passage deserves extended quotation:

It was naturally the poets who first set the movement going; for words represent things, and they had also the human voice at their disposal, which of all our organs can best represent other things [again, like Plato, we see the primacy of speech over the secondary status of writing]. . . . Even now most uneducated people think that poetical language makes the finest discourses. That is not true: the language of prose is distinct from that of poetry [but now, prose becomes the better kind of writing]. This is shown by the state of things to-day, when even the language of tragedy has altered its character. Just as iambics were adopted, instead of tetrameters, because they are the most prose-like of all metres, so tragedy has given up all those words, not used in ordinary talk, which decorated the early drama and are still used by the writers of hexameter poems. It is therefore ridiculous to imitate a poetical manner which the poets themselves have dropped. (*Rhetoric* 166)

Here, almost as if Aristotle had anticipated Havelock's and Ong's discussion of the shift from oral to literate culture, education is now associated with those who have passed out of a reliance on the old mnemonic oral tradition, dominated by the performance of poetry with tetradic meter, and moved on to a new historical phase in which the distinct language of prose description and dialectical analysis has become the new norm. In Aristotle's own words (we hope), it is "ridiculous" to try to imitate the oral manner if one is aspiring to the literal realm of the dialectic.

Aristotle proceeds with his analysis of poetry (as we will see in the *Poetics*) as if he were speaking primarily about a text rather than an oral performance, and it is the dialectic that provides the terms to analyze the characteristics of good poetry. In these terms, the very process of "speaking naturally" is placed in op-position to the now-outmoded, artificial, and repetitious clichés of an oral performance. Different perspectives, whether of social class, age, or race, call for their appropriate formal styles: "Even in poetry, it is not quite appropriate that fine language should be used by a slave or a very young man. . . . We can now see that a writer must disguise his art and give the impression of speaking naturally and not artificially" (167). To disguise the art would be to hide the repetitions and formula of oral verse; or better yet, to avoid them as inappropriate and unnatural. That slaves or young men should not use fine language suggests some early signs of the anti-universalism in this foundational text about universalism. Ironically, we can observe that Aristotle's approval of "natural writing" appears akin to Plato's "soul writing" as referred to in the *Phaedrus*.

In the process of these systemic revisions, Aristotle rescues imitation from the context of poetic memorization in which Plato had situated it, and gives us a definition much more compatible with our modern meanings for the term: "It is clear that the general origin of poetry was due to two causes, each of them part of human nature. Imitation is natural to man from childhood, one of his advantages over the lower animals being this, that he is the most imitative creature in the world, and learns at first by imitation. And it is also natural for all to delight to view the most realistic representations of them in art" (226–27). Here we find the twin pillars of imitation and delight, which will later become, as in Horace, the two missions of poetry, to "instruct" and "delight"; and as we can see the oral conditions of mnemonic devices for memorization have little to do with these positive definitions. Aristotle is simply not worried about those historical conditions that have receded in the even more literate world he inhabits.

Figuration and metaphor also get redefined in a literate habitat linking their use in poetic and prose texts: "metaphor is of great value both in poetry and in prose. Prose-writers must, however, pay specially careful attention to metaphor, because their other resources are scantier than those of poets. Metaphor, moreover, gives style clearness, charm, and distinction as nothing else can. . . . Metaphors, like epithets, must be fitting, which means that they must fairly correspond to the thing signified" (168). Thus, even metaphor is ruled by the correspondence theory of signification, as if it too could be ruled by the laws of prose: clarity, brevity, and sincerity (the CBS model of good writing we inherited from William Strunk Jr.'s 1918 classic, *Elements of Style* [revised in 1959 by E. B. White]). The only concern for justice (or fair play) immediately evident here is measured with respect to the formal correspondence theory of representation: the metaphors must "fairly correspond" to what they signify.

Like Plato, Aristotle also worries that one of the great risks of any kind of writing is succumbing to the deceptive rule of the

lower standards of rhetoric rather than the higher standards of
dialectic. In these risky cases, the language leads us astray, and
Aristotle puts the blame for these diversions even more directly on
the practices of the sophists. Indeed, it was hard not to recognize
that the linguistic play, dramatic irony, textual ambiguity, and
figural language found on almost every page of Plato resonated
with the rhetorical skills of the sophists.[10] But Aristotle takes a
position that in most regards is significantly more opposed to
sophistry than is any of Plato's texts. As he complains, "Words
of ambiguous meaning are chiefly useful to enable the sophist to
mislead his hearers" (*Rhetoric* 168). The risk of rhetoric is that
it can conceal its subordinate role as a useful embellisher of the
truth-telling capacities of the dialectic.

Aristotle insists throughout upon a singular meaning, or
monovalence, of terms, just as Plato did in his formalism: accurate
reference depends upon the correspondence theory of language,
and Aristotle opposes this strict alignment of one word with
one meaning to what he sees as the potential deceptiveness of
the sophists. Most contemporary scholars see Aristotle granting
great consideration to emotions, audience, and politics (ethos and
pathos as well as logos) in the *Rhetoric*—positions that would all
align him much more with the sophists than with the philosophers.
But Aristotle's formalism aligns him more with the philosophers.
Again, Aristotle makes far more disparaging remarks about the
potential deceptiveness of the sophists as his enemy than Plato
ever did. As Aristotle puts it, unlike the sophists, who hate to
admit this fact: "One term may describe a thing more truly than
another" (170). Aristotle offers the correct system for getting
word and idea properly aligned. The subject and the object, word
and meaning, must perfectly correspond. Likewise, pathos (emotion) and ethos (character) must correspond appropriately to the
subject and situation at hand: "Your language will be appropriate
if it expresses emotion and character, and if it corresponds to its
subject. 'Correspondence to subject' means that we must neither
speak casually about weighty matters, nor solemnly about trivial
ones . . ." (178). As we will see, he appropriately enough speaks
very solemnly about tragedy.

Rescuing the Poet in the *Poetics*

If you are not a bit scared of the *Poetics*, you ought to be, because it runs so deeply in our pan-European discourses across more than two millennia that it infects a lot of what we do when we read. This text is more than canonical, to the extent that all of us affected by European culture (which means large geographical portions of the entire world) are all sick with the aftereffects produced by the founding of literary formalism as offered in this remarkable manuscript.[11] If you have ever studied literature through an analysis of plot, character, diction, tone, or point of view (and who hasn't?), it is not too much to say you owe it all to Aristotle. He set the terms for that discourse. In so doing, he also set the terms for how we might go about disembedding universal poetic form from contingent historical realities. We are all still struggling in the twenty-first century with how to compensate for that characteristically Western kind of misframing: how can our search for universals resonate accurately (or dialectically) with more intimate historical contexts without some degree of ethnocentric narrowness?

The key question is: how did Aristotle rescue the poet from Plato's condemnation all the while using the new philosophical rhetoric that Plato had inaugurated? My answer to this question will rest on one fundamental premise: they are not talking about the same thing. Plato situates poetry within the performative educational practices of the dominant oral culture, whereas for Aristotle poetry no longer has anything to do with the experiential dynamics of orality. For Aristotle, poetry consists primarily of a set of textual objects that can be laid out in space, broken down by analysis, and descriptively explained in terms of their generic structural forms, which are visible in the texts themselves. Aristotle assumes that a poem endures primarily because of its relative stability as an unchanging text—more or less the assumptions shared by mid-twentieth-century New Critics.

Whereas Plato worried a great deal about texts getting separated from authors so that the original meaning might be lost as the text rolled around through history, Aristotle now assumes the great virtue of these same unchanging textual objects. As texts, they are portable because they retain their same basic form in different histories and different geographies: even when translated, the five acts in great tragedies can still be seen, because there they are, marked out in the text itself. So the work Aristotle performs is craftsmanlike: he describes the best examples he can find to serve as his exemplary texts, such as Sophocles's *Oedipus Rex,* and his accurate descriptions of the basic forms he finds laid out in that scroll of papyrus then serves a prescriptive function. If you want to write a tragedy, here are the basic formal features of the best that is to be found, so follow this model. And, of course, dramatists down through the ages have struggled to do exactly that as they wrestle with these terms for classic tragedy.

Noticeably, I have slipped from poetry to drama, and that slippage calls for some explanation. The simplest explanation is the influence gained during the fifth and fourth centuries BCE of the great Greek tragic dramatists such as Aeschylus, Sophocles, and Euripides, who had then taken on more cultural significance through ritual performances in open-air theaters than the older epic poets such as Homer and Hesiod. But also, once the dramatic performances appeared as papyrus texts they were shorter, and it was easier to locate organizational structures in those texts than it was in epics, which tended to be expansive and episodic rather than tightly plotted; the plays also contained a great deal of what counted for the best poetry in that age. Moreover, the dramatists tended to avoid most forms of oral repetition in their compositions—there was no longer any need for anyone but the male actors wearing huge masks to spend time actually memorizing the lines in preparation for the performances. In short, drama now stands in for poetry in the *Poetics.*

But even given those assumptions about the textual sources, Aristotle still had to account for the obvious historical situation: great plays like *Oedipus Rex* were not to be found if one looked all that far into the past. Somehow they had emerged within the previous couple of hundred years, and it was also pretty obvious that drama had tended to divide itself into two kinds. As Aristotle explains, both "Tragedy and Comedy appeared in the field" (*Rhetoric* 228). Like Plato, since Aristotle believes that the underlying forms do not change he ends up paradoxically recognizing what we would call a kind of evolutionary progression in the genre of drama, but that very historical evolution is teleological because it stops when it gets to the shape of its true form: "It was in fact only after a long series of changes that the movement of Tragedy stopped on its attaining to its natural form" (228). Evolution ends when a kind of ontogenetic apex of the adult stage or "natural form" is reached, say, in *Oedipus Rex*, so that then Aristotle's work consists of serving merely as critical handmaiden to artistic perfection of form: by describing the features of the natural form of tragedy, he ensures that that very description becomes the prescription for all other imitators, and the birth of classic drama, in a sense, ends at its beginning. Dialectical process in history culminates in textual reification of the finished absolute product that transcends history.

Now it is not at all immediately obvious what details one should be paying attention to during the act of reading a papyrus text even though Aristotle has clearly seen a lot of dramatic performances of them. His main task is to convert the temporality of dramatic performance into form, which is spatial, and he accomplishes this task by setting the two key terms, plot and character, in dialectical tension with each other: "the first essential, the life and soul, so to speak, of Tragedy is the Plot; and . . . the Characters come second" (232).

The temporal unfolding of plot, then, can be visually diagrammed as a rise in tension (arousal of pity and fear in the audience) as the character's flaw leads to complications, reaching a crisis, thus calling for a catharsis, releasing and decreasing the pressure, thus purging the imperfections as the tension dissipates in the ending, or denouement of the play. It is a linear model with beginning, middle, and end, but laid out in two-dimensional space as a graph of rising and falling tension on the vertical axis and elapsed time on the horizontal axis. In principle, we get what in 1863 Gustav Freytag will call a dramatic pyramid. The temporal struggles of the hero in the drama must be organized around this basic visual form, graphed with rising and falling emotional tensions providing the basic plot structure. Imitation is now conceived primarily as a key responsibility of the dramatist, but not, as in oral culture, based on the blind memorization and repetition of what had already been spoken and written. Instead, the dramatist had to adapt the particular actions of the hero to the universal form: one imitated the general form, not the particulars, since the latter would of course vary from dramatist to dramatist and play to play. Imitation depends, then, upon integrated, complete wholeness rather than fragmentary narrative episodes such as in epic, or, later, in picaresque. Thus, Aristotle's now classic definition of tragedy leaves very little room for rambling diversions: the structure of the plot must lead directly to the arousal of pity and fear, followed by catharsis, or the purging of those emotional impurities:

> A tragedy, then, is the imitation of an action that is serious and also, as having magnitude, complete in itself; in language with pleasurable accessories, each kind brought in separately in the parts of the work; in a dramatic, not in a narrative form; with incidents arousing pity and fear, wherewith to accomplish its catharsis of such emotions. (*Rhetoric* 230)

Of course, in this generic model, every detail must fit within the predetermined textual structure whereby "[a] well-constructed Plot, therefore, cannot either begin or end at any point one likes; beginning and end in it must be of the forms just described" (233). Ironically, what ends up being most imitated in this model is something that rarely if ever occurs in anyone's historical life: a unified plot sequence without interruptions or dislocations caused by the inevitable accidents and random occurrences of everyday living. The hero imitates not a real-life historical king, but a mythical hero of Greek legend, whose story, as a plot, already comes prepackaged as an archetypal narrative about the play of ignorance and knowledge, pride and humility, blindness and insight. "His story, again, whether already made or of his own making, he should first simplify and reduce to a universal form, before proceeding to lengthen it out by the insertion of episodes" (245). Indeed, what really seems to get imitated is the universal form of the idealized plot, a formal unity that precedes the composition of any specific play, complete and whole unto itself, that can be represented in about two hours of onstage time.

Unlike the historical life circumstances of any actual king, in a great tragedy there can be only one key action in the plot with all details integrated into that "one action, a complete whole, with its several incidents so closely connected that the transposal or withdrawal of any one of them will disjoin and dislocate the whole" (234). Structural totality of the whole textual object becomes prioritized at the point where the dialectical movement comes to an end. And the subordinate but connected properties fit within this schema: "There are six parts consequently of every tragedy, as a whole (that is) of such or such quality, viz. a Fable or Plot, Characters, Diction, Thought, Spectacle, and Melody . . . " (231). And these six formal properties, and variations of them, have dominated the formal analysis of drama and fiction and poetry for more than two thousand years. Which is to say that over those many years many people continued to be convinced that Aristotle got an awful lot of things correct in naming those categories of dramatic excellence.

Returning to the structural constraints linking plot with character, Aristotle defines the crucial concepts of hubris or character flaw. If a character were pure and unflawed, there would be no plot, action, or tension: no cause for pity or fear. So the tragic hero must follow a general type, and thus Aristotle defines the quintessential tragic hero: "a man not preeminently virtuous and just, whose misfortune, however, is brought upon him not by vice and depravity but by some error of judgement, of the number of those in the enjoyment of great reputation and prosperity; e.g. Oedipus, Thyestes, and the men of note of similar families" (238–39). In short, it has to be a leader, a man in a high place, all the farther to fall, and falling is the basic movement of tragedy.[12] But the flaw also cannot be too extreme: "the cause of it must lie not in any depravity, but in some great error in his part. . . . The theoretically best tragedy, then, has a Plot of this description" (239).

Let us now summarize this dynamic within the structural characteristics of the emerging discourse of Western metaphysics. One of the key meanings of catharsis is purgation, that is, a form of purification by which the flow or impurity in the tragic character is purged, at least in the audience and the community of viewers. Oedipus, of course, suffers deeply, at the end of the play condemned to wander about blindly now that he sees the "light": he does not get to go back, purified, to his home and community, but the audience does. In this sense, what appears as the dynamic emotional intensity of pity and fear is mapped into a structural pattern authorized by Western metaphysics: you move out of the imperfect, human, flawed world of appearances and dialectical tensions toward the pure, universal form of truth, now purged of its imperfections. The plot is a form giving rise to emotions of pity and fear, but ultimately purging and purifying the audience of those emotions in the resolution. Audience response is thus captured within the form of Platonic purification. This final re-capturing of an emotional balance or stasis mirrors the Platonic discourse with its idealized, universal forms that transcend the historical body, and the emotional intensities that lead us astray from those fixed forms.

Out of all this metaphysical formalism comes perhaps the most influential reversal ever recorded in ancient Greece, at least between Plato and Aristotle: poetry now gets elevated by virtue of its very freedom from historical contingency, exactly the opposite of Plato's situating of poetic performance within the dominant educational practices of an oral culture. This foundational sev-ering of the poetic from the political/historical will have many reverberations throughout European, and even global, history. But once poetry can be organized into a formal text that emu-lates universal form, Aristotle can then claim: "Hence poetry is something more philosophic and of graver import than history, since its statements are of the nature rather of universals, whereas those of history are singulars" (235). According to this crucial definition, poetry, now freed from history, can be so composed as to emulate in its textual form the ahistorical universal precisely because it does not have to be tied to the accidents of history. Despite his insistence on the dependence of the ideals on sensory perceptions of particular instances (such as *Oedipus Rex*), his poetic theory implicitly reinscribes some measure of Platonic idealism: correspondence goes up to the universal (ideal form), and not necessarily down to the particular (empirical fact). How-ever, given the striking difference between Plato's analyses of the role of poetic performances in an oral culture and Aristotle's contrasting assessment of the formal properties of unity of ac-tion in poetic texts, Aristotle clearly insists that the poet's social function of imagining probable ideals and alternatives is a highly rational activity, aligned with the dialectic of the philosopher.

Such a view is distinctly the opposite of Plato's consideration of imitation as irrational emotional identification for purposes of remembering the lines necessary to preserve the cultural archive in an oral culture.

We here witness the founding moments in Aristotle of the traces of Western metaphysical formalism. As we will see in Part 2, we could not really have entities like English departments as they emerged in the late nineteenth century until we could get some stable objects, the canon of great literary works exemplifying formal unity, which could then be preserved and disseminated as a disciplined body of knowledge. And not just English departments, because Aristotle, more than Plato, positively laid out the map of the basic disciplines of knowledge in his *Metaphysics,* where he distinguishes among three kinds of sciences: productive, practical, and theoretical.[13] He then further subdivides these categories such that the theoretical sciences include physics, mathematics, and theology.

We can see some of the contemporary divisions of knowledge emerging here, although those terms had to be deeply adapted and rewritten since the social history of eighteenth- and nineteenth-century Europe was so different from that of ancient Greece. But, as we will see in Cultural Turn 2, by adapting Aristotle's basic terms, it became possible at least for the Romantic idealists to claim that the great works of literature exemplify exactly that kind of universal transcendence, and the main evidence was that, in contrast to all other fleeting and disappearing texts, the canonized ones have "stood the test of time" because of their remarkably shared characteristic of formal unity within the texts themselves. As we will see in the Epilogue, in the mid-twentieth-century the New Critics adapted the transcendent version of Romantic idealism by combining Aristotle's rigorous formal analysis of textual properties in their methodology of close reading with the more transcendent, spiritual, and Platonic realm of the transcendent literary "simulacrum of experience" made available to the reader in the "unparaphrasable," "verbal icon," and "well-wrought urn" of the text itself. Aristotle himself aided these potential syntheses with his former teacher even as he clearly sought to distance himself from many of Plato's ideas.

The poet, dramatist, and artist (all analogs of one another) are now all situated within this philosophical discourse, and gain a privileged position with respect to any random events in history or nature. Neither war nor earthquake can dislodge them, so that, according to this theory, the poet/dramatists' perfect plots provide a kind of improvement on the flawed historical models. As Aristotle puts it: "For the purposes of poetry, a convincing impossibility is preferable to an unconvincing possibility; . . . as the artist ought to improve on his model" (263). Even if poets or sculptors, say, were to take a historical figure, they need not represent that figure as an exact, mimetic replica via some version of realism, because their powers of diverging from the historical can lead toward improvements, insofar as the textual object, or sculpture, imitates the universal form of ultimate truths unencumbered by the weight of historical singularities.

Once we get to this point we can begin to see that rather than being structurally at odds with Plato's critique of the poet in the *Republic* Aristotle resituates the poet within a literate culture as producer of universally truthful texts with only some slight twists on Plato's model of the thrice-removed status of the poet. Structurally speaking, the change can be represented as a dislocation in the content of the structure, rather than as a modification of the underlying principles of organization. Consider, for example, the following sentence with my insertions in brackets: "The poet being an imitator just like the painter or other maker of likenesses, he must necessarily in all instances represent things in one or other of three aspects, either as they were or are [the carpenter's bed], or as they are said or thought to be or to have been [the sophist's bed—not the poet's], or as they ought to be [the poet's bed as an equivalence of god's bed]" (*Rhetoric* 260). In short, the rhetorical instability of the sophist comes off badly in Aristotle's *Poetics,* but the poet gets elevated to a status just below that of the philosopher-king, and thus becomes a new kind of hero who has the freedom to represent things as they "ought to be."

Unlike the lowly sophist or rhetorician who practices in the courts of law and the houses of politics, the poet has now been disembedded from these encumbering domains. As Aristotle puts it, "It is to be remembered, too, that there is not the same kind of correctness in poetry as in politics, or indeed any other art" (260). Recall from our discussions about Plato that he never really distinguished between poetry and politics (at least not in the *Republic*)[14] because for him the object of attention is the whole poetic/oral/mnemonic/political tradition and the educational plan that established and perpetuated the oscillations between oligarchic and democratic sociopolitical order in ancient Greece. In contrast, Aristotle puts Plato's metaphysic into the service of rescripting the role of the poet within a philosophical register. Like the philosopher (but not quite so powerfully), the poet gets divorced, by definition, from the political and social. Consequently, once so released from the need to be accurate with respect to any historical reality, the poet is free to represent the universal form. "Any impossibilities there may be in his descriptions of things are faults. But from another point of view they are justifiable, if they serve the end of poetry itself" (260); and that end is the attainment of the universal. Communality and hierarchy potentially seem to join hands in these formulations: in the ideal community based on universal poetic values we get a hierarchy presumably unquestioned by everyone in the community so that they create the basis for shared principles of social organization. Unfortunately, only the hierarchical condition seems to have materialized in recorded history: the poets elevated to universal status tended to be European males, and Aristotle's political desires were clearly for aristocratic males to rule the uneducated populace of peasant-citizens, women, artisans, and slaves.

In the end, of course, dialectical difference culminates in metaphysical sameness: "The contradictions found in the poet's language one should first test as one does an opponent's confutation in a dialectical argument, so as to see whether he means the same thing, in the same relation, and in the same sense" (263). The criteria of formal sameness (following the "laws of logic") must be attained through empirical testing, philosophical rigor, and dialectical argument, until you reach the endpoint in the Absolute—the underlying philosophical criteria that establish the basis for judging the merit of poetry. So, once again, the dialectic trumps the poetic just as it did the rhetorical, but only if you reach the ultimate goal of fixed generic form. We need to come back to earth now by examining briefly Aristotle's elaboration in the *Politics* of his basic point that "man is by nature a political animal" (*Politics* 28).

The *Politics* of the Polity

Aristotle's political views are based on his ethics, so we need to begin with a look at *Nicomachean Ethics,* where we will see that the ethics of virtue lead to the models of the hierarchically more virtuous kinds of political states. As the most famous (and most influential) of his many writings on the subject, the *Ethics* was apparently dedicated to his son, Nicomachus, though his father bore the same name. The book itself develops a logical progression from personal to political notions of virtue, but in the end the good life of virtue can only be accomplished by "something greater and more complete," which is, ultimately, the "finer and more godlike" world of the city-state or nation (book 1, chap. 2; *Basic* 936). Ethical virtue and the political economy are deeply linked, although we do not fully get to the latter until the *Politics.* Indeed, jumping to the final pages of the *Ethics,* we find Aristotle turning to the laws and constitutions necessary for social organization, all as a kind of necessary transition toward the *Politics.*

In Books 2 to 5 of the *Ethics* Aristotle elaborates on the many qualities of moral virtue, but it is in Book 5 where he provides detailed analysis of his conceptions of personal, social, and political justice. Significantly, the attainment of justice is the "greatest of virtues" (*Basic* 1003), and he goes on to develop his iconic doctrines about the proportional mean, a moderate position deliberately intended to avoid extremes of any kind that can otherwise disturb personal, social, and political equilibrium. Unlike Plato, who rarely identified justice with concerns for equality, Aristotle directly connects unjust behavior with inequality: "the unjust is unequal" (1006). These ideals are important, although they will come to seem ironic, if not severely limited, when we get to the *Politics.* But in the *Ethics,* "Justice is a kind of mean . . . because it relates to an intermediate amount, while injustice relates to the extremes" (1012). Using abstract mathematical models of the intermediary "mean" (completely distinct from his logical stipulation about the "excluded middle"), he goes on to elaborate and justify those necessary inequalities such as between father and son, the lawful and the unlawful, the fair and the unfair. By analogy with geometrical proportion and arithmetical progression, Aristotle explains that there are, therefore, quite different kinds of justices, and he makes a clear distinction between what he calls distributive and rectificatory justice. These very terms will have a long history, since distributive justice raises questions about the social distribution of money (surplus value), material and symbolic goods, and other potentially maldistributed elements of wealth and power. Rectification also remains to this day a crucial kind of consideration, as for example in questions about reparations for war crimes, criminal actions of all kinds, and racial, gender, and ethnic violence. Indeed, Aristotle concludes Book 5 by distinguishing between what he calls natural and legal forms of political justice. Natural political justice is based on universal principles that always apply equally to all people, whereas legal justice refers to more specific instances of the application of the law, and so depends on the more historically contingent forms of constitutional and criminal law. In any given example, both kinds of justice are always engaged.

Although there are ten books in the *Ethics,* it is Book 5 that leads most directly to the concerns of the *Politics,* so I will now make this jump from political justice to the more elaborate forms of the political state envisioned by Aristotle. We will almost immediately encounter what by contemporary standards can only be seen as remarkable kinds of injustices for which Aristotle, however, finds logical justifications. What he will claim as "natural political justice" will seem entirely unnatural, especially when slavery is justified as a natural condition of human life.

The *Politics* begins in Book 1 with the first systematic attempt to describe the various domains of what today we would call the political economy. Aristotle conceptualized some of the key gender and racial differences found in ancient Greece as "natural hierarchies," and therefore the maintenance of these hierarchies was justified on the basis of his version of "natural justice." In his systematic description of the social life of his day, he divided the organization of production into three tiers: the first was the *oikos* or home, where basic daily biological needs were organized into sets of hierarchical relations between husband and wife, master and slave, and parents and children; the second tier was the village, with its larger association of multiple households organized around economic production, mainly farming, artisanry, day labor, and slave labor (especially for mining and the minting of coin); and the third was the *polis,* or state, and, ironically, the only domain based on a supposed equality of the citizenry, even though the only men who could be classified as citizens were the ruling military elite who had the time to educate themselves (*Politics,* book 1, pp. 25–53; see also Wood, *Citizens* 93–94).

The state is "natural" because it "is by nature clearly prior to the family and to the individual, since the whole is of necessity prior to the part" (*Politics* 29). Slaves and women do not come off well in these hierarchies. In speaking of the "natural" relations between "master and slave" (30), the "slave is a living possession" (31) of the master of the household. Slavery is a "natural hierarchy" because at "the hour of their birth, some are marked for subjection, others for rule" (32). In the case of women, "the male is by nature superior, and the female inferior; and the one rules, and the other is ruled; this principle, of necessity, extends to all mankind" (34). And these hierarchies depend on a scientific methodology: "There is likewise a science of the master, which teaches the use of slaves" (37), just as science tells us that in "the relation of the male to the female," "the inequality is permanent" (49). In general, then, "the slave has no deliberative faculty at all; the woman has, but it is without authority, and the child has, but it is immature" (51). On these issues, therefore, he takes exception to Plato's articulations, particularly in the *Republic,* where the "courage and justice of a man and of a woman" are said to be equal (51). For Aristotle, "the courage of a man is shown in commanding, of a woman in obeying" (51). It can seem only too painfully familiar to every critic of patriarchal societies when Aristotle quotes Sophocles's famous line from the play, *Ajax,* that "[s]ilence is a woman's glory" (52).

Later, in Book 7, Aristotle will describe the natural hierarchies of race that inhere in his notion of justice according to the mean: the extremes are those races that live "in [northern] Europe" who are "full of spirit, but wanting in intelligence and skill" and are "incapable of ruling over others. Whereas the natives of Asia

. . . are wanting in spirit, and therefore they are always in a state of subjection and slavery" (270–71). In contrast, the just mean is represented by "the Hellenic race, which is situated between them" and is therefore "intermediate in character, being high-spirited and also intelligent" (271).

Given these staunchly defended hierarchies, it may come as something of a surprise that Aristotle begins in Book 2 the systematic description and comparison of different kinds of state organization by first addressing the key notion of communality. In seeking the best form of "political community," he proposes to make distinctions based on three variations in social *commonality*: "The members of a state must either have (1) all things or (2) nothing in common, or (3) some things in common and some not" (54). He immediately admits that option (2) is "clearly impossible, for the state is a community, and must at any rate have a common place" (54), and so his basic analytic procedure engages the fundamental dialectical tension between communality and hierarchy that I outlined in the introduction.

As might be expected, the discussion about what counts as common turns immediately to "arrangements about property: should the citizens of the perfect state have their possessions in common or not?" (61). Aristotle names the basic problem of social life: "There is always a difficulty in men living together and having things in common, but especially in their having common property" (61). In contrast to Plato, who advocated many kinds of communal sharing of property and even of child care, Aristotle argues that it "is clearly better that property should be private." Yet he also offers significant qualifications to privatization since he argues for the social uses of private property in "common"; "and the special business of the legislator is to create in men this benevolent disposition" (62). Legislative benevolence is crucial to protect against the extreme forms of private property, or, properly speaking, the loss of such property as happens with poverty. "Poverty is the parent of revolution and crime" (70), so Aristotle advocates what he calls a "polity," a state organization that actualizes the mean between the extremes of democracy and oligarchy: "The whole system of government tends to be neither democracy nor oligarchy, but something in a mean between them, which is usually called a polity" (70).

   The last half of Book 2 is devoted to a historical description
of the many forms of government developed around the Mediterranean. Aristotle acknowledges that Solon was "thought by some
to have been a good legislator, who put an end to the exclusive-
ness of the oligarchy, emancipated the people, [and] established
the ancient Athenian democracy" (96). In Book 4, he goes on to
offer a systematic classification of what he describes as the three
main generic forms of government: "kingly rule, aristocracy, and
constitutional government, and three corresponding perversions—
tyranny, oligarchy, and democracy" (147). In his descriptions of
the differences among these systems, his goal is to demonstrate
that what he calls a polity, a version of a constitutional government, is the happy mean between the liabilities of the other forms
of state. From a contemporary perspective, it would seem that
kingly rule is, in fact, a version of aristocracy, although Aristotle has in mind rule by a single individual who can therefore be
relatively wise and benevolent, or violent and tyrannous. The
perversion of aristocracy into an oligarchy occurs when the ruling
powers make wealth, as in a plutocracy, the exclusive measure of
political power; and the perversion of constitutional government
occurs when it degenerates into an "extreme" democracy in which
the poor and the uneducated can destabilize the organic mean
represented by the more limited forms of participatory government found in a polity. Democracy can permit dangerous forms
of "intemperate demagogues" who can lead the people to violent
forms of revolution or rebellion. The polity avoids the extremes
of both oligarchy and democracy so that "the best political community is formed by citizens of the middle class" (169), rather
than leadership by either the extremely wealthy or the extremely
poor. Among the risks of extreme democracy is that the people
can become "supreme even over the laws" (178), thus defeating
the deliberative forums of the legislature and the courts. Despite
these qualifications, Aristotle also admits that "[s]till democracy
appears to be safer and less liable to revolution than oligarchy"
so it "is the safest of the imperfect forms of government" (190).
Even then, it runs the risk of chaos, because "every one lives as
he pleases," and "this is all wrong; men should not think it slavery to live according to the rule of the constitution; for it is their
salvation" (216). Ask women, slaves, and foreigners in ancient

Athens if they thought that the constitution that silenced them served for their salvation—well, Aristotle does not consider that question a fair one to ask given his sense of "natural justice." But it remains a fair question to ask today of women and immigrants.

In Book 6, Aristotle elaborates the differences between democratic and oligarchic forms of justice. Clearly, the main principle of "democratic justice" is "that all should count equally; for equality implies that the rich should have no more share in the government than the poor" (241). But Aristotle rejects that democracy will "secure equality and freedom in [the] state" (241) because "where absolute freedom is allowed there is nothing to restrain the evil which is inherent in every man" (244). The polity of a constitutional government with an enlightened ruler and limited kinds of democratic courts and legislatures is the only ideal, and despite his repeated criticisms of Plato's *Republic* there are clear overlaps between the ideals of the philosopher-king and the wise leader of a polity. Indeed, I have drawn out these connections in this section partly because Aristotle's (and Plato's) reservations and qualifications about democracy will be remarkably similar to those expressed by some of the leading Enlightenment thinkers, such as Immanuel Kant and Georg Wilhelm Friedrich Hegel. Both of these men, like many others of their time, favored enlightened monarchs to what they saw as the chaotic disorder of democracies. There is, indeed, a long tradition of resisting the forces of democracy.

Despite these parallels, Aristotle's descriptions of the potentially wise ruling class in a polity can be incredibly classist: for example, the rulers "must not lead the life of mechanics or tradesmen, for such a life is ignoble and inimical to virtue" (*Politics* 274). Citizens will only include the male "warriors and councilors" (275), who alone "should be the owners of property, for they are citizens, and the citizens of a state should be in good circumstances" (275). We might recall here that of the 300,000 people in fourth-century-BCE Athens, only about 40,000 were citizens, so Aristotle's plan for the polity may seem like little more than justification for conventional social life in his adopted city. When he goes on to justify the elimination of unwanted children such that there should "be a law that no deformed child shall live" (295); that lawful forms of abortion should be used not for women's rights but to ensure limits on the population; and that laws should be formulated limiting the acceptable ages for women to bear children—Aristotle can be difficult to accept by modern standards.

Interestingly, however, the final Books 7 and 8 turn to the standards for education, and they are related directly to Plato's focus on recreating a new kind of philosophical education suitable for citizens of the ideal republic or polity. As Aristotle argues, the kind of education in a society corresponds to the kind of political organization of the state: "that which most contributes to the permanence of constitutions is the adaptation of educa-tion to the form of government" (215). Laws are useless unless the citizens are educated about those laws so that the young are "trained by habit and education in the spirit of the constitution" (215). In the closing pages of Book 7, Aristotle elaborates on the developmental processes of acculturation appropriate for rearing and educating children. In this context, he almost directly reiter-ates the arguments made by Plato in Book 2 of the *Republic*. He advocates the establishment of a board of directors of education whose responsibility will be to determine "what tales or stories the children hear" (297), thus advocating for some kind of cen-sorship exactly as Plato did. "The young especially should never be allowed to repeat or hear" any kind of "indecency of speech" (298), and "all that is mean and low should be banished from their sight or hearing" (297). The educators and rulers must "also banish pictures or tales which are indecent," and they should "take care that there be no image or picture representing unseemly actions" (298). Aristotle is even more specific about the stages of educational development: ages one to five are the crucial formative years; children from ages five to seven must learn basic pursuits equipping them for social life; and more formal kinds of education should be divided into two periods: from seven to puberty (very much like our primary education); and from then onwards to the age of twenty-one (very much like our secondary and tertiary stages of education).

In the concluding Book 8, Aristotle specifically advocates educational equality: "education should be one and the same for all, and [. . .] it should be public, and not private" (300)—this is a quotation that every contemporary progressive educator might champion. He goes on to say that "the training in things which are of common interest should be the same for all" (300), and that education should be "the business of the state" so that it can "be regulated by law" (300). This may be the first-ever formal argument for socialized education. Given our current rage for privatizing education, these statements might be wise cautions, even though we must radically qualify Aristotle's limitations on the range of "everyone" who can be counted as a citizen. Perhaps equally haunting are Aristotle's divisions between "liberal and illiberal" education; and of the four "branches of education," he places the highest value on "reading and writing" (followed by gymnastic exercises, music, and drawing) (302). Finally, he may be the initial precursor to Kant's famous advocacy of "disinterested inquiry," whereby learning and education "are to be valued for their own sake" (303). The bottom line is that "habit must go before reason" (304), which is a general way of saying that culturally dominant habits that promote injustice must be critiqued by every resource available to rhetoric and dialectic.

Jumping Scales and Changing Frames to a New Geopolitical System

Aristotle had a more troubled relationship with the city-state of Athens than did his mentor, Plato. Born in Stageira, Macedonia, in 384 BCE, Aristotle was himself rather unusual, a kind of non-native citizen, although he was not called a metic (the name for foreign-born Athenians). He spent two long-term residencies in Athens. The first, twenty-year, period began in 367 BCE when at the age of seventeen he enrolled in Plato's Academy, where he became a student and later a teacher. The second, thirteen-year, residency began after Philip II of Macedon died in 336, when in 335 Aristotle returned to Athens and set up his famous Peripatetic School of Philosophy at the Lyceum. Whereas Plato's Academy focused its curriculum on mathematics, metaphysics, astronomy, and politics, the Lyceum was devoted to the natural sciences, especially botany, zoology, and medicine, as well as mathematics and politics. Just as Aristotle had broken with his mentor, especially in his critique of the Forms, the two schools were rivals, and this split between idealists and empiricists has persisted over the long history of Western philosophy and science. But there was also a very tangible political conflict, and Philip's twenty-three-year reign over Macedonia (359–336 BCE) was really the source of the tensions.

Philip was only two years younger than Aristotle, and these two men had a lifelong relationship. Aristotle's father, Nicomachus, had served as the physician for Philip's father, Amyntas III, and Aristotle would serve for four years as the tutor of Philip's son, Alexander. Basically, the political economy of the Aegean was deeply affected by Philip's and then Alexander's military aggressions, especially since they put enormous strain on the Greek city-states. By the time Philip had completely sacked the city of Olynthus (which was in alliance with Athens) in 348, and sold the remaining population into slavery, the entire Greek confederacy had become increasingly incensed at the Macedonians, and Aristotle undoubtedly felt threatened. When Plato died in 347, Aristotle left Athens, partly for his own safety given the anti-Macedonian feelings there, and lived for five years in Asia Minor. At first he lived in Assos, in what is now northwestern Turkey, where he devoted himself to biological studies, composing several texts on animals such as *The History of Animals,* and in all he classified more than five hundred species and genera of animals during the course of several years' work, in Assos and later when he lived on the island of Lesbos. Aristotle's descriptions and observations are remarkable for their detailed observations and empirical comparisons, so this period represents one of his most rigorous scientific investigations. He left Lesbos in 342, when he was appointed by Philip to be the tutor for Philip's son Alexander, who later conquered territory that covered much of the Mediterranean, including Persia, and extended all the way to India. During his stay in Macedon, Aristotle was actually appointed to direct the royal academy there. Yet he clearly yearned to return to Athens, and his patience was rewarded, paradoxically, by the death of his longtime friend. After Philip was assassinated in 336 it became possible for Aristotle to return to Athens, where he lived until 323, when, after the death of Alexander, intense anti-Macedonian sentiments again led Aristotle into retirement back in Macedonia, where he died a year later, in 322 BCE.

Even this brief survey of the links between philosophical and military leaders in ancient Greece suggests more potential connections between Western metaphysics and colonial conquests than can be definitively ascertained from the historical record. But we do know that Aristotle encouraged Alexander's colonial ventures in Persia and Egypt: the ethnocentric tutor considered most of the population east of the Mediterranean to be barbarians in need of conquest and rule, so he egged his tutee on, encouraging him to become a despot "to deal with the latter as with beasts or plants" (Green 58–59). Aristotle's dedication to "universalism" as the source of human commonality did not seem to have a very wide geographic scope, hardly extending beyond the Greek archipelago. It is hard to blame a metaphysic alone as the root of such barbaric attitudes, but it does at least suggest that Aristotle had clearly extended his philosophical concern for conceptual hierarchies to include social hierarchies, except that he didn't see them as sociocultural at all. Rather, these observable differences were in his mind clear indication of "natural hierarchies," all based on his own years of detailed fieldwork documenting different species of plants and animals. Aristotle's natural classification of things will evolve during the Christian era into the Great Chain of Being, with God at the top, angels and heavenly creatures just below, and then human beings (above the animals and plants). But "man" is not a single category, and, as we have seen in Aristotle's *Politics*, instead we find a whole series of subdivisions with kings, princes, and nobles above soldiers, farmers, and slaves, in that order, with women tending not to have a place within the subdivisions. As we will see, Darwin and his compatriots will shake up this rigidly hierarchical classification scheme, and with that in mind, I will now shift the scale from the relatively narrow time frame in ancient Greece and prepare to make an enormous historical leap of about two thousand years.

Beginning with Alexander's empire, the West began to rule the world for a few hundred years, first from Athens, and later Rome (at least the world as seen and known to Grecian eyes in those days, a world that certainly extended well into Asia). By the time he had conquered the Persian Empire, Alexander had also named about a dozen cities along the way after himself: there were more Alexandrias in ancient Persia than any modern postal service would be able to cope with. To be fair, the plunder did, however, raise the standard of living in most parts of the Mediterranean. The riches of the bounty led also to increased agricultural output, as crops from the Fertile Crescent were transposed to new climates and geographies around an expanding Europe, along with its growing urban centers, especially Rome. Ian Morris documents this steady rise of social development, which really occurred from about 800 BCE right up through the Alexandrian and Roman Empires, with an especial rise from around 100 BCE up to the time of Christ. The first hundred years CE began a slow, then steeper decline until about 500 CE. Morris takes this decline as yet one further instance of what he calls the "paradox of development": a society's increasing development ends up seeding the problems that bring about its downfall. Morris claims this is a paradox in the sense that social development ends up producing the very conditions that then lead to decline. This seems plausible, although it may seem less paradoxical when we consider that at the height of the Roman Empire, with social development as measured by Morris at an all-time high, the ratio of economic inequality in Rome has been projected to be on the order of 10,000:1, and with so many peasants having been converted into soldiers for the conquering armies, slavery had had to be increased so dramatically that there were more slaves in Rome than citizens. Any society with this degree of hierarchy and inequality will face enormous pressures from below, and the disintegration of the reigning powers began in earnest by around 200 CE; by 550 the palpable sense of collapse was widespread.

Around 541 CE (Morris loves the play on a false sense of precision), a key turning point occurred in the relations between East and West: for the first time ever, social development in the West fell below that of the East, at least that of the fertile valley in Eastern China between the Yellow and Yangtze rivers. Europe entered what many have called the "Dark Ages," and for about twelve hundred years the West fell behind social development in the East. Particularly if you were a farmer, artisan, or commoner, life for you and for most other such nonelite populations was better in China than in Europe. Highly significantly, democracy, which had seen its first organizational experiments in Greece (and, somewhat later, in China) was basically wiped out: potential democratic forces for communality degenerated, partly because of what Ian Morris calls the "four horsemen of the apocalypse—climate change, famine, state failure, and migration" (224). As democracy disappeared, standards of living declined. And the decline happened in both the Eastern and Western cores, although more rapidly in the West.

Preceding the decline, empire building in both East and West had charted similar patterns. Centralized control of these vast cores had occurred in roughly the same years and in roughly the same brutal way. Between 340 and 221 BCE, the Qin dynasty came to rule most of China by sheer military might: they developed bigger armies than the other Warring States so that, for example, in a period of about thirty years between 264 and 234 BCE "Qin generals killed about a million enemy soldiers" (Morris 266). It was about the same time (220–167 BCE, following the weakening of the Alexandrian empire centered in Greece) that Rome also developed the military might to consolidate its empire over the entire Mediterranean region. In short, both the conquering Qin dynasty in China and the Roman emperors followed a similar path: they "each slaughtered, enslaved, and dispossessed millions" (Morris 264), and new levels of brutality were reached: "'The Roman custom,' said Polybius, was 'to exterminate every form of life they encountered, sparing none . . . '" (270). Such violence would, of course, have significant consequences in succeeding generations, but for about two hundred years, social development actually improved in the consolidated empires of both East and West, partly because of the increased geographical range of market exchanges.

But the fourth horseman arrived in the form of climate change when "[a]verage temperatures fell about 2 degrees F between 200 and 500 CE" (297). By 500 CE, European social development had declined by more than twenty percent (281), and most everyone was worse off. The Bubonic plague in 541 decimated Europe's population, especially in the urban centers. The split in the West between Christianity and Islam that began in the seventh century further weakened the Western core: "The West, split between a Muslim core and a Christian periphery, now lagged far behind [China, in the East], and would not match this level of social development until the eighteenth century, on the eve of Britain's industrial revolution" (382). Significantly, the East's relative rise in social development follows a pattern of decreasing social hierarchies, as the royal administrations developed modest plans for increasing communality through redistribution plans such as nationalizing the land and redistributing it to registered citizens. The period also witnessed a dramatic increase in poetry and the arts during what became known as the "Golden Age" of Chinese literature in the period from 600 and 800 CE. Of course, in the East, rice paddies also began to boom, and even iron output in China reached about 125,000 tons per year by 1100—"almost as much as the whole of Europe would produce in 1700" (380).

For practical reasons, we're going to leap over that twelve-hundred year gap and land in late-eighteenth-century Europe, where a transformative economic system was about to be launched. An amazing new kind of energy capture that had its source below the sun-drenched, wind-swept, powerfully wet surface of the earth enabled the West to catapult its control around the world. With the discovery of the great coal fields in England—inaugurating the Carbon Age—together with the steam engine and the expansion of the new economic system of capitalism, European development was about to skyrocket. With all these remarkable changes in the global geopolitical economy, one might expect that the discourse of ancient Greece had disappeared. But, as we will soon see, Plato and Aristotle now regularly turn up as characters in the enormous explosion of philosophical, literary, scientific, and political writings that now characterize what we generally call the Romantic Revolution. We now turn to moments in and around the French Revolution and the Haitian slave revolt known as the Haitian Revolution, key moments of transition out of the Enlightenment faith in reason and science, when even as the Carbon Age was fueling up in England, France was left mired in debt, depression, and political unrest. Cultural Turn 2 places the French Revolution and the Haitian Revolution as the central political events that accompanied the biggest global event of all: the transition out of the Holocene and into the Anthropocene.

When you skip two thousand years into the future you might well expect to lose the storyline in the very act of making the leap. It is indeed a risk, so I have sought throughout to keep a focus on the underlying features of the discourse as they get modified for a new age. In Cultural Turn 1, Western metaphysics emerged in the sweeping cultural turn from orality to literacy, as the growing domestic economy was also fueled by the invention of coinage (so it was easier to pay mercenaries and soldiers), increasingly larger-scale wars, and easier patterns of migration in and around the Mediterranean. But when we turn to a transitional moment in the world system of capitalism, late eighteenth- and early nineteenth-century Europe, we can also see how the changing geopolitical economy began the dramatic shift to a whole new geological epoch.

───── Cultural Turn 2 ─────

REWRITING WESTERN METAPHYSICS: AESTHETICS AND POLITICS IN THE AGE OF CAPITAL

CHAPTER SIX

Rewriting Western Metaphysics for a Revolutionary Age

The lust of the goat is the bounty of God.
—WILLIAM BLAKE

Naming (and Framing) the Revolution

Between the sixteenth and nineteenth centuries, some fundamental things happened in the way that human beings organized social life, especially in the northwestern European nations. Karl Polanyi called it "the great transformation"; Raymond Williams called it "the long revolution"; and Michel Foucault called it "the birth of biopolitics" (as reflected in their books with those titles). More recently, in 2000, the Nobel prize–winning chemist Paul Crutzen and the biological ecologist Eugene Stoermer proposed the term *Anthropocene* (the age of the human) for the epoch beginning in the late eighteenth century when activity of the human species began to deeply affect the planetary ecology, and as Will Steffen, Crutzen, and John R. McNeil put it in 2007 "the Earth has now left its natural geologic epoch" (614). Indeed, many people have argued about how best to frame these dramatic ruptures, but nearly everyone agrees that they have involved epoch-making changes.[1]

   In terms of the political economy, the shift during this same time period was from feudalism to capitalism and from aristocracy to democracy. What emerged was a whole new social world based on principles of nation-state regulation of market economies utilizing mechanized human labor with competition for scarce resources, particularly fossil fuels. It also involved a dramatic rise in the uses of wage labor; a shift from immobile land and rent in an agricultural economy to mobile products and capital financing for an industrial economy; the deforestation of Europe for buildings, ships, and fuel; and the escalation of mass warfare and rising national debt, especially for increased militarism to aid the colonial appropriations of foreign resources. In market terms, the numbers are staggering: global capital accumulation "grew by a factor of 134 between 1700 and 2008" (Bonneuil and Fressoz 222). But this general overview conceals the historical differences: the global changes all happened at very different rates and in very different conditions depending upon geographical location, even within the three most powerful nations in Europe: Great Britain (later the United Kingdom), France, and Germany. The initial shift from agrarian capitalism to industrial capitalism really took place in Great Britain; the ideological challenge of the revolutionary doctrines of freedom and democracy were dramatized in France, even as this country remained primarily an absolute monarchy with a largely feudal peasant population; and the philosophical discourse of modernity had its roots in Germany (Prussia) even as the region retained absolutist rule and noncapitalist economic conditions. This section of the book will therefore address writers and historical events in all three of these nations.

Furthermore, it was the age of a great contradiction. On the one hand, the Age of Liberty: the revolutionary rise of the discourse of freedom, liberation, and human rights with the return of limited forms of democracy; on the other hand, the Age of Imperial Oppression with the rise of slavery as the underlying labor force for the colonizers—oppression against which the Haitian Revolution launched itself even as the French Revolution continued. These transformations affected the way most people on earth went about their daily lives.

In 1782, when James Watt patented his improved "double-action" version of the steam engine, the Industrial Revolution could truly be launched in Great Britain (Crutzen cites this invention as the beginning of the Anthropocene).[1] Whereas virtually all forms of energy capture prior to this time drew from sources above the earth (sun, wind, water), quite suddenly the ten-horsepower steam engine could replace the water wheel in all kinds of applications, none more significant than in pumping water out of the huge coal fields in Great Britain. A hundred years later, steam engines could produce up to ten thousand horsepower. The fossil fuels that had taken millions of years to form beneath the surface of the earth could now be tapped in what seemed like an unlimited supply accessed by mechanized labor. The Carbon Age began, propelling us into the Anthropocene. By the eighteenth century, more than 80 percent of the world's coal supply came out of Britain.[3] Suddenly the age of carbon fuels triggered an explosion in the political economy of the capitalist system, one that would increasingly alter the global climate.

In the long eighteenth century, from about 1648, when the Holy Roman Empire came to an end in the Treaty of Westphalia, the newly formed nation-states began their competitive control of the emerging global markets. By the time of the French Revolution, the imperialist world-system had shifted the center of hegemony from Spanish/Iberian, to Dutch, and then to British. Over the eighteenth and nineteenth centuries, the British Empire came to rule the world partly on its transformation of social relations into competitive markets based on compulsory submission to wage labor and the maximizing of profits; partly on the basis of its energy capture from the coal fields; and partly, at least in the first half of the nineteenth century, on its power to expand the slave market as a source of free labor. For the previous twelve hundred years, Asia had been the leader in the world in terms of social development and living standards. The European nations now inaugurated a remarkable rise of wealth around the globe, although the riches were terribly maldistributed.

The resulting social and economic inequalities were magnified by the commodification of land, labor, natural resources, and human beings. For millennia, land had merely designated the physical locale used by various peoples for different purposes such as farming and grazing, and many of these lands were simply part of the commons, areas that anyone could use. But beginning especially in the Tudor and Stuart reigns in England (in the fifteenth and sixteenth centuries), powerful and wealthy individuals began to enclose the land for themselves and charge rent to the peasants, thus turning the land into a profit-making venture for themselves. Hierarchies of private property diminished the regions of communality. The various Enclosure Acts continued right through the nineteenth century, and by turning land into a source of private profit the shift from feudalism to capitalism also led to the creation of wholly new groups of the poor, called paupers, who owned no land, could not afford to rent it, and could find no work. Socioeconomic hierarchies took on a new character. Often roaming the countryside, these newly displaced poor people posed significant threats to the rising capitalists, who first depended on parishes, and later the Poor Laws of 1834, to solve the problem.[4] The new groups of displaced poor could only sell themselves as human labor for the emerging capitalist classes and their industries, and their own labor marketability was diminished by the equally growing markets in slavery and indentured servitude. Indeed, the "free market" in England was neither a free choice nor an elective opportunity for those without capital.[5] Competition, profit maximizing, and the compulsion to reinvest capital transformed social relations, especially in Great Britain. Money became the nearly exclusive means of exchange for rent and pay, and the nation-state became the issuer of national currency.

Political revolutions went hand in hand with the economic revolution, especially across the English Channel. The French Revolution dramatically signaled two major changes in the ideological landscape characteristic of modernity; while almost simultaneously, the Haitian Revolution "lies at the crossroads of multiple discourses as a defining moment in world history" (Buck-Morss 13). As Wallerstein explains with respect to the former, this event introduced into the Western world two radically new social formations (*World-Systems*). The first was that social change, rather than stasis, became the new norm: whereas aristocracy and feudalism rested on the reproduction of the same hereditary social order, the new geopolitical economy of capitalism ushered in the idea that social change was not only possible but inevitable. And the second was that it became possible for large numbers of people to believe that they could become citizens participating in significant social and political decisions, rather than subjects of a king who autocratically made all such decisions: sovereignty became a human condition not a divine right, even though France reverted to absolutism when in 1796 Napoleon proclaimed himself Emperor. On the other hand, the Haitian Revolution tested the limits of the universalist discourse of equality. These contradictions in the geopolitical economy are enmeshed within the history of theory, literature, science, and art, yet those links have often been suppressed. As Susan Buck-Morss argues, "the history of philosophic scholarship" (analogous to the history of theory) is that "the colonial experience has been excluded from the stories . . . [that] . . . Western thought tells about itself" (16). Yet, "By the eighteenth century, slavery had become the root metaphor of Western political philosophy, connoting everything that was evil about power relations. Freedom, its conceptual antithesis, was considered by Enlightenment thinkers as the highest and universal political value" (21).

The conflicts between "the discourse of freedom and the practice of slavery" (Buck-Morss 23) became the paradigmatic contradictions of Eurocentric discourse within the expanding world-system. The modern discourse of progress based on science, technology, and rationality—Western metaphysics rendered now in the secular discourse suitable for capitalist expansion fueled by endless natural resources—turned a blind eye to the practice of slavery upon which that economic progress was based. Nevertheless, after nearly two thousand years of slumber, democracy reemerged in transformed, modern, limited forms of representative state governments, principally in the United Kingdom and the United States. Some of the subjects within a few powerful nations became citizens, and revolution, resistance, and enfranchisement became the new normal: progress meant the expansion of the ability of citizens to contribute to the social process, even if weakly through voting. Representative government was limited to landowners, mostly wealthy white men who really did not want democracy but used exclusive property ownership as a criterion for voting eligibility so that they themselves could maintain plutocratic control of power. As Timothy Mitchell explains, voting rights were granted to "no more than 30 to 40 per cent of adult males, or less than one fifth of the adult population" (17). So the idealized claims for democratic universalism were pretty restrictive from the beginning, even as the last two hundred years have witnessed the struggle for expanding enfranchisement of citizens everywhere.

One of the most notable discursive transformations that followed from the French Revolution was the invention of "right" and "left" as political designations, mostly because supporters of the king all sat on the right side of the president to avoid all the hectoring from the revolutionaries on the left. But the new political situation really made possible the formation of three basic ideological positions, and their permutations have shaped the modern world. The three strands are conservatism (right), liberalism (center), and radicalism (left). As we will see, the fundamentally progressive nature of the Romantic movement was internally torn between its radical and liberal strains. None of these positions was even possible in the Middle Ages. But now, conservatism emerged primarily from among the aristocratic old guard as a fear of the new discourse aiming for universal enfranchisement and bourgeois rule of market economies: a fear of mob rule and chaos if the uneducated could become citizens, and thus a whole discourse to preserve centralized authority, hierarchy, and social stability. Such centralized power could be vested in a king, or in a neoconservative state that could ban gay rights, women's rights, and social entitlements such as welfare and healthcare for everyone. Tories and the Tea Party have a common ideological root despite the latter's chanting of libertarian freedom.

The liberals were those carrying the Enlightenment banner who championed change, voting rights, individualism, free markets, and progress through science and rationality, although there were a few, like Hegel, who addressed the crucial issue of slavery even though his later racism is deeply troubling. The version commonly attributed to the humanities is called liberal humanism: the secular charge was that human beings, not God, orchestrated social life. It is also the case that liberalism almost always involves a belief in the progress of capitalism as a free and liberating market economy even though these economic commitments often lie hidden, unmentioned in the humanities version of great art and literature as well as in the scientific belief in technological progress.

Michel Foucault describes this whole new discursive formation as characterized by a shift in the function of what he calls "governmental reason": from absolute rule to market logic, whereby civil society and the state now function merely as a handmaiden to what he calls "homo œconomicus" (*Birth* 147). Human value in the dominant culture was reduced to the logic of market pricing, the extraction of surplus value, and the dominance of the commodity form. Human beings were now administered and disciplined by a wide range of institutional and ideological formations.[6] Foucault quotes from an anonymous 1751 article in the *Journal economique* in which a merchant is asked by a statesman what the state can do, and the merchant (le Gendre) replies, "Laissez-nous faire" (quoted in Foucault, *Birth* 20); thus began the moniker for the "laissez-faire" market system. Governmental reason, according to Foucault, now emerged as a way for some privileged citizens of the nation to limit the state's power from interfering too deeply in the economic order. Yet, as Ellen Wood explains, "Coercion by the state . . . was required to impose the coercion of the market" (*Origin* 69)—the reality was the coordination of state and economy, not their idealized separation in a reputed "free" market. The new domain for this coordination of the state and market was called the "political economy," because the *polis*, the state's reason for being, was to be found in its ways of securing and establishing the systems of economic exchange. For the first time in history, a newly emerging group of writers set the terms for what would later become the specialized academic field of economics, separate from history or politics, per se, and so now we refer to Adam Smith, Thomas Malthus, David Ricardo, Jeremy Bentham, and a few other British men as the "classical economists," partly because, as the nineteenth century proceeded, these writers (or their followers) tended to drop the "political" from the designation.[7] While they had not actually conceived of the economy as fully independent of social values, they had inaugurated the possibility of isolating economics so that it became conceivable to argue that all social life should be based on economic calculations of profit and loss, markets and trade, whereas previously the latter conditions were envisioned as deeply enmeshed in traditional social values and organizations—although it is equally true that those traditional values were not necessarily more socially just (see Polanyi; Graeber; Patel; Wood, *Origin*).

In contrast to the dominant views of the liberals, the radicals pushed back against the hegemony of the liberal faith that justice would be served best by the "free market" and the exploitation of an "inexhaustible" supply of natural resources. Radical countermovements struggled against the dehumanizing effects of market logic by insisting on a view of human justice that would involve some form of economic redistribution, social recognition, respect for our symbiotic entanglements with the natural world, and political representation at all levels. There were a wide range of local (and sometimes national) resistance movements protesting all kinds of injustices from labor disputes, misuse of resources, women's rights, deforestation, tariff laws, poor laws, and housing, among others. I will focus on only three of the most influential international traditions, anarchism, socialism, and communism, all of which developed contrasting views with respect to how communality, redistribution, and representation could ameliorate the extreme forms of hierarchy and inequality. Indeed, these traditions were distinctly non- or anticapitalist. Even though these radical alternatives were a crucial phase of what we call Enlightenment "modernity," they are often suppressed when modernity itself is largely equated with the dominant capitalist world system. Karl Marx and Friedrich Engels were among those most insistent on keeping the political tied to the economic, and thus the political economy became the focus of their work (see Wood, *Origin*, 55–56, 171–81). As we will see in this chapter, radical Romanticism emerged as a part of these countermovements, and some of these writers posed a direct challenge to the market economy of industrial capitalism—right from the beginning, "the major technologies of the Anthropocene . . . aroused opposition both general and sporadic" (Bonneuil and Fressoz 254). But there was also a liberal strain of Romanticism that I call Romantic idealism, and this strain adapted Classical idealism in such ways as to join with the free-market liberals to defeat some of the revolutionary consequences of the more radical strains of Romanticism. These reversals often seemed to happen unconsciously with respect to the ostensible intentions for social change voiced by the writers themselves.

In terms of the new discourse of "political economy," Marx is, of course, the most commonly taught version of radicalism, but it is historically accurate to see that the international countermovements to liberal capitalism and conservative oligarchism diverged along the lines of socialism, communism, and anarchism, and that there were, as well, many indigenous populations of the poor that struggled against their exploitation by wealthy minorities. The trajectories of theory that I try to capture in this section of the book deliberately aim to compensate for the omission of these alternative movements from most accounts of the Western tradition. Chapters 8 and 9 will therefore focus on the consequences of these countermovements.

For those of us in humanities and English departments, a major consequence of this age of revolution is the striking emergence of the discourse of aesthetics and its problematic relations to history, economics, and politics. The British Romantic authors will make extraordinary claims for the social and universal significance of poetry rather than philosophy or politics, and the radical Romantic version of these efforts to resist the ruthless damage of the commodity forms of capitalism resonates with revolutionary fervor. To this extent, radical Romanticism is deeply influential in the countermovements of anarchism as well as in many strains of socialism, communism, and localized resistance movements. But despite the best of intentions, radical Romanticism could slide into Romantic idealism, following some of the idealizing tendencies of the underlying metaphysical discourse.[8] By adopting the terms of Classical idealism, Romantic idealism sustained an unfortunate categorical separation (rather than dialectical interaction) between universal aesthetics and particular politics, literature and society, imaginative art and political economy, science and politics, human history and natural history—and these binary divisions will, in effect, mute the radical potential for social revolution it might otherwise have carried.

The emerging discourse regarding the relations between aesthetics and politics deeply affected how English departments could begin to institutionalize themselves later in the century: the Romantic writers set most of the terms that we continue to wrangle over in debates about the disciplinary status of our field. For instance, a new meaning emerged for the term *literature* as a special kind of creative, imaginative, and highly valued writing, and this new definition stands alongside the older meaning of *literature* as a more general term for writing, or literacy in general. The Latin root for literature is *litteratura,* which refers to writing and grammar, and it is based on the etymological root *littera,* or letters, thus "an acquaintance with 'letters' or books" (*Compact*

Edition 1638; see also Raymond Williams, *Keywords* 150–54): in short, literature meant literacy. Since the late eighteenth century, we have inherited this double meaning, so today we can use both of the following sentences and make perfect sense: "Check out the literature on brake pads before you try to repair them"; and, "Did you read any great literature this summer?"

The remarkable new discourse of aesthetics, whose special mission was to justify the heightened social value placed on literature and the arts, developed sophisticated philosophical theories relating to both the radical and the liberal strains of Romanticism.[9] Those theories will lead to a new split between "high culture" (literature and the arts) and "low culture" (mass culture or popular culture): those "cultural" hierarchies will become deeply problematic in the twentieth century. We can begin to see the remarkable durability of the founding rhetoric regarding universalism over more than two thousand years even as we can highlight the tactical differences between the two periods. The founding fathers in ancient Greece do not disappear: they now show up as characters, and the aftereffects of their discourse infects and sustains every text from the Romantic period.

William Blake as Revolutionary Hero

As a compelling example of this complex process of Romantic resistance to both the Enlightenment versions of liberal capitalism and the long-standing discourse of Western metaphysics, we can first turn to William Blake's famous poem, "The Marriage of Heaven and Hell," where we find a quite explicit rewriting of Plato's cave together with a poetic anecdote about the dangers of Aristotle's metaphysics. Indeed, in Plates 17–20, when the Angel in the poem leads the narrator/poet down into the cave, we get one of the most gory and gruesome images ever to have appeared in anything one might call a poem. We will get to that gore in a minute, but we should first note that Blake's form and style register as a radical discontinuity with Aristotelian expectations for the universal, textual unity demanded of poetry. Blake provocatively violates every principle of formal unity so that the poem itself works on one level as a critique of Western metaphysical formalism. Rather than Aristotle's orderly exposition, this "poem" contains iambic pentameter lyrics, prose parables, aphorisms, expository analysis, Biblical proverbs (or their inversion), and philosophical arguments, all in what appears to be a completely disjunctive narrative structure replete with visual images on every page.[10] These stylistic extravagances suggest a deliberate ploy to rewrite Western philosophical hierarchies where the mind, the idea, and the form are more important than the body, the emotion, and the context.[11] How does Blake do this? And why? And to what extent, and for whom, does it work? As we will see, the classical formal principles do not entirely disappear, although they surely get modified. Let's begin by following the narrator as he and the Angel descend into the cave, but we will certainly want to get out of there even faster than we did from Plato's allegorical cave of ignorance.

The entry into Blake's cave seems to reverse the light and dark images in Plato's version: going into the cave is a process of seeing the light, or truth, of the current human condition, which is pretty well mired in this cave; the passage into it represents the descent into hell, mimicking also Dante's descent into the inferno in *The Divine Comedy*. As the Angel tells the narrator, "do not presume O young-man but as we here remain behold thy lot which will soon appear when the darkness passes away" (Plate 17) once they get into the cave. On the way down, there is a lot of fire, smoke, "vast spiders," "terrific shapes of animals sprung from corruption," "terrible noise," "a black tempest," a "cataract of blood," a "monstrous serpent," "raging foam," and a lot of other awful stuff perhaps appropriate for a vision of hell when the natural world has been exploited and damaged. In order to get to the cave, the Angel and the narrator pass through a "mill" that might be a reference to the newly formed factory mills in England (the "satanic mills"), and the horror of the cave becomes a metaphor for the suffering of workers in the mills. This version of hell is a kind of artistic spectacle rendering visible the otherwise invisible exploitation of labor and nature under capitalism: the brutal market economy based on the commodity form devours bodies and resources, uses them up, and discards them. Cries of freedom and democracy may have been ringing out, but workers had no democratic voice in the conditions of their employment, the procedures for production, the destruction of the fields and forests, or the distribution of the surplus they produced for the owners of the new industries. Indeed, once the travelers actually get to the cave, we encounter a kind of bestiality and sadomasochism that cannot be rendered in a paraphrase:

> [A]nd lo! it was a deep pit, into which I descended driving the Angel before me; soon we saw seven houses of brick; one we enter'd; in it were a number of monkeys, baboons, & all of that species, chain'd by the middle, grinning and snatching at one another, but with[h]eld by the shortness of their chains; however I saw that they sometimes grew numerous, and then the weak were caught by the strong, and with a grinning aspect, first coupled with & then devour'd, by plucking off first one limb and then another till the body was left a helpless trunk; this after grinning & kissing it with seeming fondness they devour'd too; and here & there I saw one savourily picking the flesh off of his own tail; as the stench terribly annoy'd us both we went into the mill, & I in my hand brought the skeleton of a body, which in the mill was Aristotle's Analytics. (Plates 19–20)

The mill that seems to be the source of all this suffering turns out to be based not just on the literal iron and textile mills in England. The industrial image refers also to a kind of metaphorical factory, as if the scientific rationalism for producing the real factories was derived from an even more fundamental ideological process: the mechanical manufacturing of philosophical abstractions and mathematical models for the impersonal commodity system of setting market prices based on quantitative measures of profit and excluding all other social values. The suffering of human beings with bodies capable of physical labor serves as the grist for the metaphorical mill of mental labor (the commodity form) that grinds life into abstractions (like abstract labor, in Marx's terms), disembeds reason from the body and humanity from nature, a discursive practice that Blake now names as "Aristotle's Analytics." The evil embodied here is a kind of rationality that succeeds only by devouring the body with all its emotional, sexual, and physical needs. And so the conclusion of the parable is summed up by its moral:

So the Angel said: thy phantasy has imposed upon me & thou
oughtest to be ashamed.
I answer'd: we impose on one another, & it is but lost time to
converse with you whose works are only Analytics. (Plate 20)

Philosophical abstractions and mathematical models of the
market get severed from the social lives of human beings who
have no participatory power with respect to the basic systems
for organizing production and exchange under industrial capitalism. Dialectical processes, or *contraries* (Blake's term), come to a
violent end in the fixed mechanics of the economic system in the
effort to ground all decisions in narrowly conceived profit-loss
ratios. In these cases, the abstractions claim universal status but
function rather like linguistic levers, crude rhetorical tools that can
then be wielded by powerful groups, imposed as the rule of law
to ensure their own cultural dominance. Individual "self-interest"
gets reduced to calculations of market profit "draining life from
persons and embodying life in things" (Simpson 34). The exclu
sive principles of commodity exchange join together to become
the universal myth of the "free market." Here then, in Blake's
poem, we find what I have been calling the most powerful strains
of radical Romanticism: the valuing of lived experience, bodily
life, cooperative sharing of resources, and resistance to oppression
and tyranny through critical resistance and dialectical contraries.

Blake abhorred the reduction of human life to economic markets. He further understood that institutionalized religion could
also contribute to the project of industrial capitalism. Although
Blake was a devout radical Christian, he saw institutionalized
religion as a source of hypocrisy to the extent that repression
by institutionalized religion could join forces with repression by
market logic. Like "little Tom Dacre" in the *Songs of Innocence*
version of Blake's famous poem "The Chimney Sweeper," if Tom
would just do his job of cleaning chimneys and not complain, he
would go to heaven, even though that might be sooner rather than
later since many young boys were suffocated or burned to death,
or died from cancers and other diseases acquired while cleaning
chimneys. Religious rationalizations thus also serve the owners of
capital: workers would not resist their exploitation in this world

since their compliance assured their salvation in the afterworld. Capitalist hierarchy triumphed over social communality: "Till a system was formed, which some took advantage of & enslav'd the vulgar by attempting to realize or abstract the mental deities from their objects; thus began Priesthood" (Plate 11). The Priests serve as a metaphor for any group of people claiming to have authoritative knowledge of God (or the market economy) through their ability to elevate the abstractions above other competing social values.[12] Blake especially, but the other Romantic writers as well, pretty clearly intended a social critique of the vulgar materialism of the industrial revolution where mechanical form turns into dehumanizing factories and social injustices are magnified rather than relieved.

Blake understood the built-in liability in the priestly claims to transcendence that emphasized the end point of the universal/absolute rather than the dialectical movement. Something unfortunate happens when this discourse aims to transcend history, politics, and society.[13] For many Romantics, nature became the end-all goal of such transcendence: following the binary formulas, we aim for Nature so we can escape corrupted Society and nostalgically recover our own lost nature. But unlike Plato's invisible Forms, the convenient thing about nature is that we could see it, over there, outside ourselves, in the fields and streams—the outside. It's admittedly still hard to shuck our artifices, and sometimes it can only happen in death that the synthesis with nature is complete, as in Wordsworth's famous poem "A Slumber Did My Spirit Seal." "No motion has she now, no force / She neither hears nor sees"—but at least now she is fully immersed in nature: "rolled round in Earth's diurnal course / With rocks and stones and trees" (Collected 218). Nature became a kind of this-worldly absolute, and poetry and art were the vehicles to return us to our true "nature," healing us from our artificial, "unnatural" social life. But in practice, nature served more as a normalizing force, providing a kind of convenient pseudo explanation for just about anything: "It's my nature to do things this way"; "It's just human nature"; "If we return to Nature, we will do things this way." As Timothy Morton explains, "nature is often wheeled out to adjudicate between what is fleeting and what is substantial and permanent. Nature smooths over uneven history, making its struggles and sufferings illegible" (*Ecology* 21).

When these ideological shiftings have their way, we get the slide to Romantic liberalism or idealism. I am deliberately using the two strains of Romanticism, radical and liberal, as dialectical opposites for heuristic purposes, although in practice it is more of a sliding scale of overlapping issues. In their efforts to challenge the Enlightenment's Age of Reason, the Romantic idealists get captured by the systemic processes of idealization built into the very discourse they are trying to resist: poetry replaces philosophy, but they both aim for transcendence above the historical ugliness of the geopolitical economy and above the environmental degradation of the natural world. Nature stepped in for the universal. Capital and state could go on about their business of producing profit.

Blake was better than most in resisting these flights away from physical realities. His plan was to rescue energy and "eternal delight" from the abyss of abstractions. For this purpose he invokes not the voice of God as authority, but the inverse, the "Voice of the Devil," who names the "Errors" of both religion and philosophy. Blake does not exactly reverse the hierarchy but synthesizes the polarities or, what he calls the "Contraries": instead of elevating the body and reducing the soul, the "True" discourse joins them together in a kind of dialectical interaction so that "Man has no Body distinct from his Soul; for that call'd Body is a portion of Soul discern'd by the five Senses, the chief inlets of Soul in this age" (Plate 4). Indeed, it is a "Marriage of Heaven and Hell," not a plan for getting out of hell and into heaven.[14] As Jim Morrison could have told us before he died, the "doors of perception" (Plate 14) needed to be cleansed, but certainly not closed. We live interdependently and in symbiotic relationship with other organisms and the natural world. Repression of our human lusts invokes an unnatural system that would be no different from trying to repress the lust of any creature, such as the goat, and viewed in this light desire becomes holy and infinite rather than troublesome and unworthy. As Blake puts it: "Those who restrain desire, do so because theirs is weak enough to be restrained; and the restrainer of reason usurps its place & governs the unwilling" (Plate 5).[15]

Once Western metaphysics gets rewritten according to the terms of this new marriage of contraries, one reads texts differently. For example, Blake supplies an exemplary instance of this Romantic rereading of a canonized author, John Milton, when *Paradise Lost* gets interpreted as an allegorical history representing the story of how "Desire was cast out" (Plate 5) from the empire of Reason and the Kingdom of God. According to Blake, Milton's genius is that, however unorthodox his own religious beliefs as a Puritan may have been, and however much he struggled against the mind/body dualism of Classical idealism, his conscious religious beliefs in the inviolability of the conscience sustains the socially acceptable view of the absolute authority of God as final arbiter of truth. At the most literal level of the poem, God always has the upper hand. But in Blake's reading of *Paradise Lost,* Milton was so deeply attuned to unconscious forces, and he so successfully tapped into the powers of the imagination, that the poem itself revealed the contrary truth.

For anyone who has read *Paradise Lost,* ask yourself: whom would you rather have coffee with, God or Satan? And the answer is almost always "Satan." As a character in the poem, God is rigid, uptight, rule-bearing, and unyielding—just plain unpleasant, even if he is God; whereas Satan is so much more energetic, fallible, interesting, and, in short, more humanly divine, to use the oxymoron. Poetry, not philosophy, seems to cut through the dominant metaphysic ruled by the God of Reason, and that is the source of the sublime power of the poetic imaginary. Accordingly, as a poet, "The reason Milton wrote in fetters when he wrote of Angels & God, and at liberty when of Devils & Hell, is because he was a true Poet and of the Devil's party without knowing it" (Plate 6). The cliché "He was a poet but didn't know it" acquires a quite unstereotypical meaning to the extent that poetry now taps the unconscious powers, the exact opposite of the oral poet memorizing external formulas. We have, of course, inherited this Romantic view of the poet, and we have naturalized it within English departments as the power of the individual, imaginative, poetic text. This latter, and familiar version, of the creative but often isolated poet is the one most of us bring "naturally" to our first reading of Plato's *Republic,* a view that made it impossible to understand his arguments about poetry as a vehicle for cultural reproduction in an oral tradition.

Since Blake is also a visual artist, he offers numerous images that figure the horrors that happen when reason usurps emotion and the imagination. One of the most powerful is the famous image "The Ancient of Days," which appears as the frontispiece to his long poem "Europe a Prophecy," where he depicts one of his mythical gods, Urizen (suggesting "Your Reason"), looking down from on high, with his fingers extended like the points of a compass measuring the observable size of the Earth below him. Urizen appears as an old man, his hair swept by the wind, but with an angry expression, the perfect image of a dictator claiming all-knowing power over the objective data by which he captures the world below him. He represents an image of the ultimate isolation of objective knowing from the waywardness of subjective experience—a powerful image of the hubris necessary to believe that at the dawn of the Anthropocene humans control the planet. The facial features of Urizen resonate with remarkable likeness to those of Sir Isaac Newton, the icon of Enlightenment rationality whereby science could take the universal measure of all things, unperturbed by our misleading senses, and the laws of nature revealed the true mechanisms of the universe. (In Biblical discourse, Urizen can also be seen as Moses, the patriarchal lawgiver.)

Yet one of the key themes of the poem "Europe a Prophecy," as with the "Marriage of Heaven and Hell," is what Polanyi would call the countermovement, the resistance of many people to the oppressive constraints of the dominant discourse and political regimes. Blake called it the "Orc cycle," configuring a kind of dynamic, dialectical, and historical process with Orc being the youthful mythological figure of revolution carrying the banner against the rule of imposed law and repression administered by Urizen insofar as he represents both the ancient regime and the new industrial system. One of the key themes of the poem is that the suffering masses in the new Europe would rise up against the despotic rule of mechanized industry and economic oppression in the age of revolution spreading around the world. That is the hope, anyway. Blake published the "Marriage" in a small edition of etchings at his own printing press in 1792 when the French

Revolution was raging (only nine of the original etchings have survived). His hope was that the poetic imaginary could be carried out as a form of social justice in the political and economic domains of everyday life, so he ends the poem with "A Song of Liberty." England is "sick silent" but the "new born wonder" of the revolutionary cycle of rebirth of freedom is shaking off the shackles of oppression, and the Romantic ideal shall be realized: "Empire is no more!"[16] Did this Romantic rewriting of Western metaphysics enable the social revolution it prophesied? Or did it appear on the scene, belatedly, as a kind of rearguard reaction to the mechanistic worldview of Enlightenment rationalism? Could the proponents of universal emancipation through formal enfranchisement as voting citizens turn a blind eye on the total lack of democracy within the capitalist factories and workplaces? How quickly could the radical Romanticist strain of literary, artistic, and political freedom, with its belief in the universalist discourse of citizen's rights, collapse into the classist, racist, and sexist discourses of anti-universalism? These are the key questions for this period. But Blake was certainly not the only Romantic to share these universal ideals.

The Preface to Poetic Revolution

William Wordsworth wrote a preface to the second edition of *Lyrical Ballads* (1800) with a similar claim about the political consequences of his poetics: the new kind of lyrics he and Coleridge had composed called for "revolutions, not of literature alone, but likewise of society itself" (433). It seems fair to assess the way these powerful claims for poetic innovation and social revolution worked themselves out in the geopolitical economy of their time as well as their persistence over the coming two centuries. *Lyrical Ballads* was, without doubt, a new kind of poetry, and even though it was published anonymously, the first edition was so popular it sold out within two years, and Wordsworth was, as he puts it "advised . . . to prefix [in the second edition] a systematic defense of the theory upon which the Poems were written."[17] Interestingly, the whole idea of replacing the brief "Advertisement" in the first edition with a much expanded

"Preface" seems to have come from Coleridge (see Watson, ix), who actually abandoned the idea of composing it and turned over his notes to Wordsworth. The systematic theory entails another rewriting of Western metaphysical idealism to suit the new context, though, as we will see, it also highlighted some of the critical differences between the two poets, as Coleridge will make especially clear in his 1817 *Biographia Literaria*. But the overall aim of the "Preface" shares a great deal with Blake's vision, even though it will be carried out in a much different idiom and diction than we find in Blake: as Richard Simpson argues, "Wordsworth too is of the devil's party, and he knows it" (139). The unique features of Wordsworth's poetic revolution can be characterized best by looking at what it deliberately aimed to overthrow: the late-eighteenth-century decline of poetry into what they saw as the artificial, false, and superficial verse whose lyrics emanated from the social vanities of the aristocracy rather than the universal nature of humankind. The enemy in short is "poetic diction" now conceived as the shallow, formulaic, decorative diction—the "gaudy and inane phraseology" characteristic of the trivial, ornamental varieties of poetry pervading the courts and serving the aristocracy.

There is, of course, a class war at work in these distinctions, although it sometimes tends to get subordinated to the universal declarations of poetry's "spontaneous overflow of powerful feelings . . . recollected in tranquility" ("Preface" 441). So it is helpful to resituate the poetic distinction in the social context: the "artificial" poetry of Wordsworth's immediate predecessors in the eighteenth century was often produced under a patronage system whereby the aristocratic landed gentry funded through their inherited wealth the production of the poets by giving them a legitimizing role in the daily lives of the enthroned kings and queens, princes and princesses, nobles and lords. Peasants, farmers, and workers (especially in rural areas) were subjects of the aristocracy, but with no tangible voice as citizens and no practical decision-making powers over the organization of production. The tradition of courtly love lyrics was quite literally from out of the courts—it would not be found down on the farm. But with the great transformation underway in industrial capitalism, poetry was now entering a new system of production in the private marketplace. It was a small business enterprise, a printing house, independent of the crown, that printed and sold *Lyrical Ballads* for a profit, and it was a kind of best seller when it first appeared in 1798. The freedom of the new privately owned printing presses could reach a wider audience than the landed gentry. This hope for a broader cultural base resonates with Wordsworth's commitment to a new kind of poetic hero: the farmer, the peasant, or as he prefers to romanticize it, the rustic. The "common man," not the courtly aristocrat, has a more immediate relationship to nature, and thus his language will be more natural and less artificial. The commoner should become a poetic citizen of the nation and the planet: communality should ameliorate ruthless hierarchy.

Coleridge took issue with what he saw as Wordsworth's over-stated claims for the supposed value of the "natural" language of the "rustic," as if it could emerge directly "from the mouths of men in real life, a language which actually constitutes the natural conversation of men under the influence of natural feel-ings" (*Biographia Literaria,* ch. 17, p. 189). Indeed, he devotes most of Volume 2 of the *Biographia* to an extended critique of Wordsworth. Rural might mean back to nature, but rural labor could hardly step in for universal humanity. Ironically, Coleridge appears to have been the primary proponent of the idea of com-posing *Lyrical Ballads* in a more conversational diction, and in Chapter 17 of the *Biographia,* he praises Wordsworth's poetic accomplishment in his verse as a triumph in the artistic battle against the "poetic diction" of his predecessors. But in the same book, Coleridge also went to considerable length explaining why Wordsworth's analogy of poetry with common or rustic language was simply untenable: even when he used ordinary language and a simple vocabulary, Wordsworth himself did not speak like a peasant in his lyrical poetry, even if his word choice echoed more closely with the voice of a commoner than did that of Milton's narrator in *Paradise Lost.* Coleridge accused Wordsworth of what we would now call essentializing, and thus disengaging poetry from the social contexts in which it was produced, even as Wordsworth, ironically, championed the lower classes that had been excluded from virtually all versions of poetry practiced by his predecessors. In contrast, Coleridge explicitly believed in a "literary aristocracy, or the existence of a tacit compact among the learned as a privileged order" (*Biographia*, ch. 9, p. 79). He argued that the peasant or rustic was often tied to nothing but sensuous particulars and thus had no access to universal thoughts or reflections.

Coleridge's qualifications explicitly acknowledge the relatively privileged position required by anyone finding time to write poetry. Not many farmers got to do it.[18] Nevertheless, although Wordsworth never explicitly stated it, his sympathies in this early stage of his life lay with the disenfranchised, and thus *Lyrical Ballads* represents an implicit critique of England's increasing levels of poverty, which were creating enormous injustices since people had to lose virtually all their material possessions in order to receive any kind of assistance from the government or the local parishes.[19] Not just factories, but workhouses for unemployed "paupers" were on the rise, enclosure acts continued to dispossess the poor of their common lands, and many of these dispossessed persons could be seen walking by Wordsworth's cottage in Grasmere. So the question of just how much of Wordsworth's criticism reflected a genuine commitment to a critique of the changing conditions of England's industrial revolution remains both provocative and sometimes troubling. It is crucial to investigate the resonance between the proclaimed poetics and the intended politics.

We can begin by examining a key passage that resonates in every sentence with Western metaphysics, even if it gets turned into a Romantic version of it. In contrast to Blake, Wordsworth here takes Aristotle as his hero in order to formulate his version of poetry as "the image of man and nature" that triumphs over history, law, medicine, and even science:

> Aristotle, I have been told, has said, that Poetry is the most philosophic of all writing: it is so: its object is truth, not individual and local, but general, and operative; not standing upon external testimony, but carried alive into the heart by passion; truth which is its own testimony, which gives competence and confidence to the tribunal to which it appeals, and receives them from the same tribunal. Poetry is the image of man and nature. The obstacles which stand in the way of the fidelity of the Biographer and Historian, and of their consequent utility, are incalculably greater than those which are to be encountered by the Poet who comprehends the dignity of his art. The Poet

writes . . . not as a lawyer, a physician, a mariner, an astrono-
mer, or a natural philosopher, but as a Man. Except this one
restriction, there is no object standing between the Poet and the
image of things; between this, and the Biographer and Historian,
there are a thousand. ("Preface" 438)

Basically, in the characteristic move of the Romantics, poetry
becomes more philosophical than philosophy, more universal
than prose, as it must be in order to serve as the unmediated
access to the truth—a goal that is, after all, entirely set up by
Western metaphysical dualism, with the emphasis on "the image
of *things*" in themselves (not just the image) when the dialectic
reaches the absolute end in the Truth. Poetry provides access
to universal knowledge of human Beings, with the capital "B"
registering the universal nature of Being (or Nature). Poetry thus
emphasizes human immersion in the natural world, so this view
directly resonates with many contemporary environmentalist
concerns, even if man rather than woman seems to get a better
deal.[20] Nevertheless, the poetic emphasis on the universal goal
rather than the dialectical processes and historical contingencies
elevates art above both history and politics.

In the end, poetry has to trump science as well, and the latter
becomes a kind of practical handmaiden to the greater scope of
poetic universality. Again, the Romantics do not want to abandon the wonders of science, but they do want to put them under
poetic supervision to avoid their descent into abstract mechanics
and inhumane technology:

> The Man of science seeks truth as a remote and unknown bene-
> factor; he cherishes and loves it in his solitude: the Poet, singing
> a song in which all human beings join with him, rejoices in the
> presence of truth as our visible and hourly companion. Poetry
> is the breath and finer spirit of all knowledge; it is the impas-
> sioned expression which is in the countenance of all Science. . . .
> the Poet . . . is the rock of defense for human nature, . . . the
> Poet binds together by passion and knowledge the vast empire
> of human society, as it is spread over the whole earth, and over
> all time. . . . Poetry is the first and last of all knowledge—it is
> as immortal as the heart of man. ("Preface" 439)

This truly "sublime notion of Poetry" (439) pretty obviously carries with it a less than universal gendered characteristic with men "speaking to men," and we will highlight the gender issue when we get to William's sister, Dorothy.[21] But we should not miss the literary revolution that Wordsworth's "Preface" both announced and inaugurated insofar as it set the stage with respect to providing license and authority for a new kind of verse: basically, Walt Whitman, Emily Dickinson, Gertrude Stein, William Carlos Williams, and Alan Ginsberg, among many others, are not really possible without the precedent set by Wordsworth and his opening to new kinds of previously nonpoetic materials drawn from disenfranchised social classes. Free verse and poetic experimentation open the door to literary representations of everyday life for many people besides the heroes, gods, and public figures of classical and courtly poetry. These transformations, as Wordsworth himself argued, would inevitably lead to a revision in the canon of what would be considered the great works of literature, and for the most part we have inherited his sensibility as the naturalized process for determining the periods and genres of great literature that would constitute the core curricula for English departments. But in his articulation of the new criteria for poetic value, the class issues sometimes slide out of view in favor of the universal virtues of proximity to nature. Wordsworth articulated this transformation of taste as a process of purification, almost as if the "spontaneous overflow of emotion" became an aesthetic criterion by following the same dynamic echoed in Aristotle's theory of catharsis as purification:

> If my conclusions are admitted . . . our judgements concerning the works of the greatest Poets both ancient and modern will be far different from what they are at present, both when we praise, and when we censure: and our moral feelings influencing and influenced by these judgements will, I believe, be corrected and purified. (437)

In short, Wordsworth anticipates a whole new kind of poetic production: "a species of poetry would be produced, which is genuine poetry; in its nature well adapted to interest mankind permanently" (443). Just what counts as "genuine," what those "moral feelings" might be, and how they work in the social and political domains in which they are inevitably situated remains a crucial concern. In his own life, Wordsworth acknowledged that his own moral center of gravity had much to do with his particular circumstances, especially those involving his beloved sister, Dorothy, and their relationship has been one of the most intriguing sibling relationships in literary history.

From Prose to Poetry: Who Owns the Daffodils?

That a woman author does not finally appear until more than a third of the way through this book says a great deal about gender, authority, and authorship with respect to the transformations of Western metaphysics. And even then she does so by writing a text not meant for publication, in a personal journal, unpublished during her lifetime. These are not minor, but significant points of observation with respect to gender in the traditions of Western ways of knowing.

The remarkable thing is that while many find Wordsworth's "Preface" to be relatively boring reading, a bit too dry and abstract, I have yet to find a student or colleague who has not found some way to appreciate Dorothy Wordsworth's Alfoxden (1798) and Grasmere (1800–03) journals. There are so many reasons for that common judgment, but underlying them all is the palpable sensitivity of her descriptions of both natural and social scenes in the journals, as well as her unwavering love for her brother. Given her brother's standards for avoiding artifice and pretension, Dorothy succeeds in composing what appears to be such unaffectedly natural prose that it takes on a poetic quality that her brother appreciates, as did their close friend Samuel Coleridge.

But imagine this situation played out in the twenty-first century: you are a young woman who writes regularly in a personal journal (not Facebook) that you also regularly share with your brother and his closest male friend. You love to share your journal with these men, and they have a tremendous appreciation for your writing. In one passage you describe a walk with your brother:

When we were in the woods beyond Gowbarrow park we saw a few daffodils close to the water side. . . . [W]e saw that there was a long belt of them along the shore. . . . I never saw daffodils so beautiful they grew among the mossy stones about and about them, some rested their heads upon these stones as on a pillow for weariness and the rest tossed and reeled and danced and seemed as if they verily laughed and the wind that blew upon them over the lake, they looked so gay ever glancing ever changing. (D. Wordsworth)

You then showed these passages to your brother, who clearly enjoyed reading them, and a couple of years later your brother published a poem that became quite famous, and it read, in part:

> . . . all at once I saw a crowd,
> A host, of golden daffodils;
> Beside the lake, beneath the trees,
> Fluttering and dancing in the breeze . . . .
>
> They stretched in never ending line
> Along the margin of a bay:
> Ten thousand saw I at a glance,
> Tossing their heads in sprightly dance.

W. WORDSWORTH, *Prelude* 143

How would you feel when you read these lines? It is not unreasonable to assume that you might be distressed. For a good reason: your brother's verse is not exactly a direct quotation, but even as a paraphrase there is little doubt that this "original" poem would constitute plagiarism according to contemporary intellectual property laws. You might feel betrayed by your brother for his unacknowledged appropriation of your writing. Now, turning back about two hundred years, is there any sign that Dorothy was similarly distressed by William's poem? The answer is, of course not. Dorothy's response shows every sign of loving it when her brother (and sometimes Coleridge also) adapt her prose to their verse. She sees such appropriations of her language as acts of appreciation and signs of the intimacy they shared. And it is a unique kind of journal. Unlike a diary intended exclusively for oneself as reader, Dorothy's journal was clearly written with an audience of three in mind: herself, her brother, and their friend.

The poem becomes a sign of the fruition of her intermediary role since her prose serves as the source located between her physical experience of coming upon the daffodils and the culminating poem produced by the man who reworks her language into the recognizable form of the published poem.

The radical differences in our perceptions of these linguistic behaviors highlight the shifting historical contexts regarding our understanding of gender and authorship. That individual authorship of public texts is predominantly a male prerogative had been so deeply naturalized in late-eighteenth-century England that no one then made a peep about what today we see as a crime. It can be useful, therefore, to look over the historical context regarding the intellectual property debates during that period so we can situate the ideological battles of literary production within the material realities of the political economy.

The idea of plagiarism evolved over a long time, but the issues became acute during the eighteenth century, beginning in 1710 when Britain passed the first copyright law, the Statute of Anne, which formalized the existing trade practices of booksellers and printers, though it was not particularly concerned with author's rights. Plagiarism required something new: the myth of authorship as the creation of unique, individual genius—an ideological construct built on the foundations of the Western metaphysical separation of form and content. That is, copyright laws came into existence during the eighteenth century as one phase of the broad transformation of public commons into private property. It really took place slowly over several centuries, and progressively when the printing press emerged during the fifteenth and sixteenth centuries. For example, in 1557, King Philip and Queen Mary established a Royal Charter for the Stationers' Company, a guild formed out of two earlier manuscript brotherhoods, the Brotherhood of Manuscript Producers (formed 1357) and the Brotherhood of the Craft of Writers of Text-Letters (formed 1405). This new guild operated a near total monopoly by placing rigorous restrictions on publication and printing rights for printers and booksellers: the Royal Charter even empowered the Stationers' Company to confiscate and burn all unauthorized books and to imprison the printers of such manuscripts. So it was not as if there were some kind of free and open textual commons preceding its enclosure in copyright laws. Nevertheless, even with these restrictions, there was considerable latitude in what authors could appropriate from other texts and manuscripts. As Mark Rose puts it, "Shakespeare, for example, had no hesitation about appropriating others' works in ways that would clearly constitute infringement today" ("Nine-Tenths" 75).

It was, therefore, a somewhat different situation for authors in the precopyright era. Significantly, in early modern Europe, prior to the printing press, writing in general was conceived of as a collaborative process with the individual writer working as one craftsman among many others including copiers, proofreaders, booksellers, and parchment makers. And in the medieval period, "a claim to knowledge as one's own possession was a denial of God as the ultimate source of enlightenment and authority" (McSherry 38). With the invention of the printing press, the wider production and circulation of print made possible a heightened role for the individual author as original source of the text as it circulated in a secular world of capital exchanges. But clearly the concern in medieval and early modern Europe was with the challenges posed by unorthodox ideas such as Protestantism and other threats to the authority of the church and state. There was no particular concern about specific textual language being "pilfered" and copied without recognition of original authorship, because authorship was not seen as an individual act of creation, but rather as a collective, collaborative process. Restrictions with respect to what should count as "proper" manuscript production had to be orchestrated in obeisance to the word of God and the rule of the king.

It took the Romantic rewriting of Western metaphysics with renewed attention to individuality and subjectivity to establish the force of the intellectual property laws of late eighteenth-century England and Germany (see Woodmansee).[22] The history of the newly legislated intellectual property laws was tied to the rapid expansion of the scope of the Enclosure Acts in England, and thus the shrinking of the public commons as a space for the sharing of land for agricultural and grazing uses by peasants. Again, this history should not be read as an idealized version as if it were the case that once upon a time there were free open public lands and texts everywhere, and then the enclosure ended that idyll.[23] Given this qualification, however, the consequences of the enclosure of land goes hand in hand with the granting of private rights to individual authors, whose original works were now protected as private property regulated by the rules of commodity exchange.

In order for this linking of authorship and ownership to be successful, two things had to happen. First, there had to be a synthesis of author and text in the sense that evidence for the author's unique subjectivity could be found embodied in the specific language of the textual object. Mark Rose refers to this process as the "objectification of a writer's self" (*Authors* 121). Coincidentally, this synthesis of subjectivity and objectivity could best be exemplified in truly unique texts such as those authored by poets. And, then, secondly, there had to be an analytic split between the particular expressive text owned by an individual (or corporation) as a piece of private property circulated for profit, and the general ideas contained in the text that could circulate free of private profit as knowledge accessible in the public domain.[74] Since it appeared that ideas were intangible and thus could not be counted as property, copyright law had to be based on the work as textual object.

Western metaphysical formalism aided both the synthetic and the analytic work. The original spiritual genius of the individual author was located in the unique textual expression as an object embodying a specific linguistic form. The author/text dualism was united in the textual form but clearly distinguished from the content of ideas that could be circulated freely in the public domain, so long as they did not "plagiarize," or steal the linguistic expression (i.e., the exact words) of the author. Foucault called this the "author function," ("What" 125) whereby the author is a kind of inviolable ghost animating the specific features of the textual object. Author/text forms an inseparable bond, and the law could protect the author by protecting the specificity of the text itself: pilfering somebody's language meant using exactly the same words, hence plagiarism the etymological root, *plagiarius,* means "kidnapped," implying that when you steal a text you steal a person.

It's similar to Plato's worry in the *Phaedrus* about the gap between the true meaning intended by the speaker/writer and the wayward text that "rolls all over the place," except that for the

Romantic idealists the practical solution to the problem goes in the opposite direction—not toward the author/speaker, who is clearly absent from the text, but toward the primacy of the text. Since texts circulate outside the presence of the original author, authenticity had to be located in the originality of the linguistic features of the text itself. Nevertheless, original authorial intention is still held sacred, as in Plato's model, so the text serves as the tangible vehicle carrying the more precious spirit of the author. As we will see, this theory of meaning in the text itself will resonate powerfully for the New Critics in the mid-twentieth century, when poetic texts become sacred objects, "well wrought urns" or "verbal icons."

On the surface, these distinctions between author/text and ideas may seem simple. For example, knowledge of the theory of evolution as natural selection might be widely adapted and disseminated but no one can copy direct passages from Darwin's *Origin of Species* and claim to have authored those sentences without being accused of plagiarism. But in many cases the distinctions are not so clear-cut. Indeed, the boundaries between author/text and ideas, just like the boundaries between the public and private domains, are contestable, blurred, and uncertain, all determined by the legal and customary practices in any given social circumstance. Jumping scales for a moment, this is particularly the case in the contemporary period, when digital media hugely complicate intellectual property laws, a whole legal industry has been produced to litigate copyright and patent issues, and infractions of ownership laws are both common and complex.

Nevertheless, when we return to the situation with Dorothy Wordsworth, we can see that the textual object, the poem, "I Wandered Lonely as a Cloud" could be properly owned by William, as it was "natural" for men to own such property, while at the same time the spiritualized and transcendent meaning of the poem could pass through Dorothy so that it could be reworked (in what Coleridge called the "secondary imagination") by William until the specific language of the final poem truly corresponded with the spiritual truth that waited only for its "purified" manifestation in a work of imaginative art.[25] Dorothy, as a kind of midwife for the transcendent meaning, never had to worry about owning the text as a tangible piece of property, especially since women did not have legal rights to own property. Generally speaking, the laws authorized men as authors and women as the spiritual media whose private role need not enter the public marketplace of books. It seems totally foreign to both sister and brother to think that such language practices could be seen as a purloining, or as a violation of any individual's rights: there was just nothing in the discourse that would make what William did seem immoral or inappropriate to either of them, even as the male Romantic writers developed the discourse of authenticity, originality, and individual authorship as the source of creative genius. For the Wordsworth siblings, the movement from sister's journal to brother's poem appears as an honorable textual migration. But as we can now see, the Romantics' "return to nature" is a gendered passage, since nature is predominantly represented as a female, so it is only natural for the language to pass through Dorothy. To be an author was to be an owner of property, and since women did not own property, there was no need to worry about any pilfering.

Nevertheless, William worried considerably about the problems of ownership and authorship, and as Peter Jaszi and Martha Woodmansee point out, "Wordsworth attempted to enlist the law in support of his authorial vision by intervening directly in Parliamentary debates over copyright law reform" (4). Wordsworth argued for an author's rights to perpetual copyright, in contrast to the fourteen years of protection (mostly for booksellers, not authors) offered by the Statute of Anne, which was still on the books at the time of the "Preface." By 1842, the new copyright law passed Parliament, granting forty-two years of copyright privileges to authors (or lifetime plus seven years), even though William lobbied hard for sixty years, already a compromise position in his mind. Since authors were generally men, women authors like Ann Radcliffe, Aphra Behn, Germaine de Staël, Mary Shelley, and Mary Wollstonecraft were remarkable exceptions to the dominant patriarchal machinery of textual production and distribution, even as an emerging countertradition of women authors who focused on women's experiences, gothic narratives, small-press tabloids, street-circulated pamphlets, and domestic fiction created a growing market for printing houses.

Kant's Copernican Revolution

Not long after the publication of *Lyrical Ballads* in 1798, both William and Dorothy Wordsworth, as well as Samuel Coleridge, traveled to Germany, and Coleridge ended up spending much of the next year at the University of Göttingen. Coleridge came to master the German language, but he also came to admire and adopt many of the ideas of the German poets and philosophers, especially Immanuel Kant, Friedrich Wilhelm Joseph von Schelling, and Friedrich Schiller.[26] This experience gave to Coleridge a philosophical sophistication that exceeded that of any of his peers in the British Romantic movement. But it is to Kant that we must turn first since he supplied for generations afterwards the terms *disinterestedness* and *transcendental aesthetic* that, for him, represented the apex of what for us seems oxymoronic because it enabled individuals to attain the "subjective universal" (*Critique of Judgment* 38). He also developed the frameworks for the new theories of aesthetics, beauty, and the sublime; and, despite his influential theories on the autonomy of art, he also recognized the social and political impact that these activities could have on social life.

Kant provided perhaps the most influential discourse for modernizing Western metaphysics, theorizing a conceptual resolution intended to heal the famous Cartesian splits between mind and body, subject and object. It is fair to say that in his monumental book, the *Critique of Pure Reason* (1787; this book is often referred to as the "first *Critique*"), he also very self-consciously set out, in faithfulness to the Enlightenment enthusiasm for science, to resolve the conflicts between the long-standing philosophical tradition of rationalism in René Descartes, Baruch Spinoza, and Gottfried Wilhelm Leibniz and the more recent discourse of empiricism, especially in the work of John Locke and David Hume. As he says in the "Preface to the Second Edition,"[27] "We are here in a similar situation as Copernicus" (first *Critique* 18), and, like the world-changing effect of the Copernican revolution, Kant's ambitious aim was to "change the old order of metaphysics, and to bring about a complete revolution after the example set by geometers and investigators of nature" (21). In his mind, Western metaphysics was never going to be the same, and to some degree that is true: his influence has stretched across so many fields that all of us coming after him are called "post-Kantians."

Many of Kant's writings are so abstract and complex that they can be very intimidating for the uninitiated. Indeed, in the first two years after the publication in 1781 of the *Critique of Pure Reason*, it was almost completely ignored, partly because it was so long (eight hundred pages in the original German edition) and also so intricately obscure. Although during the 1760s Kant had developed a popular reputation for some of his books on astronomy, the beautiful and the sublime, morality, and cosmology, once he attained the position of professor in 1770 at the University of Königsberg, he published very little during the next decade, until his magnum opus appeared. Kant himself recognized the difficulty of what is called the first *Critique*, so in 1783 he published a short overview of his entire system, *Prolegomena to Any Future Metaphysics*, and in 1787 he published a heavily revised edition of the first *Critique*. The *Prolegomena* is indeed short (barely one hundred pages), but it is still not particularly easy to follow, although he does start from more particular examples, such as mathematics, and analyzes the consequences of how we come to know these truths. He proposes to answer the basic question, "Whether such a thing as metaphysics be at all possible?" (Preface to *Prolegomena* 1), which, of course, he argues in the affirmative, arguing furthermore that it should have the status of a science. In any case, the series of many books that followed in the 1780s quickly established Kant's reputation as the preeminent philosopher of his day.

Basically, Plato spoke of subjectivity by referring to the *soul*, but such an archaic term was of little use in a modern, technological age. As we saw in the "Allegory of the Cave," he proclaimed that "the power and capacity of learning exists in the soul already," although he provided no rational form or content to this ineffable proclamation about the soul. Plato never addressed issues of perception, per se, but it was the role of the senses in the process of acquiring any kind of knowledge that Locke and Hume had emphasized.[28] Unlike the idealized discourse of the soul, Kant granted the empiricists their basic starting point in the first sentence of the first *Critique*: "[A]ll knowledge begins with experience" (37). How could one know or recognize an individual soul if the only access to it was through individual bodies, in short, through any given subject's idiosyncratic perceptual experience? The problem with perception is that different individuals perceive the same things from different perspectives, and thus subjective sense experience defeats the claims of objectivity. We cannot just access "things in themselves" because the subject or self intervenes in all forms of knowing.

The empiricists insisted that all knowledge came by way of experience through the senses; the rationalists insisted that it came by way of reason. The rationalists could appear more certain, but they tended to ignore the mediating effect of perception; the empiricists could be more accommodating to perceptual mediation but so highly skeptical (especially David Hume) regarding any epistemological certainties or universals as to defeat the possibilities for objective knowledge. The rationalist tradition ran from Descartes, through Spinoza, to Leibniz—the great seventeenth-century mathematician, supposedly one of the inventors of calculus, along with Isaac Newton, and a philosopher whose idealism was often criticized by Kant. Leibniz's controversial theory of monads, fundamental elements that united mind and matter, was, for Kant, fundamentally illogical and little more than an illusion. Indeed, Kant continues to offer radical critiques of almost any form of illusory idealism. In the Second Division of the first *Critique*,[29] he offers an extended analysis of the limitations of any form of reason to logically prove the existence of such teleological concepts as God, freedom, and immortality: such proof is beyond the limits of our knowledge. Even though Kant calls himself a transcendental idealist, he was highly critical of all delusory idealisms. Transcendental idealism was, for him, the basis of his realism, as he granted the reality of the *noumena* ("the things themselves") of the world outside ourselves even as he explained how we could only have knowledge of such objects by way of the *phenomena* represented in our understanding following our experiential perceptions.

But for Kant, neither the rationalists nor the empiricists offered satisfactory resolutions to the epistemological conflicts between the subjective and the objective. His arguments against the empiricists, particularly Locke, are as rigorous as his arguments against the rationalists and idealists. They occupy much of the nearly five-hundred-page Part 1 of the book. Kant's basic reconciliation hinges on his articulation of a complex philosophical notion: what he called the "transcendental unity of apperception." Few contemporary critics accept Kant's resolution, but we still struggle with the problems involved in all claims for universality and objectivity.

Kant's resolution rests on a kind of circular reasoning because he posits what he calls the "a priori," or, translated from Latin, "before perception," prior to the senses "apperception." That is, even when a group of people sit around a bed, all viewing it from different sides (in a sense, seeing different beds), none of them have trouble accepting the fact that there is only one bed in the room. Perceptual differences of individuals tend to magnify the quality of subjectivity as idiosyncrasy, but these differences dissipate when you dig beneath the surface. For Kant, as you head deeper into the subjective you end up reaching a foundation, what he called "apperception," an a priori way of knowing, a fundamental structuring principle for unifying perception shared by all human beings: the ultimate human commonality. Many followers of Kant's work have called this a priori knowledge the *transcendental ego,* though Kant himself never used this term. The more ungainly, but accurate, *transcendental unity of apperception* evokes the oxymoronic notion of "subjective universality."

This fundamental ground of apperception is constructed according to proper Western metaphysical binary logic. For Kant, the "synthetic unity of apperception (124)" was based on "two pure forms of sensible intuition" (61): space and time. Second, those intuitions were "*forms* of intuitions" (my emphasis), following a basic principle of Western metaphysical formalism, and they were accompanied by two other intuitive properties: substance and causality. In adapting Aristotle's fundamental category of substance, Kant acknowledged a kind of bedrock of universal abstraction for objects that were acknowledged in time and space: you can begin with a specific object, say, a bed; you can begin a series of abstractions to more general categories of the particular bed (furniture; household good; commodity; etc.), but substance was the name for the ultimate limit of categorical abstractions because you can't go any more general for anything that existed in space and time. In turn, causality was the intuition about how particular substances can change, evolve, or disintegrate in the space/time continuum. This causal intuition served as a fundamental principle, common to all human beings, and thus prior to any actual perception we may have that there are specific causes for specific events. In short, when you go all the way down into subjectivity what emerges is a bedrock very much mirroring objectivity: the transcendental apperception appears identical in all human beings. Subjectivity, which had always disrupted universality, now appears grounded in its own universality as structural intuitions in the transcendental apperception of time and space, substance and causality. But "transcendental" in Kant's usage did not denote an idealized realm, such as the Platonic Forms, existing above and beyond the empirical world. Rather, as Marcus Weigelt explains, Kant uses the term *transcendental* "to denote a mental realm that precedes the empirical and which makes experience possible" (xxxiv).[30]

In the 1788 *Critique of Practical Reason* (the "second *Critique*"), Kant expanded on the practical applications of his metaphysic to the realm of morality. In this much shorter text (less than two hundred pages), Kant more fully explained that the mental faculties of reason, understanding, and sensibility have as their teleological goal the attainment of human freedom. Issues of morality and politics always lie close to Kant's understanding, even though he does not raise those issues in the *Critique of Pure Reason*. But as he explains in the *Critique of Practical Reason*, "The concept of freedom is the stone of stumbling for all *empiricists*, but at the same time the key to the loftiest practical principles for *critical* moralists" (7), and in this work he develops his famous doctrines of the categorical imperative, free will, and moral judgment by reason, doctrines that have influenced philosophers and theorists for the last two hundred years. Kant reconsiders the function of the regulative ideas of God, freedom, and immortality as rational justifications for the truths of the Christian religious traditions. I will return to the implications of these theories for his beliefs regarding the crucial need for political and religious freedoms, but before we get to the political economy, we need to consider Kant's remarkably influential book on aesthetics, *The Critique of Judgment* (the "third *Critique*"), which he published in 1790, as the French Revolution was making news all around Europe.

Kant's new discourse proposed solutions to some long-standing philosophical conundrums, but the first two *Critiques* had not directly addressed the enormously important kinds of imaginative syntheses possible in the aesthetic experience of art and literature (Kant much preferred poetry to the visual arts). Likewise, the critical judgment of subjective taste had to be rearticulated in terms of universal properties. The individual purpose, or purposiveness, of literary activities ultimately had to derive from necessary a priori principles that transcended individual differences in achieving universal synthesis in the work of art—the literary canon would depend upon nothing less. Kant addressed exactly these issues in *The Critique of Judgment* (1790), where he divides the first part, "Critique of the Aesthetical Judgment," into two books, the first being the "Analytic of the Beautiful," followed by the "Analytic of the Sublime." Despite the apparent rigorous structure of the book as outlined in the table of contents, this book tends to be ragged and somewhat repetitious, but these faults never impinged on its impact as founding the discourse of aesthetics. Actually, Kant adopted the use of the word *aesthetics* from his predecessor, Gottfried Baumgarten (1714–62), principally from Baumgarten's 1750 book *Aesthetica,* where he shifted the traditional meaning of the term by adding the "a" to its Greek root in the term *esthetics* or *aesthesis,* which meant sense perception. Significantly, one of the consequences of these new meanings was that a whole new branch of philosophy, aesthetics, now came into being as the study of the roots of all artistic endeavor and achievement. Actually, for Kant, the term *aesthetic* had less to do with art than we generally assume to be the case: the transcendental aesthetic for Kant was primarily an epistemological category whereby the faculty of sensibility could be integrated with the mental faculties of reason and understanding. As he puts it in *The Critique of Pure Reason,* "the science of all the principles of a priori sensibility I call *transcendental aesthetic*" (60). Despite these qualifications, the Romantic idealists moved the term *aesthetics* firmly into the domain of the literary and artistic, and Coleridge's adaptation of many of Kant's theories continued to affect many versions of literary criticism throughout the twentieth century. The crucial relations between aesthetics and politics have ever since these times been problematic for subsequent writers, artists, and critics.

Key to the new meaning of aesthetics was the concept of beauty that, for Kant, was the basis for taste and judgment. Such judgments depended upon criteria for aesthetic discriminations that could be based on "that which pleases universally, without a concept" (*Critique of Judgment* 40). But beauty involved both perception and apperception: empirical experience of form synthesized with apperceptive categories that are antecedent to any possibility for sensory impressions. The judgment that some particular object was beautiful could not mean that it was just beautiful "for me," but that it carried universal claims: as Kant puts it, "he must not call it *beautiful* if it merely pleases himself" (*Critique of Judgment* 34). What he seeks as universal must be common: "We ask for the agreement of everyone else, because we have for it a ground that is common to all" (55). This focus on commonality is crucial because Kant also sees both reason and beauty as fundamentally related to the possibilities for human freedom: neither external political power nor idiosyncratic desire can influence the ultimately universal judgment of the truly beautiful: what he calls the "subjective universal communicability" (38) of the judgment of aesthetic beauty.

The power of judgment is to synthesize the faculties of reason and imagination through a critical integration of universal laws and particular works of art. As Kant puts it, the "satisfaction which determines the judgment of taste is disinterested" (28), and this "pure disinterested satisfaction" (29) registers as a kind of paradoxical "purposiveness" that he distinguishes from our ordinary, individual sense of subjective "purpose" (64–65). This is, indeed, a difficult argument to follow, and he develops it at greater length in the "Second Part: Critique of the Teleological Judgment." Here, according to Kant, we must ascribe a teleological "purposiveness" to nature: natural forms clearly were not random accidents but had purposiveness as the effective cause of those forms (an acorn will not become a maple tree), even when we cannot identify any single or individual cause for them. Indeed, in all these articulations, Kant's principles derive from the fundamental value of Western metaphysical formalism, even though Kant has so modified them that we can lose sight of their significant links to Aristotelian and Platonic notions of form. The discourse of disinterestedness became fundamental not only to some of the Romantic idealists, but also to subsequent writers such as Matthew Arnold, T. S. Eliot, and the New Critics. As Kant himself made clear, however, one can be disinterested in one's critical judgment of the value of a work of art even as one finds the work itself very interesting. As he puts it in the third *Critique:* "A judgment upon an object of satisfaction may be quite disinterested, but yet very interesting, i.e. not based upon an interest, but bringing an interest with it; of this kind are all pure moral judgments" (29). It is the crucial links between aesthetic experience of art and moral judgment of social values that enable aesthetic experience to have clear social and political functions even as our perception of it remains disinterested. In short, aesthetic autonomy and the social consequences of art are certainly distinct but not opposing domains.

In order to understand those connections, we need to understand some of Kant's evolving political theories during the 1780s, but I have found it best to approach the political writings by first considering some of his key texts of the 1790s, where Kant directly addressed the institutional relations between philosophy and politics as crucial to the educational and social function of the modern university. Many have pointed to Kant as the root source for modernity's tendency to separate science from politics, the laboratory from the statehouse, the human from the natural, but Kant never saw these domains as radically disconnected. We can clearly see these relations at work in his political struggles for his own work at the University of Königsberg.

Indeed, during the early years of the French Revolution, the military expenditures of King Frederick William II of Prussia were compromising the educational mission of the emerging modern university. Although during the previous reign of Frederick the Great (whom Kant greatly favored and idealized as an enlightened monarch), the imperialist expansion of the Prussian empire had been based on belief in discipline, authority, and "might makes right," the academic community had enjoyed relative freedoms from both theological and state interventions, at least compared to most other European countries at the time. But with Frederick's death in 1786, the accession of his nephew did not bode well for liberal reformers. Although it was far from the capital of Berlin, tradition had it that the new king would be crowned in Königsberg, and as then rector of the university, Kant helped organize the 1786 coronation ceremonies for the new king, who publicly praised the great philosopher. But Kant undoubtedly had private reservations about the new regime. And sure enough, by 1788, "the King, his favorite minister [Woellner], and the coterie of likeminded officials they gathered around them launched a campaign to 'stamp out the Enlightenment'" (Gregor ix). The first enactment of that campaign was a new Censorship Edict dealing with any writings addressing religious matters. This ideological battle against the scholarly community went hand in hand with the coalition forces uniting Prussia with Austria, Britain, Spain, and Russia, all of whom waged war against the ongoing French Revolution's perceived threat to European forms of monarchical government. Although for his own safety he had to veil the full force of his criticism of these imperial activities, Kant was, as Mary J. Gregor explains, distressed by "kings who spend on war the money that might better be used for education" (viii).

It was during the unfolding of these war campaigns that Kant himself became the direct enemy of the new regime's attack on the "so-called enlighteners" whose intellectual and ecclesiastical freedoms were seen as a direct threat to state power. The "enlighteners" could be characterized as the liberal wing of the newly emergent advocates of European universalism. With his 1793 publication of *Religion within the Limits of Mere Reason,* Kant raised the ire of the biblical theologians who saw the philosopher invading their territory and attempting to adjudicate divine law by human reason. Kant's version of transcendental critique threatened religious authority at the very same time that the French Revolution threatened both ecclesiastical and aristocratic power. In Prussia, the ecclesiastics got the Censorship Commission to put all kinds of obstacles in Kant's way, even issuing an order forbidding faculty from lecturing on Kant's philosophy of religion. Kant responded to these attacks by drafting in October, 1794, the essay, "The Conflict of the Philosophical Faculty with the Theological Faculty," which became the first of the three parts of *The Conflict of the Faculties,* published in 1798 after Frederick Williams's death the year before. As many have now argued, this text, although one of Kant's lesser-known volumes, can be seen as a founding document for the formation of the modern university. The philosopher's rewriting of Western metaphysics combined the radical Romantic resistance to dominant forms of political oppression with idealist strains of transcendent truths.

Kant established a set of rights justifying the "division of labor" (*Conflict* 23) between competing segments of the university community, all of which in turn gain their legitimation as autonomous spheres for the production of knowledge on a contractual set of obligations delimited by state power and religious orthodoxy. "The university would have a certain autonomy since only scholars can pass judgment on scholars as such, and accordingly it would be authorized to perform certain functions through its *faculties*" (23). What we have here is an unprecedented Enlightenment version of Western metaphysics that would later become scripted into twentieth-century versions of academic freedom based on the principle of disciplinary self-regulation and autonomy, which in Kant's day meant autonomy from state and church interference. Noticeably, the political economy of business and capital play no part in these contractual relations.

For Kant and his Enlightenment heirs, the juridical guarantor of these domains of freedom depended on the purification of reason and universality: the well-educated, mature, autonomous subject could, via his version of transcendental critique, exercise the principle of reason in the labor assigned to the philosophy faculty. Well-educated meant literate in the Western traditions of philosophy and dialectic. As Bill Readings argues, "The University becomes modern when all its activities are organized in view of a single regulatory idea, which Kant claims must be the concept of reason" (14–15). Plato and Aristotle would have been pleased with this invocation of their legacy. The humble virtues of reason and universality justify the position of the "lower faculty" of philosophy that, paradoxically, serves as the final arbiter of the juridical truth claims put forward by the "higher faculties" of theology, law, and medicine. In this version of epistemological hierarchies, they are "higher" because they have more direct public consequences. No doubt, also, these claims for universality and reason open themselves to all the forms of deconstruction that Derrida and others have subjected them to in Richard Rand's collection, *Logomachia: The Conflict of the Faculties Today*.[31]

But the focus on the "single regulatory idea" can miss the multiple, material relations within the political economy that Kant was negotiating among the state, the church, the public, and the university, and, internally speaking, the divisions of labor that keep lawyers, doctors, clerics, and philosophers working on their own territorial claims without interfering unduly with one another. In short, Kant did not just found a university on reason as a category transcendent to the material world, but he also justified higher education as a contractual relation of powers distributed by the rights of reason, theological tradition, state power, and citizenship. Kant's version of universality emerges then as a contested term immanent to the political economy as a struggle for autonomy from both the disintegrating powers of theological certainty and the collapsing forms of state-sanctioned aristocracy. The newly emergent forms of capitalist colonialism are not yet on his radar. Of course, the "lower faculty" of philosophy must not be interfered with, because the principle of reason alone must protect the state and the public uses of the "higher faculties" from abuses of power such as Kant had experienced in the form of censorship and repression. A concern for social justice was engaged with, not absolutely divorced from, the principle of reason, but also the political economy of his day.[32] The contractual divisions of separate fields of knowledge became the basic epistemological justification of the modern disciplines, whose professional obligations were not quite so radically divorced from public forms of communality: peer review might not seem philosophically exciting, but it was institutionalized as a social practice of searching for the truth.

Kant's articulation of the domains of professional autonomy expected of university teachers and researchers directly aided the subsequent emergence in nineteenth-century German universities of the discourse of "academic freedom" whereby the three basic principles were the freedom to teach, the freedom to learn, and the freedom to do research. These basic principles of academic freedom have been adapted, rewritten, and revised many times in different historical circumstances and in different geographical regions for many different nations of the world.

We are now better prepared to consider Kant's social and political views, which were always important to him, even though they tend to be only obliquely addressed in his three major *Critiques*. In many ways, Kant will appear as the essential Enlightenment thinker who believes, as Hans Reiss puts it, "in the power of reason to judge politics" (38). Given my focus on the political economy and social justice, I will first selectively attend to the sometimes startlingly prescient and even radical positions Kant articulates, but we also have to consider those views in contrast with what will in other instances seem like troublesomely reactionary and even racist positions.

Let me begin with a brief (six-page) but important essay, "An Answer to the Question: 'What Is Enlightenment?'" which Kant composed in 1784 during the time he was revising his first *Critique*. Enlightenment calls for freedom, both intellectual and political; but at the same time, revolution is not an acceptable option to attain freedom. Kant distinguished between public and private uses of reason: "The *public* use of man's reason must always be free, and it alone can bring about enlightenment among men; the *private* use of reason may quite often be very narrowly restricted, however, without undue hindrance to the progress of enlightenment" (*Kant* 55). By public he means addresses of any kind directed at the entire social public; by private he means not just private homes, but also certain limited domains, such as a church. Thus the clergyman might be expected to conform to his duties as pastor in all *private* articulations he makes; but as a citizen speaking to the public at large, thus "making *public* use of his reason" he "enjoys unlimited freedom to use his own reason and to speak in his own person" (57). Kant desires a version of "universal history" aimed at enlightenment and freedom, and thus based on human progress toward those goals. He firmly believed that his own age was clearing the way for that very progress: "the obstacles to universal enlightenment, to man's emergence from his self-incurred immaturity, are gradually becoming fewer. In this respect our age is the age of enlightenment, the century of *Frederick*" (58). As noted earlier, Kant always honored Frederick the Great (King of Prussia, 1740–86), nicknamed "Old Fritz," who served for Kant as the image of the enlightened monarch, or what he called a constitutional monarchy, a form of government that Kant, very much like Plato and Aristotle, preferred over open-ended enfranchisement of all citizens in democratic states, where the threat of unenlightened voters, the "unruly mob," could defeat his idea of the rational, lawmaking state. Any form of revolutionary overthrow of a government would be an action defying the use of reason as the basis for social policy.

Interestingly, in a later, 1793 essay[33] where Kant is arguing for the integration of theory and practice, it appears that his own theory of freedom contradicts his own political practice of favoring constitutional monarchies. In his explication of the social contracts necessary to underwrite the "common" purpose of civil constitutions, he argues that "in all social contracts, we find a union of many individuals for some common end which they all share," (*Kant* 73), thus clearly favoring a kind of universal commonality. And that commonality rests on three basic freedoms that would seem to echo right out of the ideals of the French Revolution: first "the *freedom* of every member of society as a *human being;*" second, the "*equality* of each with all the others as a *subject;*" and third, the "*independence* of each member of a commonwealth as a *citizen*" (74). Consequently, it follows that "no member of the commonwealth can have a hereditary privilege" (76). Yet his principle of favoring constitutional monarchies such as that led by "Old Fritz" was based on exactly such hereditary privilege. This paradoxical conflict between universal ideas of commonality and restrictive limits on those common grounds recur in Kant's thinking, but it never stopped him from believing in the "freedom of the pen," a version of academic freedom, and a very cosmopolitan belief in freedom of speech in the public arena as the best safeguard for a rational society.

Kant directly addresses these conflicts in a more famous essay, "Perpetual Peace: A Philosophical Sketch" from 1795, and here he emphasizes some of the more radical dimensions of his political philosophy. During the 1790s Kant was deeply at odds with Frederick William II, who in almost all ways seemed the antithesis to his predecessor, Frederick the Great. But what is striking about "Perpetual Peace" are Kant's clear oppositions to standing armies, national debt, restrictive immigration laws, and war policies. The aim of the enlightened state was the sustaining of "perpetual peace," and that required a leader like Frederick the

Great, who "at least *said* that he was merely the highest servant of the state" (*Kant* 101). Kant, therefore, distinguishes the different kinds of states, focusing primarily on autocracy, aristocracy, and democracy, where his main effort is to make sure his version of the best forms of monarchy (a version of autocracy), based on a republican constitution, should not be "confused with the democratic one" (100). Indeed, in this passage democracy comes off very badly: "democracy, in the truest sense of the word, is necessarily a despotism, because it establishes an executive power through which all the citizens may make decisions about (and indeed against) the single individual without his consent, so that decisions are made by all the people and yet not by all the people; and this means that the general will is in contradiction with itself, and thus also with freedom" (101). We can see in this passage reflections very much like Plato's belief in the enlightened philosopher-king and Aristotle's preference for a similar kind of aristocratic polity, as he calls it. But Kant makes clear distinctions from his ancient predecessors: "It is not expected that kings will philosophize or that philosophers will become kings," but (clearly thinking of Frederick William), "Kings . . . should not, however, force the class of philosophers to disappear or to remain silent, but should allow them to speak freely" (115).

In "Perpetual Peace" we also find some of Kant's most forward-thinking articulations of the goal of cosmopolitan transnationalism and human rights, where, for instance, in terms pertinent to contemporary immigration issues, he argues forcefully that "*hospitality* means the right of a stranger not to be treated with hostility when he arrives on someone else's territory" (105). It is therefore necessary for nation-states to form international alliances to secure "perpetual peace," and to ensure that "all men are entitled to present themselves in the society of others by virtues of their right to communal possession of the earth's surface. . . . no-one originally has any greater right than anyone else to occupy any particular portion of the earth," because in all social intercourse, "the human race shares in common" these fundamental rights to live peacefully in a "universal community" (106–07).

Given these theoretical principles regarding commonality, it can be discouraging to see Kant also expressing some terribly unfortunate (and contradictory) views, such as that "while some American tribes have been entirely eaten up by their enemies, the Europeans know how to make better use of those they have defeated than merely by making a meal of them" (103). Or from a 1784 text, "one may prove that Americans and Negroes are races which have sunk below the level of other members of the species in terms of intellectual abilities" (217).[34] Nor is Kant particularly kind to violations of some forms of conventional morality, such that "The child born outside marriage is outside the law. . . . and it is therefore also outside the protection of the law" (159).[35]

Unfortunately, then, in some instances Kant's own version of the transcendent was not really universal, as his own racism excluded people of color from those very forms of transcendence. Emmanuel Chukwudi Eze has collected a number of Kant's most racist theories and expressions in Chapter 4 of his *Race and the Enlightenment,* and just to use one egregious example from this collection, Kant is quoted as saying: "This fellow was quite black from head to foot, a clear proof that what he said was quite stupid" (57).[36] But, as Eze also documents, many other Enlightenment philosophers, as well as large portions of the general public in Europe, also shared such sentiments, and partly for that reason the racist theories never suppressed the ascension of Kant's widely influential philosophical theory. At the same time, it is also fair to say that in our age of the Big Bang theory, string theory, and global climate change, Kant's secure bedrocks of time and space seem more dreamlike than real.

Kant had hoped to establish metaphysics as a reputable science, "a completely isolated and speculative branch of rational knowledge" (*Critique of Pure Reason* 17). With respect to those ambitions, he was clearly disappointed that no one in his day, or after, ever adapted his complex critique as a self-contained metaphysical system. Blake, Nietzsche, and many others have abhorred this rigid system of analysis when seen as fixed and determinative. Nevertheless, Kant's distinctions between pure and practical (or applied) reason hold even today in the distinction some continue to make between pure and applied sciences. Many contemporary critics are indebted to his critiques of the rigid dogmatisms and idealistic illusions that, in Kant's words, abound as "groundless groping and uncritical rambling" ("Preface to the Second Edition," first *Critique* 26).

Coleridge's Imaginative Synthesis in the Infinite "I AM"

> *Poetry, even that of the loftiest, and, seemingly, that of the wildest odes, had a logic of its own, as severe as that of science; and more difficult, because more subtle, more complex, and dependent on more, and more fugitive causes.*
>
> —*Biographia Literaria* 3

Enlightenment thinkers like Kant still held the highest value for reason and philosophy, although aesthetic experience was crucial because of its synthetic function. The Romantic theorists took from Kant many of his articulations about art, but they also ended up elevating aesthetic experience based on the creative power of the imagination above the cognitive capacities based on the principles of reason (although, as we will see, this statement must be qualified given Coleridge's difference from most of his Romantic compatriots). After 1801, Coleridge found the Kantian doctrines compatible with his poetical goal of realizing his famously phrased "Infinite I AM," the oxymoronic moment of aesthetic experience when the self or ego becomes not particular, as it is in ordinary life, but infinite and universal.[37] It is hard not to hear in these formulations a rewriting of Plato's claim that the truth exists in the soul already, as a precondition, before we get lost in the cave of human ignorance—a Western metaphysical emphasis on the universal goal rather than the dialectical process. We are well on our way to a highly sophisticated version of Romantic idealism.

Early in his life, especially during the few years he spent at Cambridge University (1791–94), Coleridge was excited by some of the more radical political ideas of his day, such as William Godwin's *Enquiry Concerning Political Justice*. Indeed, the trajectory of Coleridge's career can be seen as a kind of template for an early engagement in ideas associated with radical Romanticism, followed by a sharply more conservative version of Romantic idealism. For example, even as a seventeen-year-old when the

French Revolution broke out in 1789 with the storming of the Bastille, Coleridge wrote a poem, "Ode on the Destruction of the Bastille," where he celebrates the revolutionary fervor for liberty and equality: "Liberty the soul of Life shall reign" (*Poetical Works* 11). Less than a year after the beginning of the Haitian slave revolt, Coleridge published a prize-winning "Ode on the Slave Trade," directly addressed to "the wretched lot of the Slaves in the Isles of Western India." In his undergraduate years at Cambridge, Coleridge appears as a staunch abolitionist, and during that time he met the revolutionary leader and Unitarian, William Frend, who actively supported the French Revolution. He also met his good friend, Robert Southey, and in 1794 the two of them developed a plan to form what they called a "pantisocracy," an ideal of communal rule by all citizens, and even hoped to find a place for their utopian community on the banks of the Susquehanna River in eastern Pennsylvania. Southey soon realized the impractical nature of the plans for Pennsylvania, and he proposed Wales instead, but Coleridge could not agree, and in 1795 the plan collapsed. Nevertheless, that same year Southey and Coleridge married the Fricker sisters (Edith and Sarah), although it was not a good marriage for Coleridge, and after prolonged periods of turmoil, he and Sarah separated in 1815. But, also in 1795, he met Dorothy and William Wordsworth, and by 1797 he had settled in Nether Stowey, Somerset. The Wordsworth siblings specifically chose to live about three miles away in Alfoxden Park, and, over the next two years, thus began the incredibly fruitful friendship and collaboration with the Wordsworths. All three of them were appalled at the betrayals of the French Revolution during the Reign of Terror, and Coleridge began his retreat from his radical ideas with a poem he had planned to call "Recantation," although he ended up calling it "France: An Ode" (*Poetical Works* 244). Here he chronicles his early hopes but later his shock and remorse at his earlier blind idealism. After he and William had published *Lyrical Ballads,* in the fall of 1798, the three friends travelled to Germany. In 1800, Coleridge would also settle in the Lake District, near the cottage in Grasmere where Dorothy and William then resided.

Unfortunately, however, this brief period of productivity rather rapidly deteriorated, as did his marriage and his friendship with Wordsworth. Coleridge had long suffered from depression, and from childhood illnesses that some have conjectured could have been rheumatic fever, for which he took laudanum, a form of opium to which he became addicted. He came to have deep doubts about his own poetic powers, even as he composed his well-known poem, "Dejection: An Ode," in which the speaker laments not only his bodily afflictions, but his loss of "My shaping spirit of Imagination!" However, during the first three decades of the nineteenth century, we can see Coleridge steadily move to conservative religious and political beliefs, evidenced in such works as *The Statesman's Manual* (1816; often called the first "lay sermon," *Lay Sermons* 3–114); *A Lay Sermon* (1817; the second "lay sermon," *Lay Sermons* 117–230); he never completed his projected third sermon); his much more influential, *Biographia Literaria* (1817); and, just a few years before he died, *On the Constitution of the Church and State* (1830).

As the first of the "lay sermons," *The Statesman's Manual* expressly addresses itself on the title page to "The Higher Classes of Society" and announces its theme as "The Bible the Best Guide of Political Skill and Foresight" (*Lay Sermons* 3). Coleridge argues in a December 1816 letter to George Frere that the subtitle should have been "to the Learned and Reflecting of all Ranks and Professions, especially among the Higher Class" (as quoted by the editor, R. J. White, in 3n1), except that his publisher chose the simpler phrase. Nonetheless, the author's increasing identification with the "higher classes," rather than with Wordsworth's rustic commoners, becomes transparent, even though, as advertised on the back wrapper to the book, his projected third lay sermon would be directed "to the Lower and Labouring Classes of Society" (White, "Editor's Introduction," *Lay Sermons* xxxi). But around this time, in 1816, when Coleridge settled into Dr. Gillman's house on High Gate Hill in London, where he was to remain the rest of his life, he was of the belief that it was only through religion that the masses could be brought to engage philosophy. As he explains in the appendix to *The Statesman's Manual*, "Reason and Religion differ only as a two-fold application of the same power" (*Lay Sermons* 59). Interestingly, in an inscription in a copy of *A Lay Sermon*, presented in 1819 to John Gibson Lockhart, Coleridge contends that the "express object" of

The Statesman's Manual had been to consider the Old Testament "as a Code of true political Economy, and a specimen of bona fide philosophical History; and secondly, a defence of ancient Metaphysics, (principally, the Pythagorean, Heraclitic and Platonic)" (*Lay Sermons*, letter included in "Editor's Appendix C" 244). It certainly wasn't a view of the political economy recognizable by the classical economists. Nevertheless, the first Lay Sermon does contain an explicit critique of the commercial world of business and industry, a critique based not on empirical analysis of the political economy, but on moral grounds, as a kind of jeremiad against the commercial degradation of spiritual life. Coleridge rejects his earlier advocacy of the French Revolution, and looking back at those events from High Gate Hill, London, he now ties the Revolutionary interests expressly to those crass, utilitarian, business calculations that led to the organization of the state. Indeed, he snipes at the entire range of what he calls the "mechanic philosophy" of those who have presented "the histories and political economy of the present" (*Lay Sermons* 28). He is really referring here to the Enlightenment empiricists like John Locke, David Hume, and David Hartley, but he sweeps wide and dismisses out of hand all political revolutionaries with even more fervor. Indeed, much of the two *Lay Sermons* read like a diatribe against materialism, "the impostures of that philosophy of the French revolution," where "Jacobinism is *monstrum hybridum*, made up in part of despotism" (*Lay Sermons* 63). The statesman's manual should be the Bible, not the vulgar materialist philosophies of the revolutionary political economists.

Shortly after he published the second Lay Sermon in 1817, Coleridge also published his most influential book, the *Biographia Literaria*, a text it might be fair to say was fifteen years in the making since much of it is devoted to clarifying his differences with Wordsworth following upon the 1802 publication of the preface to the second edition of the *Lyrical Ballads*. The real breach in their friendship began in 1810, after which time there were long periods during which there was no intercourse between them. The significance of the *Biographia* is that, despite all its unevenness (Coleridge himself refers to it as the "immethodical miscellany"[38]), there are passages of great philosophical lucidity in the ways that Coleridge articulated what became widely influential precepts for Romantic idealism. In general, Coleridge developed a rigorous organicism whereby the imagination serves to unify our particular sense perceptions with the universal concepts of our understanding. The "organic" integration might conceivably have been worked out as an integration of aesthetics and politics, but instead it was the reverse: it turned out to be an integration of subjective and objective in the formal unity of aesthetic experience, with political considerations pretty well cordoned off from poetry and art.

Actually, Coleridge remains closer to the Enlightenment thinking of Kant than any of the other Romantics, because he holds, like Kant, that reason remains the ultimate arbiter of the path to the universal.[39] Coleridge also places a higher value than Kant on aesthetic experience for its organic synthesizing function, whereby the finite artistic/poetic object symbolizes the infinite; the imagination, for Coleridge, extended the cognitive faculty of the understanding in ways that Kant would not have accepted Kant articulated a more circumscribed role to the imagination partly because he was wary of the imaginative ties to sensuality, emotion, love. Also, Kant would never have recognized Coleridge's famous distinctions between the imagination and the fancy. Kant's system of critical philosophy was also essentially Stoic, demanding a devaluation of any epistemological status for feeling and emotion, and Coleridge saw these limitations as philosophical faults, even as he agreed that reason was still the highest faculty.

In all these formulations, Coleridge follows basic Western metaphysical formalist principles whereby the integrative capacity of the imagination resides in the formal relations of the poetic text rather than the poet or the cultural context, and this attention to intrinsic formal unity will migrate as a basic principle of the twentieth-century New Critics.

Kant's version of natural philosophy justified a significant role for poetry as an important vehicle for achieving the ultimate "purification of the mind" (Critique of Pure Reason 147), and Coleridge sought to fortify this assessment of poetry. In Chapter 14 of the Biographia, the poet reaches such "ideal perfection" (173) through "synthetic and magical power" (174) that these dualisms can be integrated, sort of like the synthesis of Blake's contraries: "in the balance or reconciliation of opposite or discordant qualities: of sameness, with difference; of the general, with the concrete; the idea, with the image; the individual, with the representative; the sense of novelty and freshness, with old and familiar objects; a more than usual state of emotion, with more than usual order" (174)—here the dialectic meets its final resting place in the organic synthesis of formal unity in the literary text. In characteristic Western metaphysical fashion, the *unity* of organic *form* wins the day. Kant would have agreed with the emphasis on form, but he certainly would not have agreed that you could integrate "more than usual . . . emotion, with more than usual order."

In Chapter 12, Coleridge articulates the fundamental philosophical dialectic, with the aim of demonstrating how poetry will get us a long way toward the universal goal. You can start at either pole, so long as you end up in the same place: the universal. Given our concern for copyright laws, it might seem ironic that much of Chapter 12 of Coleridge's *Biographia Literaria,* from which I have been quoting, consists of little more than a translation from Schelling's *System of Transcendental Idealism* even though Coleridge published it under his own name. In many ways, Schelling was even more directly influential on Coleridge than Kant, but given those qualifications, here's the central epistemological problem: "All knowledge rests on the coincidence of an object with a subject" (*Biographia* 174). Thus, as Coleridge puts it, you can start with either pole, so that "Either the Objective Is Taken as the First, and Then We Have to Account for the Supervention of the Subjective, Which Coalesces with It" (175), or vice versa. But when you bring them together "[d]uring the act of knowledge itself, the objective and subjective are so instantly united, that we cannot determine to which of the two the priority belongs" (174). No chicken-egg dilemma here. Nature will stand in for "the sum of all that is merely objective," and "the *self* or *intelligence*" will stand in for "the sum of all that is subjective" (174). Schelling aimed his aesthetics toward the goal of the Absolute, and Coleridge follows his lead. In the end, the move from the primary through the secondary imagination describes the aesthetic function of poetry as the creative power to join nature and self in the ultimate coalescence that will have to be divine, and to that extent based on reason.

Basically, Coleridge utilizes Kantian epistemology with its emphasis on the individual and the "subjective universal" to generate an apolitical aesthetics. But, at the same time, Coleridge never considers any of the potentially more radical political implications of some of Kant's ideas. Indeed, this implicit depoliticizing of aesthetic theory became a widely influential pattern when the political implications of radical Romanticism could be mitigated by the idealizing tendencies of Romantic idealism.

Yet Coleridge modified Kant's analysis in his distinction between the primary and secondary imagination. The primary imagination "is the living power and prime agent of all human perception, and . . . a repetition in the finite mind of the eternal act of creation in the infinite *I am*" (167). The oxymoronic "infinite *I am*" draws on Kant's formulations about the a priori "transcendental unity of apperception," but modifies them quite significantly. For instance, in the first *Critique,* Kant explains that the transcendental universal was based on "pure apperception, in the representation *I am*" (*Critique of Pure Reason* 132). Here we find, to a large extent, a version of the "subjective universal" that mirrored Coleridge's own sense of the powers of art to accomplish this feat. For a Romantic idealist like Coleridge, these were exactly the kinds of theoretical justifications to elevate the powers of art above the powers of cognitive understanding (although that was certainly not Kant's intention). Yet, and here's the key difference, Coleridge would not accept what he saw as the ultimately subjective idealism of Kant, whereby the reality of the noumena could only be presumed, but we had no direct access to them. In his mind, Coleridge retranslated the subjective Kantian epistemology by elevating the imaginative powers of poetry to synthesize internalized perceptual phenomena and the externalized reality of the noumena. His description of the more voluntary and willful processes of the second imagination could aid that process.

Indeed, the secondary imagination is somewhat like Kant's description of the productive function of the imagination in creating a newly imagined synthesis following acts of perception: the "conscious will" of the poet is now the source of poetic agency to transform in language the effort it takes to get from the perception of the daffodils to the symbolic beauty of the poem, "recollected in tranquility," in which they later appear. This vital secondary imagination "dissolves, diffuses, dissipates, in order to recreate. . . . [I]t struggles to idealize and to unify" (*Biographia* 167). In short, the secondary imagination provides an avenue to a genuine knowledge of the noumena, and thus toward the infinite and divine unity in the text itself (but not for Kant).

Fancy is the term Coleridge gives to everything else that is merely subjective, pertaining only to memory, which is, of course, often faulty, and dresses up reality in all kinds of fanciful ways having nothing to do with "real" reality. Coleridge has here reversed a long-standing tradition from the Renaissance of valuing Fancy above the Imagination (see Habib, *History* 447)), as the former was conceived as the true avenue to universal truth. Coleridge completely reverts this hierarchy so that the fancy is the nonuniversal and more idiosyncratic faculty. Coleridge had been struggling for years with this key distinction between imagination and fancy, and it is one of the distinctions that he accuses Wordsworth of failing to make. To some degree it may appear that Coleridge recognizes in the fancy a name for one of Kant's worries about the imagination itself as he expresses it in the *Prolegomena:* "The imagination may perhaps be forgiven for occasional vagaries and for not keeping carefully within the limits of experience" (55). In short, fancy is a bit like a daydream, a drifting off into the trivial and insignificant, Kant's "vagaries of the imagination," and this weakened version of the imagination, yield only the kind of poetic diction that Wordsworth and Coleridge so oppose in *Lyrical Ballads.* A genuine dream can yield "Kubla Khan," Coleridge's famous fragment of a poem, which he wrote upon waking from a dream and which reveals the universal poetic truth in harmony with nature and thus completely detached from the commodity forms of production. To this extent, Coleridge offers a philosophical defense of poetic autonomy that would prove to be highly influential for later writers such as Matthew Arnold, F. R. Leavis, and the New Critics.

The form a poem takes in this new model is analogous to the growth and development of an organism, say a plant, as it transforms itself from a seed, to a shoot, to the final flower, a development orchestrated by its own innate nature. Coleridge's Romantic organicism plays off just this analogy, as he offers a critique of the mechanical imposition of form on potential poetic content while advocating the greatness of organic form. The mistake of any kind of "poetic diction"

> lies in the confounding mechanical regularity with organic form. The form is mechanic, when on any given material we impress a predetermined form, not necessarily arising out of the properties of the material. . . . The organic form, on the other hand, is innate; it shapes, as it develops, itself from within, and the fullness of its development is one and the same with the perfection of its outward form." ("Shakespeare's Judgment Equal to his Genius," Adams 462).

This version of poetry as enacting in language the sublime integration of the human and the natural was widely shared among the Romantics. Coleridge tends to philosophically wedge himself in between the Enlightenment and Romantic views of poetry, but, in general, the Romantics elevated poetry as the ultimate synthesizer of reason and feeling; and Percy Bysshe Shelley became its greatest champion.

How Plato Became a Poet

Although Shelley composed his famous "Defense of Poetry" in 1821 as a response to a satirical attack on poetry by his friend, Thomas Love Peacock, it was not published until 1840. In any case, Shelley is a bit younger than most of his British Romantic peers, and his "Defense" consolidates most of the Romantic theory that had preceded him, so it stands as a paradigmatic expression of Romantic idealism. What we will find is that Shelley is, paradoxically, the most radical and the most Platonic of all the Romantic writers to the extent that he borrows repeatedly the universal goals of "the eternal, the infinite, and the one" (500) whereby the poet, not the philosopher, could embody "ideal perfection." Indeed, the latter term he attributes to Homer: given our analysis of the oral conditions in which the Homeric epics were composed, Shelley's attributions may seem highly ironic today. But, needless to say, Shelley had no access to the research of Milman Parry and Eric Havelock. His way of reading Homer is paradigmatic of the way most everyone has been reading and appreciating Homer for the beauty and uniqueness of his language.

Shelley is clear that he is initially going to separate social analysis from formal considerations. As he puts it, "let us dismiss those more general considerations which might involve an inquiry into the principles of society itself, and restrict our view to the manner in which the imagination is expressed upon its forms" (500).

Poets are not just anybody but special people, "those who have employed language as the hieroglyphic of their thoughts" (501), and the notion of "hieroglyphic" here registers with particular significance. This notion of poetic "genius" follows Kant's famous pronouncements in *The Critique of Judgment* that "Beautiful Art is the art of genius" (112; cf. 111–123), and, of course, mirrors what we found in Wordsworth's notion of poetic genius, whereby the individual imaginative act expressively links itself with the universal beauty of nature. The emergence of this discourse of genius is taking place also right around the time of an important historical discovery. In 1799, when the Rosetta Stone was discovered, it drew international attention, especially since inscribed in the stone was a decree written in 196 BCE by Ptolemy V; but the distinguishing feature of this stone text was that it was written in ancient hieroglyphics, Demotic script, and, below those lines, the same meaning in ancient Greek. In short, the stone was the first trilingual text from the ancient world, and it provided the key to deciphering the hieroglyphics, even though it was not until 1822 that Jean-François Champollion successfully did so. The hieroglyphs were of two main kinds: pictographs and ideographs. Pictographs clearly seemed to include rudimentary images, pictures as it were, of the objects they referred to; ideographs were more abstract representations where the visual component did not necessarily correspond to the meaning of the hieroglyph mark and was thus much more difficult to translate. What fascinated the Romantics was the idea that there had existed a language more closely connected to nature—a natural language that we had somehow lost touch with. Given their concern for harmonizing poetry and nature, here, in the Rosetta Stone, was evidence for just such a language. For anyone like Shelley who believed that "in the infancy of the world, neither poets themselves nor their auditors are fully aware of the excellence of poetry" (502), the ancient poets were themselves so close to nature that they did not have to cope with an alienated modern self-consciousness that had to be brought back to nature.

Poetic greatness and proximity to nature must coalesce for liberty and freedom to occur. Without such poetic harmony with nature, society will inevitably register a period of degradation, and so, mirroring Wordsworth's attack on "poetic diction," Shelley laments that "in periods of the decay of social life, the drama sympathizes with that decay. . . . The period in our own history of the grossest degradation of the drama is the reign of Charles II, when all forms in which poetry had been accustomed to be expressed became hymns to the triumph of kingly power over liberty and virtue. Milton stood alone illuminating an age unworthy of him" (505). So, like Blake, Shelley understands Milton's Satan: "Nothing can exceed the energy and magnificence of the character of Satan as expressed in *Paradise Lost*. It is a mistake to suppose that he could ever have been intended for the popular personification of evil" (508). The radical Romantic side of Shelley registers in these passages, where poetry resists both aristocratic power and crass commodification—as Kir Kuiken puts it, Shelley attempted "to rethink the limits and conditions of the political with its various conceptions of the imagination" (209).

Plato and Homer, of course, both have to be wrapped into all versions of Romantic poetics since their greatness is indisputable, and it quite naturally follows, therefore, that: "Plato was essentially a poet—the truth and splendour of his imagery, and the melody of his language, are the most intense that it is possible to conceive" (Shelley 501). Only in retrospect can we see Havelock's "method of reduction," as I described it in Chapter 2, working beautifully: Shelley reduces the unpalatable conclusions Plato draws about excluding poets from the Republic by sweeping so widely that Plato himself becomes a poet in his search for truth because of the "splendour of his imagery," the very terrain of the imagination and creativity. Homer likewise falls under this spell: "Homer embodied the ideal perfection of his age in human character" (502)—a far different picture from the one we get of the formulaic, repetitive, mnemonic functions of oral poetry. Of course, my point is that we have inherited Shelley's version of the "method of reduction" so we tend to appreciate Homer and Plato in those Romanticized terms by which Shelley translated the ancients into modern vocabulary.

Indeed, in this light it can appear quite remarkable how successfully Shelley rewrites Western metaphysics for a Romantic age by deploying the Platonic metaphors almost exactly to describe the essence of poetry: "it strips the evil familiarity from the world and lays bare the naked and sleeping beauty, which is the spirit of its forms" (512). Poetry now replaces philosophy as the method to get past the world of appearances to the underlying Forms that constitute reality. What more can one say than: "Poetry is indeed something divine. It is at once the center and circumference of knowledge; it is that which comprehends all science, and that to which all science must be referred. It is at the same time the root and blossom of all other systems of thought" (511). In these terms, Western metaphysics has indeed been rewritten for the Romantic Age, and it is now possible to summarize the differences between Classical idealism and Romantic idealism in a chart, something like that in Figure 6.1.

What I have tried to visualize in the diagram is that the same overarching goal of transcending the historical world of contingency, represented by the vertical arrows on the right and left margins aiming for the universal and absolute truth, stays the same, but the binary relations between reason and emotion get modified by the Romantic idealists through a kind of 90-degree rotation. The aesthetic discourse evolving in the late eighteenth century with respect to the integration of reason and feeling, abstract and concrete, enabled them to rescript poetry from Plato's lowly banishment to the heights of enlightened idealism.

The parallels and inversions can also be listed in comparative columns:

PLATO	SHELLEY
Doctrine of inspiration—Muse arrives from outside—external—visitation of Gods—*heights*.	Muse arrives from inside—unconscious *depths*—beyond conscious control.
Poetry depends upon blind imitation and uncritical memorization—consists of clichés. Poetry prohibits transcendence.	Poetry depends upon insightful imitation, creativity, originality, and vivid recreation. Poetry is a mode of transcendence, an alternative sovereignty.
Poetry *binds* citizens to accidents of tradition, authority, the past, history, and the state. Poetry is a form of submission.	Poetry *liberates* citizens from oppression, from the "accident of surrounding impressions," from the political authority of the state, from market commodification.
Poetry is dominant and incapable of being *critical* of forms of cultural dominance. Doctrine of inspiration.	Poetry is marginalized in an oppressive culture, actualizes the forces of cultural *criticism*.

Whatever idealism we can so clearly find in Shelley, we should also remember that in terms of politics, he was one of the most consistently radical of the Romantics. He was the follower, and son-in-law, of the anarchist and political theorist, William Godwin. So his form of poetic idealism meant that, for instance, "The abolition of personal slavery is the basis of the highest political hope that it can enter into the mind of man to conceive. The freedom of women produced the poetry of sexual love" (Shelley 507). Shelley, therefore, incorporates the revolutionary fervor of radical Romanticism (cooperation, community, and empathy) with the transcendent versions of Romantic idealism (transcendence, truth, and the absolute). Poetry and the aesthetic acquire hierarchical privilege over philosophy, and their clear elevation to the pinnacle of epistemological as well as spiritual

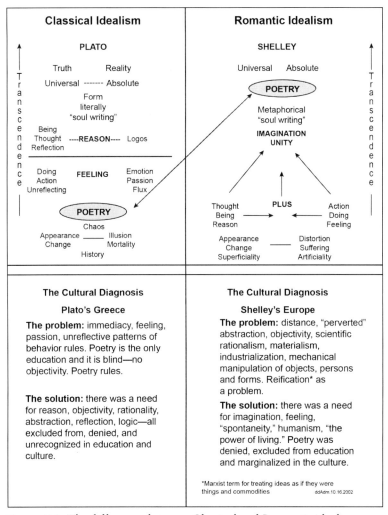

FIGURE **6.1.** *The differences between Classical and Romantic idealism.*

knowledge remains one of the distinguishing characteristics of the Romantics, which explains why, despite their enormous influence on the Romantic writers, Kant and Hegel remain Enlightenment figures: for them, philosophy retains its preeminent place in the epistemological and metaphysical hierarchies. But following Shelley we might say "if only"—if only it were the case for all of us students and faculty who inhabit English departments that

"Poets are the unacknowledged legislators of the world" (513): all we would then need is a little recognition from the rest of the world of our incredible powers. The geopolitical economy might then be transformed into our Romantic ideals for human justice. Looks as though we have a way to go on that score.

The Prelude *to the Revolution: The Limits of Literary Freedom in a Market Society*

From Opposition to Incorporation

In late September 1792, after the brutal slaughter earlier in the month of hundreds of priests, women, prisoners, Swiss guards, and aristocrats at prisons all over Paris, including in front of the Abbey of Saint-Germain-des-Prés, William Wordsworth walked across the ground that had now been cleared of "[t]he dead, upon the dying heaped" (*Prelude,* Book 10, l 57). He was horrified with the ensuing Reign of Terror, and, like many liberals, appalled that a Jacobin like Robespierre could cite liberty, virtue, opposition to war, and the end of the death penalty in one breath and in the next justify terror as a necessary act of purification in defense of revolutionary ideals.

I will return to this moment where the living poet encounters the violent deaths of the revolutionary terror. Both radical Romanticism and Romantic idealism share their opposition to the terror. Yet the political consequences and theoretical possibilities of the two strains of Romanticism veer quite sharply from each other. This chapter focuses primarily on the possibilities and limitations of Romantic idealism.

The British Romantic writers opposed both the inequalities of landed aristocracy and the cruelties of industrial capitalism, although they did not use those terms exactly. The language of opposition upon which they drew most heavily was the newly emerging discourse defining the relations between aesthetics and politics. The classical economists, beginning with Adam Smith, began to talk about political economy, labor, and capital. But in the late eighteenth century, the new terms of the bourgeois "political economy" signaled mostly the reign of private property: as Franco Moretti phrases it, "The triumph of political economy was a discourse registered in the possessive: it was *his* wheat, not yours" ("Fog" 72)—in short, if you owned valuable food in times of crisis, there was no moral obligation to share it or redistribute it, no matter what the need of others who had no wheat. Smith died in 1790, in the early stages of the French Revolution, and hardly anyone noticed, perhaps because of the turmoil of the times.[1] But he was not widely known until after 1800, so his landmark book seemed to have only marginal impact on the British poets. In Britain, the aesthetic discourse of Romantic idealism was put to work by the poets themselves to yield a new meaning for "Literature." The older sense of literature as a reference to a general "literacy" appropriate to "men of letters" shifted to those special kinds of imaginative writing ascribed to authors of unusual genius whose ability rose above the limitations of historical context. The radical Romantic version worked to resist the ruthless reductions of the commodity forms of industrial capitalism, but the idealist version aimed to be a transcendence of history and politics altogether. The problem is that what transcends politics cannot do much political work, and so the literary could easily be defanged by the conceptual force of the Western metaphysical binary.

To understand the dynamics of such political enfeeblement in some of the greatest works of English literature requires that we read against the grain of the author's intention. For that purpose, I will be juxtaposing Wordsworth's *Prelude* with Gayatri Chakravorty Spivak's theoretical rereading of that iconic poem, which Wordsworth had originally penned as "a poem to Coleridge." As a well-known postcolonial critic, Spivak in her challenging essay exemplifies the rising influence of symptomatic or depth reading in the 1980s charging many of the Romantics with idealistic evasions of history and politics. Several contemporary critics have worked to correct this overstatement by a more rigorous analysis of Wordsworth's political imagination as a phase of radical Romanticism. But Spivak's essay effectively highlights the internal tensions between aesthetics and politics, and her analysis can be a real challenge for those lovers of Wordsworth's great poem.[2] Spivak has asked us neither to doubt the noble intentions nor slight the remarkable poetic accomplishments of Wordsworth; rather, her critique points back at us: she has asked us to put aside the "unquestioning reverence" and "credulous vanity" that has shaped our discipline to the extent that literary critics after the Second World War had only too systematically cordoned off the political economy from the domain of the literary.

This opening to the social and political is the basic premise behind the shift from literary to cultural studies in the 1970s and 1980s. We can value Wordsworth not just for the formal beauty of the poems but also for the sociocultural work he performed as an interpreter of his society, even if our reading seems to go against the grain of his own conscious intentions. At the same time, as David Simpson argues: "No one works harder than Wordsworth to mount an exemplary critique of these forces taking on seemingly irresistible powers in the years around 1800 and no one registers with greater clarity the extent and depth of their capacity to remake human beings in their own image" (233). Nevertheless, like those of most educated Europeans, his own subjectivity was so deeply shaped by the discursive structures of Classical idealism that we can expect to find some troubling contradictions, especially as he turns to a more conservative political stance in his later years.[3]

Wordsworth's personal crisis in revolutionary Paris became a poetic crisis that, within the next few years, he rendered in one of the most famous poems in the English language, *The Prelude, or the Growth of the Poet's Mind*. There will be significant institutional consequences that follow from Wordsworth's (and other Romantic idealists') aesthetic theories about the function and value of poetry. For one thing, English departments could eventually claim an independent status as a discipline with a distinct body of knowledge on the basis of defining their objects as those kinds of valued writing that rose above the accidents of history. By the late nineteenth century, English departments became normalized as Literature departments, and, as a part of this ideological process, the important pedagogical task of teaching writing slipped into its familiar subordinate status as a service function where nonetheless most of the labor, if not the spiritual calling, of the profession took place. The true "calling" of our discipline would be grounded in Literature, the capital "L" signifying the select group of canonized peaks of universal value that would constitute the basic objects of our discipline, as opposed to the mass market for all kinds of "popular" literature. High and low culture became relatively distinct terrains. So we have to see tandem movements at work: the depoliticization of rhetoric by the subordination of its social function as persuasive acts to formal rules of composition and the depoliticization of literature by its elevation above the historical fray. Western metaphysics can be altered so as to aid both reductions: by digging deeper beneath the surface to find the underlying grammatical forms; and by rising higher to attain the formal unities of beauty and truth embodied in the aesthetic object, the canonized text. In each case, thick descriptions of historical context tend to slide out of view, dialectical movement comes to an end, and the universals then function as quite exclusionary, anti-universal discourses. We can find the former process at work in the emerging tradition of rhetorical theory and belles lettres in eighteenth-century Scotland, somewhat prior to the quintessential Romantic movement in nineteenth-century England. These were nearly simultaneous but reverse operations: the rise of Literature as art in the elite, highbrow cultural quarters of the discipline and the subordination of writing as craft in the labor-intensive servant's quarters of composition.

So before we look more closely at Wordsworth's exemplary Romantic text, let us first backtrack a bit into Edinburgh, Scotland, around the mid-eighteenth century, where we can pick up a crucial precedent. The institutionalized split between literature and composition that has to this day controversially structured the disciplinary habitus of our field has at least one of its roots in this very contrast between the Scottish Enlightenment rhetoricians and the English Romantic poets. In Scotland, rhetoric got sidetracked into formal principles of composition rather than the more politicized version of social persuasion; and in England, belletristic versions of good taste morphed into the more philosophically sophisticated, metaphysical version of the poetic sublime.

What Happened to Rhetoric in a Literary World?

Although Hugh Blair began his intended career as a Presbyterian minister in 1759 at the age of forty-one, he began to teach a course in the principles of composition at the University of Edinburgh. This might be the first composition course in the world, and he can be credited with highlighting the term *composition,* seldom in use before he popularized it, to refer to written works and the rules and genres about how they should be constructed (see Connors, 216). At first Blair was unpaid, but he was so popular that he ended up being appointed by George III of Scotland as the first professor of Rhetoric and Belles Lettres, a position he maintained until his retirement in 1783, when he published his most famous book, the title of which echoed his own professional position, *Lectures on Rhetoric and Belles Lettres.* Interestingly, given our consideration of copyright laws in the previous chapter, Blair felt compelled to publication because unauthorized versions of his lectures were being circulated without his permission, and he felt that such actions might threaten the authenticity of his own legacy. One might imagine, therefore, that Blair was an abrasive accumulator of literary capital, but it appears that Blair himself was a beloved, mild-mannered man whose greatest foibles seemed to be traces of vanity and pomposity. In any case, his work represents the culmination of the Scottish Enlightenment tradition with its focus on articulating the underlying principles of rhetoric and belles lettres.[4]

The belles lettres tradition emerged primarily out of Scotland during the eighteenth century, and it was intellectually grounded in the Enlightenment search for universal laws governing rhetoric, that is, language uses of all kinds. Although we think of Adam Smith more as a founder of classical economics with his 1776 publication of *The Wealth of Nations,* his earlier work on rhetoric was immensely influential. As a young man in his twenties, he left the University of Oxford, where he felt that he had been stifled for four years and ostracized from his intellectual roots, and returned to the University of Edinburgh, where, prior to Blair's arrival, Smith composed a series of lectures on rhetoric and belles lettres. These lectures were compiled by Smith's students into a text in 1762, but it was not actually published until the twentieth century; it bore the same primary title as Blair's book, *Lectures on Rhetoric and Belles Lettres.*[5] Smith established the principles of this new discourse on rhetoric that would be refined and developed especially by George Campbell in *The Philosophy of Rhetoric* (1776), and then, of course, Blair's more widely influential *Lectures* in 1783. Significantly, the man who later articulated the mathematical principles and laws of the capitalist market was also the man who first articulated the universal laws for composition and rhetoric.

All these writers drew on models of classical rhetoric, from Aristotle through Cicero and Quintilian, and they managed a particular way of rewriting Western metaphysical discourse as a search for the universal laws of good speech and good writing. Indeed, they tended not to distinguish between speech and writing, as if the principles were the same whether in an oral or a literate mode. But the situation in eighteenth-century Scotland favored their working out those predetermined laws as manifestations of good taste and good manners that presumably represent the common good. Good taste led to the appreciation of the best kind of writings and speech found in belles lettres, or those more beautiful texts that exemplified the universal laws that could, in turn, be perceived by men with refined taste—a perfect version of circular reasoning. The basic methodological principle draws on Aristotle's practice: examine the best work in a given genre (say, *Oedipus Rex*), describe its underlying formal properties of style and organization, and then generalize that particular description as a prescription for the genre itself. Dialectical process subsides in the endpoints of universal forms and genres. Belles lettres included what later will be seen as the canonical writers of poetry and drama, but the belletristic tradition was a distinctly wider category including well-written essays, histories, and philosophies of the "polite" arts. Recall, this is a time before the more specialized meaning of "Literature" had been circulated in general use. As a social conservative, Blair believed the moral virtue of fine writing could be identified through the merging of good taste and good manners since they provided the best models for improving one's lot in life. His exemplary models of such elegance were drawn from the history of classical rhetoric such as Quintilian, and, given the proper mix, the combination of virtues would lead to upward mobility through the social hierarchies. Good taste could, therefore, ensure an entry into the emerging bourgeois classes, so this version of rhetoric fit well with the rise of the market society. Like Aristotle's, Blair's entire project is prescriptive, an explication of the good rules necessary for successful composition: belles lettres were polite, cultivated, and high-minded. They had little to do with critique and resistance other than bad manners and weak grammar, and that was the basic problem for the more revolutionary-minded Romantics.

Despite their noticeable differences, the common project for Smith, Campbell, and Blair was that they all reduced the social function of rhetoric to rules that served as preexisting laws for good writing. The rules were independent of, and thus external to, the more subjective acts of composition, just as the classical economists will later develop the argument that the rules of competition for capital work more or less independently of the messy social variables of the historical moment. Drawing on a basic Aristotelian sense of fixed genre, the Scottish rhetoricians also concerned themselves with elaborate taxonomies outlining the forms that predetermine the basic characteristics of each type of writing. For instance, Blair outlined a general category, say, historical writing, and then described each of its subgenres such as history, annals, memoirs, lives, biography; on the belles lettres side, poetry was subdivided into dramatic poetry, pastoral poetry, lyric poetry, didactic poetry, epic poetry, etc. This detailed attention to proper generic form was, for example, quite the opposite of Blake's stylistic and formal experimentation because the rhetoricians had little to say about individual acts of creativity—so for the most part the British Romantic poets ignored the rhetoricians entirely. Belles lettres has, indeed, passed down to us as a category often meant to signal less serious or more trivial kinds of beautiful writing, not the profound literary masterpieces represented by the new canon of universally great talents. "Belletristic" now carries some negative connotations of being aesthetically effete, removed from the practical world of affairs. For the Romantics, belletristic had much the connotation of the poetic diction that Wordsworth and Coleridge attacked: superficial, fanciful, and sometimes entertaining, but nothing like the Romantic sublime with its discourse of transcendence. Nevertheless, back in the eighteenth century, the Scottish rhetoricians found it quite convenient to join the rules for rhetoric with the genres of belles lettres.

But it was the rhetorical side of things that ended up being most consequential. Since the British Romantics let rhetoric go its own way, its influence turned out not to evaporate but rather to materialize in the educational system. That is, as Robert Connors explains, "instruction in formal English grammar" began "in both England and America around 1750," and the instructional handbooks of the rhetoricians could be hard-boiled into the production of grammar primers to be used in schools. This institutional basis will serve as the groundwork for its own inevitable expansion so that by the end of the nineteenth century, rhetoric and grammar had moved well into the precincts of higher education as well. Matthew Arnold will proclaim that literature can replace religion as the basis for social cohesion even though in his role as school inspector he also made sure the kids got their grammar.

The high-minded Literature of the British Romantics never had much of a place in educational practice until toward the end of the nineteenth century, when it entered college curricula, although many kinds of literature had been circulating among the bourgeoisie, even if these works never made it into college classes. What smacked of the Literary had little to do with the practical tasks of mass education, learning the language and becoming literate, and so the latter, not the former, was the main mission in the uneven but increasingly wider establishment of laws for compulsory educational systems. Thus it was for all these reasons that, during the French Revolution, when the British poets turned not to Scotland but to Germany for their aesthetic theories, it was because the German philosophers offered a resolution to the split between subjective taste and universal truths through the notion of organic form. In contrast to the Scottish rhetoricians' search for universal laws of form external to any individual act of writing, "organic" signaled for the Romantics a version of formal unity that was internal to the process of artistic creation, tied to nature, and intrinsic rather than extrinsic to the "growth of the poet's imagination." The aesthetic theories worked out with great precision in Germany supplied the English Romantics the discursive tools whereby the poetic moments of beauty took over the criteria for literary excellence. In this latter process, the more general category of rhetoric inevitably got subordinated as an inferior relative, suitable for prose and other kinds of nonfiction—the less imaginative or creative kinds of writing. Rhetoric, that is, could be conveniently reduced to mundane rules, a kind of formal attention to the principles of grammar, especially since the Scottish rhetoricians had already accomplished the task of disarming rhetoric of its persuasive effects in the social and political realms. So Literature went the way of the poets and rhetoric went the way of the students: the former toward an elite group of extraordinary individuals; the latter toward the masses learning to read.[6] Those of us who identify ourselves in social settings as English teachers still do so with the risk of having someone say, "So I'd better watch my grammar." A lot of people still know what we're good for.

However, Enlightenment rhetorical theory had its limits even though those very limits served it well in the educational marketplace. Six years after the publication of Blair's *Lectures,* the French Revolution began with the storming of the Bastille, and the political climate in Europe changed dramatically. Blair's polite version of belles lettres just would not serve the more revolutionary-minded British Romantics. By August of 1789, when the first "Declaration of the Rights of Man and of the Citizen" was proposed by the Marquis de Lafayette, and adopted by the National Constituent Assembly in France, no discourse of manners was likely to be very helpful for the revolutionary forces. It is true that even though it spoke of citizens as "all men without exception," it still did not include women or explicitly address slavery. So even universal declarations can be deeply at odds with their own nonuniversal hierarchies, sometimes in what can only be seen as a cruel irony. As Frederick Douglass articulated in his famous 1852 speech, "What to the Slave Is the Fourth of July?" "All men are created equal" is not so universally fine if the subtext is except women, slaves, and other non-Caucasians. The poets espoused the revolutionary ideals of political as well as poetic liberty. But we should see how the plans for transcending the political got worked out in a poem that addresses one of the major political events of its age.

Reframing Aesthetics and Politics in *The Prelude*

What, after all, could be more revolutionary than a long poem whose central historical event is the French Revolution? As an exemplary Romantic poem, one of the most famous ever written, Wordsworth's *The Prelude, or the Growth of a Poet's Imagination* theorizes what it means to become the kind of poet Wordsworth became. At the heart of that poetic transformation is the key historical event of the age: the French Revolution. Imagination and politics seem to be joined in the verse, if not at the hip.

This palimpsest effect of textual layering is no more apparent than in Gayatri Spivak's complex analysis of the poem. Spivak's most notable methodological principle involves tracing some of the sociohistorical contexts that remain otherwise buried beneath the heavily revised 1850 version of this canonized text. She locates in key passages the traces of a history that has been lost, often from sheer lack of contradictory evidence, but sometimes with skillful avoidance of a troubling past.

Recall from previous chapters that a recurring methodological procedure has been the recovering of lost traces such as investigating the shift from oral to literate culture in order to reframe the meaning of Plato's term *poet*. Recall also Derrida's method of etymological tracing through the recovery of the double meanings of the pharmakon as both remedy and poison, and the significance of that double meaning as evidence for Plato's ambivalence about writing in the *Phaedrus*. Likewise, Spivak refuses to restrict herself to the embodiment of canonized intention, as if the authority of the final edition should in no way suppress consideration of earlier versions. She therefore compares the earlier 1805 edition with the final 1850 edition, searching for traces of ideas and materials that were edited out of the final version, as well as continuities between them.[7] Of course, these extended traces can get pretty complex through a linking of Wordsworth's personal psychological history, including his affair with Annette Vallon, his intimate relationship with his sister, Dorothy, and the early deaths of his parents and two of his own children; the sociohistorical context of late eighteenth century France and England; the economic history of industrial capital; the political history of the French

Revolution; and the textual history of Wordsworth's own revisions to the *Prelude* over a course of forty-five years. The point is that all of these discourses leave traces, but you have to look very carefully because they are not always self-evident.

Spivak's counterreading of the *Prelude* shows that in the process of revision Wordsworth actually edited out of the 1805 text many of the details regarding his love affair with Vallon and his daughter, Caroline, who was born in 1792. In the process of eliminating these personal complications he was able to achieve in the 1850 edition a more perfectly formal, poetic unity since uneven historical contingencies could no longer interfere in the imaginative transcendence of poetic form. But more important, and following the same pattern, Spivak argues that Wordsworth's Romantic idealism also reduced the recognition of class struggle and gender relations in the production of poetry. In other words, as he ages, Romantic idealism suppresses radical Romanticism. This all sounds very doctrinaire, but we can get a better sense of the depth of close reading required to arrive at these conclusions by focusing on a couple of specific examples.

The key issues can be framed in terms of the tensions between aesthetics and politics. On the very first page, Spivak herself offers concise statements of her three main theses, and the second and third points are not difficult to comprehend:[8] first, that Wordsworth "coped with the experience of the French Revolution by transforming it into an iconic text that he could write and read"; and, second, that Wordsworth "suggested that poetry was a better cure for the oppression of mankind than political economy or revolution and that his own life had the preordained purpose of teaching mankind this lesson" (*In Other Worlds* 46). This powerful poetic rendering of Romantic idealism demonstrates how the sublime objects of literary imagination triumph over both rhetoric and politics, preparing the grounds for the subsequent disciplinary divide characteristic of the history of English studies. But let's now turn to just one specific example and trace out the consequences of the comparative methodology.

As Spivak points out, the language of the 1805 edition sometimes more fully dramatizes the idealistic presumptions of the poem, but with a significantly more radical bent than in the final version. One passage from Book 12 serves as an illuminating example. Not long after Wordsworth refers to "[t]he wealth of Nations" as a false idol to worship, he asks a rhetorical question: "Our animal wants and the necessities / Which they impose, are these the obstacles?" Wordsworth rhetorically assumes that the answer is no, but even so he answers his own question: "If not, then others vanish into air." In short, the material world of needs vanishes since it can be transcended by a new poetics of the imagination. But we could resist this presumed affirmation by reading against the grain, and answer, that, yes, indeed, the "animal wants and needs" of us humans are considerable obstacles to transcendence: in conditions of poverty and deprivation, the world may not always look so beautiful as when you are well-fed and well-clothed. Such a counterreading leads to a much different theory of the dialectical relations between aesthetics and politics. That is, as Spivak puts it, by the end of this poem the claim is that the "social relations of production cannot touch the inner resources of man. The corollary: revolutionary politics, seeking to change those social relations, are therefore superfluous; poetry, disclosing man's inner resources, is the only way" (*In Other Worlds* 96). In short, "Wordsworth offers his own poetry as a cure for human oppression and suffering because it teaches one where to look for human value" (70). Wordsworth revised this line for the 1850 edition so the final version reads: "Our animal appetites and daily wants, / Are these obstructions insurmountable?" (Book 13, lines 91–92). What seems noticeable in the revised version is a muting of the material claims of the body: "necessities" become "appetites" and "wants" (as opposed to pressing needs); the power of the verb, "impose," has been eliminated; "obstacles" have become mere "obstructions" that are clearly not "insurmountable." Later in his life, by 1850, the more politically conservative Wordsworth edited his more youthful expression of imposing needs to better fit the idealist discourse of poetry.

Returning to the French Revolution as the setting for the poem itself, Wordsworth offers a pretty clear interpretation of what went wrong. Basically, his analysis is very much like that offered by many of the Jacobins with whom he felt allied. The revolution failed because its leaders betrayed the ideals of freedom and liberty, and he witnessed that betrayal in person when he walked across the ground that had only shortly before he arrived been cleared of "[t]he dead, upon the dying heaped" (Book 10, line 57). This moment of recognition of violent betrayal of ideals became a poignant moment in the *Prelude* itself, as well as a turning point in Wordsworth's own life, a turning to poetry and, to some degree, a turning away from the terrifying historical realities of betrayal and violence (and from France, leaving his lover, Annette, and his daughter, Caroline, behind). Wordsworth's answer to these betrayals of ideals when terror could be called a virtue was to create his own poetic ideas as a turn away from the material history of the revolution to the more subjective theory of value which climaxes with the triumph of the poet's imagination, not with political revolution. This is not a necessary transition: it could be that the immanent powers of art and literature could fully resonate with the political realities and the geopolitical economy, as they often do, but not in this instance, in one of the most celebrated poems in the English canon.

Since Spivak has drawn on Marx's critique of class struggle in her reading of Wordsworth, we can directly turn to this writer, whom we will consider at greater length in Chapters 8 and 9. In the context of the French Revolution, Marx offers a remarkably contrastive interpretation of this crucial event. And here's the problem: Wordsworth and Marx offer opposing views, and you can't simply assimilate them in some easy kind of pluralism. That is, whereas Wordsworth believed that the ideals of liberty and democracy were betrayed by the leaders of the revolution because they failed to live up to those ideals, Marx counters that it was never a question of betrayal. For evidence, we can turn to Marx's ironically titled polemic of 1845, *The Holy Family*, where he succinctly reevaluates the political consequences of the French Revolution. As he puts it, "the interest of the bourgeoisie . . . far from having been a 'failure,' 'won' everything and had 'effective success,' however much the 'pathos' of it evaporated and the 'enthusiastic' flower with which that interest adorned its cradle faded. . . . The Revolution was a 'failure' only for the masses which did not find in the political 'idea' the idea of its real 'interest,' whose real life-principle did not therefore coincide with the life-principle of the Revolution" (McLellan 155). Of course, this is a basic practical lesson in materialist history: whose interests are really being represented by which specific historical actors in any given event?[9] Those hierarchies will not disappear except through the fog of an illusory idealism. Without the idealist blinders, we can better see that violence and terror are not just misguided betrayals of the true ideals championed by the leaders of the new political economy but collateral consequences of the capitalist world-system's need for endless accumulation of land, resources, and profit through the expropriation of surplus labor magnified by the slave trade.

Now, in the final two sections of this chapter, I will contrast two kinds of interpretive framing. First, I will proceed by framing my analysis in terms of Wordsworth's influential version of Romantic idealism, trying to read key passages in their own terms as faithfully as I can rather than deliberately against the grain of the author's stated intentions. And, second, in the final section I will offer a brief reading of the political economy that led up to the French Revolution, paying particular attention to the economic theories of the infamous John Law, whose financial speculations sent France into economic insolvency for the entire seventy years preceding the revolution. In other words, I will first attempt a close reading of select passages based on the literary aesthetics of Romantic idealism before we turn to a radical Romantic reading of the geopolitical economy that shaped the sociohistorical context, a contrast that mirrors the professional shift from literary to cultural studies.

The point in the contrast of these two interpretive frames is that Wordsworth's aesthetic theory and Law's economic theory seem to have nothing to say to each other. That's the point: both the aesthetic theory and the economic theory are dissociated from the lives of most people because the theories work only within isolated, compartmentalized domains of the aesthetic and the economic. It is as if such domains do not in principle touch each other, art and the market forever sundered; as if they could both be disentangled from the social and political contingencies of the world, and, eventually, disciplined into separate departments as they are in the modern university, where practitioners of the two fields rarely speak to each other. What joins the two sections is that Wordsworth's disentanglement of individual aesthetic principles from political action resembles in certain uncanny ways Law's disentanglement of economic principles based on individual power from the social values of cooperative human relations and interdependencies. These brief case studies will, I hope, serve as paradigmatic instances of the highly significant disciplinary divisions that became institutionalized later in the nineteenth century: literature became a separate discipline from history and political science, just as economics also became independent of history and political science. As we will see in the epilogue, the mid-twentieth-century New Critics fulfilled these departmental ambitions by developing this version of Romantic idealism into a triumph of disciplinary autonomy based on the aesthetic autonomy of the literary object. Strikingly, Wordsworth's idealism may be a clear antecedent to the New Critics' aesthetic formalism whose residues persist in our profession; and Law's "system" echoes exactly the premises of neoliberal theory in the contemporary moment. Although Law operated during the final stages of mercantilism (the sixteenth to eighteenth centuries, when merchants rather than industrialists [or financiers] ruled the economic system), the basic principles for financial speculation remain hauntingly familiar in our age of leveraged buyouts. Neither Law nor neoliberalism has a great deal to say about the exploitation of labor, the maldistribution of the surplus, the degradation of the environment, and the hierarchical, noncommunal organization of production.

The important lesson is that aesthetics, politics, and economics may indeed call for discretely different kinds of investigations, but these discourses are all produced in deeply enmeshed sociohistorical contexts. To that extent, their interdependencies should be evident, insofar as the aesthetic theories should speak to the social, political, and economic theories, and vice versa.

Plato in the *Prelude*

What happens when we try to close-read the poem in its own aesthetic terms, to read "with the grain," more sympathetic to Wordsworth's intentions as embodied in the formal unity of the poem? Wordsworth's grain turns out to be mostly in line with Western metaphysics and especially Plato, mainly because their ideals resonate with each other. As we saw in Chapter 6, Wordsworth rewrote Plato's version of Western metaphysics into the poetics of Romantic idealism. Whereas Aristotle was much more congenial for the Scottish rhetoricians, Plato's more figurative language proved far more compelling for Wordsworth, as it did for Shelley. And Plato (or at least Platonism) is, for all practical purposes, in the text in a lot of ways in a lot of places. For the sake of convenience, I will refer only to Books 9–14 of the 1850 edition of *The Prelude,* but those culminating sections highlight the key issues.

Book 9 actually exemplifies the political ideals Wordsworth emulates where he can imagine "a Republic, where all stood thus far / Upon equal ground; that we were brothers all / In honour, as in one community" (lines 226–28). Here, he clearly champions communality over hierarchy, resonating well with the strains of radical Romanticism. In this republic "wealth and titles were in less esteem / Than talents, worth and prosperous industry" (lines 231–32). This meritocracy of value would be governed by "equal rights / And individual worth" (lines 242–43). To have such equality, you would have to end poverty, and Wordsworth makes it clear that the government would have a role in ensuring such "equal rights." He is quite explicit that they are fighting so "that poverty / Abject as this would in a little time / Be found no more" (lines 520–22). And that there would be an institutional and legal basis for the new government, "that we should see . . . " (line 524)

> All institutes for ever blotted out
> That legalized exclusion, empty pomp
> Abolished, sensual state and cruel power . . .
> Should see the people having a strong hand
> In framing their own laws . . . (Book 9, lines 526–31)

Indeed, we see in the above passage the most democratic principle of all the lines in the *Prelude*—that the people should have "a strong hand / In framing their own laws." Those are the radical Romantic strains of the poem, reflecting exactly Simpson's assessment that Wordsworth demonstrates "a poetry of concern, comfortable neither in the rhetoric of subjectivism nor in an assumption of objectivity; it is permanently engaged in an encounter with the world wherein either kind of resolution is proven inept and insufficient" (141). The dialectical process is alive in radical Romanticism. Wordsworth here joins his poetic ideals with his political hopes, but, unfortunately, this communality is at the level of formal political enfranchisement, without explicit reference to the economic organization of production whereby the capitalists still seem to have their antidemocratic decision-making powers left untouched. Nevertheless, Wordsworth's sense of betrayal and disappointment regarding his own democratic ideals reaches a peak when he returns to Paris shortly after the September massacres, an experience he represents in Book 10, when he saw

> The dead, upon the dying heaped, and gazed
> On this and other spots, as doth a man
> Upon a volume whose contents he knows
> Are memorable, but from him locked up,
> Being written in a tongue he cannot read,
> So that he questions the mute leaves with pain,
> And half upbraids their silence. (Book 10, lines 57–64)

Clearly, Wordsworth admits to having some difficulty interpreting the depth of this betrayal since the events are so heinous as to be "written in a tongue he cannot read."[10] He hopes, however, "that there was, / Transcendent to all local patrimony, / One nature, as there is one sun in heaven" (book 10, lines 155–57). The suffering is so unimaginably great that Wordsworth yearns for a universal oneness with Nature to heal these wounds, and even, a bit later, in Book 11, suggests that "wild theories were afloat," that the ideals of liberty were exchanged for conquest, or, as he puts it, "Frenchmen had changed a war of self-defence / For one of conquest, losing sight of all / Which they had struggled for" (lines 207–09). Unlike Marx, however, Wordsworth believes that the Third Estate, whether peasants, sans-culottes, or bourgeois, were all still fighting for the same ideals of liberty, with shared interests. Those shared interests were based not on class affiliations but on a deeper political premise regarding individualism, and, ultimately, "self-interest": the revolution aimed to "[b]uild social upon personal Liberty" (line 240), but it had betrayed that principle for the merely individual. The individual comes first in these equations, even though the goal is universal transcendence. Given his frustration with these political betrayals, Wordsworth begins to turn from the political situation toward the answer in the poetic imagination. From the end of Book 11, through the remainder of the poem, Wordsworth's belief that the leaders of the French Revolution betrayed their earlier ideals leads the poet away from the historical event itself: the actual political revolution slides out of sight as the philosophical and poetic moments in the growth of the poet's imagination now come more into focus. That focus unfolds in language almost directly out of Plato's dialectic between reality and appearance. The world of appearances has veiled the underlying reality from our eyes. As Wordsworth puts it, "A veil has been / Uplifted; why deceive ourselves?" (lines 266–67). Science, but not politics, can aid this task of unveiling because once "abstract science" and "the reasoning faculty" have been "enthroned," "the disturbances of space and time . . . find no admission" (lines 328–30). That was Plato's point: reason can get us beyond the circumstantial disturbances of our historical lives in space and time.

In Book 12, Wordsworth explains that the mind can be "perverted" when, "even the visible Universe / Fell under the dominion of a taste / Less spiritual" (lines 88–91), when the senses gain control of the mind. The metaphysical dualism between mind and body is exactly the theoretical reference point, and the problem arises when the senses become despotic:

> A twofold frame of body and of mind.
> I speak in recollection of a time
> When the bodily eye, in every stage of life
> The most despotic of our senses, gained
> Such strength in *me* as often held my mind
> In absolute dominion. (lines126–31)

These are perfectly Platonic, binary formulations such as we saw in the "Allegory of the Cave," with the corrective to the misleading visual sense coming from the more powerful intellectual process of metaphorically "seeing" the invisible truth. The mind must become "lord and master" so that "outward sense" becomes "[t]he obedient servant of her will" (lines 222–23). Wordsworth honors Plato's hero, the philosopher of "right reason," but, as in Shelley, the hero's path out of the cave will come from the "pure imagination" of poetry (lines 414–15). Despite all the obstructions,

Wordsworth never gives up hope that poetry can overcome any "bars" that "are thrown / By Nature in the way of such a hope" for transcendence of our physical condition. Then follows the lines Spivak refuses to affirm even though Wordsworth must have felt confident that his readers would of course agree with him: "Our animal appetites and daily wants, / Are these obstructions insurmountable?" (lines 89–92). The argument of the poem here makes the rhetorical affirmation, that, no, the body, history, and politics cannot stand in the way of our divine quest for Nature.

Wordsworth now frames his own plan for poetic transcendence within the very problematic Plato addressed in the *Phaedrus:*

> Speaking no dream, but things oracular;
> Matter not lightly to be heard by those
> Who to the letter of the outward promise
> Do read the invisible soul. (lines 253–56)

Recall that in the *Phaedrus,* Socrates placed the most value on "the living, animate discourse of a man who really knows" (Plato, *Phaedrus* 70), "inscribed with genuine knowledge in the soul." Wordsworth has, in effect, rewritten Plato so that poetry (rather than philosophy) becomes the exemplary vehicle for awakening the "arche soul" or "over-soul," which attains to universal knowledge when "life's every-day appearances" dissolve and we "gain clear sight / Of a new world . . . / Made visible; as ruled by those fixed laws / Whence spiritual dignity originates" (book 12, lines 366–78). Like Plato's ideal forms "those fixed laws" resonate with the universal:

> In one continuous stream; a mind sustained
> By recognitions of transcendent power,
> In sense conducting to ideal form,
> In soul of more than mortal privilege. (lines 74–77)

As the *Prelude* reaches its climactic moments of synthesis in Book 14, we find reason wedded to feeling (as we saw in Shelley), what Wordsworth calls "the height of feeling intellect" (book 14, line 226). "Reason in her most exalted mood" (line 192) will be united with the "absolute Power" of poetry: "This spiritual Love acts not nor can exist / Without Imagination, which, in truth, / Is but another name for absolute Power" (lines 188–90). For this organic synthesis to take place, it will require a female tenderness when the poet's heart

> Be tender as a nursing mother's heart;
> Of female softness shall his life be full,
> Of humble cares and delicate desires. (line 431)

The mediation of the woman as synthetic effect, enabler of "man's" transcendence in the beauty of poetry, calls for the arrival of Dorothy, "Child of my parents! Sister of my soul!" (431). And the synthesis succeeds: "And now, O Friend! This history is brought / To its appointed close: the discipline / And consummation of a Poet's mind" (lines 302–04). When transcendence is achieved through consummation and coalescence, the poem can conclude with the word *divine,* a divine registered in those poetic moments of sublime beauty when

> . . . the mind of man becomes
> A thousand times more beautiful than the earth
> On which he dwells, above this frame of things. . . . (lines 448–54)

Just as Plato's forms rose above the mundane, everyday world of beds and battles, the *Prelude* ends in the divine fabric, "above this frame of things," that is, above the visible, material world. The quintessential Romantic idealist leaves the everyday world of social contexts far behind.

Having reached this point of poetic transcendence, in the next section we leave the poetics of the French Revolution far behind and come back down to earth through a brief investigation into a few of the key financial crises in capitalism that precipitated the revolution. As we will see, however, economic theories can also be framed outside of the social context in which they operate, although the consequences of Law's severing of economic theory from all other social values except the abstract rules of finance had devastating material consequences. Given the commitment of its poetics, the *Prelude* does not always point us toward this history, although there is no inherent reason that such a long poem could not, in principle, open a view to exactly these dimensions of social and economic history, as radical Romantics (including Wordsworth himself, in other places, other texts) would insist. In other words, now that we have given some attention to the lines of Wordsworth's poem, let's go the other way: let the text fade and the geopolitical economy come more into focus.

Of Bubbles and Busts: On the Revolution in Financial Speculation

On August 20, 1786, Louis XVI's finance minister, Charles Alexandre de Calonne, informed the King and the Assembly of Notables that the kingdom was insolvent. The royal treasury was broke. France's contribution to the U.S. cause in the War of Independence from Great Britain had left the country 113 million livres in debt. Calonne bypassed any democratic appearance of appealing to the courts and parliaments by secretly going directly to the King and the Assembly of Notables. He offered a plan: levy new taxes on landowners that would sweep away their aristocratic protections from the market economy, institute new free-trade laws, and cut government spending. Of course, Calonne's plan offended the Notables as a direct attack on their hierarchical privileges and exemption from land taxes, so they outright refused to consider such a threat. This bad judgment on Calonne's part, and the ensuing crisis, led to Calonne's being fired by the King and having to flee for safety to England.

Calonne had a reputation as an unscrupulous political opportunist, but his plan was really an effort to bring bourgeois capitalist principles to an aristocratic state capitalism. If his solutions echo with recent tensions between neoliberal plans for free trade and austerity (versus more progressive plans to raise taxes on the wealthy), all the while funding huge military ventures overseas, those echoes are worth hearing. In the end, Calonne's plan under the king failed in part because it could satisfy neither the landed gentry nor those clamoring for free markets, but mainly because as it turned out the king was powerless to enforce the new taxation laws even if they had been instituted. He was a controversial figure, and some hold Calonne personally accountable for the financial crisis leading to the revolution. But as others (for example Munro Price) have argued, this is unfair, because the entire project of an absolute monarchy attempting to manage fiscal policy on its own terms without public scrutiny or accountability was broadly seen as a form of corruption. Over the preceding century, the hereditary and authoritarian principles for perpetuating political power had been thoroughly tethered to the emerging capitalist world-system so the forces were larger than any individual human being, including the king himself. It is entirely plausible that Louis XVI may have genuinely tried to aid his suffering population with the hope he invested in Calonne's supposedly more enlightened policy changes. When they were crushed, legend has it that the king got pretty depressed, spent a lot of his time hunting and eating huge meals, and generally tried to escape the impending doom that came a few years later, in 1793, when he was beheaded.

Fiscal policy was in a shambles in France in the years preceding the revolution, and many of the protests were coming from what was called the Third Estate. Now, historically speaking, the term *Third Estate* referred to a huge group of just about everyone (97 percent at the time) who was neither noble nor clergy, consisting mostly of the commoners and since the Middle Ages including local businesses such as printing houses as well as peasants, farm laborers, and then factory workers. So this segment would appear to represent the interests of Wordsworth's "rustic" or commoner. In Paris, however, there were no peasants, so the Third Estate would have been composed primarily of the sans-culottes (those "without breeches," or those who wore long pants, in contrast to the more aristocratic knee breeches), or that mix of urban laborers, small businessmen, plus the more republican Jacobins, and other bourgeois rather than proletarian leaders. Although committed to democratic reforms, the Jacobin Club was initially formed out of deputies of the Estates General, and so many of them were lawyers, statesmen, and businessmen and consequently much closer to emerging bourgeois classes than to peasants or workers. Statistically speaking, only 8 percent of the Third Estate in France at the time of the revolution could have been categorized as bourgeois, or owners of capital, since most of the commoners had little or no money. But in terms of influence and power, this statistic can be misleading. The French

Revolution has been generally characterized as the revolt of the Third Estate against the First Estate (the declining powers of the clergy), but most notably against the Second Estate (the nobility, the kingdom of inherited wealth, and landed aristocracy).[11] In his famous January 1789 pamphlet, "What Is the Third Estate?" the Abbé Emmanuel Joseph Sieyès argued that it was the common people of France, and by far the largest segment of the French population. But as it turns out, the 8 percent minority of the Third Estate were really the ones in control of much of the politics of the revolutionary machinery, the ones who controlled the flow of debt and labor.

They were the Jacobins, the Girondists, and other bourgeois factions, not the sans-culottes, nor the rural peasants. Even so, as we will see in Chapter 9, the Jacobin leadership of the short-lived Paris Commune did include the sans-culottes, and their political program tried to institute universal suffrage, the end of the nobility's exemption from property taxes, and, most important, commitments *against* the free market. This latter feature, however, was completely lost by the time Maximilien Robespierre took over power of the Committee of Public Safety in July, 1793, and the Reign of Terror began later that year. This exactly confirms Marx's point that the actual interests of the revolution were orchestrated not by the commoners, or by communality as a general principle, but by the 8 percent of the Third Estate that could be characterized as owners of capital. As Marx points out, this class division internal to the Third Estate, between owners and workers/peasants, became crucial to the dynamics of the revolution: the "failure" of the ideas of liberty upon the collapse of the First Republic in 1795 and the subsequent rise of the Directorship and Napoleon were hardly a failure at all for the owners of capital, since Napoleon (who was himself originally a Jacobin) went on to liberalize trade and grant privilege to the emerging mercantile bourgeoisie. Just as neoliberal capitalism has depended much more on centralized control of production than on democratic decision making, industrial capitalism favored centralized, hierarchical power rather than circulating, horizontal, or distributed power.

Reframed within the emerging market society, the French Revolution has its roots deeply connected to one of the most outrageous bubbles and busts in the history of capitalism. It was not as if France's national debt suddenly went overboard in the 1780s, since the biggest crisis had to do with a fateful financial speculation seventy years earlier. After all, it was in 1719 that the word *millionaire* was coined in France, at a time when the country seems to have gone wild with financial euphoria over a plan for financial resuscitation offered by the Scotsman mentioned earlier, John Law. Anyone who thinks that finance capitalism began in the 1900s should attend to Law's speculative ventures and their aftermath. Niall Ferguson refers to Law as "[a]n ambitious Scot, a convicted murderer, a compulsive gambler and a flawed financial genius" (126). He was surely all of those things and more, but Law's System, as it was called, brought modern market economy to the struggling nation. Although supposedly based on "liberal" economic laws of the marketplace that made the adventures of capital available to a much wider spectrum of wealthy landowners, Law's System depended on an enormously authoritarian absolute monarchy, and on the power of an elite to set stock prices in the Mississippi Company. Law's System was dissociated from the real-life experiences of most people the theory might affect. As in the twenty-first century, the theories of financial speculation produced exactly what was intended: sudden, immense wealth. But they also produced exactly what was not intended: equally shocking falls from power once the schemes were exposed.

Before we even get to the gist of Law's story, we need a brief sketch of the emerging dynamics of the global economy of nation-states beginning with the formation of the first joint-stock corporation, the Dutch East India Company, chartered in 1602. In its early years there was a kind of executive board, the Seventeen Lords, who set the price for the certificates of stock. The company was not very profitable in its first decade, and it proved impossible for the corporation to liquidate the stock certificates, so the only possibility for investors to get their cash back was to sell their shares, and thus a secondary market, the first stock market, the Beurs, was established in 1608. And it appears that much like the modern trading floors, the Beurs was a place where "The anxious speculator 'chews his nails, pulls his fingers, closes his eyes, takes four paces and four times talks to himself, raises his hand to his cheeks as if he has a toothache and all this accompanied by a mysterious coughing'" (quoted in Ferguson 132). Financial speculation over ratios of credit and debt then, as it does now, produced enormously hierarchical social relations: security for a small percentage of people at the very top; for the rest, worry and insecurity. But a third basic component of the emerging market economy was necessary, and so in 1609 the Amsterdam Exchange Bank was established in order to set monetary policy by setting credit requirements and lending for the purpose of investment (Ferguson 131–37). In short, the origins of a triangulated market society were based on contractual regulations established by a small coterie of wealthy individuals who gained control of the relations among market goods, market speculation, and credit financing. World-systems analysts have documented how the Dutch took over the hegemony of the emerging capitalist world system from the Iberian/Spanish dominance of the sixteenth century.

The tie between colonial empire and the emerging market economy now organized around endless capital accumulation fueled by equally endless global resources can be pretty clearly documented early on in the Dutch East India Company's ruthless battles with their main competitor, the British East India Company. While both Dutch and British companies strove to plunder the resources of the "East," they also recognized, in the words of the Dutch commander of the East Indian fleet, Jan Pieterszoon Coen, words that resonate hauntingly with twenty-first-century neocolonial ventures: "We cannot make war without trade, nor trade without war" (quoted in Ferguson 134). Coffee, spices, and timber for the wealthy (not yet coal) were the resources to fight over. Coen went so far as to execute British company officials and virtually destroyed the indigenous Bandanese, before declaring himself the first governor-general of the Dutch Empire in Jakarta. Coen's ascension to power in the East Indies took place about twenty years before the remarkable terms set in 1648 at the Peace of Westphalia, terms that established the sovereign integrity of the modern nation-states and facilitated the rights of nations to monopolize trading markets, or at least facilitated the battles for such supremacy between the Dutch and the British. Global markets and national sovereignties thus came into being at roughly the same time, as coextensive forces coordinating the colonial control of the world's resources. Between its founding in 1602 and 1733, shares in the Dutch East India Company rose from 100 to 786 (Ferguson 136), but it was not a bubble since the growth took place over more than a century. The collapse of the Dutch empire happened with the collapse of the Dutch companies' stock when the British finally gained superiority, but that did not take place until the middle of the French Revolution, in 1794, by which time the stock had fallen back to 120. As Ferguson explains, "This rise and fall closely tracked the rise and fall of the Dutch Empire" (136).[12]

Now this historical sketch sets the stage for John Law's new economic theories, especially since he seemed to offer France a chance to compete with the more powerful British Empire. Basically, his scheme was based on the use of paper money in place of gold coins for currency. Confidence was all you needed, according to Law, and then banknotes would do all the work of precious stones, gold and diamond, a kind of ultimate disembedding of economic theory from material labor and from any social values other than financial profit; the whole event prefigures the contemporary fiascos based on financial derivatives. As Law himself was supposed to have told a friend, "I have discovered the secret of the philosopher's stone . . . it is to make gold out of paper" (Ferguson 138)—the ultimate financier's dream. A Scotsman, Law tried to get the Scottish Parliament to institute his proposal for a new, centralized bank modeled after the 1694 formation of the Bank of England, which they refused, but by 1708 he had taken his scheme to France, a country that had been bankrupted several times over the previous century, and at that time was deeply in debt as a result of Louis XIV's many costly wars of aggression. Law appeared to have the solution, even though the French knew that Law was a professional gambler. By 1716, Law had established the Banque Generale under his direction, but it was a grander scheme yet that he worked out with the Duke of Orleans who served as Regent of France between 1715 and 1723.

"Law's System," as it came to be called, was a theory based on inflating royal credit through a privatization scheme of offering stock on France's imperial ventures in the Mississippi Delta. The Louisiana Territory was a huge tract of land in the New World, roughly equivalent to a third of the landmass of what is now continental United States. Law established in 1717 a new Company of the West (Compagnie d'Occident) and granted monopoly rights to commerce in Louisiana, and shares of the company were offered at 500 livres. The city of New Orleans was named as one way to flatter the French Regent, which makes sense since Law's System was based on rigid hierarchy and absolute sovereignty. As he articulated his theory: "I maintain . . . that an absolute prince who knows how to govern can extend his credit further and find needed funds at a lower interest rate than a prince who is limited in his authority. . . . supreme power must reside in only one person" (quoted in Ferguson 140). That the cycles of capital accumulation and debt escalation, whether led by Dutch, British, or the latest U.S. hegemony, have favored dictators in other parts of the world in order to maintain stability sufficient for a market economy should come as no surprise given what we have seen in recent years. As David Harvey has argued, monopoly controls are not simply an unfortunate aberration in the truly beneficent balancing act of free market competition: the dialectical unity between monopoly and competition are at the core of the capitalist system (*Seventeen*, ch. 10). Law clearly understood the need for such "supreme powers" for France also, and by May 1719 the Company of the West had extended its monopoly, taking over the East India and China Companies to become the Company of the Indies, generally known as the Mississippi Company. The point is that the growth of the "free" market required very unfree forms of centralized authority, a point mirrored in the ironies of recent neoliberal economists: deregulation actually requires a great deal of regulation in the form of restrictions on collective bargaining at home and regulations of the international financial institutions that favor investors over borrowing nations and peoples.

Law's plan was one of the first great efforts at privatization, the conversion of public debt to a privatized equity system, a kind of grand stimulus package. And at first it succeeded in creating a bubble of assets, wildly exceeding any expectations. From an initial opening price of 500 livres in 1717, shares in the Mississippi Company reached an astronomical spike of 10,025 on December 2, 1719. French euphoria turned to mania, and Voltaire asked, "Have you all gone crazy in Paris?" while in London Daniel

Defoe dismissed the French frenzy as if they had "run up a piece of refined air" (quoted in Ferguson 145). Basically, Law had convinced many French people that Louisiana was a "veritable Garden of Eden, inhabited by friendly savages, eager to furnish a cornucopia of exotic goods for shipment to France" (Ferguson 144). The reality, of course, was otherwise: "Louisiana was a sweltering, insect-infested swamp. Within a year 80 percent [of the colonists] had died of starvation or tropical diseases" (145). But too many of the wealthy ruling-class property owners of France were convinced by Law's scheme, invested fortunes in hopes of greater fortunes, and went bust. The whole point of this particular story is that it serves as a representation *not* of an aberration of capitalism by a few ruthless individuals, but rather the essence of the capitalist system, based on monopoly control of limited competition in order to carry out debt-financed speculative ventures that have always produced more returns for the wealthy few than economic growth in the production of material goods and jobs serving the needs of the many.

In 1720, Law even converted to Catholicism, partly to demonstrate his appreciation for the French, but little good that would do. By December, the bust that followed the bubble had reduced share prices of the Mississippi Company to 1,000 livres. Panic set in; people now felt they owned worthless paper. Law was suddenly vilified, his pie-in-the-sky scheme exposed, and he was forced to flee the country to save his life. As Ferguson explains, "A series of humorously allegorical engravings were produced and published as *The Great Scene of Folly,* which depicted bare-arsed stockbrokers eating coin and excreting Mississippi stock; demented investors running amok in the rue Quincampoix, before being hauled off to the madhouse; and Law himself, blithely passing by castles in the air in a carriage pulled by two bedraggled Gallic cockerels" (153).

Now, the point of this story is that the resulting collapse of the French economy had repercussions throughout Europe, but France in particular was so devastated that it destroyed France's economic development and modernization for all the subsequent generations leading up to the French Revolution. Both Louis XV and Louis XVI struggled repeatedly with financial chaos, reeling from one impotent reform to the next, "until royal bankruptcy finally precipitated revolution" (Ferguson 154). Again, this is a model of capitalist financial ventures (even though then authorized by the failing aristocracy). It was certainly a prescient though unheeded warning that the failures of the emerging market economy were not just a case of a few rotten apples spoiling the otherwise benevolent basket of capitalist goods.

These are some of the conditions that made the geopolitical economy the fuel for the revolutionary fervor, not just a philosophical belief in the ideals of liberty shared by all members of the Third Estate, as Wordsworth suggests. These preceding events make it clear why, in 1786, Calonne could bring to the nearly bankrupt French royalty his duel scheme of taxation for the aristocrats and free trade laws for the bourgeoisie, as a reasonable-sounding plan for stimulating the markets. Calonne was also chased out of town, however, even if a bit less vituperatively than Law. A few years later the full force of the revolution would be unleashed, and in the end the bourgeoisie got both taxation for the nobles and more free-trade laws. The workers and peasants and paupers still suffered unremittingly poor living conditions.

The only kind of poetics that might resonate with these conditions would necessarily have to relate to the political economy as a form of active engagement with and against it, not a retreat to Romantic idealism. There is no inherent reason that a long poem addressing the French Revolution could not engage, or at least open the inquiry toward, an investigation of the political economy affected by both Law and Calonne (which, as we will see, is exactly what Mary Wollstonecraft did attempt). The reduction of the dialectical logic of Western metaphysical discourse to only one anti-universal pole of absolute Form allows no place for the in-between spaces of social life, the relations between local situations and their wider contexts.

The unsettling problem is that idealized individualism in poetry can be the dark mirror image of absolute individualism in economics. Ironically, "self-interest" is that odd new formation, in which subjectivity seems to gain an objective correlative in market economics that can measure one's self-interest in terms of real or potential accounting for profit.[13] I realize that articulating these structural links between aesthetic theory and economic theory can seem audacious, or even outrageous, especially given that I am comparing a great, canonized poet, Wordsworth, with a ruthless financial speculator, Law. The aesthetic theory has had little direct effect on the economic theory of financial capitalism, and it is true that the latter theory has served ruling powers as a driving force in the world historical process of the past few hundred years. That distinction alone should be a humbling moment for all of us working in the humanities wings of higher education. But the gap also speaks to how complex historical processes sometimes inadvertently but powerfully severed the literary from the historical, and demonstrates that only by investigating the historical origins of the split itself can we begin to reverse those kinds of idealism that have left us irrelevant to the market society. Given those qualifications, Wordsworth's late-life version of Romantic idealism (in spite of his grand intentions) tends to disengage art from history; and John Law's version of economic systems (because of his despicable monetary goals) tends to disengage market mechanics from history and communal social life. Just as William Blake lamented that "Aristotle's Analytics" had been reduced to a "system" that abstracted the "mental deities" so that one person could "impose on" many others, Law's System created an illusory self-regulating system of exchange out of paper, credit, and speculation, completely severed from the social and historical lives of most of the people affected by these theories. Extreme hierarchy then crushes emergent communality.

Clearly, Wordsworth opposed Law's absolutism, but his version of Romantic idealism could, ironically, serve the interests of the wealthy even as the ostensible purpose of Romantic idealism was to defeat those material vulgarities. Wordsworth is an enormously complex thinker, nonetheless, and in many instances, especially earlier in his life, his commitments to radical Romanticism contributed to the emergence of the countertraditions of socialism, anarchism, and communism. The liberal story of progress and capitalist expansion has been repeatedly told in our history textbooks (see Loewen) even as the stories about these rising countermovements have been suppressed. Understanding the relations between capitalism, socialism, and communism as differing modes of production and exchange is simply part of the historical realities that shaped the West, no matter what anyone's individual attitude toward these movements might be. While it may be possible to see the best features of Western metaphysics as a just theory and a beautiful rhetoric when reflective of our deepest interconnectedness and responsive to the vital dialectical tensions, in the misframed versions of aesthetics and economics, poetic egotism and economic greed can be structurally aligned even though the latter rules the earth.

The radical Romantics took the lead on resisting such exclusions by insisting that the imaginative arts should be deeply in solidarity with the projects for social reproduction and human justice, rather than aligned with individualistic theories building bubbles, busts, and inequality. And there were many other individuals and groups in the eighteenth and nineteenth centuries to whom we are also deeply indebted, among them Mary Wollstonecraft, Pierre-Joseph Proudhon, Charles Fourier, Henri de Saint-Simon, Mikhail Bakunin, Friedrich Engels, Karl Marx, and others to whom we will turn in the next two chapters.

Women's Rights, Class Wars, and the Master-Slave Dialectic: Signs of the Rising Countermovements

Revolutionizing Gender

In 1790, Mary Wollstonecraft anonymously published *A Vindication of the Rights of Men,*[1] and it sold so well that it was reprinted with her name on it a few weeks later. The first edition was lavishly praised in every major periodical of the day, but with the second edition male writers everywhere backtracked, considered it the work of "passion" in contrast to the esteemed "reason" of Edmund Burke, and railed against "petticoat" philosophers. Despite the patriarchal backlash, this political pamphlet represents perhaps the first widely circulated feminist critique of male writing ever produced, because a central aim of the book was not only to refute Burke's conservative defense of aristocracy and his critique of the French Revolution, but also to defeat Burke's notorious distinction between beauty, which he saw as weak and feminine, and the sublime, which he defined as strong and masculine. *Rights of Men* thus set the stage for Wollstonecraft's publication two years later of what has now become her most famous book, the monumental *A Vindication of the Rights of Woman.* The power of this text owes a great deal to Wollstonecraft's willingness to take on some of the most notable male writers in the world, including even such social idealists as Rousseau, who had argued in *Émile* (1762) that women's education should be aimed only at serving the pleasure of men. Wollstonecraft thought passionately otherwise, and her landmark text sets out to show that such patriarchal assumptions are educational problems, ones that can be remedied by recognizing the rights and needs for educating women in all the affairs of history, state, politics, language, literature, science, and, most of all, the ways of reason. Transforming education is as much at the heart of her ideas for cultural transformation as it was for Plato, who also called for the education of women.

Soon after completing *A Vindication of the Rights of Woman*, Wollstonecraft arrived in Paris, about a month before Louis XVI was beheaded. It was not long before she fell in love with Gilbert Imlay, an affair that led to the birth of her first daughter, Fanny (named after her closest friend, Fanny Blood), in 1794; and the very next year she published her own history of the French Revolution, *An Historical and Moral View of the Origin and Progress of the French Revolution and the Effect It Has Produced in Europe*, which runs to more than five hundred pages. Wordsworth had already left Paris by the time Wollstonecraft arrived, but like him she knew that the events taking place in France would change the world. Also, like Wordsworth, Wollstonecraft struggled with what she saw as the corruption of the ideals of liberty. She too was a great believer that the 1789 *Declaration of the Rights of Man* was a universal affirmation, so the Reign of Terror struck her as one "of the fatal errours of ignorance," a "perverse obstinacy" (*Historical* book 1, ch. 1), and a sign of the barbarity of the mob who gave up all reason and the law in their gut-wrenching acts of violence. Like Wordsworth, she saw the revolutionary ideals being corrupted: "The revolution . . . soon introduced the corruption, that has ever since been corroding beautiful freedom." She likens it to a kind of filial betrayal within the family: "Like the parents who forget all the dictates of justice and humanity, to aggrandize the very children whom they keep in a state of dependence" (book 1, ch. 1).

But what most distinguishes Wollstonecraft's analysis of the French Revolution from Wordsworth's poetic rendering of this historical event is her detailed consideration of the geopolitical economy. Indeed, she spends a large part of the second chapter detailing "the immoralities of Calonne" even as she recognizes that had Calonne's plan for taxing the nobles been implemented it might have gone a long way toward "warding off the tumults that have since produced so many disastrous events" (*Historical* book 1, ch. 2). And a key factor was that many people "discovered the magnitude of the deficit" when national resources were drained off by the "gigantic tyranny" of the Bourbons. She understood the basic links between war and national debt. No wonder there was a clamor for a new constitution: "An approaching national bankruptcy was the ostensible reason assigned for the convening of the *notables* in 1787" (book 1, ch. 2).

Calonne's scheme seemed to have had some merits in terms of reducing the national debt, but Wollstonecraft saw from the beginning that his vanity, selfishness, and just plain unscrupulousness had led him to "waste the treasures of his country" (*Historical* book 1, ch. 2). Although she calls Calonne a "weak, machiavelian politician," she also documents that it is not just the character of an individual man that brought about the revolution. Indeed, one of the striking things about her historical account is the sweeping nature of her story: she often circles back to fill in relevant stories from, for example, Ancient Greece, Rome, the Reformation, the politics of Frederick II of Prussia, the Austrian empire, and a huge range of historical figures such as Descartes, Newton, and what she calls the "decline of the Aristotelian philosophy" (book 2, ch. 4). But perhaps more important, in Chapter 3 of Book 4, Wollstonecraft offers a highly detailed financial accounting of the effects of the national debt, tax situation, and federal revenue. Her analysis on these points regarding the French Revolution both foreshadows and mirrors Karl Marx's analysis of the financial roots leading up to the later 1848 revolution that ended disastrously in the restoration of the monarchy. As he argues in *The Eighteenth Brumaire of Louis Bonaparte,* "The mortgage debt burdening the soil of France imposes on the French peasantry payment of an amount of interest equal to the annual interest on the entire British national debt" (McLellan, 349). As Wollstonecraft explains, the deficit of more than 56 million livres in 1789 was at the time a financial crisis (modern estimates put the debt at closer to 113 million livres). And she conjectures that, "In this posture of affairs, the enthusiasm of the French in the cause of liberty might have been turned to the advantage of a new and permanent system of finance" (*Historical* book 4, ch. 3). Without putting it in these words, it is as if she is yearning for an alternative economic system to industrial capitalism. Such an alternative system of finance would require "a just system of taxation" which, of course, never arrived.

More than any of the British Romantic writers of her day, Wollstonecraft offered a materialist account of the geopolitical economy, with the crisis squarely situated in the conflict between aristocratic versus bourgeois control of the capitalist system. That alone constitutes a remarkable accomplishment. However, it is also fair to say that she is herself deeply committed to liberty as a bourgeois promise of a comfortable life with more bounty for the middle classes, and her account of poverty will come off poorly to many contemporary ears. Her economic analysis reflects some characteristically bourgeois ideological contradictions between the language of universal rights and at the same time the claim that the middle class represents "the most natural state" (*Vindication* 140). On the one hand, it is "a monstrous tyranny, a barbarous oppression" for "any government, to preclude from a chance of improvement the greater part of the citizens of the state" because "men of every class are . . . equally susceptible of common improvement" (486). Yet, on the other hand, in her plan for instituting national educational institutions (Chapter 12 of *Vindication*) she suggests that the poor, other than those few with exceptional talents, should be educated in separate schools, a kind of an incipient tracking system ensuring the separation of social classes in education. She still offers a powerful complaint that reducing all life to market mechanisms is nothing other than "the destructive influence of commerce . . . carried on by men who are eager by overgrown riches to partake of the respect paid to nobility," and that this "most pernicious" belief only aims to produce the maldistribution of resources that she calls the "aristocracy of wealth" (*Historical* book 5, ch. 4).

When we focus on gender in *A Vindication of the Rights of Woman* (1792) we encounter the truly radical force of her arguments for the liberation and education of women. Prior to Wollstonecraft, no writer had ever made such an eloquent and impassioned plea for coeducational institutions of learning. In no uncertain terms, Wollstonecraft argues that "the tyranny of man" (143) has led to the degrading of "one half of the human species" (146) because "they are treated as a kind of subordinate beings, and not as a part of the human species" (139). The key factor is the "false system of education" (139) they have received: "the instruction which women have hitherto received has only tended, with the constitution of civil society, to render them insignificant objects of desire—mere propagators of fools!" (142). Her arguments are grounded in the Enlightenment discourse of reason so that in only slightly sardonic language she apologizes: "My own sex, I hope, will excuse me, if I treat them like rational creatures" (141). She wishes "rather to persuade by the force of my arguments, than dazzle by the elegance of my language. . . . I shall try to avoid that flowery diction which has slided from essays into novels . . . " (141). Her critique of "flowery diction" reminds us of Wordsworth's attack on poetic diction, although her targets here are not so much the poets but the growing flock of what, in Chapter 13, she calls "the sentimental novels," or more pointedly, "the stupid novelists," those narratives written expressly for women readers and deploying nothing but "sentimental jargon," "stale tales," and "meretricious scenes" (157). In contrast, Wollstonecraft herself wrote two novels that were both highly critical of the institution of marriage and the ills of patriarchy, and both based on a critique of what she felt were the false eighteenth-century discourses of sensibility and sentimentality whereby women were "heroines" for their virtuous self-sacrifice to the ways of men.

Although it has been pointed out by some contemporary feminists that Wollstonecraft places too much uncritical value on the predominantly male discourse of reason and "the law of Nature" (140), such a critical observation reflects no more than that she is, of course, situated in the sociohistorical formations of the Enlightenment. As she puts it, "What does history disclose but marks of inferiority, and how few women have emancipated themselves from the galling yoke of sovereign man?" (156). No male writers are spared from her critique. For example, while Blake provides a model of the basic Romantic rereading of Milton as an advocate for human creativity and imagination, Wollstonecraft focuses on the gender stereotypes in Milton's language so that "when he tells us that women are formed for softness and sweet attractive grace, I cannot comprehend his meaning . . . " (143). She is even more vehement about the "rants" outlining women's roles in popular guidebooks of the day such as that by Dr. John Gregory, the Scottish author of one of the most widely circulated books on women's education, *A Father's Legacy to His Daughters*

(1774). Gregory wrote his book toward the end of his life, and directs it to his three daughters, who had lost their mother at an early stage, so he worries about their education should they lose their father also. Gregory's book exemplifies the stereotypical role of the chaste, virtuous, modest woman who defers so fully to the superior male roles that even a lively wit must be suppressed because it "is the most dangerous talent you can possess." For Wollstonecraft, such manuals are "absurd and tyrannic," and enforcing them is equivalent to laying "down a system of slavery" (*Vindication* 154–55), as if women's only role in the economy is unpaid domestic labor.

Wollstonecraft's goal is nothing less than social transformation toward a more just world for both genders, and she realizes that "till society be differently constituted, much cannot be expected from education" (*Vindication* 145). Such a transformation will not simply be an inversion, whereby matriarchy replaces patriarchy: "Let it not be concluded that I wish to invert the order of things" (148). Indeed, she recognizes the limitations of women's freedom as a kind of inevitable biological essentialism based on their weaker physical bodies: "In the government of the physical world it is observable that the female in point of strength is, in general, inferior to the male. This is the law of Nature" (139–40). Thus, the Enlightenment belief in universal laws of nature provides some inevitable limits to the social transformation. But there are no "natural" limits to women's reason: even "the word masculine is only a bugbear" (142), a clear recognition that masculinity and femininity are themselves social constructions based on education and instruction. The problem, again, is that "[a] mistaken education, a narrow, uncultivated mind, and many sexual prejudices, tend to make women more constant than men . . . " (152).

In launching the first wave of feminist criticism, *A Vindication of the Rights of Woman* appears as a remarkable anomaly in an age when women could not divorce nor own property nor ever stand on equal legal footing with men.[2] In both of her novels, Wollstonecraft demonstrates that women's friendships unite them as women even across social class differences. For instance, in perhaps her most radical work, the unfinished novel, *Maria, or The Wrongs of Woman,* (published posthumously in 1798), the main character is forced by her aristocratic husband to live in an insane asylum where she sustains an intimate friendship with the woman assigned to be her servant, Jemima, a relationship that clearly crosses class lines. Indeed, Wollstonecraft is one of the first to fully understand the relationships between gender and class, and thus the economic role of women in the national economy: gender is produced, it doesn't just happen out of nature. So it is time now to focus more on the economic theory emerging in England, France, and Germany during the same period.

From Landed Gentry to Free Trade

Adam Smith often serves as the icon for free-market ideology. His massive twelve-hundred-page volume, known today as *The Wealth of Nations*, took him ten years to complete (in 1776), and it has ever since served for many people as the monumental justification for laissez-faire capitalism. The only problem is that Smith never once used the term *laissez-faire*.[3] Although he was clearly a strong believer in the rights of individuals to set the price of market goods and the virtues of free trade to stimulate profit, he never thought markets could regulate themselves without some national controls over exchange rates and protections from the self-interests of monopoly corporations. A careful reading of his magnum opus suggests that he would have been quite appalled with recent neoliberal claims that the market could completely regulate itself through the absolute freedom of private self-interest.[4] He worried a great deal about the "mean rapacity" of the rising capitalist class, who "neither are, nor ought to be, the rulers of mankind" (quoted in Heilbroner 68). He explicitly acknowledged that the government would have to invest in projects and institutions such as roads and education that would be ignored by private industry. But despite these facts, Smith's work was often misinterpreted by the ruling industrialists of the nineteenth century (as it continues to be today) to mean exactly the opposite. As Robert Heilbroner explains, "*The Wealth of Nations* was liberally quoted to oppose the first humanitarian legislation. Thus by a strange injustice, the man who warned that the grasping eighteenth-century industrialists 'generally have an interest to deceive and even to oppress the public' came to be regarded as their economic patron saint" (70). Were he alive today, Smith would have been one of the first to point out the contradiction that the free-market fundamentalists have required all kinds of national regulations such as nonprogressive taxation, restrictions on collective bargaining, reductions in social services, and massively complex international regulations, even as they also depend on public expenditures for highways, water supply, and military forces, all of which favor the creditor nations over the debtor nations.

The most commonly cited passage from Smith's book is the one where he refers to the "invisible hand," a metaphor for a kind of miraculous balancing act. Even as individual men pursue their own economic self-interest, they end up, willy nilly, benefiting society as a whole as if they were "led by an invisible hand to promote an end which was no part of their intention" (*Wealth* 572). No doubt this articulation suggests that society in general will benefit by allowing the market to seek its own equilibrium. This steady state can only occur when individuals are free to set prices, as if the "invisible hand" carefully balances out the changing relations between production costs, market pricing, and population growth, thereby avoiding turbulent boom/bust cycles. Unfettered self-interest appears to yield the greatest social benefits. But the thing is, this term, *invisible hand*, occurs only once in the volume, about halfway through, and within the next few pages Smith goes on to make many qualifications about the likelihood of a peaceful equilibrium actually being achieved. He acknowledges that regulations regarding military products for the nation fall within those instances where "it will generally be advantageous to lay some burden upon foreign" (586) imports, and in other instances tariffs "may be good policy in retaliations" (587) for foreign aggressions. He worried that monopolies could disrupt the open market and brutally lower wages below subsistence levels for workers. Smith also consistently condemned the use of slaves even though plantation slavery was fundamental to the operation of colonialist capitalism. In several places in *The Wealth of Nations,* he actually argued that the maintenance of slaves was more costly than the wages paid to freemen.[5] And, finally, Smith actually advocated that government should subsidize new and emerging industries until they could become profitable on their own business terms. In short, the "invisible hand" becomes sometimes very visible in terms of state regulatory policies, up to and including socialized, state-run start-up enterprises.[6]

Still, Smith's notion of economic "equilibrium" established by market price setting profoundly affected all subsequent economic theories about mercantilism and the production and exchange of goods in variable markets, although not until 1800 did his book become widely known. In a sense, Smith described in plain language the remarkable but often confusing changes in social and economic life that were affecting everyone in Northern Europe in the eighteenth century. Smith was the first of what has been called the "classical economists," a group that generally also includes Thomas Malthus, David Ricardo, Jean-Baptiste Say, Jeremy Bentham, and John Stuart Mill, among others. The significance of these classical economists is that they succeeded in treating the economy and the market as domains that could be analyzed as *relatively* separate from the social, cultural, and political organizations of the day. For this purpose, discrete Western metaphysical systems of classification came to their aid: universal separations between relatively independent branches of knowledge meant that the strictly economic performance of the market could be bracketed off from the political organization of the state and civil society. These writers vary considerably in their theories, but they all share a commitment to capitalism as a vast improvement over feudalism, and, in particular, they all work out their own versions of Smith's key notion of equilibrium. But Smith was an inveterate Enlightenment optimist whose underlying belief in the ability of the market to adjust itself encouraged the powerful ideology that increased accumulation of capital inevitably led to human progress via increased national wealth. Everyone might not share equally in the accumulated wealth, but his optimism in the "rising tide" theory of economic progress meant that at least everyone's boat would rise.

We will briefly return to Smith's well-known passage about the pin factory as a model for the division of labor under industrial production, but first it can be helpful to provide a brief overview of the other classical economists. Indeed, twenty years after the publication of *Wealth*, the downsides and inequalities of the capitalist system seemed to be escalating, and there were pessimists waiting in the wings. For example, in 1798, two years after Napoleon assumed his directorship, the Reverend Thomas Malthus published *An Essay on the Principle of Population*. Malthus's fear was that population growth would terribly upset the "equilibrium" maintained by the dominance of the European elite (France, the most populous nation in Europe, now had more than thirty million citizens; Britain itself had only about five million). Malthus worried that the orderly distribution of wealth would be overturned by chaos, and so he recommended a kind of eugenic control of the poor, to be accomplished by reducing all welfare aid to reduce overpopulation by the lower social classes. As Heilbroner sums up the argument: "[W]hile the number of mouths grows geometrically, the amount of cultivable land grows only arithmetically" (89). Malthus's immediate target was the naïve optimism of William Godwin (who had briefly been married to Mary Wollstonecraft before her death), who had in 1793 published a book called *An Enquiry Concerning Political Justice*, a founding book for the ensuing anarchist traditions that argued for the perfectibility of society. Godwin's popular book glowed with optimism about the possibilities of morality, truth, and communality joining in the human progress toward utopian well-being for all. So Malthus's 1798 pamphlet directly argued that even if Godwin's dreamlike egalitarian communities were to come into being, the population growth from all this human health would inevitably lead to overpopulation and ultimately famine. To give Malthus his due, he did predict the kind of famine, war, and disease that we have seen in many parts of the world when economic inequalities and population growth lead to social disintegration. However, Malthus's mathematical equations about population growth have been mitigated in many parts of the world through birth control and other kinds of economic and political restrictions.

Sticking more closely to Adam Smith's economic analysis, Jean-Baptiste Say published in 1803 his famous book *A Treatise on Political Economy,* in which he argued that the mere consumption of products leads to an accelerated production of other products. Called "Say's Law," the key point was that government intervention in the economy through supplying more money was unnecessary because the market would self-adjust through supply-

and-demand ratios of production and consumption: the producer of a product will invest his profit in the purchase of more products such that supply-side growth automatically increases demand. As Say explains it: "Thus the mere circumstance of creation of one product immediately opens a vent for other products" (138–39). Basically, this formulation represents a rewriting of Smith's notion of equilibrium, even though it accepted as natural the more bleak cycles of boom and bust that inevitably accompany capitalist progress. Say also adopted a basic Romantic idealist vision of the unlimited resources of nature, so that the separate sphere of economic calculations based on the laws of supply and demand never touched the inexhaustible resources of the natural world such as found in the "immense provisions of fuel in coal mines" (quoted in Bonneuil and Fressoz 204). The classical economists basically followed this optimistic vision of a limitless nature funding the progress of human history.

But a substantially more pessimistic analysis came from Malthus's close friend, David Ricardo, and their mutual respect and friendship also included passionate arguments about their widely differing views regarding the liabilities of the market system. Ricardo did not substantively disagree with Malthus's fear that the population growth of England, although then undocumented,[7] would overrun the ability of the island to supply food for all the hungry mouths—indeed, Malthus had vividly articulated a commonly shared fear that population and poverty were somehow related. But they did disagree on just about everything else.[8] Ricardo sought a far more abstract analysis of economic laws, and he developed some of the most influential doctrines of free trade, even between nations of unequal resources such as between European monarchies and the undeveloped countries of the East and South— theories that served the British Empire quite well. Again, similar to Say's Law, Ricardo's analysis of free trade depended on the belief that production costs of wages and resources could somehow be balanced out with exchange and consumption through the continuous seeking of new markets for goods. But Ricardo's is a *tragic system*" (Heilbroner 94), because ultimate economic and social equality is not even remotely possible. His notion of "comparative advantage" is that each nation should produce what it is best at producing so that, without tariffs or trade restrictions, the efficiency of each nation's use of resources would best achieve economic equilibrium: in short, deregulated free trade all around. As a member of Parliament, his arguments were deeply influential in affecting the shape of some of the policies of the British Empire such as the eventual repeal in 1846 of the protectionist "Corn Laws" that discouraged free trade with more corn-producing nations. Yet Ricardo's great fear of disequilibrium stemmed from his belief that land prices and rent would rise so precipitously as to disrupt economic equilibrium: basically, he saw that the tension of the new age was a bitter conflict between, on the one hand, the landed aristocracy whose income depended on agricultural yields from their farmlands, and on the other, the rising industrial capitalists in the urban centers who favored the lowest possible grain prices so they could pay lower wages. But on this point, his prediction turned out to be less accurate than Karl Marx's that the industrial capitalists would be the ones to create enormous economic inequalities.[9] Nevertheless, among other things, Ricardo's enormously influential book, *Principles of Political Economy and Taxation* (1817), reformulated in strictly economic discourse such fundamental terms as the relations between use value and exchange value and the labor theory of value. Simply put, the latter theory meant that the value of any product was determined by the amount of labor it took to produce it, and that wages for that labor should be set according to the ratios of supply and demand. Ricardo provided detailed analyses of the relations between wages, rent, profit, land, and resources. Ricardo's pessimism stemmed from his realization that whatever equilibrium the market system might attain, it would never be based on an equally shared distribution of the rising surplus that he knew could be accumulated under the capitalist's agenda: class differences would have to be accepted for any possibility of equilibrium to have a chance. "Like Malthus," as Heilbroner puts it, "Ricardo saw only 'self-restraint' as a solution for the working masses, and although he wished the workers well, he did not put too much faith in their powers of self-control" (95). The industrial capitalists interpreted Ricardo as their intellectual savant for favoring them over the landed aristocracy, although Ricardo himself championed free speech and the regulation of corporate as well as Parliamentary corruption. For all these reasons, he will be particularly singled out in many of Marx's subsequent arguments against the classical economists' position that capitalism can produce some acceptable form of equilibrium rather than the increasing exploitation of wage labor and the exacerbation of class differences.

On the other hand, John Stuart Mill's influential economic writings were virtually ignored by Marx, even though, rather remarkably it seems, 1848 was not only the date of widespread workers' and student rebellions but also the publication of Mill's two-volume *Principles of Political Economy* and Marx and Engels's *The Communist Manifesto*. What is even more striking is that it would be hard to imagine two more differing styles and rhetorics than those embodied in these two texts: Mill's is an ultimately optimistic view unfolding through a detailed, methodical analysis culminating in the idea that capitalist hierarchies will eventually move toward a more egalitarian and peaceable kind of socialism; whereas Marx and Engels offer a shrill but brilliant call to arms for the workers to rise up in violent revolt if need be to end the oppression of the ruling bourgeoisie. Indeed, Mill offered a gentlemanly, scholarly, and optimistic view based on his famous premise that only individual freedom can sustain any version of social liberty. The socialist utopians themselves (as we will see in the next section) sometimes slipped into what can only be called weirdly idiosyncratic views in their efforts to imagine not reformed capitalism, but totally alternative societies to the cruel market economy they witnessed in their lives. In contrast, Mill provided scholarly respectability as a political economist, and in many ways he bridges the views of the classical economists and the socialists. His views have often been reduced to the famous term, *utilitarianism,* that he adapted from Jeremy Bentham (a close friend of Mill's father, James), and consequently what often gets left out in the critical literature devoted to Mill's massive range of writings is that, more than any of the classical economists, he actually refused to separate economic analysis from political analysis. In short, Mill actually countered the despairing views of Malthus and Ricardo, who offered their economic analysis as if it were based on an Enlightenment faith in laws, whether of economics or nature, that appeared to be inevitable, fixed, and open only to minor kinds of regulatory controls.

In contrast, Mill saw that the economy was based on social values and political organization, so his whole analysis works out a series of optimistic, peaceful reforms that, in his view, would lead toward a kind of benevolent socialism as a newly invented equilibrium between individual morality and social well-being. It would not be entirely inaccurate to say that we owe it to Mill for offering a possible vision of progressive labor laws, welfare states, New Deal reforms, and Keynesian regulations—all indirectly derived from Mill's optimistic idea that good moral values in the leaders will ameliorate the oppressive hierarchies of capitalist ruthlessness. Significantly, in the *Principles*, Mill also offered one of the first real critiques of the liberal beliefs in economic growth and perpetual progress: instead of an "unlimited increase of wealth" he argued for a finite, "stationary" (*Principles* 128–29) economy, based on conservation and redistribution, for maintaining relative equality. Marx and Engels, perhaps more clearly, saw that such an ultimate vision of slow reform leading to a peaceful equilibrium was more dreamlike than real, and that it would require more tangible forms of labor organization and revolt to more equitably and communally redistribute the surplus. By the time of the Paris Commune, as we will see, Marx himself had much more fully recognized a need for organized labor movements to create the necessary solidarity with not only the proletariat but also workers in other spheres, including artisans, small shopowners, educators, and government workers.

In many ways, Mill was himself a remarkable educational experiment carried out by his father, James Mill. The father undertook the exclusive education of his eldest son in order to make him into one of the great philosophical and political reformers of his age. Under this plan, by all accounts, the son was a remarkable prodigy, learning Greek and arithmetic beginning at the age of three and Latin at the age of eight, so that before he was ten years old he was reading most of the ancient Greek and Latin writers in their native languages. By the time he was a teenager Mill had read most of the classical economists of his age, especially Smith, Bentham, and Ricardo, and also the British empiricist philosophers. Like Bentham, Ricardo was also a close friend of James Mill. Shortly before his death in 1873, John Stuart chronicled in his famous *Autobiography* his remarkable learning and his major influences. Significant to our interests in historical links with the ancient Greek philosophers, Mill explains that Aristotle's *Rhetoric* was "the first expressly scientific treatise on any moral or psychological subject which I had read," and his father made him study it "with peculiar care" by throwing "the matter of it into synoptic tables" (32). By the age of twelve, Mill had gone on to Aristotle's *Organon* and the *Posterior Analytics*. He also then read "some of the most important dialogues of Plato, in particular the *Gorgias*, the *Protagoras*, and the *Republic*," and, as he explains, "There is no author to whom my father thought himself more indebted for his own mental culture, than Plato" (*Autobiography* 38). The Socratic method came to mean for Mill "the perpetual testing of all general statements by particular instances" (39). James Mill might seem like a terribly authoritarian teacher, but Mill attests to how much he enjoyed his learning, even as he admits that "[t]he education which my father gave me, was in itself much more fitted for training me to *know* than to *do*" (48). But still, Mill did a lot of things, such as at the age of sixteen (1822) founding the Utilitarian Society (which lasted until 1826), and beginning his nearly lifetime preoccupation of revising Bentham's influential version of utilitarianism so that it might serve more progressive ends in social reform. It was also about this time, in 1823, that Mill accepted a position arranged by his father in the East India Company to serve as the Examiner of India Correspondence, in which capacity he served for several years.

The *Autobiography* also offers an account of Mill's well-known emotional breakdown at the age of twenty, when he came to grave doubts about his lifelong ambition to be a "reformer of the world" (111). But he also describes his meeting with Wordsworth in 1828, and how the latter's poems were "a medicine for my state of mind" (121). He was soon having regular meetings with some of the key Romantic poets and thinkers such as Coleridge, Southey, and others. Significantly, these exchanges led him to his complete commitment to political and philosophical concerns for communality and a rejection of arbitrary social hierarchies. As Mill puts it, during this period he acquired "a greatly increased interest in . . . the common feelings and common destiny of human beings" (121). He became acquainted with the Christian Socialists, particularly Auguste Comte, and by 1830 "a new mode of political thinking was brought home to me . . . [by the writers] of the St. Simonian school in France" (131). The socialist analysis of the political economy helped him to understand the St. Simonian principle "under which the labour and capital of society would be managed for the general account of the community, every individual being required to take a share of labour, either as thinker, teacher, artist, or producer, all being classed according to their capacity, and remunerated according to their works" (133). He also came to his belief in the "perfect equality of men and women" (134), a belief that he would articulate at great length in his 1869 book *The Subjection of Women,* one of the most startlingly feminist books ever written by a man in the nineteenth century, even though he never cites Mary Wollstonecraft—virtually none of the nineteenth-century male writers ever acknowledged that *Vindication* even existed. As Mill argues at length, "What is now called the nature of women is an eminently artificial thing—the result of forced repression in some directions, unnatural stimulation in others" (*Subjection* 21). His radical reformist goals were clear: "We have had the morality of submission, and the morality of chivalry and generosity; the time is now come for the morality of justice" (43). Mill became a deep advocate of free speech and universal education for all, and he sought throughout his life to address what he saw as "[t]he social problem of the future . . . how to unite the greatest individual liberty of action, with a common ownership in the raw material of the globe" (175). Likewise, in his 1859 book *On Liberty,* Mill aims to directly address "[t]he struggle between Liberty and Authority" (1). It is hard to imagine more precise articulations of the fundamental tensions between communality and hierarchy in the search for social justice.

Despite the varying degrees of optimistic hope for human progress (Smith and Mill) or pessimistic fear of rising inequalities (Malthus and Ricardo),[10] there are significant structural affinities between the classical economists' theories of the systemic equilibrium potentially achievable by the "free" market and the Romantic idealists' theories of "organic" wholeness potentially achievable in the formal properties of a work of art, just as we saw between Law's financial theories and Wordsworth's poetic theories. The imaginative integration of artistic form that emerges internal to the process of artistic creation is analogous to the idea of an economic equilibrium calibrated internally to the economic system. Ironically, Smith's own analysis of the division of labor in *The Wealth of Nations* begins in Chapter 1, "Of the Divisions of Labour," with his famous example of a pin factory, though one which exists primarily in the fictional rendering of this site as imagined by Smith. It is a kind of vivid literary fiction, providing a model of a tightly controlled economic site isolated from the messy realities of social and political life. Although, as David Graeber points out, Smith claimed to have visited such a factory, he also seems to have adapted the story from the book *Ihya,* written by the eleventh-century medieval Persian writer Ghazali, "in which he describes a needle factory, where it takes twenty-five different operations to produce a needle" (279), although in Smith's pin factory, there are only eighteen stages. In any case, Smith's fictional pin factory is also strikingly distanced from any empirical analysis of actually existing factories, and thus in a most basic way represents an attempt to provide a historical analysis of capitalism that is, in this case at least, ahistorical, based on a kind of literary fiction.[11] Among other things, Smith's imaginary factory world is "almost entirely free of debt and credit" (Graeber 353); there are no worker complaints about poor working conditions; and there are no government tariffs, exchange rates, or taxes anywhere to be found—all contrary to most existing industrial sites. This imaginary scenario balances itself out into its ultimate equilibrium through the coordination of the minutely assigned tasks configured as "the division of labor" so that the ten workers in this small factory can produce forty-eight thousand pins in a day—but in a world that never existed. And what might happen if no one actually needed forty-eight thousand pins every day? In Chapter 4, "Of the Origin and Use of Money," Smith also envisions a kind of premarket society based on bartering, prior to the advent of the market economies: as Graeber argues, this imaginary precapitalist bartering society never existed in any real world. But perhaps most significantly, these fictional stories all served as "the great founding myth of the discipline of economics" (25). The fiction, or myth, was "the very idea that there was something called 'the economy,' which operated by its own rules, separate from moral or political life, that economists could take as their field of study" (27). As Graeber concludes, the academic field of economics ultimately became an institutional reality by assuming "a division between different spheres of human behavior that . . . simply does not exist" (33).

In both the economic and the aesthetic registers, then, equilibrium and integration can appear external to or independent of other social values, such as those embodied in religious traditions, educational institutions, the ethics of groups and individuals, and other forms of reciprocity, personal care, communality, and social reproduction. Paradoxically, economic self-interest can then appear as a foundational metaphysical principle, almost like a mirror image of aesthetic transcendence; economic selfishness and aesthetic selflessness get formulated as eternal principles of human life rather than deeply historical processes of cultural communication and transaction. The classical economists prepared the ground for all their followers who have tried to separate economic production from the history and politics of social reproduction, including such vital necessities as child care, elder care, healthcare, environmental care, etc. Again, these misframings are structurally homologous to the strains of Romantic idealism that aimed to raise the timeless qualities of art and literature above the contingencies of history and politics. Both these forms of disembedding are underwritten by the binary logic of Western metaphysics: the transcendent universal form trumps the messy historical reality and ends the dialectical movement in the dream of ahistorical ideals.

Most available histories of criticism and theory have focused so exclusively on the literary that they have tended to omit any significant account of these theorists of the political economy, but to varying degrees they have had tremendous material effect on the actual shape of every phase of capitalism, including the production of literature and other kinds of writing. One clear similarity among the classical economists is that they assumed a view of the worker as rather passive: it never seemed to occur to any of them that struggles for social change could come from below. They passed on this assumption of worker passivism to many contemporary economists. The struggles of labor, union-ization movements, worker strikes, socialist states, communist interventions, New Deal regulations, indigenous resistance, and the social-welfare state—none of these phenomena pleased the neoliberal free marketeers of the Post–World War II era, such as Friedrich Hayek, Milton Friedman, and Gary Becker (see Patel 25). Nor would they have pleased many of the classical economists whose theoretical analyses served the capitalist system. The countermovements provide clear evidence that the system is neither totalizing nor seamless, and that the workers and the oppressed can acquire agency through their collective weight. Those individuals who contributed to the countermove-ments tried to imagine alternative economies whereby necessary strategic hierarchies could be integrated into public concerns for equality, participatory parity, communality, and social justice with respect to the organization of production and the distribu-tion of the surplus. The imagining of alternatives resonates with radical Romanticism when artistic and literary experimentation provides for the concrete expressions of the social imaginary so crucial to the countermovements.

The Countermovements: Socialism, Anarchism, and Communism

Not far from the border with Switzerland, the French city of Be-sançon has the distinction of being the birthplace not only of Vic-tor Hugo (1802), but also of two of the founding figures of both socialism and anarchism. Born thirty-seven years apart, Charles Fourier (1772–1837) and Pierre-Joseph Proudhon (1809–65) shared commitments to basic principles of social justice and hu-man freedom whereby communality, collaboration, and coopera-tion could better eliminate poverty than competition, hierarchy, and free trade. They both resisted the injustices of the aristocracy as much as the abuses of capitalism although neither went so far as to believe that you could eliminate hierarchy altogether. Fourier, together with Henri de Saint-Simon (1760–1825) and Robert Owen (1771–1858), came to be known as the "utopian socialists" because they all proposed specific models for ideal communities that would supposedly relieve human suffering better than any other social organization. Proudhon was the first to call himself an anarchist, or someone in principle opposed to any kind of centralized and repressive state authority that imposed hierarchy: citizens and workers had to participate in the decision-making process regarding the production and exchange of social goods. To this extent, he developed the optimistic version of anarchism proposed by William Godwin. But beyond their basic shared principles, Proudhon's and Fourier's specific ideas were about as different as can be imagined, and sometimes as strange as they were idealistic.

Of them all, Saint-Simon was the most directly tied to Enlightenment beliefs in the benefits of scientific progress as the cure for social ills, but he was also one of the oddest characters among the radical protesters against capitalist excess. Born of an aristocratic French family in Paris (his full name is almost too long to say: Claude Henri de Rouvroy, comte de Saint-Simon), he spent several years in the United States, where he fought in the Revolutionary Army under George Washington in the battle at Yorktown, Pennsylvania, where he also won the coveted Order of Cincinnatus for his valor. Most of all, he became dedicated to the anti-aristocratic values of liberty and equality. Back in France, Saint-Simon was much impressed with the idealism of the French Revolution, and the people of his home town of Falvy elected him to the National Assembly, a role which he agreed to accept while abandoning his title in favor of the simple Citoyen Bonhomme. He was imprisoned during the Reign of Terror out of fear that he was involved in counterrevolutionary activities, but, according to his own account, during his time in jail a revelation came to him in the form of a vision of Charlemagne, who appealed to him to become "a hero and philosopher of first rank" (quoted in Heilbroner 118). Saint-Simon was released in 1794 with the fall of Robespierre, and he set out on his mission to become the most well-educated man of his age. He spent his entire fortune trying to become that visionary philosopher, and it appears that his endless spirit and energy drew him a following even if he never did become the sage he had hoped to. Nevertheless, during the French Revolution he became completely enamored with the possibilities of the new scientific technologies, so that when he published his first book in 1802, *Lettres d'un habitant de Genève,* his focus was on the relations between science and politics. As was true for many Enlightenment thinkers, science was idealized as the avenue to what was truthful, and therefore common, among all human beings. His faith in science was carried out with a religious zeal (a kind of precursor to twenty-first-century versions of technocratic solutions for climate change), and even though most of his endless writings went unread, he had personally gained such a following that Saint-Simonians were more like a religious sect than a workers' organization. By 1817, with the publication of his most widely circulated book, *L'Industrie,* he had developed his socialist plans for utopian communities. His central belief was that in the proper kind of industrial society, science would produce what he called a "non-power politics" where technological innovation would help to eliminate poverty. Like many of the reformers we have discussed, Saint-Simon believed that education would be the avenue to the improved social relations, and that the main thing was to educate workers in new modes of technological production that would improve morale primarily through increased efficiency. His socialist world called for full employment, whereby workers would be the producers of both social and material goods, and nonworkers seen as "thieves" in their dependence on others, meaning that only workers could vote in his communities. But workers would vote, both in the social domain of civic government and in the organization of the workplaces. Saint-Simon's utopian socialism was based on a kind of scientific meritocracy where, echoing Plato, the wise would be the elected rulers; but, completely unlike that of Plato, his vision reflected the British Romantics' unification of science and art so that the rulers would also be artists—an organic unity of science, art, and literature. Such a synthesis of science and art, if worked out in conjunction with more gender equity, would have been highly compatible with Wollstonecraft's vision twenty years earlier, but like most of the male radicals of the nineteenth century he never seems to have encountered her books. Saint-Simon himself cycled through periods of wealth and poverty. He even spent part of 1813 in a sanatorium until he was rescued by funds from relatives. Finally, in 1823, he became so depressed at the failure of his writings to bring about the social changes he had worked so hard to invent that he tried to commit suicide by shooting himself six times in the head. Remarkably, he only managed to lose sight in one eye, although he did die two years later.

In contrast to Saint-Simon's nearly religious zeal for science, Charles Fourier abandoned his early interest in engineering and architecture, and came to have little faith in technology and industry to solve any problems other than further exploitation of workers; his version of social liberation was based instead on the elimination of repression. Ideologically, he appears much closer to the British Romantics such as William Blake with his cry that "Energy is Eternal Delight," and so Fourier favored sexual liberation and women's rights and defended homosexuality as a preference for some individuals; in these ways he was ahead of his time (again, no mention in this context of Wollstonecraft's work). Paradoxically, it appears that he himself may never have had a sexual relationship. He worked for many years as a correspondent, salesman, and merchant, but became truly disenchanted with the knavery and corruption of the capitalist business world. He believed that mutual cooperation, in contrast to hierarchical competition, would actually increase productivity. Like Saint-Simon, Fourier believed in a basic kind of meritocracy in which wages would be commensurate with effort and labor, and in which every effort would be made to align interests with job assignments. However, as with many thinkers of his era, Fourier's anti-Semitism remained strong, as "Jews" were associated with the ills of business and so in Fourier's utopian community would be assigned menial farm jobs.

The cooperative communities Fourier envisaged were called "phalanstères" or phalanxes, and they were to be four-storied apartment complexes with the floors representing the social hierarchies, so that the hardest-working, and thus richest, would enjoy the top floor, and the more indolent, and thus poorest, would occupy the first floor. Hierarchy was indeed incorporated into this form of communality. Even given these differences, wages were to be high enough to avoid suffering for anyone in the community, and he even went so far as to propose what we would call a kind of guaranteed income: even if one could not work, one would receive at least a livable income. Machinery was not the panacea envisioned by the industrialists because, Fourier insisted, the quality of craftsmanship was more important than the quantity of lesser goods produced by factories. Despite these progressive ideals, some of Fourier's beliefs will seem archaic to the contemporary reader. For example, he believed that human beings were progressing through eight stages of advancement, but so far they had only reached the fifth stage. He also believed in a kind of numerology whereby twelve basic passions organized themselves into 810 character types, and this would mean that the ideal phalanx would have 1,620 people. It seems that his version of utopian socialism included a kind of ultimate Aristotelian formalism in the extreme.

Fourier also had some even odder ideas, although some of them seem remarkably prescient. He seems to have anticipated a kind of global warming, as he believed that the North Pole's would gradually become more like a southern European climate. But even more oddly, he thought that with the melting of the polar cap the oceans would lose their salinity and become lemonade. Nathaniel Hawthorne made great sport of Fourier's juicy ocean theory. His well-known novel *The Blithedale Romance* presents a critique of what the author felt were the foggy social idealists, and at one point, the narrator, Miles Coverdale, lampoons Fourier's ideas: "When, as a consequence of human improvement . . . the globe shall arrive at its final perfection, the great ocean is to be converted into a particular kind of lemonade, such as was fashionable at Paris in Fourier's time. He calls it limonade à cèdre. It is positively a fact! Just imagine the city docks filled, every day, with a flood tide of this delectable beverage" (76). Admittedly, then, the socialists can be as prone to idealized theories about the world as any market fundamentalist, but we should not miss the most important point: Fourier offered a strong critique of the relentless exploitation of the natural world and the deteriorating effects on the planet of these basic capitalist principles of endless growth. He specifically saw the horrors of the rapid deforestation of England and much of Europe. And he was not alone: "Fourier simply drew on a large number of scientific writings and warnings of his time" (Bonneuil and Fressoz 76). Indeed, he "opposed Saint-Simon's industrialism, accusing him of spreading a false religion, a 'false progress,' and not placing the 'association of workers before that of the masters.' Fourier gave his critique

. . . an ecological dimension" (257). He aimed not at reforming the market system but at envisioning entirely new social systems and economies from the ground up—such radical utopianism always carries risks of impracticality. But Fourier's vision of a new world order based on cooperation did influence many future writers and activists.

About the same time in the early 1800s that Fourier was beginning to organize his phalanxes in France, Robert Owen became part owner and manager of the New Lanark cotton mills in Scotland. Owen became appalled at the generally deplorable working conditions in the mills, where orphaned children and destitute men and women labored long hours, oftentimes with no pay other than tokens that could be exchanged for highly overpriced goods only at the "truck stores" that were themselves operated by the mill owners. Owen set out to change everything with respect to unjust social hierarchies, and his philanthropy with respect to improving education, housing, and working conditions for the millworkers made him a legendary figure throughout Europe; even the future czar of Russia, Nicholas, visited the mills. Although Owen was himself a flourishing capitalist, he demonstrated that the welfare of the workers could enhance productivity and profitability, in contrast to the reigning capitalist belief in the lowest possible wages for workers. In short, workers should be well-treated and well-cared-for, but they would still allow business decisions to be made primarily by the owners. In 1813, Owen found a group of investors, including the classical economist Jeremy Bentham, who could completely buy out the previous owners and give Owen himself much more freedom to implement his improvements. Unlike Bentham, however, who favored a completely free-enterprise market system, Owen provided a kind of welfare and education for his workers. During that same year, Owen published his influential book *A New View of Society, or Essays on the Principle of the Formation of the Human Character,* in which, in a spirit similar to Fourier's, he argued that machinery such as Eli Whitney's newly improved cotton gin (1793) should be subordinated to human values for united and collaborative action. Moreover, like Plato, Wollstonecraft, and many others, Owen understood that there could be no improvement in human lives without education, including in the humanities and the arts and not just vocational training. He elaborated on his conception of socialist communities, "Villages of Cooperation," that would range from five hundred to thirteen hundred people, all living in shared buildings in the shapes of parallelograms with private apartments, all cooperatively rather than privately owning designated tracts of land, or townships. Also, the production factories and the shops that sold the goods produced would be cooperatively owned and operated, although it was difficult to tell how much decision making regarding production would be granted to workers. Groups of townships should be cooperatively linked, and eventually these shared communities would become global networks of socialist ventures. Several such communities were actually set up, most famously in New Harmony, Indiana, although most of them were unsuccessful, partly because they lacked the presence of Owen himself, or someone equally benevolent of spirit, to guide them. Owen brought the term *socialism* into the public imagination as one possible kind of organized countermovement to the privatization required by industrial capitalism. Although his cooperative villages failed, Owen's radical vision was most materially carried on in 1833 by his organizing of the labor movement through an incipient workers' union, the Grand National Consolidated Trades Union, that ended up having about half a million members, an amazing achievement at that time. It was a model precursor to workers' movements that arose later in the century, although the Grand National was rather violently snuffed out by the government two years after its founding—the worry was that the trades union threatened private property, and there was no nation then ready to accept that idea.

One of the most militant of the socialist activists was Auguste Blanqui (1805–81), whose version of socialism insisted on strong, centralized party organization in order to combat the capitalist state. He was, as might be expected, active in many of the nineteenth-century revolutionary movements in France, especially in 1830 and 1848, a period during which he was repeatedly imprisoned for opposing the rule of Louis-Philippe. In 1839, Blanqui led a major Paris uprising in collaboration with the League of the Just, an organization which in 1847 would reorganize into the formation of Karl Marx and Friedrich Engels's Communist League, with the slogan changing from the benign

"All Men Are Brothers" to the much stronger "Working Men of All Countries, Unite!" Blanqui believed deeply in the equitable sharing of wealth, but, contrary to Marx's views, his focus was less on proletarian masses than on small cadres of revolutionary leaders that would violently seize control from the capitalists and form a dictatorship, and only later share power with workers. But, as Plato had imagined it, education had to be the core for the new rulers: "'the great majority are mired in ignorance.' [chained in the cave] So the action of an educated minority would be required: 'There is no durable revolution without light! Liberty means instruction! Equality means instruction! Fraternity means instruction! Teachers, books, the printing press, these are the true revolutionary agencies'" (quoted in Gluckstein 66). The success of such a militant revolution was, for Blanqui, much more the focus than any postrevolutionary socialist political economy. Significantly, Blanqui would be elected in the spring of 1871 as president of the short-lived Paris Commune, even though he was imprisoned at the time by the leader of the French National Army, Adolphe Thiers, who would not release him even when the Communards offered to release all their prisoners in exchange. As we will see in Chapter 9, the tensions between the Blanquists and the Proudhonists will become quite heated during the brief two months of the life of the Commune.

Indeed, in contrast to the Blanquists (and also to the utopian socialists), the anarchists championed participatory democracy and worker control of all levels of production and social life, which often meant that they disdained any form of centralized state authority, temporary dictatorships, or hierarchical organizational principles. Pierre-Joseph Proudhon is the founding father of this movement, and calling him a "father" may be more significant than many anarchists might like to think. Whereas Fourier, much like Blake, advocated sexual freedoms and new liberation for women and minorities, Proudhon was quite the opposite. He was very puritanical, though he was the first to call himself an anarchist, against state oppression, against centralized authority. He was also, unfortunately, sexist and anti-Semitic. Despite these limitations, and besides their shared hometown, Fourier and Proudhon shared beliefs in cooperation, communality, mutuality, and social justice, although beyond that they had as different personalities as they did beliefs. Proudhon's version of anarchism would be much refined in subsequent work by, among others, the geographers Élisée Reclus and his friend, Peter Kropotkin, whose famous book *Mutual Aid* (1902) articulated his version of anarchist communism based on the end of wage labor, an emerging environmentalism, voluntary cooperation, and "mutual aid." Fourier had been concerned with class analysis, although he did not base that analysis on labor and the emerging market society, but rather with developing resistance to feudalism and the still-powerful domination of landed aristocracy, and Proudhon, too, proclaimed in his famous book, *What is Property? Or, an Inquiry into the Principle of Right and Government* (1844), that "Property is theft!"—so Marx was not the first to critique the role of private ownership of the means of production. Marx met Proudhon in 1844, and because of the latter's focus on equality and justice first responded positively to Proudhon's work, to the extent that it sought to illuminate the social ills of any system based on private property. Two years later, however, Marx changed his mind and attacked Proudhon's 1846 book *The Philosophy of Poverty* by writing a book titled *The Poverty of Philosophy,* in which he scathingly attacks Proudhon's naïve idealism—the latter's belief in "eternal" economic principles rather than in the historical development of the material forces of production.[12]

Proudhon rejected Jean-Jacques Rousseau's famous doctrine of the social contract that could best be realized by a popular sovereignty in a democratic republic. For Proudhon, "popular sovereignty" was just a replay of aristocratic statism in lamb's clothes. He favored reciprocal, decentralized forms of mutually shared democracy based on self-governance. As Kojin Karatani explains, "According to Proudhon, true democracy must be realized not only at the level of politics but also at the level of the economy. The French Revolution abolished the monarchy, but in economic terms it left in place a monarchy of money. . . . Proudhon's idea for abolishing the monarchy of money was to replace money with a system of labor vouchers and credit unions" (237). These arguments between centralized state authority, designated forms of leadership, and organizational hierarchy, on the one hand, and local governance, communality in the mode of production, and participatory democracy, on the other, have been replayed many times, and, as we will see in the next chapter, these arguments emerged in heated form between the Jacobins, the anarchists, the socialist Blanquists, and the Marxists in the spring of 1871 during the two months of the Paris Commune. These debates further characterized the tensions between Marx's version of socialism/communism and Mikhail Bakunin's version of anarchism, and later became central ideological issues in the formation of the Bolshevik Revolution in Russia.

Whereas Proudhon focused primarily on the local, communal mode of economic production through workers' cooperatives, his disciple, Bakunin, focused more attention on abolishing the state, or any form of centralized government. As Donny Gluckstein explains, Proudhon "focused on the symptoms of the disease but held back from dealing with the core of the system—the exploitation at the heart of the capitalist-worker relationship, and the state that exists to protect that exploitative process" (65). Proudhon thus tended to ignore the nonlocal organizational hierarchies required for effective political action by focusing on local worker production processes of "artisans and small-scale producers, as well as the creation of a financial system to support them" (Karatani 241). For these, and other, personal, reasons, Marx had a long history of strained relations with Bakunin, reaching a pitch beginning in the 1870s when the latter advocated immediate, violent revolution but Marx advocated peace and labor organization. Indeed, Marx also ended up as an antiwar pacifist, much like the Quaker, John Stuart Mill. In any case, Bakunin did offer a direct critique of all centralized organizations such as the state. Despite these differences of emphasis, both anarchists insisted on the basic human need for local, communal organization, participatory democracy, and nonhierarchical decision making rather than the large-scale corporations owned by the capitalists and ratified in principle by the laws of the centralized governments established by each nation-state. Anarchism became the code-word for opposing all centralized forms of hierarchy. But there are many versions of anarchism,[13] as we have seen, and though anarchists are often lumped together and accused of being not only against authority but in favor of chaos and anarchy, this is simply untrue: their basic antiauthoritarianism is based on belief in reciprocity, mutuality, and cooperation rather than in centralized authority.[14]

With Karl Marx we get the third of the three main legs of the countermovements to free-market ideology: socialism, anarchism, and *communism*. But before I summarize a few of his key theoretical ideas about the political economy, we have to backstep and pick up another crucial philosophical thread, one so influential that it could move either toward the center/right (which here includes both the liberal idealists and the conservatives), or toward the left (the radical countermovements). As a late Enlightenment thinker, Georg Wilhelm Friedrich Hegel deeply influenced both the Romantic idealists and the rising anticapitalist movements through his development of a richly historical approach to the rise of Western metaphysics with its culmination in Enlightenment philosophy. But most significant to the nineteenth-century analyses of the geopolitical economy of capitalism was his articulation of what we have come to call the master-slave dialectic as well as his commitment to the goal of human freedom. Hegel did not always fulfill the idealized promises, but his thought deeply influenced those whose theories of the political economy aided the work of the radical Romantics.

Right and Left Hegelianism: Inventing the Master-Slave Dialectic

We are still in the position of continually struggling to find out how to write history.
—G. W. F. HEGEL, *Lectures on the Philosophy of World History*

As a young man (born in the same year, 1770, as Wordsworth), Hegel eagerly sought news of the escalating French Revolution. In 1791, he shared a room at the Tubinger Stift Lutheran Seminary with the great German poet-to-be, Friedrich Hölderlin (also born in 1770), and Friedrich Schelling, then a young and brilliant sixteen-year-old philosopher-to-be. By the early nineteenth century, these three close friends would have a great deal to do with the rise of German Idealism, but during their time in the seminary, their enthusiasm for the revolution fueled their idealistic hopes for a new age of science, reason, and truth (the dream of the Enlightenment) that would witness the liberation of the spirit and the emancipation of human beings from bondage. During that same year, and a week before Hegel's twenty-first birthday, in August, 1791, the Haitian slave revolt broke out in Saint-Domingue. At that time, the French colony dominated the world's coffee and sugar industry, so it was a key to the Bourbon dynasty's financial stability and political rule. The problem was that by the beginning of the French Revolution, the more than 500,000 African-born slaves in Haiti outnumbered their French masters by a ratio of fourteen to one—a volatile situation, to say the least. After the French National Assembly passed the *Declaration of the Rights of Man* in 1789, declaring all men free and equal, the situation in Saint-Domingue would prove to be one of the great testing grounds of that hypothesis. By 1794, the revolutionary leaders of the National Convention of the First Republic in Paris banned slavery in France and all its colonies, largely as a direct response to the uprising in Saint-Domingue. In 1801, the former slave and new governor of the newly independent nation of Haiti, Toussaint Louverture, wrote a constitution officially enfranchising all citizens of the island. A year later, in 1802, Napoleon arrested Louverture, had him deported to France, and moved to reestablish the infamous Code Noir (formed in 1685 under Louis XIV) that established the legal codes for slavery. Nevertheless, on New Year's Day in 1804 Haiti's new military leader, Jean-Jacques Dessalines, declared independence from France, and in the following year, by defeating the white French population, he established "an independent, constitutional nation of 'black' citizens, an 'empire' mirroring Napoleon's own, which he called by the Arawak name, Haiti. These events, leading to the complete freedom of the slaves and the colony, were unprecedented. [According to David Patrick Geggus,] 'Never before had a slave society successfully overthrown its ruling class'" (Buck-Morss 38–39).

So it was no great surprise when Hegel and his friends paid close attention to both revolutions. Most of Hegel's writing during the last decade of the eighteenth century were essays in theology and religion, but by the time in 1804, after thirteen long years of violent struggle, the Republic of Haiti gained its independence from all European powers, Hegel was deeply affected at the very time he was composing his masterpiece, *The Phenomenology of Mind*,[15] which he would publish in 1807. The Haitian slave revolt was the only successful slave revolt in the history of the world, and it inspired one of the most influential sections of Hegel's detailed exposition of his entire system of philosophy.

In simple terms, this highly complex and influential text took Kant's dialectical system for analyzing the movement from sense perception to absolute knowledge and gave it a sweeping historical casting: Hegel brought history to philosophy. Consciousness, in Hegel's terms, was evolutionary in both an individual and a historical sense. In the individual sense, human beings acquire a sense of self, (he called it "being-for-self") in their temporal relations with others ("being-for-others"), and thus any given personal identity has a deeply social dimension arising in a historical process of development from birth, through childhood, into acculturation as an adult. How one is treated as a child is therefore directly related to how one evolves as an individual—a remarkably prescient turn that anticipates the later work of Sigmund Freud but also developmental and social psychology more generally. The individual self-consciousness is, however, deeply related to the vast evolutionary history of the rise of human consciousness characteristic of the species, but beginning, for Hegel, with Heraclitus (whom Hegel believed was the first philosopher to have understood the ultimate Oneness of Being), through Plato, Aristotle, Descartes, and Kant, culminating in the ultimate synthesis of the Absolute Spirit. Clearly, this direct manifestation and rewriting of Plato's version of Western metaphysics has a teleological goal aimed at the Absolute as an endpoint when the dialectical tensions would come to rest, but nevertheless metaphysics is now given a historical casting that has made Hegel's work deeply influential for critical theorists of the last two centuries. When push came to shove, Hegel, like Plato, was a believer in the superiority of spirit over matter, universal over particular, yet he also insisted on the synthesis of the two, rather than just an idealized break from the specificity of material history: as he puts it, "labour shapes and fashions the thing" (*Phenomenology* 111), and philosophy therefore needs to account for the labor that produced the things about which the discourse speaks.

In paradigmatic ways, then, Hegel's historical analysis of the teleological progress of Western metaphysical idealism culminating in the attainment of the Absolute will end up greatly influencing the later emergence of the more traditional forms of Romantic idealism. But the enormous range of his complex thinking also propelled a dialectical version of historical materialism that led to more socially radical theories of art, literature, and philosophy. In practical terms, his followers have often, therefore, been characterized by their political interpretations of Hegel's philosophy so we have Right Hegelians and Left Hegelians. Actually, the Right Hegelians were named derisively by a Left Hegelian, David Strauss, a Protestant theologian who pioneered the historical study of Jesus. What he called the "Right Hegelians" were the group of Hegel's students who were the conservative followers of their teacher's "abstract idealism," tending to ignore the more radical political implications of some of Hegel's ideas. As it turned out, those who fit the Right Hegelian label ended up having no real effect on philosophy or politics—indeed, they had little subsequent influence, and we never hear of them today.

In terms of my analysis of the two strains of Romanticism, nonetheless, the Right Hegelians match up with the Romantic idealists, and the Left Hegelians match up pretty well with the radical Romantics. It will be the Left Hegelians such as Marx and Engels who insist on the move toward an even more materialist critical theory, thus adapting Hegel's historical dialectic to the long history of class struggle in the battles between rulers and oppressed, although neither Marx nor Engels ever refers directly to Hegel's master-slave dialectic. Marx arrived at the University of Berlin in 1836, five years after Hegel's death, but the latter's followers were everywhere, in one of the most prestigious universities in the world.

For the Right Hegelians such as Karl Friedrich Göschel, Georg Andreas Gabler, Leopold von Henning, and others, Hegel's aesthetics will be intellectually aligned with the subsequent forms of Romantic idealism even though the British Romantics never refer to them in their work: as in the concluding sections of Wordsworth's *Prelude,* art provides the medium for the movement from the particular, sensuous dimension of perception to the attainment of the ultimate universal Idea. Like Wordsworth, Hegel also became more conservative as he aged. Hegel was indeed the great champion of what he calls the "living work of art" (*Phenomenology* 422), and therefore provided, along with Kant, some of the philosophical theories underwriting Romantic idealism. But Hegel was clearly not a Romantic, and he himself objected to his being coupled with that term. For Hegel the absolute ideal of reason retained its Enlightenment status as the highest form of knowledge, reigning supreme over the necessarily synthetic accomplishments of art. In Hegel's formulations, the concrete forms of specific artworks (such as the *Prelude*) enable us to apprehend through the senses the universal spirit that transcends those very senses.[16] As we will see in the *Logic,* Hegel's great achievement is that he disavowed nearly every one of Kant's systematic articulations of absolutes, and insisted on a historicized version of the emergence and development of philosophy—a kind of immanent critique of the kind Adorno will later champion. But the return of the same still happened: as in Kant's view of transcendental idealism, with its built-in universal basis in all human beings, Hegel sought in art the imaginative synthesis and in rational philosophy the ultimate synthesis of the uneven hierarchies between subject and object. Aesthetic experience provided a kind of sublime (Hegel called it "sublation") unification of binary tensions in the communality of universal human consciousness and particular human subjects. But we need to look a bit more closely at Hegel's influential formulations to get a better sense of what he was trying to do so we can better assess what he actually accomplished.

A few weeks before his death in 1831, Hegel was about halfway through the preface to the second edition of *The Phenomenology of Mind,* and what he left us was a reasonably accessible overview of the entire plan for his masterpiece. In terms quite similar to Kant's basic vision for Enlightenment thought, Hegel saw his work as a revolutionary fulfillment of the possibilities of basing philosophical speculation on the firm footing of science.

It was a historical watershed moment for him: "our epoch is a birth-time, and a period of transition. The spirit of man has broken with the old order of things hitherto prevailing, and with the old ways of thinking," such that the world was to be "carried along the stream of progress ever onward" (6). On the very first page of the preface, entitled "On Scientific Knowledge," Hegel stakes his central claim for the integration of the subjective and the objective: "philosophy has its being essentially in the element of that universality which encloses the particular within it" (1).

For Hegel, then, the Absolute is a synthetic moment integrating universality and difference rather than a Platonic escape from the world of appearance to the otherworldly Forms. Each concrete individuality "can be clearly interpreted only in the light of the entire system. Each mirrors the whole system in itself; and the whole system can be said to be the unfolding of 'the notion' par excellence" (Baillie xxix). To this extent, Hegel draws on the German word *Bildung*, which was to have such significance in educational theories in the nineteenth century by signifying the development of the cultured individual through increasingly higher levels of self-consciousness. Hegel took the educational task of philosophy to be "the formative development (*Bildung*) of the universal [or general] individual," but with a teleological goal: "every moment, as it gains concrete form and its own proper shape and appearance finds a place in the life of the universal individual" (*Phenomenology* 15). The latter term is not an oxymoron for Hegel, and the social value of all these intellectual processes is the achievement of freedom.

These apparent contradictions hinge on Hegel's specialized meaning of an otherwise ordinary language term, *notion*. In common parlance, we think of a notion as a kind of vague or inchoate idea, such as, "I have the notion that I may contact my old friend." But Hegel puts it to a much different use. In the 1831 preface, he tries to explicate the particular meaning he had in mind when he first used the term so often in the 1807 edition, but it nevertheless remains very difficult to understand (indeed, the entire *Phenomenology* has been called one of the most difficult books ever written). In German, the term is *Begrift*, which is commonly translated as "concept," but many translators have adopted the term *notion* as more appropriate for Hegel's special uses.

In the 1807 "Introduction," Hegel summarizes his plan for the spiritual awakening of consciousness: "Consciousness . . . is to itself its own notion; thereby it immediately transcends what is limited, and since this latter belongs to it, consciousness transcends its own self" (48–49). At the end of the book, Hegel believes that he had truly attained that degree of individual transcendence toward the Truth of the Absolute Spirit: "The goal of the process is the revelation of the depth of spiritual life, and this is the Absolute Notion" (476). In this grand sense, we can think of Hegel's use of "notion" as the Truth or essence of any concept, term, or category so that, for example, the notions of reason, truth, and spirit are their universal reality, not just the wayward and uncritical terms we often use in everyday speech without the philosophical rigor Hegel demands.

The *Phenomenology* argues that this arduous path toward the Absolute is clearly a long historical and developmental process, but in this text there is very little actual historical analysis, even as he makes reference to the French Revolution as a historical turning point: "the so-called 'Enlightenment' . . . proceeded and culminated in the French Revolution, the supreme outburst of spiritual emancipation known in European history" (283). We have to wait for the posthumously published *Lectures on the Philosophy of World History* to see the historical map laid out by Hegel. But before we get to that crucial text, we should look briefly at his second major book, *The Science of Logic,* partly because it is easier to understand than the *Phenomenology,* and he spends considerably more time clarifying "The Notion as Notion" (*Science* 190).

Indeed, the *Logic* is Hegel's clearest articulation of his philosophical method. In basic terms, Hegel's method shares much with both Plato and Aristotle, since they would all admit Hegel's assumption that "Truth is the object of Logic" (*Science* 18), but the methodological differences emerge in their procedures for getting to the goal. For Plato, the negative function of the dialectic played a kind of weeding-out role: each step of the dialectic moved higher, away from the sensuous world of appearances toward the truth of the absolute Forms. But for Hegel the dialectic of reason not only negates false appearances, but also provides an integrative function, so that we can get closer to the synthesis of material and abstract "Notions." Following the introduction, in the second chapter of the *Logic,* called "Preliminary Notion," Hegel explains that his philosophical method is aimed at getting us to the notion, or essence, of the abstract ideas we contemplate.[17] The problem is that these formulations seem less historical than Hegel might intend because it is hard to imagine reaching the teleological goal of determining the absolute notion of a finite thing without somehow evoking the preexistent nature of abstract forms as the endpoint of the intellectual journey. Hegel tries to deny this idealized meaning of the notion, and he does so expressly in his extended discussion of essentialism in the long, eighth chapter "The Doctrine of Essence" (134–86).

This chapter represents one of the first extended attempts to address the problem of "essentialism" that later became so prominent in theoretical debates in the 1970s and 1980s. This chapter is long because it is complicated: Hegel tries to resist the reduction of the essence of an object to its form: the essence may be the "ground of existence" (138), but it cannot just be reduced to an abstract form devoid of content. These are important arguments for resisting Western metaphysical formalism, and he treats these issues in the context of technical philosophical arguments about identity and the excluded middle, a crucial logical concept that as we saw began with Aristotle's distinctions. Hegel also addresses the dialectical tensions between appearance and reality, ground and foreground, essence and existence, actuality and contingency. Not everyone agrees with Hegel's formulations, but his efforts to preserve the dialectic between historical contingency and the notion of the "actuality" of Being (one of the ultimate notions), remain a source for some of the later historical materialists, including Marx.[18]

Indeed, in an earlier section of the *Logic,* Chapter 4, "Second Attitude of Thought on Objectivity," Hegel offers one of his most detailed critiques of his predecessor, Immanuel Kant. While granting the huge significance of Kant's struggles to reconcile empirical and rationalist differences in epistemology, Hegel believes that in the former's doctrine of the "transcendental unity of apperception" too much emphasis is placed on perception, sensibility, and subjectivity; so much so that Kant ends up in a kind of "subjective idealism" that neglects the integrative tension with external actuality, including historical context and material reality. As Hegel puts it, "Kant undertook to examine how far the forms of thought were capable of leading to the knowledge of truth. . . . That is a fair demand. . . . Unfortunately, there soon creeps in the misconception of already knowing before you know,—the error of refusing to enter the water until you have learnt to swim" (*Science* 53–54). It's as if, for Kant, some of the categories, or the notions (such as time and space), have their existence already in the subject or ego, or, using Kant's term, *pure apperception.*

Despite the apparent difficulty of these theoretical nuances, in the early nineteenth century Hegel's philosophical analysis was seen as more historically based than Kant's on precisely these key points. Given our interest in the political economy, this turn to history is crucial to understand. We can first get a good sense of this historical turn by returning to Chapter 4 of the *Phenomenology.*

Although famously known as the "master-slave dialectic," the concept Hegel introduces in this section of the *Phenomenology* was actually called the "lordship-bondage dialectic." In formulating this key concept of dialectical materialism, Hegel drew directly on his understanding of the Haitian slave revolt. But as Buck-Morss argues, Marxists tended to treat Hegel's master-slave, lordship-bondage analysis as a metaphor for the class struggle between proletarians and capitalists rather than as a reference to the literal reality of slavery as the quintessential underbelly of capitalism. As it had for Wordsworth, the French Revolution became the model for new forms of human freedom, and the Reign of Terror the historical lesson to be learned from the betrayal of the idealism of the human spirit. The simultaneously occurring Haitian Revolution represented the real test of the material possibilities for human freedom. The "thesis" of freedom and the "antithesis" of terror must be resolved in the dialectical evolution toward the Absolute Spirit. As we have seen with Wordsworth, the social and political implications of these new forms of idealism can lean either toward the political right or toward the political left, and some of the more radical formulations of Hegel's philosophy of history can be traced to his formulation of the master-slave dialectic.

It unfolds in Chapter 4, Section A, on "Lordship and Bondage" of the *Phenomenology,* and begins with one of the most widely cited sentences in all of Hegel's work: "Self-consciousness exists in itself and for itself, in that, and by the fact that it exists for another self-consciousness; that is to say, it *is* only by being acknowledged or 'recognized'" (104). Hegel situates the formation of subjectivity in an intersubjective "process of Recognition" (105) that would appear to be based on mutuality and reciprocity (what Louis Althusser will later call "hailing"). But Hegel emphasizes that the historical actuality of most kinds of human identity takes place in asymmetrical, hierarchical relations based on the maldistribution of political and economic power so that individual subjects stand opposed (rather than equal) to each other: "The one is independent, and its essential nature is to be for itself; the other is dependent, and its essence is life or existence for another. The former is the Master, or Lord, the latter the Bondsman" (108). Although these terms reflect the familiar arrangement of power in feudal societies, it is fair to say that Hegel means something much more archetypal or fundamental about the long-standing historical inequality in human relations.[19] We have to attend to the historical context in which he is writing to glean the more general meanings that he theorizes on the basis of concrete historical events of his age.

Two significant factors seem to have contributed almost simultaneously to Hegel's formulation of this lordship-bondage dialectic: his reading of Adam Smith in 1803 and his reading of the press reports on the Haitian Revolution. Yet few critics have drawn these inferences. As Susan Buck-Morss hypothesizes: Hegel's reading of *The Wealth of Nations* appears "to be a turning point" (52n90). In addition, "No one has dared to suggest that the idea for the dialectic of lordship and bondage came to Hegel in Jena in the years 1803–5 from reading the press" (49), yet we know that "Hegel knew—knew about real slaves revolting successfully against real masters, and he elaborated his dialectic of lordship and bondage deliberately within this contemporary concern" (50).[20] To this extent, "he used the sensational events of Haiti as the linchpin in his argument in *The Phenomenology of Spirit*" (59).

These remarkable links between philosophical hierarchies and political/economic hierarchies have often gone unrecognized in the long history of influential critical interpretations of Hegel's monumental articulation of what we have come to know as the master-slave dialectic. Yet we now know that Hegel "connected the liberation of the slave explicitly with the historical realization of freedom" (Buck-Morss 61). During these early years of the nineteenth century, Hegel was also actively involved with Freemasonry in its work against slavery.

Yet Buck-Morss also traces Hegel's movement away from the material forms of economic exploitation in the slave trade of industrial capitalism—a movement that begins in the very section of his chapter on lordship and bondage. As she argues: "But then the slaves . . . achieve self-consciousness by demonstrating that they are not things, not objects, but subjects who transform material nature. Hegel's text becomes obscure and falls silent at this point of realization" (54). Hegel turns to a more Aristotelian formalism in his dialectical distinction between the lord's being "for itself" and the bondsman's being "for others." Given these considerations of slavery, however, Buck-Morss asks: "why should—how *could* Hegel have stayed somehow mired in Aristotle?" (59). Historical reality, nonetheless, gets subordinated to the idealist strain: what Hegel calls "genuine reality" of the sensual world ends up being subsumed by "absolute universal being" until, in the end, the former material reality is shown "to be mere nothingness" (*Phenomenology* 127). In short, Chapter 4 ends with the triumph "of Reason of the certainty that consciousness is in its particularity inherently and essentially absolute or is all reality" (130). The historical conditions formed by particular master-slave relations seem to have been left far behind once we reach that absolute reality.

Thirteen years later, we find, Hegel wrote *The Philosophy of Right* specifically to address the material conditions of the newly emerging political economy as orchestrated by the nation-state. What from our contemporary perspective will seem most unusual is Hegel's apparent idealization of the modern nation. As he puts it quite strikingly, "the state is the mind objectified" (*Hegel's*

Philosophy 156); "[t]he state is the actuality of the ethical Idea" (155); "the state is absolutely rational" (155). Given the clearly irrational actions of so many contemporary nations, these ideas jar with almost everyone's conception of the nature of national governments in our global economy. Indeed, they jarred deeply with Marx's growing critique in the 1840s of the exploitive, unethical behavior of the modern state as orchestrated by the ruling bourgeois classes. Marx clearly grants that Hegel was right to articulate the relationships between the state and private property, and that it was certainly an advance to think of the organization of "the diversity of powers as organic" (*Critique of Hegel's* 12). But after these materialist beginnings, according to Marx, Hegel slips into the most tautological idealisms whereby the universal notion of the state is a totally abstracted idealization of the ultimate harmony of the state as an "organism." Hegel's ultimately formalized meaning of freedom has given this political concept nothing more than a kind of "mystical bearer" whereby the "actual subject of freedom takes on a formal meaning (63), but completely ignores the actual conditions of sovereignty and exploitation of living human beings.

Indeed, Hegel's turn toward a more conservative political philosophy took place in the last decade of his life, during the 1820s, when he delivered a series of five lectures (one every other year) at the University of Berlin that were published posthumously in 1837. Adapted by the editor, Eduard Gans, from Hegel's own lecture notes as well as notes from his students, this book, *Lectures on the Philosophy of World History*, reveals a great deal about Hegel's understanding of the political economy.

In his introduction to the book, Duncan Forbes accepts Hegel's theory that, despite its current shortcomings, the emergence of the modern state represents a new vision in the world of a government based on reason, law, and morality rather than on brute strength. He therefore takes Marx to task for missing Hegel's intentions and for failing to see that "the deeper rational meaning of the modern state suggested by Hegel's dialectic still stands" (xxxi). Forbes reverses Marx's critique with the claim that "Hegel's state is doing precisely what Marx wants communism to do" (xxxiii), and that the modern "democratic state is a standing contradiction in terms, and a perpetual tension and never-ending dialogue between freedom and order. . . . Hegel wants as much liberty as possible, and so does Marx. . . . And both want the maximum development of the individual" (xxxv). Hegel certainly did want freedom, but his acceptance of something like a hereditary monarch (in its idealized version, sort of like Plato's philosopher-king), and the concrete representations of history that take up the large part of the *Philosophy of World History* make it very difficult to agree with Forbes's positive evaluation of Hegel's historicism. Indeed, a closer look at that history will quickly reveal the problems.

In the first chapter, "The Varieties of Historical Writing," Hegel offers us a description of his three-level classification of the progressive stages of history-telling: (1) original history; (2) reflective history; and (3) philosophical history. Obviously, his version is the third, and each stage is an improvement on its predecessor. By original history, he means a basic representation of events that the author has lived through, and his examples are those historical records written by the original Greek historians, Herodotus and Thucydides. Interestingly, no version of any kind of oral history such as we saw in Chapter 3 is even recognized as having any significance to history. Reflective history arises when writers look back to construct narratives of events that preceded their own historical moment, and Hegel describes four progressively more self-reflective versions of such history leading up to what he calls "specialized history," offering as an example the work of his contemporary, Victor Hugo, especially his *History of Roman Law*—such accounts focus on narrow or specialized historical periods or locations from the past. And third is Hegel's own universal, "philosophical history of the world" (*Lectures* 23) where "the spirit, with its rational and necessary will . . . continues to direct the events of world history" (24).

It becomes increasingly clear as this text goes on that Hegel's Christian values join deeply with his narrative of world history. He speaks at length of God as the "eternal being" and the source of universality and reason. "Christianity is the religion which has revealed the nature and being of God to man," and it is the philosophical historian's task to determine how world history is "commensurate with the divine government" (41). Thus, "History is the unfolding of God's nature in a particular, determinate element" (42). When he goes on to describe this actual world-historical unfolding, the story begins in ancient Greece where "the consciousness of freedom first awoke among the Greeks . . . but, like the Romans, they only knew that Some, and not all men as such, are free. . . . Plato and Aristotle did not know this either; thus the Greeks . . . had slaves" (54). One might think that this assessment would lead Hegel to universally condemn slavery in this context (as he did as a young man), and he does somewhat head in that direction ("man is by nature free" would seem to be nonexclusionary), but the historically early stages also provided a kind of excuse for justifying slavery, as we have seen the ancient philosophers such as Aristotle clearly did.

The goal of all this history is, however, not that different from the ancient task of attaining "knowledge of the unmoved mover, as Aristotle calls it, of the unmoved motive force by which individuals are activated" (77). Coming out of the cave of ignorance is a historical project of coming out of the limitations of all preceding historical epochs and reaching the peak of universal self-consciousness now made possible by the evolving nineteenth-century version of Western metaphysics, primarily as exemplified in Hegel's own writing. However, what follows in the appendix as the "Geographical Basis of World History" will now appear shockingly racist.

There are many examples, but I will cite only a few to give a sense of these ethnocentric judgments, some just ridiculing Native Americans, Asians, Africans, and most other peoples outside the "temperate zone" around the Mediterranean that must, by default, "furnish the theater of world history" (155). With respect to the Native America that "had to perish as soon as the spirit approached it" (163), "even the animals show the same inferiority as the human beings" (163). Even those Native Americans who had visited Europe were "obviously unintelligent individuals with little capacity for education" (164). "The Americans, then, are like unenlightened children" (165). With respect to Africans, Hegel claims that they have "not progressed beyond a merely sensuous existence" and that they are "absolutely impossible to develop any further" (172). Their general "good-naturedness . . . is coupled, however, with completely unfeeling cruelty" (173). The African is said to live "in a state of savagery and barbarism

. . . an example of animal man in all his savagery and lawless-
ness" (177), and "all men in Africa are sorcerers" (179). For these
reasons, as Hegel explains, "it is easily explained why *slavery* is
the basic legal relationship in Africa" (183) so that, even for the
Europeans coming in contact with them, "this slavery is endemic
and accepted as natural" (183). By this point, late in his life, then,
Hegel is willing to believe that there are historical justifications
such that, at this stage of history, "slavery is still necessary" (184).

What Hegel calls the "Orientals" do not fare much better,
since "[w]orld history travels from east to west, for Europe is the
absolute end of history, just as Asia is the beginning" (197). In
this historical frame, then, we "find that the political structures
of Oriental substantiality are accompanied by wild hordes who
descend from the verge of the uplands into the peaceful states.
They lay them waste and destroy them" (201–02). In any case,
it should be pretty clear by now that this is a version of history
not many of us would subscribe to.

In comparison with Wordsworth's relatively modest shift to
Romantic idealism later in his life, Hegel's conversion is more
startling. As Buck-Morss summarizes, "Hegel's retreat from
revolutionary radicalism was clear. . . . Notoriously condemning
African culture to prehistory and blaming the Africans themselves
for New World slavery, Hegel repeated the banal and apologetic
argument that slaves were better off in the colonies than in the
African homeland" (67–68). Indeed, what was most striking was
"the brutal thoroughness with which he dismissed all of sub-
Saharan Africa, this 'land of children,' of 'barbarity and wildness,'
from any significance for world history, due to what he deemed
were deficiencies of the African 'spirit'" (68). Buck-Morss does
not let up: "What is clear is that in an effort to become more
erudite in African studies during the 1820s, Hegel was in fact
becoming dumber" (73).

Of course, Hegel was a very smart and exceptionally educated
man, and those who deeply admire him might be more distressed
by Buck-Morss's critique than the admirers of Wordsworth's
radical Romanticism might be at my Chapter 7 critique of his
late-life shift toward a more conservative idealism. But, just to
conjecture, the consequences of the Romantic movement might

have been different had these influential poets and philosophers not made these shifts to the right.

We will never know, but we do know that Marx and Engels appreciated Hegel's emphasis on historical process; at the same time, they were critical of Hegel's idealized version of the positive side of labor, thus ignoring the huge potential for workers to be exploited and alienated. They began their own task of creating a much modified version of dialectical materialism that they hoped would inform the international countermovement to the dominant powers of industrial capitalism. Neither Marx nor Engels had even been born when in 1806 Napoleon rode through Jena in celebration of his military triumph, yet Hegel clearly marveled at the show of state power, or at least he saw on display the remarkable world-historical transformations underway following the French Revolution, a process now represented for Hegel in the physical presence of Napoleon. In a famous letter to a friend in October 1806, about a year before the *Phenomenology* appeared, he exults: "I saw the Emperor—this world-soul—riding out of the city on reconnaissance. It is indeed a wonderful sensation to see such an individual, who, concentrated here at a single point, astride a horse, reaches out over the world and masters it ... this extraordinary man, whom it is impossible not to admire" (quoted in Pinkard 228).[21] Hegel's admiration did not seem to be abated by the devastation of the ransacked city of Jena because his fundamental hope was that the French Revolution had reached a new stage as it passed into Prussia. Although Napoleon did not close the University of Jena as he had many other Prussian universities, Hegel "was stuck with no money and no real prospects" (233) because the demolition of the city meant that most of the students had abandoned their studies: by "November 3, 1806, only 130 students returned" (232). Hegel also had his own personal problems, as his married landlady (Christiana Burkhardt, then estranged from her husband) was pregnant with their illegitimate son, Georg Ludwig Fischer, who would be born in February of the following year. The mother and son stayed in Jena when Hegel fled to Bamberg for about a year before he sought and secured a position in a Gymnasium in Nuremburg, where he stayed for eight years.

Of course, by 1806 Napoleon represented not the liberatory aims of the revolution but, rather, the power of the rising bourgeoisie and the principles of "laissez-faire" capitalism fully secured by the nation-state, now legalized by the Napoleonic codes for relaxed trade rules and reduced tariffs. Marx and Engels would devote their lives trying to move the Left Hegelians, and the rest of the world, toward a more engaged form of dialectical materialism that would oppose the exploitative hierarchies of the ruling classes, which meant the owners of capital.

From 1789 to 1848 to 1871: Revolution Redux

Mary Wollstonecraft never lived to encounter the great works of Hegel nor to see the economic transformations wrought by Napoleon as Emperor of France, but, like the socialists and anarchists, she surely would have been an adamant critic of what transpired in the geopolitical economy of Europe in the early nineteenth century. Unfortunately, she died giving birth to her second daughter, also Mary, who would later marry Percy Shelley and write *Frankenstein*, the monster created by a blind faith in scientific technology to provide, as Saint-Simon suggested, the answer to all social problems. But during the early decades of the nineteenth century, the suffering of peasants and workers actually increased. The dislocations the peasants experienced often led them to migrate to the industrializing urban areas, and that is why they appear as the impoverished unemployed walking by the Wordsworths' cottage in Grasmere and why Robert Owen found working conditions so loathsomely unjust once the migrants settled in as mill workers. Under the new laws of property ownership, the peasants now had to seek employment for wage labor, and pay rent to the bourgeoisie and taxes to the state. At first of course, this seemed like a triumph of the peasants over the landed aristocracy, at least insofar as they were no longer "serfs," or "bondsmen," but by the middle of the nineteenth century, their sense of futility and betrayal laid the ground for the huge revolutions in 1848. For example, about 85 percent of the 400,000 inhabitants of Berlin at that time were poor, with more than half of that number depending on some form of poor relief. In Paris, a two-hundred-franc voting tax was passed in 1847 when even the relatively secure artisans made only about six hundred francs per year, so that of the nine million French men, only about 250,000 could vote. The revolutions of 1848 represent one of the largest international revolts of workers, peasants, and students that has ever occurred. It began in February of the year in Paris, but by the end of March revolutions had also broken out in many nations in Europe, and several places in South America and Africa. It became known as the "Springtime of the Peoples." Marx and Engels composed the *Communist Manifesto* in order to further the causes of the worker rebellions. Communism was the name given to the main alternative for imagining a utopian classless society, the "higher phase" where "the springs of co-operative wealth flow more abundantly" because the free access and distribution of goods and services would be "from each according to his ability, to each according to his needs" (Marx, *Critique of the Gotha Programme*).

On the surface, Marx and Engels would seem to be two of the most unlikely compatriots: Marx was the scruffy, bedraggled son of a line of Jewish rabbis whose father had converted to Christianity only so he could practice as a lawyer, a profession legally closed to Jews in nineteenth-century Prussia; Engels was the son of a wealthy industrialist, fastidious in every way, and having to continue running his father's factory in order to support Marx. But they changed the world.

Both Marx and Engels clearly saw that the classical economists were, as Marx puts it, mired in an "unhistorical outlook" (McLellan 447) because they simply assumed that price equaled value, that the more or less free market determined wages and prices, and therefore missed entirely the notion of surplus labor, the amount above subsistence labor that a worker could work in a day that could be exploited and turned into more capital for the owner, irrespective of the conditions of the worker. Up until about 1848, Marx had been deeply influenced by Proudhon to the extent that the communist goal was the establishment of free associations of workers, and Marx and Engels expressed these associationist views in the *Communist Manifesto*. But by 1846, in his correspondence with Marx, Proudhon had begun to express his reservations about what he perceived to be Marx's views about the need for violent revolution by the proletariat to seize momentary control of the state. Yet a centralized state was never Marx's ultimate goal, because he consistently argued for the abolition of the state, to be replaced by worker cooperatives, although he did reassess his views about how this might happen following the 1871 Paris Commune.[22] These theoretical tensions came to a head in the dramatic events unfolding in the spring of 1848, when worker and student revolts began in Europe but spread quickly to many parts of the world. Marx had hoped for a simultaneous world revolution so he was of course profoundly disappointed that the temporary freedoms gained by the workers were devastatingly short-lived. The violent suppression of the revolutions of 1848 pales, however, in comparison to the level of brutality wrought by the suppression of the Paris Commune in 1871. Something about the latter event can be seen as paradigmatic of the major challenges of all the countermovements to the dominance of the capitalist system, so that's where we'll look in the next chapter. But first we need to look briefly at some basic Marxian concepts such as surplus value, the mode of production, and commodity fetishism.

The Geopolitical Economy of Theory; or, How to Free the Fetish

> *A commodity appears, at first sight, a very trivial thing, and easily understood. Its analysis shows that it is, in reality, a very queer thing, abounding in metaphysical subtleties and theological niceties.*
>
> —Karl Marx, *Capital*

In the course of composing his monumental volumes of *Capital*, Karl Marx creatively reconstructed a familiar term so that it acquired a new, more technical meaning adapted to his particular analysis of the political economy. *Fetish* came into European use sometime in the late seventeenth century, and according to the *Oxford English Dictionary* it was used by explorers in referring to the strange but talismanic objects believed to have supernatural properties that Africans wore around their necks (*Compact Edi-*

tion 176). In common usage today, particularly in psychology, it refers to any object that has unusual or obsessive interest, such as a sexual fetish for shoes or whips.[23] But Marx adapted the term *fetishism* to his analysis of the production and exchange of commodities under capitalism, and for many Marxist theorists fetishism is a key to understanding his dynamic analysis of the political economy. I agree.

Section 4 of the first Part of *Capital*, Volume 1, is entitled "The Fetishism of the Commodity and Its Secret," and it is both an unusual and a crucial section to Marx's entire theory. It is unusual because of its shift in linguistic register and style. As David Harvey explains, in contrast to the more dull and analytic style Marx most often adopts, "This section is written in completely different, rather literary style—evocative and metaphoric, imaginative, playful and emotive, full of allusions and references to magic, mysteries and necromancies" (*Companion* 38). It is also crucial, because the notion of fetishism embodies the central but dynamic ways that capitalism hides the human lives of the producers through an almost talismanic worship of the commodity and the monetary value by which we measure it. Fetishism is a name for this complex process whereby the human labor necessary for producing things is concealed and replaced with a relation of abstract things, what he called the commodity form, between the commodity itself and money as a measure of its value. As Marx puts it, "a definite social relation between men" becomes transformed into "the fantastic form of a relation between things" (McLellan 473).

Harvey uses a good, concrete example of going to the market to buy a head of lettuce: "Hidden within this market exchange of things is a relation between you, the consumer, and the direct producers—those who labored to produce the lettuce" (*Companion* 39). But when we purchase the lettuce all we are concerned with is the price and quality of the lettuce—we can't see the workers in the fields who planted, tended, and picked it. We can't see how the products we consume got produced in the first place. It gets more complicated when we talk about cultural commodities like theory or art, but the principles remain the same: since theoretical production requires a significant array of goods and services, not just the brain of an isolated individual, it can be very helpful to turn our analytic attention to all the various material producers engaged in what may otherwise appear to be such immaterial commodities as theories and philosophies about literature, art, and the world.

I have thematically framed this history of theory in terms of an analysis of the geopolitical economy because the latter focuses on breaking the mythical hold of commodity fetishism characteristic of consumer culture. Instead of concealing productive factors, analysis of the geopolitical economy makes visible the hidden relations of the producers that occur prior to the exchange of goods in commodity markets. More particularly, the political economy refers, among other things, to two main social functions necessary for sustaining human life: the organization of production and the distribution of the value added to any raw materials in the process of any mode of production. Whether it is an agrarian economy, feudalism, capitalism, or any other system of production and exchange, some form of increased value accrues to the goods produced. To use a specific example, for most people a coat is of more use and value than the cotton or hide out of which it is made; in turn, cotton fabric or animal hides are more valuable than the plants and animals from which the former are produced. The specific ways that any society carries out these necessary functions determines the range of social justice possible in that society.

As populations increase, the division of labor also increases so that the relations between labor, value, and price can become very complex. In the late eighteenth century, what we now call the labor theory of value emerged as a direct response to these complexities, and, as we saw in the work of Ricardo, it became a crucial concern for some of the nineteenth-century classical economists. Labor theory actually has roots going all the way back to the Middle Ages, but Adam Smith began to rework these relations for the modern age of market economies (see esp. *Wealth*, book 1, chapters 1–8, pp. 9–121). Among other things, he introduced the important distinctions between "use value" and "exchange value." He also introduced the important notion of "surplus value" : in the modern "commercial society" (*Wealth* 33) no person can produce all the goods necessary to sustain life. In short, life depends on exchange value "by exchanging that surplus part of the produce of his own labour, which is over and above his own consumption" (33). In the early nineteenth century, this key term was modified by Pierre-Joseph Proudhon and Ricardo, among others, but Marx will attack both Proudhon and Ricardo (see Harvey, *Limits* 23–24) precisely because of their failure to understand how surplus value was the central mechanism for the exploitation of workers under capitalist modes of production.

The chain of production and exchange can, of course, be very intricate so that, as Marx explained, basic use-value gets converted almost completely into market exchange-value. Nevertheless, two crucial questions with respect to the organization of production are: (1) Who makes decisions about how things get produced and exchanged? and (2): What are the conditions and human relations of those most directly involved in producing and exchanging those goods? The crucial question with respect to the surplus is: How is the value added to the products distributed among the population? That is, decisions about production can be widely and democratically shared by all those participating in the production of the goods; or decision making can take place exclusively by small groups of powerful individuals. Likewise, the surplus can be widely distributed, or, it can be appropriated by a few who control production, thus creating exploitive economic and social hierarchies among the society. Questions about the distribution of the surplus are thus also questions about the modes of exchange in terms of how the goods and services circulate within and between different societies, which Marx called the "commodity form" of exchange in a capitalist economy. He felt that one of his main contributions to economic theory was his detailed analysis of the ways that capital could appropriate the surplus value produced by labor: workers' wages could be far less than the monetary form of surplus value gained as profit by the owners of production; and the workers had very little control whatsoever over the power of capital to extract that value from them. Marx also understood that the economic principle of endless accumulation of capital would inevitably lead to increasing economic inequalities between the owners of capital and the workers. As Kevin Anderson argues, "capital accumulation devastates the global environment and the world's people" ("Marx's Capital" 6).

Nevertheless, maldistribution of the surplus, such as we find in capitalist modes of production, is not a necessity of nature but a product of history—which is to say that the organization of production and the modes of exchange can be altered through historical struggle. Analyses of the geopolitical economy can thereby aim to ensure that all people involved in production and distribution of goods get recognized in our theoretical and historical descriptions. To that extent, just theory works to break the hold of the fetishized commodity so that we can make more visible the social consequences of the system of endless accumulation.

Given the respect most critics now have for the recognition of racial, gender, class, and ethnic differences, we also have to recall that difference itself can be fetishized as a commodity to be exploited by capital.[24] That is, late capitalism systemically operates through a willful fetishizing of differences (as in "disruptive innovations")[25] that serve to customize products in niche markets and seamlessly radiate a spectrum of more "innovative" products that glitter on computer screens and TVs as spectacular images of consumer choices.[26] The key question to ask, therefore, is: innovative and disruptive for whom? Marx referred to the powers of capitalism to engulf all forms of resistance and difference into its own mode of production as a process of "subsumption." Thus, when we say that our own beliefs and behaviors are complicit with the system we wish to criticize, we acknowledged the degree by which we have been subsumed within the system.

The fetishizing of difference in complete denial of any dialectical tensions with some forms of sameness is also self-defeating: without some forms of communal sharing, we cannot even sustain what David Palumbo-Liu calls "the intersubjective nature of knowing the world and making propositions about it" (213). "Difference" itself is a rational generalization that serves, among other things, to recognize that we now live in a world where there are roughly five thousand different ethnic groups, and each of those groups is thoroughly blurred and hybrid.

The activities of producing and exchanging theory, seeking general frames for knowing, are immanent within our market economy precisely to the extent that theoretical ideas can function, both at the same time, as a cultural commodity and a critique of the political economy of commodity markets. That dialectical paradox is possible because the totality of social relations in a market society is never seamless or total in any absolute sense. Dominant cultural ideologies aim to be seamless and consistent, but critique reveals them to be inconsistent and contradictory in practice, struggling to maintain their hold over various residual and emergent discourses.[27] A good case of some of these inconsistencies can be seen in the relations between gender and labor, and Marx was one of the first to point out that, for instance, the garment factories exploited women just as the general capitalist economy depended upon the unpaid labor of women carrying out "domestic labor" necessary for social reproduction. Yet there were some pretty deep personal contradictions: some of Marx's personal difficulties and political actions in his own life can be troubling for a contemporary feminist. For one thing, Marx was highly critical of Victoria Woodhull, a noted First Wave feminist who was a member of the International Workingmen's Association (also known as the First International) and the first woman to run for the presidency of the United States (against Grover Cleveland). Marx wrote many negative things about Woodhull, and he forced her out of the First International. Woodhull did have some unusual backgrounds in arcane subject matters, but she was an outspoken feminist, and Marx derailed her work in the labor movement. Second, Marx was, to say the least, a difficult man to be married to, as he was frequently away from home, demanded a great deal from his wife, Jennifer (whom he clearly loved), had regular drinking binges, and he had an affair and a child with the longtime house maid that Jennifer's parents had arranged for when Karl and Jenny were first married. Yet, this person, Helene Demuth, known as "Lenchen," continued to live and serve in the Marx household even after the child was born—Engels claimed he was the father, to cover for Marx, and the child, Frederick Demuth, was raised by foster parents in East London. These contradictions can be difficult to sweep under the rug.[28]

Of course, Marx was a master at analyzing the ways that the "false consciousness" of capitalist ideology could sweep contradictions right out of sight. Drawing on these insights, in the late twentieth century, what Guy Debord called "the society of the spectacle" was the overwhelming power of late capitalism to create an appearance of a seamless web of spectacular images and multimedia discourses that make invisible any alternatives to the official stories. But this mystified "world of appearances" (the ultimate Platonic "simulacrum") has never been completely totalizing, as its advocates might wish. Capital, nation, and state are not seamlessly but contentiously integrated. Indeed, cultural dominants such as the commodity form also tend to produce what Karl Polanyi referred to as "counter-movements," and the general frames of our analysis must attend to the formative struggles among those multiple movements and ideological contradictions (see Harvey, *Seventeen*)—what Marx called class struggle.

Marx tended to focus on the capitalist structures of production and exchange—the economic base—with the nation, state, and culture all as secondary, an ideological superstructure added to the material base. On this latter point, Kojin Karatani's conception of the tightly woven tripartite structure of capital-nation-state is more historically accurate in our contemporary geopolitical economy. Western metaphysical idealism functioned in perhaps unconscious ways leading Marx to formulate this binary, base-superstructure model that can be misleading insofar as it tends to forecast an end of the dialectical struggle in a unified ideal. As Karatani argues, if you accept Marx's binary model, you can be led to the highly improbable belief that if we can overcome the economic system of capital, the nation and state will "wither away." Given the incredible importance of Marx's nineteenth-century investigations of the commodity form, Karatani's modifications are also highly significant: "state and nation have their own roots in the base structure and therefore possess active agency" (*Structure* 3).[29] "Capital-Nation-State" are thus best conceived as "a mutually complementary apparatus" (xiv). It also follows, then, that cultural phenomena like literature, art, and theory are also not semiautonomous "add-ons" to the economic base, but processes deeply enmeshed in the modes of production and exchange and of the social reproduction of basic human needs. Not everything, of course, can be reduced to the dialectical binary, and how we frame any dialectical contradiction becomes crucial. Marx revised his own ideas about class struggle and revolutionary praxis through his personal understanding of the dramatic but brief two months of the Paris Commune in 1871.

The Struggle between Communality and Hierarchy: Lessons of the Paris Commune for the Twenty-First Century

From Civil War to the Commune

Few events in the long history of capitalism have resonated with more symbolic significance than the two months from March 18 to May 21 of 1871, when the Paris Commune briefly came into being before it was brutally suppressed by the French National Army. On May 21, after weeks of artillery shelling, the army broke through a surprisingly undefended gate at Point-du-Jour in the southwest section of the defensive wall surrounding Paris, and Adolphe Thiers, the president of the French National Assembly headquartered in Versailles, ordered his troops, led by General Marshal MacMahon, on a savage rampage through Paris, slaughtering more than 25,000 Communards.[1] In the course of "La Semaine Sanglante," or the "Bloody Week," the relentless terror of Thiers's Army exceeded by a factor of ten the roughly 2,600 counterrevolutionaries guillotined eighty years earlier in Paris during the more infamous 1793–94 Reign of Terror. For all the self-righteous chastising of the 1794 Jacobins for their brutality, rarely do we find an acknowledgment of the far greater inhumanity of the bourgeois Thiers and the French National Army that destroyed the Commune.

In terms of sheer backlash, few revolutionary actions have been crushed so quickly and so violently. Why and how that backlash became so extreme has led to some highly provocative arguments about the powers of capitalism to eliminate any radical ruptures to the system itself. But certainly the most famous was Karl Marx's remarkable piece of critical journalism, *The*

Civil War in France, which he composed in London without any immediate access to the events in Paris during the two months that the Commune was itself fighting for survival. This pamphlet was actually the most widely circulated (to that point) of any of Marx's texts, and it instantly made him a famous and notorious figure, primarily because of the circulation in the press, both in the United States and in Europe, of misinformation and lies about the "Red Terrorist," the demon, the puppet-master, Marx, who was said to have directed the entire Commune revolt from London. Nothing could have been further from the truth. Indeed, Marx himself had at first opposed the idea of the Commune because its locus of social transformation was too narrowly tied to Paris, when he knew that any communist revolution had to have a much more international cast if it were to be less vulnerable to the massive forces of capitalism.[2] By this point in his life, Marx had come to oppose most forms of violence rather than protest, political organization, and education of the workers. But once the Commune began, he became one of its most ardent supporters. Nearly fifty years later, the Commune also became the focal point of Lenin's classic study, *State and Revolution,* wherein he elaborated upon Marx's analysis, although he completely ignored Marx's initial reservations. Most accounts of the Commune have described it as a *political* revolution, but Marx was correct to frame it within the political *economy*.

Without rehashing these complex debates about the Commune, it is possible to see outlined in this event the tensions between communality and hierarchy, grand narratives and local policies, as they affect the geopolitical economy.[3] Indeed, Marx himself altered in significant ways his entire understanding of political revolution as a result of his interpretation of the Commune. As such an exemplary moment, it was a time when the countermovements against capitalism actually gained broad control of a city of nearly two million people. In some ways, this two-month experiment based on the anarchist views of worker cooperatives condenses some of the key issues in a more genuinely communist version of social life, in which democratic decision making would extend not just to formal civic suffrage, but also to workplace production sites. This is hugely significant, because, as Richard Wolff has explained, almost all large-scale communist states have really been forms of state capitalism when viewed from the perspective of surplus value and worker participation in the organization of production. The complex stories of the twentieth-century communist state experiments have more typically served as the model for the sins of a centralized state, even if they rarely achieved the goal of worker-run associations controlling the mode of production.[4]

The significance of the Paris Commune has been lost in most accounts of the history of theory, so this chapter seeks to rectify that loss. After all, imagining alternatives to the dominant world-system has always been a crucial function for just theory. What this chapter aims to do is present a highly selective version of some of the gritty living conditions in nineteenth-century Paris, but always with an eye to the larger systemic effects framed by the capitalist world-system.

As we have seen in the key events of the French Revolution and the Haitian Revolution, the countermovements to the dominant economic system struggled with the tensions between localized, participatory democracy and the desire to universalize their values through more centralized, thus hierarchical, political and economic structures suitable for large populations. The focus on democracy at the state level often mutes any real attention to democracy in the organization of production, which is to say, worker control of production and distribution of the surplus. The Paris Commune struggled with exactly these tensions, just as activists in contemporary countermovements both in the United States and in many places around the world have recently struggled to negotiate the tensions between the open-ended collectives supporting local occupations and the larger international movements that seek to defend the public commons against private capital. But looking back from a historical perspective, we can see the systemic, triumvirate links between the nation, based on the often-cultivated fictions that populations sharing geographical domains also share cultural and linguistic homogeneity (see Benedict Anderson); the state, represented by the military and bureaucratic structures of government supported by taxation; and capital, the basis of the world's geopolitical economy. The increasing interdependence between the nation state and capital would prove violently capable of suppressing a local nineteenth-century revolution, even though it occurred in what was then the second most populous city in Europe.

Before we turn to some of the details of the Paris Commune itself, even a cursory overview of the political economy in mid-nineteenth-century France provides empirical evidence that the tensions over debt, hierarchy, centralized control, war, and violence resonate, albeit in quite different ways, with contemporary circumstances. Despite the dramatic differences between industrial capitalism and twenty-first-century neoliberal capitalism, the earlier period experienced conditions not entirely dissimilar to contemporary life—such similarities are the effects of the historically shared frame of global capitalism. In both periods we find rising economic and social inequality; deteriorating working conditions and decreasing wages brought about by intensified market competition; extravagant displays of "spectacular" power and wealth by the ruling elites through monopoly control of markets; debilitating national debts; widely increased international "free trade" policies; costly and aggressive wars; financial control of the media by the wealthy, and its corollary, restrictions on freedom of the press; and increasing debt-financed militarization.

During the nineteenth-century revolutionary period, universal claims for communality permeate both the local and international levels: universal suffrage was a specific decree passed by the Commune, but the hope was that the local enfranchisement would become the model for the Universal Republic of affiliated workers' federations around the world. Mikhail Bakunin articulated these hopes at the time of the Commune in 1871: "The future social organization should be carried out from the bottom up, by the free association or federation of workers, starting with the associations," which would then spread outwards "to the communes, the regions, the nations, and, finally, culminating in a great international and universal federation" ("Paris Commune" 84). As Kojin Karatani explains, "The Proudhonists and Bakunin naturally believed that they were mounting a world revolution. They began the revolution assuming that it would spread into a European world revolution. Needless to say, this was an utterly arbitrary assumption on their part" (*Structure* 252). In our cynical age, such a federation as Bakunin imagined may seem no more than a wildly utopian dream, but the desire for universality was real at all levels, especially for the disenfranchised such as women, racial minorities, and non–property owners. Indeed, as the influential Communard and activist Élisée Reclus put it with respect to the vision of the Commune: "Our rallying cry is no longer 'Long live the Republic' but 'Long live the Universal Republic'" (quoted in Ross, *Communal* 22). The Paris Commune therefore stands as a key moment of crisis in the nineteenth-century British dominance of the capitalist world-system, and for that reason we should undertake a brief foray into the social conditions out of which the events of the Commune emerged.

Second Empire Extravaganzas: Social Injustice in the Political Economy

One overriding circumstance characterizes both the last decades of the Second Empire in France and the first decades of the twenty-first century in the United States: rapidly increasing economic inequality. During the Second Empire's "roaring 1860s," the gala masked balls in the Tuileries Palace marked the period as a kind of libertine extravaganza. A wealthy new bourgeoisie were eager to celebrate with the Emperor, especially since Louis-Napoleon had championed industrial growth and expanded trade. As Eric Hobsbawm explains, the very word *capitalism* came into "the economic and political vocabulary of the world" (*Age of Capital* 1) during that very decade. The wealthy were growing wealthier at unprecedented rates, although, just as in the twenty-first century, in wildly disproportionate ways. The vulgar displays of wealth and pomp made less visible the deteriorating conditions for most citizens of France. Indeed, it was not hard to hide many of the grim realities since economic expansion was real during the period: according to Alistair Horne, "industrial production doubled and within only 10 years foreign trade did the same" (22). Nevertheless, the national debt had skyrocketed during the same period, so deficit financing could temporarily conceal the deeper troubles in the political economy.

The fabulous Paris International Exhibition of 1867 drew an almost unimaginable fifteen million people to sample the wonders of this new industrial age. Royalty from around the world were courted in Paris. Illustrious monarchs such as the Sultan of Turkey, the Princess of Wales, the King of Prussia, and the Czar of Russia strolled the halls with their full entourages. It was truly one of the first real spectacles of globalization: "Each nation had erected stalls and kiosks where pretty girls or ferocious tribesmen served their customers in bizarre national costumes" (Horne 6). Outside the exhibition halls, nobility could promenade down the wide boulevards, marveling at the massive reconstruction of Paris under the direction of Prefect Haussmann's remarkable new urban design. As Marx put it, a bit less enthusiastically, "financial swindling celebrated cosmopolitan orgies" (*Civil War* 56).

Ironically, at the very heart of the more than 50,000 displays was a large gallery, "The History of Labor," that glamorized workers as the noble producers of the many social achievements of the Second Empire, with not a sign of sweat, blood, or poverty from their labor. The "History of Labor" gallery can be read as a massive ideological spectacle that completely camouflaged the historical realities of production. The gallery framed workers in a false, idealized myth of perpetual progress where worker contributions to industrial capitalism were represented as the glorious incarnations of the emerging technological advances of modern civilization. At the same time, this Eurocentric ideology avoided any acknowledgment of the escalating national debt, the increasing economic inequality, and the continued necessity for slavery in the Americas to supply the cotton for the European garment factories. As we have seen in the last chapter, the classical economists such as David Ricardo and John Say (just like twentieth-century free-market theorists Friedrich Hayek and Milton Friedman) had provided the theoretical justifications to separate the economic from the political: the idealized myths about self-regulating markets justified the false image of worker satisfaction in those market successes glorified in the "History of Labor" gallery. Outside the Exhibition park, they had even built many model "workers' homes"—neat, sturdy buildings completely unlike the shabby dwellings in the slums of Paris. One can only imagine workers wondering how anyone could have invented these houses so alien to their actual habitations. In short, the focus on market logic and consumable products kept the actual mode of production out of sight. The workers' lived experiences were quite otherwise than the fabled display would have its visitors believe. In a general way, the idealized workers have an ideological function similar to the idealized poets we find in some versions of Romantic idealism: labor and art are not real problems so long as they transcend the vulgar realities of poverty, debt, and war.

Beneath all the glitter of the 1867 exhibition, "seldom had France known a year with more industrial stoppages" (Horne 6). Worker's wages had modestly increased during the Second Empire, but nowhere near enough to keep up with inflation, so they experienced increasing poverty in the appalling slums, especially in the northeast quarters of the city, an area particularly important during the life of the Commune. Child labor meant that thousands of boys as young as eight years old worked in factories; disease and malnutrition contributed to the malaise; there was no secure employment, no sickness benefits, and no pensions; there were restrictions on the rights to affiliate and organize; and freedom of the press was virtually nonexistent (Horne 285). Marx understood clearly what Napoleon III had done with the economy: "The Second Empire had more than doubled the national debt, and plunged all the large towns into heavy municipal debts. The [Franco-Prussian] war had fearfully swelled the liabilities, and mercilessly ravaged the resources of the nation" (*Civil War* 44).[6] In the brief armistice agreement that ended the war with Prussia on January 27, 1871 (two months before the Commune broke), the National Assembly agreed that within four years they would pay Germany five billion francs—around a billion dollars. Nothing like that would have been remotely possible, even in the best of times.

It was not quite meant to be so disturbingly unjust. When Napoleon III appointed Georges Haussmann Prefect of the Seine in 1853, the idea for the redesign of Paris included many progressive features: more sanitary conditions with a new sewer system; reduction in the overcrowded population density; and wide streets to improve the transportation network and allow massive military maneuvers (thus making it easier to crush any demonstrations or rebellions). Napoleon III had been influenced by the socialist utopian Saint-Simon,[7] but the actual implementation of the plan followed the basic capitalist system: authoritarian state control for organization and implementation without any public input, and the hiring of private enterprises to do the actual work. There was nothing local or participatory about these decisions. Indeed, the most authoritarian phase of the Second Empire occurred during its early years prior to the 1857 depression, and during the 1850s many Parisians were ordered to move in order to accommodate the new boulevards. The windy, narrow, congested medieval Paris was converted to its modern image in a kind of massive gentrification project: plans to relieve poverty in many instances actually increased it through displacement since there was no adequate compensation for those forced to move. Haussmann was himself well aware of the problem so that even in 1862 he judged that "over half the population of Paris lived 'in poverty bordering on destitution'" (Horne 25; see also Harvey, *Paris* 87).[8]

The grand new avenues were enjoyed by the increasingly wealthy shipping and industrial bourgeoisie at the same time that comfort was disappearing for the workers. "The wealth of nations" might have been on the rise for a small minority of nations, but it was equally clearly a case of the rich getting richer and the poor getting poorer. As Eric Hobsbawn puts it, "the increasingly uneven distribution of national incomes" had clearly shown that the capitalist system was not merely "unjust, but that it appeared to work badly and, insofar as it worked, to produce the opposite results to those predicted by its champions" (*Age of Revolution* 242).

Financial inequality was also being magnified by the kind of capitalist free-trade agreements that would later become the cornerstone of contemporary neoliberal policies for international financial systems. As Hobsbawm explains with respect to the nineteenth century, "a series of 'free trade treaties' substantially cut down the tariff barriers between the leading industrial nations in the 1860s" (*Age of Revolution* 37). For example, the 1860 Anglo-French Treaty of Commerce inaugurated a movement toward free trade throughout Europe. As John Nye argues, this agreement became "the strategic linchpin of European liberalization" (10).

Although in the mid-nineteenth century there were no international financial institutions (IFI) such as formed after the Second World War, the two dominant capitalist nations in the 1860s, Britain and France, set the agenda for the global market.

The Anglo-French consensus, not completely unlike the contemporary Washington Consensus, protected and favored the dominant capitalist nations over the peripheral zones in other parts of the world. These new "free" trade laws "took the form of a European expansion in and conquest of the rest of the world" (Hobsbawm, *Age of Capital* 3). Clearly, the nineteenth century expanded through direct colonial invasions, centralized imperialism, and slave labor, whereas the more recent postcolonial period depended more on financialization of the world system.

Indeed, nineteenth-century private industrial expansion led to British dominance of the global capitalist system, just as the late twentieth-century IFIs orchestrated the U.S. hegemony over the multinational world-system. About the time the Civil War in France broke out in 1871, the European hegemony was reaching "a temporary domination of the entire world" but one that "was about to reach its climax" (Hobsbawm, *Age of Revolution* 26). Increasing social tensions in both Britain and France meant that counterattacks such as registered in the Paris Commune were gaining force to alter that dominance. In both the late nineteenth and the early twenty-first centuries, rapid economic expansion fueled a small, but remarkably wealthy elite more and more distant from the lives of average citizens.

Whereas the 1867 exhibition clearly celebrated the triumphs of capitalism, as did the installment that year of the stock ticker at the New York Stock Exchange, four other events also took place during that same year, each a signal that countermovements to the dominant political economy were gaining power. On September 2, the Congress of the International Workingmen's Association met in Lausanne (remarkably, as it may seem, Louis-Napoleon supported this organization—another sign of his contradictory belief that he could support both capital and labor at the same time); in Jena, Germany, Ernst Haeckel coined the term *ecology*, or ökologie (derived from the root word *oikos*, or home); in early 1867 Louis-Napoleon issued a decree granting greater freedoms of the press, repealing "the tough laws of 1852" (Horne 32), which had denied publication rights to antimonarchist, antiempire views; and later that same year, Marx published *Das Kapital*.

By 1870, conditions in France had completely deteriorated, especially during and after the disastrous Franco-Prussian War with its four-month siege of Paris. The Prussians literally starved the Parisians to capitulation during the siege by surrounding the walled city and cutting off all food supplies. During the siege, economic inequality had been further exacerbated through the unequal distribution of the dwindling food reserves. By the time of the final capitulation to the Prussians in January, 1871, most of the remaining monarchists and bourgeois had abandoned Paris because of the deplorable conditions. This left an opening for radicals, socialists, and the new worker movements led by the Proudhonists, Blanquists, and Bakunin to gain political control, at least within the city.

To make a long story short, the Paris Commune began with peaceful resistance to a military action by Thiers's army: when, on the night of March 18, the National Assembly soldiers reached the hills of Montmartre, with the intention of seizing the two hundred cannons the Parisian National Guard had sequestered there, the soldiers refused to fire on the largely unarmed women and men standing before the cannons. Here we see a momentary instance of the people of the nation standing in solidarity against the state military led by Thiers. Instantly realizing that the situation was now precarious, with many of his own soldiers deserting the army to join with the Parisian armed militias, Thiers quickly withdrew all his forces to Versailles. The door was now left open for the radicals to establish the Commune, which they did in an amazingly brief space of time. On March 26, the Commune officially came into being as Parisians voted for their new government.

On March 29 the Communards set up ten commissions for the provisional life of the Commune. Two social transformations stand out that are worthy of attention. First, by eliminating the police force, the Communards openly challenged every bourgeois and monarchist fear that crime would run rampant without the protections offered by a police state. But the opposite seems to have happened: even as they were almost continuously under attack by the Versailles forces, the crime rate in Paris seems almost to have disappeared during the brief duration of the Commune. As Marx explained, "no more corpses at the morgue, no nocturnal burglaries, scarcely any robberies" (*Civil War* 67). Second, Paris had rarely looked so clean: the workers and Communards apparently now taking control of the conditions of their own lives took great care in cleaning the streets and disposing of trash. Self-governing clearly had not deteriorated into mob disorder and filth as predicted and inaccurately described by the bourgeois presses in the provinces outside Paris. This is an enormously important point because it provides clear evidence that an active citizenry participating in the social means of production leads to better results than any private enterprise with respect to some very basic everyday living conditions such as sanitation and a reduction in violence.

Of the ten commissions, one of the most important was the Finance Commission. Their key task was to organize the financing for all aspects of the Commune, from the pay for the arming of the citizen-based National Guard, which had now expanded to about 400,000, to the salaries for government officials, to the operation of basic human services such as water, food, education, and healthcare. Merely because of his age, the seventy-five-year old Charles Beslay served as Chair of the Commune, but he also became one of the chief members of the Finance Commission. Even though he had failed as a banker, his first real task was to take control of the Bank of France. This powerful institution had been left in the hands of the Marquis de Plœuc, who organized his staff to stand guard against Beslay when the latter arrived at the bank to execute the takeover. The marquis had over four hundred employees armed with sticks, and when Beslay arrived with his four compatriots, they were easily intimidated and retreated hastily to the Hotel de Ville, where the Commune had centered its activities. According to Horne, the aging Beslay told the members of the Commune that the marquis had successfully made the case "that if the Commune laid hands on the Bank there would be 'no more industry, no more commerce; if you violate it all promissory notes will become worthless'" (302). Remarkably, the Commune somehow acceded to this claim, a kind of self-blinding belief in the narrative frame espoused by the capitalists: take this money, and the workers and peasants throughout France will all suffer. Nothing could have been further from the truth—as if funding for the truly disenfranchised would upset the entire system.

Nevertheless, the Finance Commission had managed to borrow 500,000 francs from the Rothschilds, and they had also managed to secure another 9 million from the Bank itself. The

Commune thus momentarily had enough resources to survive, so it might seem reasonable that there was less immediate pressure to take over the bank. Both Marx and Lenin argued that one of the great failures of the Commune was its reluctance to appropriate the huge sources of funding that lay in the National Bank. What Marx didn't know at the time was even more distressing: the head of the bank, the Marquis de Plœuc, was, quite literally, sneaking out the back door, and clandestinely carrying more than 250 million francs to Versailles along with the plates for printing more money and banknotes. Without these massive funds, Thiers could never have rebuilt the military might of the Versailles forces so rapidly and so powerfully.

The myth of the sanctity of private property was crucial: the money slipping out the back door of the bank was primarily public, as it was explicitly based on tax revenues from the people of the nation, yet it went almost exclusively to rebuilding the state army in Versailles so that they could better execute the wishes of the private, monied classes who sought to crush the rebellion and take even greater control of the political economy. Not one working person or peasant benefited in any direct way from these misdirections of national public resources: both the rural peasants and the urban workers in 1870s France bore the brunt of the debt for financing the state army that crushed the Commune.

Without those funds, and surrounded by Versaillais in the south and west, and the Prussians on the north and east, the Commune was doomed. Thiers made sure of that through the sheer brutality of la Semaine Sanglante. With respect to any attempts at negotiations, he would accept no compromises: "I shall not listen to you. . . . I have no conditions to accept, nor commitments to offer. The supremacy of the law will be re-established absolutely. . . . Paris will be submitted to the authority of the State" (quoted in Horne 362). In his eyes, his mission was to save the republic from lawless anarchy, so much so that afterwards, he crowed over his victory: "we have got rid of Social-ism" (Horne 430). On that score, at least, he was wrong many times over, although it was true that the pure anarchist belief in a truly decentralized, stateless system of cooperative production could rarely thereafter affect labor struggles except in local and sporadic circumstances. All subsequent socialist reformations tended toward some form of state-run organization of an otherwise capitalist market economy. In fact, the violent crushing of the Commune fueled the rising force of the socialist movement, organized labor, and worker resistance to capitalist exploitation leading to the creation of socialist democracies and welfare state policies for redistribution of wealth. Despite various ideological rifts within the International Workingmen's Association, its membership expanded exponentially over the coming years as the global economy between 1873 and 1896 entered what many have called the "Great Depression," even though it was never as precipitous a fall as the 1930s depression. Nevertheless, capitalist expansion in general slowed in the years following the Commune (just as global expansion diminished after the 2008 crisis). Marx had himself presciently predicted what he called the "falling rate of profit" [FROP]) that would afflict the capitalist enterprises during the late decades of the nineteenth century even as British imperialism increased in the effort to compensate for sagging local markets (see Hobsbawm, *Industry* 126–33). Marx also seems to have correctly deduced the remarkable powers of capitalism to restore its systemic contradictions between market freedom and state/capital domination through powerful reassertions of monopoly control linking production, finance, and state powers.[9]

The terrifying ferocity of Thiers's orchestration of the bourgeois backlash against the alternative to capitalism represented by the Commune took on a kind of patriotic nationalist ring in the French press, as if Thiers, provisional president of the new French Republic, had saved the country from terrorist rebels who deserved their violent fate. It is a cruel irony with respect to who actually served up terror: Thiers's centralized, authoritarian, nearly dictatorial takeover as president was represented as a form of liberation from the potentially oppressive alternatives to capitalism embodied by the Commune.

Spectacular Tales: Media Ownership and Freedom of the Press

From its ill-fated beginnings, the Commune faced an insurmountable public-relations problem. The National Guard troops in Paris were often depicted by the bourgeois press as drunken and disorganized, which, of course, they were at times, given their difficult situation. At the time of the Commune, while writing drafts of *The Civil War,* Marx complained in a letter to Engels of the "wall of lies" (quoted in Ross, *Communal* 86) put up by the French and German presses, which reported only the Versaillais version of the events and vilified Marx. But these popularized distortions illustrate the ideological problem: the French General Ducrot decried the Communards as "the conscienceless mob, what M. Thiers rightly called the 'vile multitude'" (Horne 229). These latter views were being disseminated by most of the newspapers around France, thus serving as an early sign of the "society of the spectacle" whereby the private media serve the state-authorized ruling classes by creating images deliberately concealing the actual conditions: fake news has had some powerful progenitors. Capital and state can thereby gain ideological control of the people of the nation so that in a feedback loop, the people of the nation yearn for the stability of the centralized state. Capital-Nation-State, as Karatani explains, became more integrated domains during the late nineteenth century.

In 1871, the Communards had little practical ability to control what was said outside the city about their own occupation within the Parisian city walls. As Kristin Ross argues, the Communards made extensive efforts to explain their solidarity with the peasants and all oppressed peoples through extensive printed documents that could only be distributed outside Paris by carrier pigeon, balloon, or secret couriers, but the Versaillais was able to destroy almost every one of these communication efforts (*Communal* 83–85). Even though the 1867 Freedom of Press Act made theoretically possible the publication of dissenting views, the bourgeoisie still managed the dissemination of news.[10] The Republican forces controlled the newspapers outside Paris because the large printing presses were mostly owned and operated by wealthy magnates so they could say what they wanted not only to win the favor of their fellow bourgeois but also to garner the allegiance of the peasants in the rural areas throughout the country, who came to fear the insurgent revolutionaries more than the stability of the monarchy. And it was quite a show for the conservative presses: *Le Figaro* screamed "No clemency is possible for these monsters, these ferocious beasts[!] eliminate these . . . vermin" (quoted in Gluckstein 158). This attitude was carried around the world so that the *New York Herald* likewise cheered on the powers of Versailles to "[m]ake Paris a heap of ruins if necessary, let its streets be made to run rivers of blood, let all within it perish" (quoted in Gluckstein 158). That pretty well sums up what did come to pass.

Despite these uproars, the 1867 repeal of the tough censorship act of 1852 had opened a crack in the door for a rapid growth in free press publication, and alternative leaflets and magazines began to emerge, not completely unlike the impact for the contemporary countermovements of alternative online news sources and social networking. Significantly, the expansion of publication venues became one of the most noticeable characteristics of the period immediately preceding and during the brief life of the Commune. Indeed, various clubs, associations, committees, and informal organizations began to buzz with activity (Ross, *Communal* 14–18). Nearly every Paris printing house in the city began to devote itself to news stories and pamphlet production to serve the cause of the Commune, or, perhaps more accurately, to get the diverse news and points of view internal to the life of the Commune spread throughout the urban area. They were also particularly concerned with trying to communicate to the peasants outside the city the idea that they shared the same basic commitments, contrary to everything the latter had been told by the bourgeois presses.[11] Differences abounded, but within the city at least the relative freedom of the press made participatory democracy possible because such democracy requires an informed citizenry.

In fact, one of the first things the Commune set up was an official journal to communicate its actions. Many decrees and resolutions had been passed after the election of the Executive Council on March 26, all of them enacting specific policies. But on April 19, 1871, the "Déclaration au peuple français" (or what some have called the "Program of the Commune") was published in their journal. The declaration was of a different order from earlier decrees and resolutions because it included not just a summary of the particular demands established by the Commune but also some of the key philosophical justifications for those policies. Although it was only three pages long, in many ways it is a remarkable document, partly because of the sheer audacity of its ambitions but also because it sought to rectify the many egregious misrepresentations of the Communards as scoundrels and madmen perpetrated by the conservative and monarchist forces that dominated the national and international press.[12]

Although the Communards faced an insurmountable uphill battle, they still had hopes that their declaration might be circulated outside the city and the country, and it did find its way to London and other metropolitan areas both in and outside France. So it is worth taking a closer look at the document itself. In many ways, because of its invocation of universal human rights, it can be considered as an explicit precursor of the 1948 United Nations Universal Declaration of Human Rights (UDHR) and of the 1962 Port Huron Statement of the Students for a Democratic Society, as well as of the 2011 statements by leaders of the Occupy movements and other resistance movements.[13] The Commune's declaration insists on the autonomy of the citizens to administer their own government and their own economy, and it articulates the universality of human rights, foreshadowing the UDHR's basis for "the promotion of universal respect for and observance of human rights and fundamental freedoms" ("Preamble" to the *United Declaration*).[14] In addition to the many practical organizational policies, the declaration articulates the "inherent rights of the Commune" to establish and preserve "the absolute guarantee of individual liberty and liberty of conscience, the permanent intervention of the citizens in communal affairs by the free manifestation of their ideas and the free defence of their interests" (Fetridge 151). The aim was clearly to establish broad-based forms of communality through nonhierarchical, participatory forms of democratic social life.

Particularly significant among these accomplishments was the active participation of women in all stages of the Commune's activities. On April 11, 1871, the Union des Femmes (Women's Union) was formed under the leadership of the twenty-year-old Russian Elisabeth Dmitrieff. Several thousand women attended the meetings of this organization, and at one point they drafted a manifesto that they brought to the Labor Commission: it "was a magnificent combination of political strategy, women's emancipation, immediate practical steps and the overcoming of the alienation under capitalism" (Gluckstein 23). Whereas women's wages had been no more than 50 percent of men's wages, the manifesto put in place a policy of "equal pay for equal work"; they reduced the exploitive work hours; they eliminated the distinctions between "legitimate" and "illegitimate" relationships; and they assured that pensions would be paid to all dependents regardless of their marriage status. Mary Wollstonecraft's vision of gender equality seems to have materialized in the Commune. As Donny Gluckstein summarizes: "The Women's Union was not patronized and sent away after lobbying. It was quickly incorporated into the fabric of the Commune. . . . With Labor Commission backing it began setting up an entire structure of syndical chambers out of which would emerge production units under workers' control and a Federal Women's Chamber" (24).

The Commune's reformation of education was also remarkable. Most forms of institutionalized education at the time were under the control of the Catholic Church, whose curriculum consisted of little more than reciting the catechism (and about one-third of school age French children attended no formal schooling at all), yet the Commune insisted on the separation of church and state, and established the basic principles for public school systems that would be free to all citizens. Religious beliefs were left open to families, but religious oaths were banned from the public schools. Several of the Paris newspapers stressed the need for education for girls. They had many plans for the development of professional education and higher education, but of course they never had time to implement these ambitions.

The Commune also envisioned the liberation of workers as tied equally to the liberation of culture and the arts of free expression. Consequently, more than four hundred people met to establish the Artists' Federation, which organized a festival and celebration of their new-won rights as enfranchised citizens. The Artists' Federation included sculptors, painters, engravers, architects, writers, and many others; the well-known painter Gustave Courbet served as president. In fact, as Donny Gluckstein explains: "In a move a century ahead of its time the federation overthrew the elitist division between fine arts and applied arts [a product of Romantic idealism] and promised that both would enjoy equal status in future communal exhibitions" (32). They even tried to eliminate the gender-based addresses of "monsieur" and "madame" in favor of the term *citizen,* which had emerged in the 1790s from the French Revolution. Theater companies put on daily performances; there were concerts and events celebrating the arts right up to the crushing last weeks of the Commune.

As the general declaration for the Commune stipulated, no one was to be excluded from the common rights that all citizens had when assured that "produce, exchange, and credit have to universalize power and property according to the necessities of the moment" (Fetridge 152). Because the anarchist factions of the Commune had largely authorized the document, they critiqued the Versailles government as "nothing but centralization, despotic, unintelligent, arbitrary, and onerous" (152). In contrast, the Commune represented itself as a new kind of "political unity . . . a voluntary association of all local initiative, the free and spontaneous co-operation of all individual energies with the common object of the well-being, liberty, and security of all" (152). Again, what is so striking about these claims in 1871 is their demand to abolish unnecessary and unjust forms of hierarchy in favor of the more just practices of communality.

Local Associations and Global Hopes

Singularly striking about the Paris Commune was that, for the first time in history, workers and the disenfranchised took control over the occupation of a major metropolitan area; Paris had a population of nearly two million people, the second largest city in Europe at the time, after London. A measure of communality became a historical actuality, not just a theoretical possibility. The event, for all its two months' brevity, has resonated through history as both myth and reality, paradigm for freedom and model of insurrection, depending on your politics. Before I look a bit more closely at some of the tensions embedded within the political activities of the Commune, it is worth pausing a moment to highlight the scope of what they did enact. In the course of its brief two months, the Commune Council actually passed more than 390 resolutions, including universal suffrage (for women as well as all other citizens); the establishment of worker pensions; the reduction of working hours; the abolition of a standing army and police force; the separation of church and state; the elimination of the death penalty; the legalization of divorce; the limitation of all government officials' salaries to no more than 6,000 francs; the worker-based organization of factories in the city; and many other reforms.

Every previous major revolutionary action (1789, 1830, 1848—a period Eric Hobsbawm calls the "Age of Revolution") ended up with concessions from the monarchy for the bourgeoisie, not the workers or the peasants. In stark contrast, the Paris Commune represented, however briefly, the first genuine self-governing assumption of power by the workers and many otherwise dispossessed citizens. Understandably, then, Marx recognized the Paris Commune as having momentous consequences for his account of class struggle. It was, for a brief time anyway, as Marx put it, "a government of the people by the people" (*Civil War* 65). For many of the Communards, the ultimate ambition of the Civil War was to extend such worker controls throughout the nation, and eventually around the world, as a revolutionary alternative to the capitalist system. Indeed, when Marx addressed the First International in 1870, he cited the manifesto of the organization drafted in July of that year, which explicitly claims to seek "peace, labour and liberty!" and he endorsed their unmistakably international intentions of aiming for the Universal Republic: "Workmen of all countries! . . . we, the members of the International Working Men's Association . . . know of no frontiers" (Marx, *Civil War* 24).

Of course, the historical realities were more compromised than the idealized accounts, and Marx certainly had contributed to those idealizations, but the revolutionary action had such a dramatic impact on him that both he and Engels later came to wish they could have amended the *Communist Manifesto;* and later they did, in fact, compose a new preface to that work.[15] His basic claim was that the Commune was "the political form at last discovered under which to work out the economical emancipation of labour" (*Civil War* 60). But he gradually came to make some major revisions to his theories of class struggle. First, the Commune made clear that social revolution could not just be an emancipation of labor, at least not labor narrowly conceived as employed proletarian workers;[16] second, the Commune provided concrete evidence that the proletariat could not just seize control of the state by way of a violent revolt, and make the state serve workers' interests. Even more than he could have known from London, the actual political orientations of the Communards differed dramatically on both ideological and material levels. Ideologically speaking, there was a wide range of political beliefs represented, from the anarchists to the Jacobins, and they often got in heated arguments.[17] In terms of material circumstances, there were not only employed workers, but small craftspeople and artisans, shopowners, liberal lawyers and judges, restaurateurs, teachers and professors, bakers, artists, writers, and various kinds of small merchants and businesspeople.[18] These divisions within the Commune are worth attending to because they prefigure some of the most divisive issues that countermovements have struggled with ever since.

First of all, the Commune was noticeably not "communist," at least not in the narrow sense, although it was thoroughly communal/communist in the broad sense. The First International had little to do with it directly, although twenty of ninety members of the Commune Council were Internationalists, and this latter group served as a strong majority on the important Commission on Labor, Industry, and Exchange; so there was certainly a proletarian coloring to many of the important actions of the Commune. Nevertheless, many of the anarchist leaders following Auguste Blanqui, Pierre-Joseph Proudhon, Mikhail Bakunin, or the great geographer and activist, Élisée Reclus were in constant interaction with the revolutionary Jacobins, who distrusted the startling new philosophy advocated by the followers of Karl Marx, as well as with the socialist utopian followers of Charles Fourier or Henri de Saint-Simon. As Alistair Horne puts it, "from the day it assumed office, the danger was apparent that the Commune might be overloaded, indeed overwhelmed, by the sheer diversity of desires as represented by so polygenous a multitude of personalities, ideologies, and interests" (299). Given this broad range of differences, it is quite amazing the degree of consensus through participatory democracy that the Communards did in fact achieve, as evidenced in the many decrees issued by the council.

Marx himself even lamented that sometimes the Commune was wasting time in unproductive debates without action. As he wrote in May 1871 to two of the Internationalist leaders of the Commune: "The Commune seems to lose too much time in trifling affairs and personal quarrels. . . . none of this would matter, if you had the time to recover the time already lost" (quoted in Horne 332). But as the pressure from Versailles mounted, the tensions within the Commune took identifiable binary form between the radical anarchists and the liberal Jacobins.

These powerful divisions within the Commune between participatory democracy and more centralized infrastructures mirrored what later became manifest in the conflict between Bakunin and Marx. This same division later became paradigmatic of the rift within the Left between bottom-up participatory democratic models of social organization and top-down centralized forms of state command.[19] By simple inversion it is also possible to use this division to characterize Left and Right: the Left socialist orientation has generally advocated the former even as it has sometimes slipped heavily into the latter; the Right capitalist orientation has generally tended toward top-down, hierarchical, and centralized forms even as it has sometimes produced (and mythically advocated for) "free," anarchic, and decentralizing forces. Michael Harrington articulates well these "counterposed phenomena: the growing centralization and interdependence of capitalist society under the control of an elite; and the possibility of a democratic, bottom-up control by the majority" (8).[20] His main point is that despite all their differences, many of the anarchists, socialists, and communists all have shared a common aim of establishing a bottom-up, nonauthoritarian social organization. The Commune clearly represented the latter even as it slid toward centralization in the last weeks of its life. In short, the Commune brought to a head the tensions between communality and hierarchy internal to the countermovements: the struggle for local, participatory democracy, and the need for a centralized infrastructure of state institutions to orchestrate that democracy.

Indeed, on April 28, 1871, an old Jacobin from the 1848 Revolution, Jules Miot, put before the Commune Assembly a move to create a Committee of Public Safety to exercise executive functions. The anarchists, the socialists, and the members of the

International among the Assembly strenuously opposed this move, which seemed far too much like a resurrection of the infamous 1793 Committee of Public Safety, but in the end, with growing fear of their own safety under Thiers's bombardments and threats, "the Commune Assembly voted, 45 to 23, in favour of Miot's proposal" (Horne 333). This was clearly a turning point, as the Jacobins sought centralization, hierarchy, and control rather than bottom-up democratic participation. Unfortunately, with their demise only a few weeks away, there was little any of them could do to prevent the backlash that was about to be mounted by the Versailles forces. The new dictatorial committee ineffectively tried to take action by rounding up about three thousand counterrevolutionaries as hostages by May 15, but these desperate measures had no effect when the collapse came a week later.

Once the Commune had been crushed, differing interpretations of the events heightened tensions between the antistatist anarchists and the political organizations of the communists. The historical event of the Commune prefigured in powerful ways the key dialectical tensions—local and global, decentralized and statist, communal and hierarchical social organization—that would beset nearly all countermovements ever since that time. For instance, these very tensions over the political significance of the Commune precipitated Marx's 1872 expulsion of Bakunin from the Hague Congress of the International Workingmen's Association.[21] In 1870, Bakunin had organized a failed revolutionary action in Lyon, and even though he was not an active participant in the Paris Commune he was one of its strongest defenders, seeing it as an exemplification of workers taking revolutionary action against both the centralized state and capitalism. Marx was likewise a strong defender of the Commune, but on different terms. The conflict between Bakunin and Marx stemmed from Bakunin's deep fear of a creeping authoritarianism in Marx's version of the communist state even though it was Bakunin arguing for violent revolution and Marx decrying the resort to immediate violence. The "dictatorship of the proletariat" was something he feared, not something he sought to achieve by organizing workers to create a centralized state. But, clearly, Marx also distrusted Bakunin and thought of him by that time as an imposing, overweight lout whose critical thinking was shallow at best and lacking in the scientific rigor regarding the analysis of the political economy that Marx had brought to the four volumes of *Capital*.

Bakunin had, for the most part, underestimated Marx's deeper commitments to democracy and communal life, especially as Marx modified his views after the Commune, but the former's fears certainly seem prescient with respect to world history given the twentieth- and twenty-first-century rise of many centralized, authoritarian, nominally left-wing regimes. It was the Commune that significantly changed Marx's thinking about the role of the proletariat. Basically, Marx came to more deeply appreciate that the universal values of social justice carried out by the Commune were diametrically opposed to hierarchical state rule; he subsequently gave up as ahistorical his earlier theories that the proletariat could simply assume hierarchical control of the state mechanisms. As Michael Harrington explains, "To the very end of his life . . . [Marx] . . . insisted that the state would eventually 'wither away' [Engels's term, actually], a utopian formulation if there ever was one. And when he once tried actually to describe the 'dictatorship of the proletariat,' Marx saw it prefigured in the Paris Commune, a quasi-anarchist body that provided for the immediate recall of all elected officials" (20).

Nevertheless, it now appears clear that Marx's binary separation of the economic base from the cultural superstructure had the fatal effect of making the state appear as a mere ideological "superstructure" that would "wither away" once the cooperative economic base had been established on communistic principles. This theoretical liability concealed the deeply integrated realities of capital, nation, and state. Nations of people governed by state military bureaucracies could facilitate capitalist forms of production and exchange to serve the will of an elite plutocracy: as Karatani puts it, "state ownership and capitalism are not incompatible" (*Structure* 249). Marx would agree with that assessment as he never put faith in a centralized state, but his way of formulating the historical dialectic of class struggle as primarily a base-superstructure model still tended to theoretically separate the economic from the political/ideological at a deep level so that, according to his theoretical assumptions, the state might conceivably wither away as easily as Plato's ultimate Forms could dispel the world of appearances. This binary model calls out for some significant reframing.

But the historical reality regarding the Commune was never so polarized with respect to communal participation and central hierarchical organization. Even the Commune had to form an Executive Council of representatives, although they were duly elected on instant recall. What remains striking in the Communards' actions is the effort to dialectically unite the grand, universal aspirations for communal social life with the contingent struggles of the local associations that inevitably called for leadership as well. Marx continued to favor the integration of local and universal aspirations as exemplified in the Commune, but his support of those radical efforts split the International movement. The Commune failed because it ended up having no international traction and very little communication with the peasantry outside Paris despite its idealization of them. After this event, "Marx would become extremely cautious about the idea of leaping over historical stages" (Karatani, *Structure* 255). Indeed, as Kevin Anderson has now made eminently clear, Marx took from his interpretation of the Paris Commune a more complex sense of history, revolution, and cultural difference. Anderson argues that by the 1880s Marx had "created a multilinear and non-reductionist theory of history" whereby he more fully "analyzed the complexities and differences of non-Western societies, and [. . .] refused to bind himself into a single model of development or revolution" (*Marx* 237).[22] No longer was Marx's "theory of social change . . . exclusively class-based," but it became much more attuned to the "intersectionality of class with ethnicity, race, and nationalism" (244). Contrary to what many people have often thought about Marx, he refused later in his life to collapse "ethnicity, race, or nationality into class" (245). Although Marx is clearly "not a philosopher of difference in the postmodernist sense" (244), these significant revisions in his own theories suggest a richer attunement to the dialectical interaction between large-scale frames and deeply historical particulars than most assessments of "Marxism" have been willing to acknowledge. In short, Marx understood how the new powers of capital "reached into every society and created a universalizing worldwide system of industry and trade for the first time, and with it a new universal class of the oppressed" (244). On this score, Marx should be given credit for so often sustaining an ongoing dialectical analysis aimed at making warranted generalizations while avoiding "formalistic and abstract universals" (244) that radically disengaged theory from the rich contexts of social life.

Reenvisioning Communality and Hierarchy for the Countermovements

Here we leave this brief sketch of the Commune for the long and complicated history of the countermovements that followed, but the gist of those complications can be briefly characterized as growing out of the basic tensions that emerged late in the life of the Commune. First, the revolutionary anarchist hope that local cooperative modes of production and exchange could be internationalized came to a tactical closure: It was evident after the events of the Commune that the interlocking hegemony of capital, state, and nation was far too powerful to be displaced by idealized dreams of reciprocity and mutuality, no matter how crucial such visions of cooperation might be to human life. In short, anarchist revolutions had proven not to be viable in the European centers; or at least, any revolutionary hopes now had to move to the periphery, which is what large tracts of Russia was as a developing nation. Consequently, new forms of socialist organization came into being, mostly pinned on reformist hopes of working within parliamentary democracies in England and Germany: regulating capitalism and working toward welfare-state forms of redistribution were the best hopes in this scenario. Marx objected to the aims of "state socialism," as he made especially clear in his 1860s rebuttals of the arguments put forward by his sometimes-friend, sometimes-rival, the German political activist Ferdinand Lassalle, who was killed in a duel in 1864, and in his scathing critique of the German Social Democratic Party's Gotha Program.[23] Indeed, beginning especially with the 1889 formation of the Second International, a sharp rift widened between the German Social Democrats (SPD) led by Karl Kautsky and the rapidly expanding Bolshevik movement in Russia, which was led by Vladimir Lenin beginning in the early twentieth century. Both Kautsky and Lenin claimed to be the true followers of Marx, but their split exemplifies what we found in the split within the Commune.

In simple terms, Kautsky came to believe that Marxism could only come about through the establishment of a democratic but centralized state. He recognized that the bourgeois state worked from authoritarian, top-down models, so his commitment was to the creation of social democracy from the bottom up. Kautsky's model was binary but not really dialectical since it was an either/or situation with just two end-point possibilities: capitalist state or socialist state, but always a state, and no in-between mixture or radical alternative and no dialectical oscillation. Socialism for Kautsky became "ownership by the democratic state of the large-scale industry, which is the inevitable outcome of capitalist development" (Harrington 50). Kautsky's definition became enormously influential, but it was vigorously opposed by Lenin, who saw Kautsky as the betrayer of the radical potential of communism.

For Lenin, in *State and Revolution,* Kautsky's fateful definition would lead to the centralization of authority in Communist states, which Lenin opposed at least until the final years of his life.[24] In the 1917 "Preface" to the first edition of *State and Revolution,* Lenin therefore calls Kautsky the "great distorter" (6), and goes on to explain that Kautsky's goal is "to perfect the state machinery, whereas it must be shattered, broken to pieces (25)."[25] Lenin's fear was, of course, to a large extent realized. There would come into being not decentralized communes, socialist working associations linked by loose networks of affiliation and worker-run sites of production for both peasants and proletarians aiming for a post-national Universal Republic, but modern state-run enterprises and bureaucracies that dictated tasks for workers (rather than the reverse) in the inevitable competition with other capitalist nation-states. Lenin's arguments that the violent revolution by workers would lead to a temporary dictatorship of the proletariat that would then "wither away" follows from Marx's and Engels's theories about the ultimately disappearing state, but they clearly call for a new mode of production based on worker-controlled industries—an ideal contrary to the role that Lenin found himself in at the end of his life. As Harrington explains, "In the years between the October Revolution in 1917 and his death in January, 1924, Lenin acted first upon the most utopian, antistatist definition of socialism, then moved abruptly to a statist, anti-utopian model and, in the last months of his active life, turned toward Asia for the solution to difficulties he found all but insuperable" (62–63).[26] In either case, we again see Lenin's reliance on Marx's somewhat misframed model of economic base and cultural-state superstructure leading him to mistakenly come to believe that the "withering away" of the state could become an actual possibility, even though any version of a Universal Republic would necessitate some forms of affiliation and hierarchy on both a local and a grand scale. This too seems like another trace of ahistorical idealism akin to the Romantic idealism we have seen in other circumstances, which tends to underestimate the deeply interwoven dimensions of culture, capital, nation, and state in the geopolitical economy. Inevitably, any concrete event or individual action may take place within one dimension more than another, but a strong materialism requires that we consider the effects (or lack of effect) in all of those entwined domains.

Without elaborating on the details of these debates, their historical significance should not be missed. Kautsky's statist version of socialism came to dominate the formation of most socialist states. The historical shifts in the twentieth century of the Soviet Union and the People's Republic of China, among others, to socialist statism came to stand in for the universal essence of *all* versions of socialism and communism.[27] Socialism and communism could then be more easily demonized for the relative failures of these centralized states (which is exactly the strategy that Friedrich Hayek took in his famous 1944 book, *The Road to Serfdom*), but conversely this ideological bias prevented most people in the West from fairly assessing the real achievements of the socialist and communist states. The right wing has benefited widely by representing socialism as always and everywhere tied to the historical dictatorships that called themselves Marxist, communist, or socialist nations. While most all of these historical manifestations struggled with the idea of worker-run enterprises and communal affiliations, to varying degrees many of them also slipped into repressive, centralized state bureaucracies that destroyed participatory democracy by workers and disenfranchised people. These slippages are also understandable, as Immanuel Wallerstein argues, because the communist and socialist nations had no choice but to compete with the capitalist world-system that sought to crush them (see *World-Systems*). However, by focusing on the centralized oppressions of the socialist states, we have failed to assess the degrees of communality that were in many instances achieved, and, conversely, we have often neglected to account for the oppressive degrees of hierarchy established by corporate controls. In order to do that, we have to more fully theorize the interlocking system of capital, nation, and state, rather than an economic base producing a cultural superstructure.

Even with this brief look back at the Paris Commune, we can see that although Louis-Napoléon had ludicrous fantasies that a state-sanctioned war with Prussia would aid his empire, instead the war precipitated economic collapse throughout France, especially in Paris, whose citizens were left hungry and destitute, eating rats and vermin to survive during the four-month Prussian siege of the city in 1870–71. But the capitalist world-system calls for an interlocking system of nation-states with one nation typically gaining some form of hegemony, and the French demise made it possible for the British Empire to become that center. As we have seen, Napoleon III took on the mantle of the rising bourgeoisie (as had his famous uncle seventy years earlier) and consequently initiated many of those same capitalist goals even though they were orchestrated around a political economy based on expanding industrial monopolies. He created a huge backlash that would not go away.

Even today we see many twenty-first-century resistance movements harking back to a rhetoric reminiscent of the Communards' "Declaration" from another moment of crisis. David Harvey asks the crucial question about the various localized irruptions that have taken place in the twenty-first century in many cities around the world: "if these various opposition movements did somehow come together . . . then what should they demand?" And his answer to his own question is "simple enough": "greater democratic control over the production and use of the surplus" (*Rebel* 22). That remains a demand widely shared by many people engaged in the slow-motion revolution for a more just kind of social, political, and economic life.

The lesson of the Paris Commune is that there was no social justice when the reign of capitalists could be integrated with the state and the national identity so much as to destroy the possibility for bottom-up democratic processes such as the Commune represented. There is no social justice when the will of the vast majority of citizens for social reproductive security in the areas of child care, healthcare, education, and participatory parity in the public sphere gets crushed by austerity measures serving private capital interests. As Marx clearly understood, capitalism seeks to enclose the public commons, but the Paris Commune sought to establish the common good for all citizens of Paris. Their failures were not internal to their own organization so much as imposed upon them by the brutal repression of the bourgeoisie, who sought to restore the system that had given them the power to control the political economy. But another key lesson we might carry away from even this brief sketch is that the resistance represented in the spring of 1871 Paris did not die with the Commune. As Kevin Anderson argues, any positive alternative to capitalism will come out of "dialectical imagination, where Marx takes revolutionary aspirations and trends inside the present order—like the Paris Commune of 1871—and moves them much further" toward what Marx called "'an association of free human beings'" ("Marx's Capital" 4). Even though many of the Communards were buried alive in mass graves, and contrary to the false myth that the universal free market lives on, there is also a long tradition of countermovements that seek a "new society," one more just and equitable, and based on participatory democracy. Such critical-utopian wishes have some important material consequences if we hope to avoid the destruction of the planet by market-driven exploitation of dwindling resources.

We have now moved deeply into the contemporary period, but before we conclude our story of Cultural Turn 2 we need to consider two very different kinds of writer, one a wealthy Victorian gentleman and the other an impoverished radical philosopher, whose theoretical and practical work appears remarkably prescient with respect to contemporary concerns. Charles

Darwin's theories of evolution may not have directly altered the geopolitical economy, but they did have profound indirect effects across a huge range of social, philosophical, artistic, and political domains. As John Dewey put it, "the *Origin of Species* introduced a mode of thinking that in the end was bound to transform the logic of knowledge, and hence the treatment of morals, politics, and religion" (*Influence* 2).[28] And in a different register, Friedrich Nietzsche shook up the "quest for certainty" (Dewey, *Quest*) that had for so long been the main mission of Western metaphysics.

From God's Great Chain to Nature's Slow-Motion Evolution: Reframing Our Regulative Fictions

A breed, like a dialect of a language, can hardly be said to have had a definite origin.
—Charles Darwin, *On the Origin of Species*

Lack of a historical sense is the original error of all philosophers.
—Friedrich Nietzsche, *Human, All Too Human*

Hence one should consider the teacher . . . a necessary evil, an evil to be kept as small as possible.
—Friedrich Nietzsche, *The Wanderer and His Shadow*

"A Mere Fragment of Time"

When Charles Darwin published *On the Origin of Species* in 1859, deep time became an imagined possibility and the category of "species" became profoundly destabilized. These challenges to the foundations of Western metaphysical formalism are among the many reasons that help to explain why this book has sold more copies and been translated into more languages than any book other than the Bible. But it didn't all happen as fast as one long and famous trip to the Pacific Ocean.

In 1837, the year after Darwin returned from his remarkable five-year voyage (1831–36) to the Galapagos Islands and many other places in his circumnavigation of the globe, he gradually began to scope out perhaps the world's first realistic account of a phenomenon so big you couldn't observe it, measure it, or test it. Of course, his theory had a deeply empirical basis, but today we can look back and understand that the book, originally called *On the Origin of Species by Means of Natural Selection, or the Preservation of Favoured Races in the Struggle for Life* (more on the title, later), deconstructed the very notion of species whose origin he otherwise sought to describe. That is, indeed, the heart of the evolutionary paradox: you can't see species change and evolve, but the deep-time historical evidence makes it clear that they have. Before Darwin, there were cats and dogs, tulips and daffodils, and you couldn't cross one with the other because what you saw was what you thought you got: radically separate species that could not crossbreed. You could load up the ark with two of each animal species, but once the ark hit dry land, you still ended up with the same number of exclusive species even if the pairs had multiplied.

But Darwin upset all these fixed categories: rather than God authorizing a stable Great Chain of Being, the reigning regulative fiction for universal history, you got uncertainty, randomness, and blurred boundaries. Western metaphysical formalism took a big hit. Something called "natural" selection meant that chance differences could lead to alterations in species-being, and so much so that it now appeared that human beings emerged out of, if not cats and dogs, well, apes and amoebae, depending on how far you wanted to go back. Darwin's Victorian society was not ready to accept this radical reframing. Indeed, after 1862, when Darwin grew his famous gray beard, many cartoonists lampooned him by picturing his heavily bearded face atop an ape body. The disbelievers and the cartoonists had their empirical as well as religious grounds for objection because, as could be readily satirized, none of these evolutionary theories can actually be seen: it is not really a "phenomenon" emerging out of our senses, but a piecing together of bits and pieces of evidence, traces of a long-ago past that neither Darwin nor anyone else could point to in the physical world. Evolution is much bigger than what we see before our eyes.

After all, what exactly was it that twelve-year-old Mary Anning and her brother, Joseph, unearthed in 1811 when she discovered the first dinosaur fossil (an ichthyosaur skeleton) buried in the dangerously unstable limestone of the Blue Lias cliffs of Lyme Regis, in Dorset, England? During the nineteenth century, no woman could join the Geological Society of London, so Anning rarely received recognition for her striking findings. Fossils were curiosities that fueled the auction business, and Mary made a living at selling such rarities as she could dig out of the cliffs, so it is no surprise that the four-foot ichthyosaur skull, along with the rest of the skeleton Mary had unearthed, were auctioned in 1819 for 23 pounds sterling. And of course the only way to frame the odd remains was in familiar terms, as a huge crocodile. It seemed impossible to figure out how and why these giant creatures had somehow appeared and then disappeared. Eventually, however, after a few exchanges, the fossil made its way to the Egyptian Hall in London, a private museum, where it was put on display "as a fish and then as a relative of a platypus before being recognized as a new kind of reptile—an ichthyosaur, or 'fish-lizard'" (Kolbert 39).

To return to Darwin's famous voyage, even then he himself didn't "see" in the Galapagos Islands the evidence for the revolutionary theory he later pieced together. In fact, he was so blind to it that on the return voyage, he and his shipmates ate their way through some of the key evidence for an evolutionary theory and tossed it overboard.[1] As Stephen Jay Gould and others have now made clear, Darwin himself was such a creationist when he first headed to the South Pacific (still believing that he would follow his chosen profession as an Anglican parson) that much of the evidence for his world-shaking theory appeared trivial to his observant eyes, because changes in tortoiseshells and mockingbird beaks had no significant meaning within the deductive theoretical frame with which he sought to isolate the evidence for different species. Creationists see species as fixed essences so that variations on the surface such as the size or shape of a bird's beak are trivial differences that do not affect the deeper rational plan laid out by God's Great Chain of Being. As John Dewey explains, Western metaphysics depends upon "the assumption of the superiority of the fixed and final" so that elements of "change and origin" can only be seen "as signs of defect and unreality" (*Influence* 1). In Darwin's inherited metaphysic, the world of confusing appearances could not touch the underlying absolute Forms, yet evolution upended this version of universalism.

Even so, Darwin did briefly entertain some heretical thoughts in his journal aboard the HMS *Beagle,* when, several months after he left the Galapagos, he registered some doubts about his creationist views because the different varieties of mockingbirds and finches led him to admit that "such facts would undermine the stability of Species" (quoted in Gould, "Darwin" 573). As Gould explains, "The myth of the *Beagle*—that Darwin became an evolutionist by simple, unbiased observation of an entire world laid out before him during a five-year circumnavigation of the globe—fits all our romantic criteria for the best of legends" (571), but it has little to do with historical reality. Before he even landed back in England in October 1836, Darwin had dismissed his brief conjectures about evolutionary possibility as mere heresy. No surprise there, especially given that throughout the entire five-year voyage he had shared a cabin with the odd young captain of the *Beagle,* Robert FitzRoy, whose eccentricities and short temper clearly made for some pretty steady quarreling and generally difficult times in small spaces, all thoroughly reported in Adrian Desmond and James Moore's 1992 biography of Darwin. But, most important, FitzRoy was such a devout Christian that even though the ostensible purpose of the entire voyage was to chart coastal waters, his constant obsession was to find evidence for the biblical version of creation. The twenty-three-year-old FitzRoy had even selected the twenty-two-year-old Darwin as a companion because the latter was in training for the ministry, and he ap- parently also liked the shape of Darwin's nose. Quite pointedly, FitzRoy gave Darwin a gift: a copy of Volume 1 of Charles Lyell's three-volume *Principles of Geology.* Lyell was the groundbreak- ing geologist (later a close friend of Darwin's) who opposed any of those renegade scientists of the day who leaned toward what was called "transformisme" in Paris and "transmutation" in London: both were terms for the evolutionary theory that Lyell thoroughly rejected. Darwin was so taken by Lyell's book that he had both the second and third volumes of the *Principles* sent to him for pickup, the second at Montevideo and the third in the Falkland Islands. In any case, there were lots of reasons that Darwin might not have been leaning toward evolutionary theory. As Gould sums it up: "Darwin entered and left the Galapagos as a creationist, and his style of collection through the visit reflected his theoretical stance" (577). Despite these difficulties, the voyage was a transformative experience for Darwin, as his new direction in life was as a naturalist, and the voyage itself was spectacularly successful. Besides the bird and tortoise specimens from the famed Galapagos Islands, the ship also returned with a huge collection of giant fossils; they identified a previously unknown species of dolphin; they had conducted detailed studies of coral atolls; and they had gathered important geological data regarding the Andes Mountains. Darwin returned with enough data and specimens to last a lifetime without ever having to risk his scientific reputation on theories of evolution.

Darwin actually had to reinterpret all the evidence from the specimens he had collected once he moved to London as a young man now wholly dedicated to making his name as a man of science. Since his original collection of finch and mockingbird specimens from the Galapagos failed to note many significant characteristics (and on which islands they had been located), even when he tried to rearrange the evidence within the parameters of his emerging evolutionary frame more errors cropped up. For these reasons, evidence regarding finches and mockingbirds never shows up in *On the Origin of Species*.

We can also note the many material realities of the day that enabled Darwin to complete his work. For one thing, his father, a wealthy British doctor, could afford to fund his son's voyage on the *Beagle*, including the additional resources of a personal servant (Syms Covington) and others (shipmates) to assist him in collecting and recording the specimens. On his return from his voyage, Darwin could also relocate to London without having to worry about securing a job or professional position. London was necessary because it was the location of the scientific community of his day, especially such notable figures as the naturalist Lyell, who was delighted with Darwin's report upon his return to London; the highly esteemed ornithologist John Gould; the famous paleontologist Richard Owen; and many others connected to the network of institutional supports in London. Darwin had gained considerable fame through his reports from the *Beagle*, so he was well-received within these elite circles. London was the site of such influential organizations as the Royal Society

(Darwin became a Fellow in 1839 and in 1853 won the society's Royal Medal, which secured his reputation), the Royal College of Surgeons of England (where Owen worked), the Geological Society of London, and the Zoological Society of London, all of which expressed interest in Darwin's work. But, rather remarkably, none of his awards and recognition came by way of *Origin* or his work on evolution, because the scientific community of his day was still loath to recognize its veracity.

When we take account of these institutional networks, we can more fully see that Darwin's work as a naturalist was sanctioned and supported by a wide range of material practices that both directly and indirectly had a great deal to do with the geopolitical economy of Victorian England. Evolutionary theory did not just emerge from some unbiased, clearsighted observation on a famous voyage. Recognition of the highly stratified scientific community and social institutions of Darwin's day reveals the remarkable intellectual and political intrigue as well as the personal and social stress that swirled around the evolution of evolutionary theory. For one thing, the *idea* of evolution had been around since before the beginning of the nineteenth century. Darwin's own grandfather, Erasmus, a noted British physician and abolitionist, had made reference to evolutionary theory in a long footnote to his 1789 poem "The Loves of the Plants" (reprinted several times under the title "The Botanic Garden"). More famously, his poem "The Temple of Nature" was published posthumously in 1803, and describes an evolutionary progress of life from microscopic organisms to human beings. But it appears that his grandfather's poems made far less impression on Charles than did his reading, upon his return from his voyage on the *Beagle,* of Thomas Malthus's *Essay on the Principle of Population.* Malthus had clearly articulated a view of life as a competitive struggle in which some kind of natural selection determined which species would survive. But Darwin's first job on returning to London was the arduous work of sorting through all his many crates of specimens.

It took about six years (1842) before Darwin was ready to sketch out his emerging theory of natural selection, and another two years before he actually had a roughly 230-page manuscript, or "sketch," outlining the entire theory. But he was so unnerved by his recognition of the terribly frightening impact his new ideas would have on both the scientific community and the general public that he did what now seems unimaginable: he put the manuscript away for more than a decade, devoted himself to raising a family of ten children, and wrote a series of studies on barnacles, published between 1851 and 1854. His friend Joseph Hooker had suggested that Darwin would be wise to study one species extensively first before revealing his ideas about natural selection and evolution. The trepidation might have been warranted in retrospect, because in 1844, the very year Darwin retired his revolutionary "sketch," an anonymously published book, *Vestiges of the Natural History of Creation,* argued that humans evolved from earlier primates rather than suddenly from a divine act of creation. The truly vicious nature of the attacks on this book not only from the pulpit but also from the scholarly community might indeed have given Darwin pause. Ironically, the book had been written, it turned out, by a publisher of Bibles, Robert Chambers, so it is also understandable that he did not want to put his name on the book.

But the historical record regarding the "origin" of the theory of natural selection becomes even more complex and confusing (see Bryson 386–88). For example, a Scottish fruit farmer, Patrick Matthew, had published in 1831 (the year Darwin had left on his voyage) a book called *On Naval Timber and Arboriculture,* and in a five-page appendix described the basic concept of natural selection as an evolutionary mechanism. But no one noticed for the obvious reason that it seemed to have little relation to the title of the book. It only came to Darwin's attention in 1858 by way of another naturalist, Alfred Russel Wallace, an admirer of Darwin who had sent the latter a manuscript called "On the Tendency of Varieties to Depart Indefinitely from the Original Type." Darwin immediately noticed that Wallace's ideas were, although independently arrived at, almost a mirror of his own basic theory of natural selection as he had outlined them fourteen years earlier in the neglected 1844 "sketch" of his theory. As Bill Bryson describes it, "Darwin had discreetly warned Wallace that he regarded the subject of species creation as his own territory" but "Wallace failed to grasp what Darwin was trying to tell him" (387). Darwin's distress was magnified by the sudden death by scarlet fever of his youngest son (also Charles). At this point, his friends Lyell and Hooker suggested a "compromise solution" whereby the two of them would present "a summary of Darwin's and Wallace's ideas together" (387). The event came off on July 1, 1858, with a presentation to about thirty people of the Linnaean Society of London, even though neither Darwin nor Wallace was present. Darwin and his wife were burying their son; Wallace was "still in the distant East" (388). There was barely a ripple among the crowd as they listened politely to the most revolutionary of ideas because those ideas were so easily dismissed as false. Wallace never even learned about the presentation of his ideas until long afterward, but even he came to refer to evolutionary theory as "Darwinism." In short, "the theory became, essentially by default, Darwin's alone" (388).

Darwin then rather rapidly prepared his book for publication, and when John Murray published 1,250 copies in November, 1859, it sold out on the first day. Ever since then, *On the Origin of Species* has seen more editions, translations, and reprints than any book other than the Bible. Yet the book was not well-received by the scholarly community, mainly because Darwin had proposed such huge, suprahistorical time frames (and with each edition in his lifetime, he expanded the periods of evolutionary history), and the fossil evidence at the time did not seem to support these claims. Even his friends, Charles Lyell and others, felt that Darwin had overstated the case, and the latter's conversion to evolutionary theory strained the relationship with Lyell. Darwin could barely reconcile himself to his own arguments: he "never ceased being tormented by his ideas. He referred to himself as 'the Devil's Chaplain' and said that revealing the theory felt 'like confessing a murder.' Apart from all else, he knew it deeply pained his beloved and pious wife" (Bryson 388).

When we turn to the text itself, what is most striking about *Origin* is how often and how thoroughly Darwin concedes the difficulties of defining the notion of species (almost as hard as Plato's efforts to describe the Absolute Forms). Once he truly became an evolutionist, after his return to London, those previously trivial variations of characteristics became crucial: they now provided signs of the random genetic differences significant for evolution under the principles of natural selection. As a taxonomist, Darwin could see that all the blurred boundaries and conflicting evidence for evolution upended all the fixed categories of classical taxonomy. Under the frames of Western metaphysics, for example, the very terms *origins* and *species* seem contradictory. Species should not have origins because they should be fixed, timeless essences characterized by their underlying forms. Aristotle began this way of thinking, as we have seen in Chapter 5, with his early work in biological taxonomy. As John Dewey explains, "Aristotle gave the name *eidos*. This term the scholastics translated as *species*" (*Influence* 5). Its biological uses then extended across all of epistemology: for the Classical thinkers "species, a fixed form and final cause, was the central principle of knowledge as well as of nature. Upon it rested the logic of science. Change as change is mere flux and lapse; it insults intelligence. Genuinely to know is to grasp a permanent end that realizes itself through changes, holding them thereby within the metes and bounds of fixed truth" (6). Again, we see the collapse of the dialectic in the end point of the Absolute or "final cause": the potentially endless chain of inductive evidence disappears under the strict deduction of everything from the Forms.

In contrast, Darwin knew that in evolutionary theory there is "no law of necessary development" (*On the Origin* 673). So even as a naturalist Darwin repeatedly had to confront these deeply theoretical and philosophical conundrums. He did just that, often, and in many places in *Origin*. Much like Derrida's notion of the linguistic "trace," Darwin proclaims that with evolutionary theory "we shall surely be enabled to trace in an admirable manner the former migrations of the inhabitants of the whole world" (758). Let us look at just a few examples of how the evolutionary traces clearly destabilize any ultimately fixed sense of species, or genre (the homologous term in the humanities for recognizing generic "species" of literature).

Darwin begins Chapter 2, "Variation under Nature," by analyzing the relations between species (which indicate underlying sameness) with variations (which indicate differences). Just as Socrates had had a lot of trouble finding a fixed definition for *justice,* Darwin records his similar reservations regarding the definition of *species*, which you might think would be a good bit less abstract and thus easier to define than *justice:*

> Nor shall I here discuss the various definitions which have been
> given of the term species. No one definition has as yet satis-
> fied all naturalists; yet every naturalist knows vaguely what he
> means when he speaks of a species. Generally the term includes
> the unknown element of a distinct act of creation. The term
> "variety" is almost equally difficult to define; but here com-
> munity of descent is almost universally implied, though it can
> rarely be proved. (477)

Three pages later he confesses, "I was much struck how entirely
vague and arbitrary is the distinction between species and variety" (480).[2]

Darwin repeats these admissions throughout the text, reiter-
ating the theoretical problems at great length in both Chapters
5, "Laws of Variation," and 6, "Theoretical Difficulties," and
he returns again to these issues in his concluding chapter, where,
within a few pages of his famous last sentence ("There is grandeur
in this view of life . . . "), he reiterates more than once that "no
clear distinction has been, or can be, drawn between species and
well-marked varieties" (754). Darwin's questioning of species'
uniqueness is prescient with respect to recent understanding about
multispecies, "holobionts" (Gilbert), and the symbiotic nature of
most living beings, which are more entangled with one another
and with nonliving matter than the idea of the "individual"
species allows. There can also be no sudden leaps or creationist
moments where a species appears all at once, or in seven days,
because evolution moves very slowly through deep time, with the
chance variations having a great deal to do with the "struggle
for existence" (Darwin's title for Chapter 4). Indeed, there are
no big ruptures in evolution, because "she can never take a leap,
but must advance by the shortest and slowest steps" (574). But
although mighty slow, evolution is also clearly hierarchical,
with the "higher species" coming last: "The inhabitants of each
successive period in the world's history have beaten their predecessors in the race for life, and are, in so far, higher in the scale
of nature, and this may account for that vague yet ill-defined
sentiment, felt by many paleontologists, that organisation on the
whole has progressed" (668). Evolution thus both demonstrates
our commonality of ancestors at the same time that it registers
the increasing hierarchies to be found in the natural world. The

struggle for life (the "race" for survival) turns out to yield as a result of those competitive battles the higher "races" as the hierarchies of evolution work themselves out even within the species of homo sapiens. However, Darwin himself never even used the word *evolution* in the entire book, and the only variant of the term (*evolved*) that appears occurs once, as the last word in the magnum opus.

As he nears the end of the book, Darwin quietly unfolds in his gentlemanly and elegant Victorian prose the vision of deep time that his theory had opened: "The whole history of the world, as at present known, although of a length quite incomprehensible by us, will hereafter be recognised as a mere fragment of time, compared with the ages which have elapsed since the first creature, the progenitor of innumerable extinct and living descendants, was created" (759). In 1859, even to imagine such deep biological and geological time was a revolutionary gesture.

The *Descent* into Race and Sex

Despite its being frequently attributed to him, Darwin never actually used the phrase "survival of the fittest" in the first four editions of *On the Origin of Species*. That famous expression actually came five years later from Herbert Spencer's 1864 volume *Principles of Biology*, where Spencer responded to Darwin's masterpiece by mistranslating natural selection into the moniker that most people would henceforth associate with Darwin. To be fair, Darwin himself eventually came to accept the phrase, specifically ten years later in the 1869 fifth edition of the book, where he inserted it once. But by 1874, when he published *The Descent of Man* (nearly 50 percent longer than *Origin*), he more pointedly adopted Spencer's catchy expression, using it several times, most notably exclaiming in the last sentence of Chapter 4 that "through the survival of the fittest, combined with the inherited effects of habit" human beings had risen to their "present high position in the organic scale" (866).

We might conjecture that the terms *survival* and *fittest* seemed more appropriate to a historical epoch Eric Hobsbawn referred to as the *Age of Capital*. Ruthless competition for industrial profits demanded a language of brute strength rather than the more nuanced and less masculine sense of "natural selection," whereby arbitrary genetic variations serve as the motor force in evolution. In an 1862 letter to Engels, Marx also came to the same basic assessment of Darwin: "It is remarkable how Darwin rediscovers, among the beasts and the plants, the society of England with its division of labour, competition, opening up of new markets, 'inventions,' and Malthusian 'struggle for existence.' It is Hobbes' *bellum omnium contra omnes* [or war of each against all]" (quoted in Ross, *Communal* 72). When he finally rushed *Origin* into publication, and ever after that, Darwin did not let his worries about offending Victorian society prevent him from taking him where his evidence led him. All the evidence assured Darwin that creationism was blatantly false and that humans had certainly descended from lower life forms over long periods of evolutionary history. But in some unfortunate ways, Darwin never had to shed some of the dominant forms of cultural ethnocentrism characteristic of his time. That plants and animals had evolved was no problem; but that humans had evolved clearly tipped the scales in mid-nineteenth-century England.

Given his own social milieu, Darwin could read the evolutionary evidence as he saw it so as to fully ratify what today we can only see as remarkably unfortunate versions of racism and sexism familiar in the dominant culture. Adopting the anti-universal discourses of Western metaphysics enabled him to grant to his own race and sex certain seemingly inalienable hierarchies of superiority. Given the ideological power of the notion of progress so widespread in European thought during the nineteenth century, it was not hard to see that although homo sapiens had taken a long time to evolve into the hierarchical position humans occupy in nature, it was also not hard to believe that variations also exhibit this progressive sense of hierarchical variation as improvement in human attributes according to racial characteristics. Epistemic violence had its way. Darwin's very theory of divergence among varieties pretty clearly led to the divergence of the races and the genders and thus the superiority of the white race and the male gender. These unfortunate expressions of bigotry are only too apparent in *Descent*, whereas the technical focus on the principles of natural selection in *Origin* pretty much kept these values at bay. As a young man, Darwin had traveled the world (although after his 1836 return he never again left England), and in all his visits to alien lands he accepts the common Eurocentric distinction between civilized and savage.

In *The Descent of Man,* Darwin continues to insist on the underlying commonality of all life forms, and he notes that such continuities become especially evident in embryonic forms: "the embryos of a man, dog, seal, bat, reptile, etc., can at first hardly be distinguished from each other" (*Descent* 795). But even as ontogeny recapitulates phylogeny, once the individual species reach maturity all the differences become relatively stabilized in distinct species and subspecies. Darwin elaborates race as a distinct variation at the level of varieties of the species homo sapiens, although these racial distinctions took a long time in reaching their present state of indubitable hierarchies: "Difference of this kind between the highest men of the highest races and the lowest savages, are connected by the finest gradations" (798).

In one sense, Darwin was, of course, a man of his time, and we have seen rather egregious instances of these unfortunate kinds of racism and sexism in many famous philosophers and poets. In this instance, Darwin found powerful ways to script a kind of biological basis for racism out of what he saw as the evidence of human variations. He devotes Chapter 7 to defining "the Races of Man," and he vacillates a bit about whether the races should be designated as constituting distinct species or rather as subspecies. After some fairly extended discussions weighing the evidence of racial differences in physiognomy, skin color, and intellectual abilities,[3] he settles on the definition of races as subspecies within homo sapiens: "So again it is almost a matter of indifference whether the so-called races of man are thus designated, or are ranked as species or sub-species; but the latter term appears the most appropriate" (910).

These theoretical categories provide justifications for what most contemporary readers will see as outlandish forms of racist othering: "Most savages are utterly indifferent to the sufferings of strangers, or even delight in witnessing them" (831). The North American Indians are seen to exemplify "the conduct of animals" who leave "their feeble comrades to perish on the plains" (821), and even worse: "The American savage voluntarily submits without a groan to the most horrid tortures to prove and strengthen his fortitude and courage" (831). The different races are even seen to have a credible empirical basis because Darwin shares a widespread acceptance among naturalists of the practice of phrenology: "Dr. J. Barnard Davis has proved by many careful measurements, that the mean internal capacity of the skull in Europeans is 92.3 cubic inches; in Americans 87.5; in Asiatics 87.1; and in Australians only 81.9 inches" (859).

The hierarchies of the races parallel the hierarchies of the sexes. Darwin's account "proves" that man has "[t]hus . . . ultimately become superior to woman" (1205). So many Victorian stereotypes abound in Darwin's text that a few examples will suffice: "Woman seems to differ from man in mental disposition, chiefly in her greater tenderness and less selfishness" (1203). But there are not only emotional differences but clear intellectual differences: "The chief distinction in the intellectual powers of the two sexes is shewn by man attaining to a higher eminence, in whatever he takes up, than woman can attain—whether requiring deep thought, reason, or imagination, or merely the use of the sense and hands. . . . the average standard of mental power in man must be above that of woman" (1204). Darwin must not have read Mary Wollstonecraft.

Darwin may be the man who unsettled the stability of the species but he also reestablished some socially dominant racist and gender hierarchies within the new evolutionary paradigm that too often continue to pervade our contemporary postcolonial geographies. Given the international significance of Darwin's work, this is not a minor reinforcement of patriarchal injustice. Just theory works to transform these limitations and inaccuracies, but we can only begin that work when we recognize that some of our most venerable traditions of Western ways of knowing, including our general high esteem for the authority of science based on the espousal of unbiased objectivity, can themselves be so steeped in these prejudices that they reinforce injustices. For that reason alone, it is useful to turn now to a man born thirty-five years after Darwin, but a man who gained little fame in his own lifetime in the last half of the nineteenth century. Whereas Darwin was deeply esteemed within the scientific community of his day, Friedrich Nietzsche was often isolated and denied access to his intellectual communities. The latter's views became so radical that, even though at twenty-four he was hired as the youngest-ever faculty member at the University of Basel, he had to give up his position in 1879 because of his health problems, and after that time, for the rest of his life, no university in Germany would hire him—but for ideological, not health, reasons. Despite these difficulties, after his death in 1900, Nietzsche was recognized during the twentieth century as one of the most challenging thinkers of his day.

Less Godlike and *All Too Human:* Science as Regulative Fictions

Friedrich Nietzsche offered such a powerful critique of Western metaphysical prejudices that he seems more a man suited for postmodern times than a nineteenth-century philosopher. Darwin certainly destabilized the Great Chain of Being, but Nietzsche destabilized so many shibboleths of the philosophical tradition that he often appears as the progenitor of deconstruction before Derrida even invented that word. Nietzsche undertook one of the most scathing critiques of Western metaphysical anti-universalism ever offered. He rejected all versions of rigid "systems" of thought as they emerged in classical and Enlightenment thinkers, but he also rejected all forms of mass conformity and the herd mentality—a kind of culmination of radical Romanticism. To this extent, he is often associated with the anarchist movements of the nineteenth century in their rejection of authority and what Louis Althusser would call the repressive state apparatus, but unlike the anarchists who often espoused equality and egalitarianism, Nietzsche argued that hierarchy was as necessary, and often more fundamentally common to human life, than the uncritical championing of equality alone. W. B. Yeats saw the key links between William Blake and Nietzsche in the focus on energy, intensity, and social transformation by art. They were all great debunkers of the bourgeois liberal pretensions and mystifications proclaiming freedom as the "rational" telos of an unrestrained free market capitalism. However, some have argued, as Terry Eagleton has, that Nietzsche arrives at a version of human life completely compatible with capitalism, especially in some of his formulations whereby individualistic competition reigns supreme. Indeed, in some of Nietzsche's more virulent expressions of individual autonomy, it would be hard to deny that "[f]ew more explicit theorizations of capitalist competition could be imagined" (*Ideology* 252). The main problem with Eagleton's interpretation is that it treats Nietzsche's entire life as if his body of work were a consistent set of "fundamental values" (245) when, in fact, few writers have been so variable and willing to change their views, as we will see Nietzsche did regarding his critique of science: also, sometimes he was just wildly inconsistent, not just richly paradoxical.[4] But it certainly remains a deep irony that, from a political perspective, he was a revolutionary philosopher without any political ties to revolutionary movements. He also seems to have had a lifetime aversion to democracy, and to this extent he shared the values of his Enlightenment predecessors, Kant and Hegel, who, as we have seen, distrusted voting by "uneducated" citizens.

Although Darwin suffered throughout most of his life with troubling illnesses such as heart palpitations, recurring stomach pains, and severe headaches, Nietzsche experienced far greater health problems from terrible physical ailments such as severe short-sightedness, migraine headaches, violent indigestion, insomnia (for which he took huge doses of opium beginning in 1882), syphilis (perhaps, although this has been disputed), and probably a hereditary stroke disorder so that in the last two years of his life he could neither walk nor speak. He also suffered from mental disturbances (perhaps manic-depressive disorder, or bipolar disorder, but of course they went undiagnosed in his day), and he spent more than a year (1889–90) in psychiatric wards in Basel and then Jena. In the last decade of his life, until his death in 1900, the combination of physical and psychological difficulties clearly disabled Nietzsche to such an extent that he was unable to take care of himself and had to be cared for by his mother and then his sister.

Combine these difficulties with Nietzsche's antisystemic, aphoristic stylistic exuberances, as well as the changes in his own views at different times in his life and the uneven quality of his writing—well, it is no wonder that many people have drawn radically different interpretations about Nietzsche. The complexity of his views also makes it virtually impossible to provide a brief synopsis of his lifework. So I will not even attempt such paraphrasing, but, following my own framing principles, I will focus on several key issues pertinent to this history of theory, with the intention of correcting what I believe are some widely circulated but inaccurate beliefs about Nietzsche. Many people have described him as a depressing nihilist, as an advocate of a willful anti-Semitic doctrine based on a kind of Fascist "super-man," or as a mystical maniac. He was none of these, although he was often a skeptic, and he did have a real mental collapse in 1889. What he was, in the context of this history of theory, was a dedicated historical materialist who was simultaneously a great critic of doctrinaire thinking, whether strictly materialist or idealist. As Eagleton puts it, Nietzsche keenly understood "the body as the enormous blindspot of all traditional philosophy: 'philosophy says away with the *body,* this wretched *idée fixe* of the senses, infected with all the faults of logic'. . . " (*Ideology* 234). For Nietzsche, any kind of thinking was symptomatic of material force" (235), and it is this radical Romantic and materialist side of Nietzsche that I will emphasize. As he puts it in a short section called "On the Despisers of the Body" in *Thus Spoke Zarathustra,* "There is more reason in your body than in your best wisdom" (Kaufman 146–47).

In what follows, I will offer just a few succinct investigations into some of Nietzsche's radical views on science and art, and his oppositional critique of Western culture generally. Nietzsche was especially critical of the oppressive ways that common goods, services, and ideas were produced by blind adherence to the dominant powers controlling the geopolitical economy. He also wrote against most of the philosophers of the Western tradition, including Socrates, Plato, Aristotle, and Kant, but he saw as precursors to his own thinking the radical work of Heraclitus (the world is flux and change) and Baruch Spinoza, the radical seventeenth-century Dutch philosopher, among a few other notable kindred spirits. It is also true that Nietzsche could be dogmatic about his resistance to dialectic, as when late in his life, in his brief, but heavily sarcastic autobiography, *Ecce Homo,* he proclaims that "I consider dialectics a symptom of decadence" (Kaufmann 658). As usual, it is hard to tell the depth of the irony, so it may be wise to view Nietzsche's proclamation as a radical Romantic resistance to the Western tradition's frequent flights to an immaterial, disembodied "reason."

But a good place to begin a view of Nietzsche is in Leipzig in 1865, shortly after he transferred from the University of Bonn. He made the move in order to follow the well-known classical philologist Friedrich Wilhelm Ritschl, and, at the age of twenty-one, Nietzsche was now a serious philology student. That same year, while perusing a local bookstore, he accidentally discovered a copy of Arthur Schopenhauer's *The World as Will and Representation,* and this book made a huge impression on him. Nietzsche shared Schopenhauer's keen sense of the limitations of reason and the dialectic. They both shared a much more pessimistic view of the powers of the intellect, and they saw as delusional the Enlightenment faith in the steady path of human progress based on reason and science. They also both saw as hugely mystifying and misleading the systematizing of world history they found in Hegel.

Although Schopenhauer lampooned Hegel, he had much more respect for Kant, and, especially in the appendix to the first volume of *The World,* Schopenhauer offered a rigorous critique of Kant that had considerable impact on Nietzsche. Schopenhauer also situated the critique of Kant in the context of Plato's "Allegory of the Cave" with which we began our history of Western metaphysics. As Schopenhauer argued, "All previous Western philosophy . . . had failed to recognize the truth, and had therefore in reality always spoken as if in a dream. Kant first suddenly wakened it from this dream" (*World* 420). The central dialectical division is between the world of perceptible appearances and the reality of the thing-in-itself. Plato's "Allegory of the Cave" now appears as "the most important passage in all his works" (419) because it configures this very division between appearance and reality. According to Schopenhauer, however, Plato presents this basic epistemological conundrum "mythically and poetically rather than philosophically and distinctly" (419). Even so, Plato's Axial Age representation of the fundamental problem of knowledge parallels in many ways, "although presented quite differently," the same basic dynamic as also represented in India through the "teaching of the *Vedas* and *Puranas,* namely the doctrine of Maya" (419). The *Mahabharata,* referred to in the introduction, was composed during Plato's lifetime, but in this long text the much earlier *Vedas* were attributed to Brahma; and, Vyasa, the narrator of the *Mahabharata,* is credited as the transcriber into Sanskrit of the many oral versions of the *Puranas.* The Sanskrit term *Maya* has many meanings, but in these ancient texts it most often meant "illusion," whereby something would seem to be real when it was not, very much like Plato's world of appearances, the shadows on the walls of the cave.[5] The relative simultaneity of these Eastern and Western doctrines regarding the deceptive world of perception suggests to Schopenhauer a sign of their universal significance. Schopenhauer will make multiple references to the Sanskrit texts throughout his book. The appeal of Kant was that he seemed to have worked his way out of the illusions of Maya and the appearances of the shadows on the walls of the cave.

In Schopenhauer's view (so compatible with Nietzsche's at this point), Kant "effected the greatest revolution in philosophy" (425), "which the new age awakened," (425), even though Schopenhauer highlights "Kant's great mistake" (437). "that he did not properly separate knowledge of perception from abstract knowledge" (437). Because of this basic mistake, Schopenhauer rejects "the whole doctrine of the categories, and number[s] it among the groundless assumptions with which Kant burdened the theory of knowledge" (452). As a young man, Nietzsche was greatly impressed by the rigor of Schopenhauer's critique of Kant. The corrective effort of Schopenhauer, as Nietzsche saw it, was his radical critique of the limits of reason and of the illusions of science as the progressive answer to all forms of human suffering. Instead, Schopenhauer began from Kant's basic starting point that all knowledge of the world only comes from our representations of the world as phenomena. But much more than Kant, Schopenhauer was pessimistic about the Enlightenment faith in reason's transcendent ability to guide us through the deceptive world of shadows, and, in contrast, he emphasized the powerful role of the will and the passions in all our forms of knowing.

Nietzsche found this radical alteration of Kant to be completely compatible with his own emerging formulations of what he will describe as the powerful tensions in ancient Greek life between the Apolline and Dionysian forces. But before we get to Nietzsche's famous first book, *The Birth of Tragedy,* we can retrospectively appreciate the many ways that Schopenhauer's theories helped pave the way for Nietzsche's creative account of what, as a young man, he saw as the great tragedy of Cultural Turn 1. Among other things, Schopenhauer's critique foreshadowed Freud because, for the former, reason was not some ultimate faculty, but only a small segment of human life, most of which was driven by the will over which we have only minimum conscious control—thus, humans were much more susceptible to unconscious motivations, to the unruly drives of sex, and to wildly rationalized idealizations and myths. Nietzsche will associate these powerful forces with the tragic power of Dionysian art. But he will also draw from his friend Richard Wagner, whom he had met in 1868, less than three years after discovering the work of Schopenhauer.

Nietzsche recoiled later in his life from his devotion to both Wagner and Schopenhauer. Many writers have offered explanations for this dramatic change in attitude, but one way to conceive of it is that Nietzsche rejected what he came to see as an illusory kind of Romantic idealism based on the mythical ideals of aesthetic objectivity and the liberal beliefs in some kind of ultimately pure "human nature," a teleological goal that was the historically progressive task of the Enlightenment to fulfill. Nietzsche gradually came to understand that, despite his apparent antihumanist radicalism, Schopenhauer ended up himself in a highly ascetic world of idealism, far from the engaged, energized, and materialist emphasis that Nietzsche had so appreciated as a young man. He came to see Schopenhauer's philosophy as a withdrawal from rather than an engagement with the material world.[6] Ultimately, despite Schopenhauer's radical beginnings, his philosophical project ended up representing a retreat to idealized forms of art and aesthetics, a kind of ultimate Platonism. Nietzsche remained committed to a version of radical Romanticism, and to this extent he fully anticipates a wide range of twentieth-century critiques such as pragmatist, poststructuralist, and deconstructionist resistance to liberal humanism and any version of transcendent philosophy. Nietzsche developed a much more nuanced account of the relations among reason, science, ethics, morality, and politics later in his life. But in the 1860s and early 1870s he was still deeply under the influence of Schopenhauer and Wagner.

As the Franco-Prussian war escalated, Nietzsche left his recent appointment in 1869 as a professor of classical philology at the University of Basel to aid the war efforts.

For two months in 1870, Nietzsche served as a medical orderly in the Prussian Army not long before it began its assault on Paris later that fall, leading up to the March, 1871, formation of the Commune. He had to leave the Army because of a serious illness, but almost immediately upon his release and relative recovery, he returned to his position at Basel and composed an exploratory essay called "The Dionysiac World View." Within the next two years, Nietzsche would expand this essay into his famous first book, *The Birth of Tragedy out of the Spirit of Music* (1872), written when he was twenty-eight years old. From Schopenhauer, Nietzsche adapted the doctrines of will and representation, and clearly his deepening relationship with Wagner intensified his own interests in music. Nietzsche himself was an accomplished pianist, and he had already composed several short piano concertos. He had also fallen in love with Wagner's wife, Cosimo, so tensions among them all developed early. Wagner made sure Nietzsche knew that he saw his music as insignificant and dilettantish. Even following the later rift in their friendship, when Nietzsche came to see Wagner as decadent and as representative of some of the worst excesses of the modern age, there is still considerable evidence that Nietzsche continued to love (and also perhaps hate) the Dionysian powers of his former friend's music because of the influence it had over him. Among other things, Wagner had integrated music and drama in his operas, and as a young man deeply in awe of Greek tragic drama Nietzsche clearly experienced those connections as profoundly moving.

In *The Birth of Tragedy*, Nietzsche developed in richly lyrical prose his famous pronouncements about the rift between what he called the Apolline (or Apollonian) and Dionysian forces as represented by the Greek gods, Apollo and Dionysus. He therefore offered a memorable critique of the epistemic violence at the heart of the history of Western metaphysics. But he was also making a grand argument about reforming modern society into what he called a "tragic culture" (*Birth* 87) based on something like Wagner's music-drama (he dedicates the book to Wagner in the forward to the first edition). Nietzsche returns to the origin

of Western art and philosophy in ancient Greece, and he casti-
gates Western metaphysics as a concerted effort to cut off the
Dionysian roots of tragedy, energy, emotion, art, and sexuality
through an idealizing of Reason: the Apollonian desire for order
and Form tried to conquer the violent and precarious contingencies of history. It will appear rather ironic in light of our consideration of Homer (and Plato) in terms of the orality-literacy
debates (which were obviously not available to Nietzsche), that
Nietzsche represents the epic poet as the apex of individualism,
fixed identity, and the order of Apollo. Certainly, the technology
of oral memorization through repetition and recitation required
a sense of order and submission to tradition, but the emotional
investment of the poet or rhetoric in the oral tradition plays no
role in Nietzsche's vision of epic poetry. Even more contrary to
Eric Havelock's interpretation of Homer, Nietzsche claims that
Homer was recognized as the best epic poet on aesthetic grounds,
when, as we saw in Chapter 3, aesthetics had no role to play in
ancient Greece because the term itself was an invention of the late-
eighteenth-century Romantics. Nevertheless, it is the rise of the
tragic drama in ancient Greece that, for Nietzsche, integrates the
order of Apollo with the music of Dionysus. Nietzsche therefore
emphasizes the Archaic period of Greek culture between Homer
and Socrates as the best historical example of an artistic culture,
rather than one based, like nineteenth-century society, on the
illusory claims of reason and science, a historical epoch that for
Nietzsche had its origins in the Classical Greek period beginning
with Socrates and the rise of Western philosophy.

Indeed, Nietzsche appears as the ultimate radical Romantic,
whereby the great works of ancient Greek tragedy had fused the
mythical elements of both Apollo and Dionysius—the God of
Reason and the God of intoxication, passion, and the body. Very
much like Blake's synthesis of Energy and Reason, Nietzsche saw
in Greek tragic art the fusion of the elemental suffering of the
human body with the struggle to create reason and order, but
always in deep, living tension. Western metaphysics as developed
by Socrates (who is the real villain for Nietzsche)[7] therefore comes
off as the ultimate Apollonian illusion (like Blake's Urizen, the
"God of Reason"). The effort to escape suffering through the
illusion of fixed, ahistorical Forms becomes the pattern for all

versions of Western metaphysics: the lived body disappears into the ghostly skeleton of lifeless form. As in Blake's harangue against Aristotle in "The Marriage of Heaven and Hell," we may find, following Nietzsche, that all we are left with is "the skeleton of a body . . . Aristotle's Analytics," a systemic analysis imposed on us in our own day by a banking system of education (Freire) authorized by a rigidly hierarchical, ethnocentric, and spurious claim to "value neutrality." Nevertheless, not once in *The Birth of Tragedy* does Nietzsche directly consider political issues such as the role of democracy or aristocracy in the social order. Throughout his life he had little but contempt for democracy as a kind of rule by the masses, so from a contemporary perspective we have to read Nietzsche selectively because he is so unsystematic and so inconsistent—both traits that he might have seen as positive attributes of critical thinking.

Nietzsche had high hopes that his first book would be deeply appreciated by the classical philologists of his day, so much as to alter some of the basic principles of his discipline. But in this he was deeply disappointed. Although Wagner was, of course, delighted that his own music-drama was then envisioned by Nietzsche as the antidote to modern social ailments, the academic world rejected the book on almost every count. The then-twenty-four-year-old Ulrich von Wilamowitz-Moellendorff (who would go on to become a renowned classical philologist) wrote a scathing critique of the whole project as unscholarly, an effort to turn philology into an art rather than a science. Even Nietzsche's former academic mentor agreed with Wilamowitz, and communicated his personal disappointment to his former student.

Fourteen years later, in 1886, Nietzsche wrote a preface to the publication of the second edition of *The Birth of Tragedy*. Called "An Attempt at Self Criticism," this short essay certainly lives up to its title. He now claims that his first, youthful book "is badly written, clumsy, embarrassing, with a rage for imagery and confused in its imagery, emotional, here and there sugary to the point of effeminacy, uneven in pace, lacking the will to logical cleanliness . . . " (5–6). Indeed, that sentence goes on for another half page in its vilification of Nietzsche's own work. What may be most striking about this preface, however, is that it seems to offer a radically different thematic focus for the project than virtually any reader had recognized. That is, as we have seen, the ostensible central argument seems to be about the need for art and aesthetics; but Nietzsche now casts the focus of the book as "the problem of science . . . science grasped for the first time as something problematic and questionable" (4–5). He even quotes Plato from the *Phaedrus* (where the latter revalues emotion and madness, as we saw in Chapter 4): "to quote Plato, it was precisely madness which brought the greatest blessings to Hellas" (7). Nietzsche had begun to revalue his earlier visions of the strictly Apolline character of the illusory trust in science as a manifestation of reason, and to this extent he began to see a much more social, transactional assessment of science as a modest, but crucial, dimension of human inquiry. But before we get to that version of science, we should turn to one of Nietzsche's most notorious nineteenth-century pronouncements.

In the prologue to Nietzsche's 1883 publication, *Thus Spoke Zarathustra,* the protagonist utters the famous words "*God is dead!*" Now forty years old, Zarathustra emerges from his mountain cave after ten years of solitude to descend, to "go under," and to reenter social life. As he begins his descent, he meets an old man or saint who has also been living outside of town and society to "love God" (Kaufmann 123). After this brief encounter, Zarathustra reflects to himself: "This old saint in the forest has not yet heard anything of this that *God is dead!*" (124). Nietzsche uses this expression several other times (three times in *The Gay Science* alone). Many people have interpreted it to mean that Nietzsche did not believe in God, did not believe in morality, and did not believe in any human values more generally, so much so that they believe Nietzsche was the ultimate nihilist.

But Nietzsche fought most of his life *against* nihilism, against the deadening effects of conventional beliefs, against illusory beliefs in an afterlife that justified complacency toward the injustices of this life. In many strands of his thinking he developed what he himself called "affirmative philosophy," nearly the opposite of Schopenhauer's withdrawal from the world: indeed, by the 1880s, he completely rejected Schopenhauer's "whole philosophy of resignation" ("An Attempt" 10). He offered a philosophy based on a much more committed engagement with suffering, pain, and injustice, so it recognized a necessary (or tragic) pessimism, but not the emptiness of nihilism. He despised any view of individual freedom based exclusively on the shibboleths of wealth, reason, Christian morality, or "the pompous pretext of founding an empire" (10). It is true that in some of his expressions he honors the warrior as a necessary phase of resisting the violent operations of a repressive society. But, contrary to many views, he was outraged at the prevalence of anti-Semitism in Europe: in *Human, All Too Human*, he saw as an absolute "obscenity" the idea "of leading the Jews to slaughter as scapegoats of every conceivable public and internal misfortune" (Kaufmann 62). He argued in the same book against the ills of narrow-minded nationalism, and recognized instead that "continual intermarriage" must lead to a "mixed race" (61), and that such hybridity was a virtue. Part of the reason he broke with Wagner was over the latter's anti-Semitic views, which Nietzsche found abhorrent.

At the same time, Nietzsche never engaged in direct political actions; nor aligned himself with any social movements; nor felt that democracy led to anything other than "mediocrity"; not ever considered labor and economic analysis worthwhile. But he certainly opposed the bourgeois belief in inevitable progress through technology and capital accumulation. Where he most directly seemed to offend people was in his conviction that the conventional belief in God was, likewise, just such an illusion to justify our living with oppression and what he called "ressentiment" without ever having to engage in the struggle to free ourselves of these illusions and injustices. Such ressentiment often arose from a slave-based economy where profit was terribly, unjustly maldistributed. Zarathustra's descent into human life can be seen as a heroic struggle to get beneath the illusions, to engage in radical revaluations of everything, to literally get out of the cave in the mountains and the "cave" of illusory appearances and sustain a complete *"revaluation of all values."* The latter phrase Nietzsche used repeatedly in the last (and most) productive year of his writing life, 1888, when it first appears in the *Twilight of the Idols* (Kaufmann 465). Nietzsche planned to use the phrase as the title of a planned four-part major work; but he only got to write the first section, called *The Antichrist*. He last uses the phrase a bit later in *Ecce Homo* (Kaufmann 465, 659). Nietzsche clearly didn't like Plato's method of escape from the cave by means of reason and dialectic alone, but he certainly did share with Plato his powerful metaphors of ignorance when lost amidst the false idols of the conventional world, the illusions of everyday appearances, and the hegemony of the dominant military and political order (even if he would not have used the latter set of terms).

In the end, as we have seen, Nietzsche also fought against the pessimism of resignation, and in *Human, All Too Human,* even argued against the reduction of life to theological battles between pessimism and optimism. For Nietzsche it was only after shattering traditional illusions about a paternalistic God keeping watch over his flock that one could begin the real work of his "affirmative philosophy," which he always distinguished from the illusory optimism of a comforting faith in reason or a benevolent God. As he put it in *The Gay Science,* "Indeed, we philosophers and 'free spirits' feel as if a new dawn were shining on us when we receive the tidings that 'the old god is dead'; our heart overflows with gratitude, amazement, anticipation, expectation" (Kaufmann 448). Nietzsche famously recognized that truth in conventional garb was mainly "A mobile army of metaphors, metonyms, and anthropomorphisms . . . illusions about which one has forgotten that this is what they are; metaphors which are worn out and without sensuous power" ("On Truth" 146). But in his radical Romantic moments, Nietzsche saw that the new dawn he imagined would not come from a cynical denial of the importance of seeking the truth through honest inquiry, but rather that "nothing is needed more than truth and in relation to it everything else has only second-rate value" (Kaufmann 448). He wrote these words in 1873, although this now famous essay, "On Truth and Lying in a Non-Moral Sense," was never published in his lifetime.

Nietzsche understood that much of what had gained power and authority through the discourse of science was indeed "second-rate": one could claim to have objectivity and universality when in practice this more often meant an assertion of the subjective will of the scientists, such as we have seen in Darwin's own reinforcing of familiar biases. More than anyone of his day, Nietzsche found abhorrent Darwin's story of racist supremacy as a "natural" consequence of the "survival of the fittest." His subsequent attack on the ahistorical claims made on behalf of the universal values of "science" led many people to believe that he was attacking all scientific endeavors *tout court*. Nothing could be further from the truth. Especially in his later works, such as *Beyond Good and Evil* (1886), *Human, All Too Human* (1886), and *The Gay Science* (1887), Nietzsche never argued that we should abandon the best kinds of scientific inquiry, he just gave it more humble aims.

Nietzsche's view of science was in many ways a direct precursor of twentieth-century American pragmatist versions of inquiry as well as more recent forms of actor-network theory of inquiry such as found in science and technology studies (see especially Latour, *Reassembling*). It is true that pragmatist concerns for establishing consensus seem completely alien to Nietzsche, who so often seems to champion an aggressive, hypermasculinized sense of the autonomous, isolated heroic Übermensch that, as Eagleton explains, "Nietzsche brings low any notion of social consensus" (*Ideology* 255). But, again, there are many different ways to read Nietzsche, depending on what texts one reads. In the passages I cite, science was for Nietzsche a particular kind of social practice grounded in provisional hypotheses that always bear a hypothetical, contextual, and contingent historical specificity. In *The Gay Science,* he was quite emphatic that scientific inquiry was one important phase of the network of human relations, a connectivity and communality much deeper than "herd-like" social conventions and institutional procedures: "In science, convictions have no rights of citizenship, as is said with good reason. Only when they decide to descend to the modesty of a hypothesis, of a provisional experimental point of view, of a regulative fiction, may they be granted admission and even a certain value within the realm of knowledge—though always with the restriction that they remain under police supervision, under the police of mistrust" (Kaufmann 448). The latter term registers a rigorous hermeneutics of suspicion; the "regulative fiction" registers a hermeneutics of recovery and reparation.

For these reasons, Nietzsche has often been called a "perspectivist," and that is true to the extent that he is always open to acknowledging the limitations of one's partial perspective and, therefore, recognizing that inquiry often requires Herculean forms of not just courage but humility so as to remain open to truths contrary to our own customary beliefs. The term *regulative fictions* is evocative in its conjoining of two terms: science has a fictional, mythical quality partly because of our modern devotion to it, but also because scientific findings as the latest hypotheses about the world are not completely unlike narrative fictions or myths because of their necessarily provisional status. Newtonian physics, for example, might be supplanted by Einstein's relativity. In his own words: "It is clear that science too rests on a faith; there is no science 'without presuppositions'" (Kaufmann 449). Second, though provisional, such fictions are both necessary and indeed regulative in that they serve as ways we construct meaning and knowledge through the social and communal presentation of evidence and argument, metaphor and narrative: regulative in the way that we need such frames to understand the world as best we can—but always, as Nietzsche says, open to question and transformation as new evidence arrives on the scene. In *Human, All Too Human,* Nietzsche emphasizes the practical significance of scientific inquiry without overinflating the claims to neutrality and objectivity: "On the whole, scientific methods are at least as important as any other result of research: for it is upon the insight into method that the scientific spirit depends" (Kaufmann 63). And the method is not a Godlike neutrality and an unbiased observation of the world, but rather a progressive seeking and testing of inferences: "The greatest progress men have made lies in their learning how to draw correct inferences" (57). Science, in this sense, is a particular, self-conscious, and methodical social practice enabling some people to reach tentative consensus with respect to how to read and interpret some specially demarcated arenas of knowledge. Implicitly, at least, such hypothetical understandings radiate within the social and political domains depending on the mechanisms of exchange and reciprocity available within the given society.

What is especially striking with Nietzsche is that scientific inquiry is as much as any other kind of theoretical or practical work tied to issues of morality. Questions about the function of science inevitably engage considerations of social justice even though in some contrary passages in *Beyond Good and Evil* (and elsewhere) Nietzsche ridicules any conventionalized notions of a "common good," and he finds conventional morality based on laws and "categorical imperatives" (Kant) repressive of human possibilities for flourishing. Nietzsche would never buy into what he felt were the false myths of "disinterested knowledge" and knowledge "for-its-own-sake": instead, education, knowledge, and research are all deeply connected to possibilities for the fulfillment of "common" human capabilities. We may not always agree with his version of those capabilities, given his not infrequent slide into some pretty masculinist rants in some passages, but that's only to say that we always have to read critically and selectively in the Western tradition.

Jumping ahead, in 1959, when C. P. Snow formulated his famous hypothesis of the "two cultures," science and humanities, he seemed to have consolidated the Enlightenment belief that modern science transcends history, politics, and social values insofar as it seeks objective data, verifiable truths, and empirical realities. So the sciences were "hard" and the humanities were "soft."

In contrast, from Nietzsche's perspective, the very term *humanities* is a kind of misnomer: it implies that other kinds of study, say, science, are "inhuman," not part of the humanities insofar as they claim (falsely) to be ahistorical. But all kinds of inquiry are human, and thus really a part of the vast historical project of the "humanities" broadly conceived. In Nietzsche's eyes, that would be a more accurate use of the term, although it's true that these differences are so built into the institutional structures of higher education (as well as general public expectations) that they have acquired enormous material force. But even more radically Nietzsche argues that the whole concept of "humanity" seeks to separate the human from nature, and it is a completely illusory division: "When one speaks of *humanity*, the idea is fundamental that this is something which separates and distinguishes man from nature. In reality, however, there is no such separation: 'natural' qualities and those called truly 'human' are inseparably grown together" (Kaufmann 32). Nietzsche here foreshadows the contemporary work of what many have called *posthumanism*, a strange word that Nietzsche helps us to see really means resisting deceptive distinctions between the human and natural (and the cybernetic) worlds. But, more important for our future life in the Anthropocene, Nietzsche's critique of the human-nature split anticipates the need for a "new environmental humanities"

(Bonneuil and Fressoz 288) whereby "scholars in the humanities need to rethink human action *also* on a geological scale of tens of thousands of years" (67).

Nietzsche also offers us a more humble view of science completely compatible with Naomi Oreskes and Erik Conway's "new view of science" as a social practice freed from the limitations of the positivist tradition: "History shows us clearly that science does not provide proof. It only provides the consensus of experts, based on the organized accumulation and scrutiny of evidence" (268). The social value of science is not that it represents some especially idealized access to the "Truth," but that in practice it represents one of the best ways we have found to mitigate hierarchy by way of peer review: at its best, science represents, then, a view of inquiry as a kind of participatory democracy where the community of those knowledgeable in the field all have a say in what counts for knowledge. No one individual, no one hierarchical center of power, whether economic, social, or political, can, in principle, defeat the voices of all eligible participants. Those principles can as easily apply to the mode of production: workers in any given manufacturing process can potentially participate in the decision making and share in the distribution of the surplus. Hierarchies of decision making will, of course, emerge for practical reasons, but it certainly need not be the extreme hierarchies we now find wherein CEOs take one thousand times more of the surplus than the workers.

Indeed, "the question 'Why science?' leads back to the moral problem . . . " (Kaufmann 450) because any time, effort, or resources devoted to scientific inquiry always raises the question of who benefits from those endeavors? Whose well-being is improved or affected? That is a difficult question to answer: we often don't know the social consequences of any given form of knowledge, but that hesitation need not prevent us from the inquiry. When the crowd mentality fails us, we often then have to draw on the resources of our own will to overcome conventional habits. It is in this context that Nietzsche's famous championing of the "will to truth" has often been misinterpreted to mean that he licensed the most robust forms of egotistical self-interest in gaining power over others. His notion of the "Übermensch" has been translated as the "superman," but the term is better translated as "overman," suggesting someone who can overcome the pull of conventional beliefs and dominant ideologies. To this extent, the "overman" is the opposite of the usual consideration of self-interest and ego-centeredness. In fact, it is possible to read Nietzsche's heroic "overman" as someone trying to overcome the capitalist self that justifies private profit, narrow-minded cultural nationalism, and anti-Semitism over rigorous cultural critique: in Nietzsche's terms, these cultural illnesses are all phases of the "crowd mentality." In these terms, "self-interest" is a form of self-delusion, and that is the most immoral form of inquiry. The "will to truth" is not a license for political power over others but a quest not to deceive others and to avoid self-deception.

In *The Gay Science,* Nietzsche is very precise about this moral dimension of the will to know:

> Consequently, 'will to truth' does *not* mean 'I will not let myself be deceived' but—there is no other choice—'I will not deceive, not even myself'; *and with this we are on the ground of moral ity.* For one should ask oneself carefully: 'Why don't you want to deceive?' especially if it should appear—and it certainly does appear—that life depends on appearance; I mean, on error, simulation, deception, self-deception; and when life has, as a matter of fact, always shown itself to be on the side of the most unscrupulous *polytropoi.* (Kaufmann 449).

One thing we can be sure of is that we will be deceived at various times in life: we cannot prevent those deceptions from happening because they are often out of our control, and we are vulnerable. So the moral dimension over which we can exercise some willfulness is our ability to choose not to deceive others: the "will to truth" also depends to a considerable degree on our willingness not to deceive ourselves. It is not easy work: as Nietzsche puts it, we constantly face error, deception, and "the most unscrupulous polytropoi." We live in what some have called the Plutocratic age or the "post-truth era," where truth itself no longer seems to matter. But moral inquiry requires that we not deny but confront the multiplicitous and polysemous nature of language uses. Nietzsche offers a relentless philosophy of opposition to the powers of manipulation that assault us. For this reason, I have concluded my account of Cultural Turn 2 with Nietzsche because in many ways he has already ideologically propelled us into our contemporary moment. Nietzsche never had to worry about the devastating effects of climate change. But were he alive today, I suspect that he certainly would have been a harsh critic of the illusions of market fundamentalism and the deceptions of the climate-change deniers. We have to read Nietzsche critically and selectively, as we have all the authors in this book, but if we do, we can understand that this nineteenth-century critic began to unravel for us all the ways that, as Naomi Klein puts it, "we are trapped in linear narratives that tell us . . . we can expand indefinitely." Such myths of progress at all costs sustain the delusion "that there will always be more space to absorb our waste, more resources to fuel our wants, more people to abuse" (*This Changes* 168). Those linear narratives are vestiges of a reductive version of Western metaphysics called neoliberalism that have converted all communal and social relations to competitive enterprises measured exclusively by the economic metrics of the market. This is a disastrous logic that has collapsed the public sphere and exacerbated both social inequality and global warming. We need some alternative narratives, and this history of theory has sought to reconsider the Western tradition within, rather than severed from, anthropological and geological perspectives. But there is no possibility of simply importing the traditions of resistance directly into the vastly different circumstances of the twenty-first century. The central point of this book has been that some phases of the Western tradition are a rich resource, but only when critically reassessed and selectively rewritten to serve contemporary needs. Too often, for example, Nietzsche's diatribes against politics must be revised or rejected because in some passages he clearly voiced total skepticism of our collective ability to assess any version of the common good; but in many other places, he insisted on the need to assess our shared (and divergent) historical trajectories. We will need such nonlinear narratives to aid any efforts to alter the dominant cultural stories of the past so that we can better work toward a more bearable future grounded in reciprocity, communality, and interdependence. These potentialities for human flourishing should remain on our wish list.

——— Cultural Turn 3 ———

SURVIVING THE SIXTH EXTINCTION AND RESOLVING THE CRISIS OF CARE

Epilogue

What Is the Crisis of Care?

We live in truly extraordinary times. The Arctic ice cap now "covers just half the area it did thirty years ago, and thirty years from now, it may well be gone entirely" (Kolbert 150). Since the 1970s, Caribbean coral reefs have declined by almost 80 percent, and in the last thirty years the Great Barrier Reef has diminished by 50 percent. Scientists estimate that because of the burning of fossil fuels, the atmospheric carbon dioxide concentration is higher (400 ppm) than at any time in the past three million years. Total global temperature increases for this century are about the same as the temperature variations during the ice ages, which took thousands of years, but today's rate is at least ten times faster than during any of the twenty ice ages. But it isn't just the atmosphere we need to worry about. Ocean acidification is about 30 percent greater than in 1800, and by 2050 is likely to be 150 percent higher, deeply affecting almost all forms of marine life. Consequently, the loss of biodiversity is astonishing: 24 percent of all species wandering around Planet Earth today will be headed to extinction by 2050, just about the time many of today's undergraduate students will be at the peaks of their careers.

Indeed, as Elizabeth Kolbert explains, we are living in the "age of the Sixth Extinction." To put this in perspective, since the arrival on Earth of complex species with backbones about 500 million years ago, in the late Triassic Period, there have been five episodes in geological history of massive, global extinction. They are called the Big Five (thus we are the Sixth). Each of the previous five represents a sudden (on a geological timescale) loss of biodiversity. In contrast, species extinctions generally take place very slowly, at an average rate of what scientists call background extinction rates, something like one species disappearing about every seven hundred years. Mass extinctions are very different. Although Darwin developed his evolutionary theory without a clue about these dramatic events, today we are all familiar with Number 5: the extinction of the dinosaurs 66 million years ago, marking the end of the Cretaceous Period. But the biggest mass extinction was Number 3, called the "End-Permian Extinction" or "the mother of all extinctions," about 250 million years ago, when about 96 percent of the species alive on the planet died. We don't always know the exact causes of these mass extinctions, although we do know that Number 5 had something to do with the catastrophic impact of an asteroid (or comet) near what is now the Yucatan Peninsula, and Number 6, just getting under way, is largely caused by human activity such that about five thousand species are vanishing each year—about fourteen species per day. The extinction rate for amphibians (the most endangered class of animals) is calculated to be about 45,000 times higher than the background extinction rate.[1] In general, "the total number of nondomesticated vertebrates alive in the world (individuals, not species) declined by some 52 percent over the period 1970–2010. Half of all wildlife. Three-quarters, among freshwater animals" (Davies 33).

In short, we (or, I should say, some people) haven't *cared* very well for the planet on which we live. The Anthropocene represents an irreversible geological event that brings death not just to other species: "Global warming means that people will die and countries disappear.... In the time of the Anthropocene, the entire functioning of the Earth becomes a matter of human political choice" (Bonneuil and Fressoz 24–25). The threats to human life via climate change can be linked to a dangerously reductive version of Western metaphysics where falsely ethnocentric versions of universalism serve the vested interests of economic and political leaders. We can trace that discourse all the way back to Cultural Turn 1 in ancient Greece, where Aristotle developed his remarkably influential system for the objective classification of everything that exists. This strand of the Western tradition reemerged in the Enlightenment and was transformed during Cultural Turn 2, when the earth began its transition into a new geological epoch. We depend upon the positive strands of Enlightenment thinking—reason, science, and data analysis—especially for our knowledge of climate change. But there is also much at risk. The dangerous philosophical strands of such thinking emerged as a blind faith in human ability to control nature as a passive "object," and thus to extract energy sources from deep beneath the earth without ever having to worry about any unintended consequences. Binary metaphysics served vested interests. From its beginnings, one of the basic splits of the capitalist world system has been that between humanity and nature, human history and geological history.[2]

Climate change is perhaps the most visible sign of what Nancy Fraser (and other writers[3]) have called "the crisis of care" that has characterized the history of the capitalist world-system since Cultural Turn 2. In simple terms, it means that concern for profit and markets have counted for more than care for our social bonds and common good. Or, as Fraser argues, the crucial contradiction is between economic production and social reproduction. The former depends upon the latter, but it tends to conceal that dependency. Fraser's insistence on the importance of caring for others through social reproduction has its direct antecedents in nineteenth-century countermovements such as Radical romanticism and First Wave feminism, as part of which, as we have seen, Mary Wollstonecraft insisted on caring for the rights and education of women. In Fraser's terms, "the capitalist economy relies on—one might say, free rides on—activities of provisioning, caregiving and interaction that produce and maintain social bonds, although it accords them no monetized value and treats them as if they were free" ("Contradictions" 101). Social reproduction includes necessary caretaking activities such as childcare, healthcare, elderly care, education care, etc. The reciprocal bonds of communality for the many often get broken by the hierarchies of unlimited accumulation for the few.

These formulations revise the more restricted sense of "social reproduction" that Marx first formulated as a name for the reproduction of socioeconomic inequalities. In the late twentieth century, Pierre Bourdieu refined the dynamics of social reproduction in such books as *Distinction*, where he detailed through his empirical research the connections between what he called "symbolic capital" and the forms of "symbolic violence" that reproduce social inequality.[4] Idealist aesthetics (a version of Romantic idealism) could thus serve to reproduce a social elite. But some feminist theorists, particularly Fraser, have offered a richly qualified analysis of the contradictions that inhere in the processes of social reproduction. In their eyes, the concept of social reproduction has been developed too exclusively in the masculinist discourse guided by the hermeneutics of suspicion, whereby social reproduction always refers to the negative reproduction of unjust hierarchies such as the "separate spheres" of women's work *inside* and men's labor *outside* the home. As I suggested in the introduction, those feminists committed to the dialectics between negative critique and reparative criticism have argued that there are significant positive dimensions to the necessary processes of human reproduction even though they have too often been cordoned off to the domestic sphere as women's unpaid labor. In these activities, human beings need nonviolent, nonsexist, and nonexploitive forms of caregiving suitable for our interdependent, symbiotic relations with others. In short, you cannot just eliminate all forms of social reproduction and expect human beings to survive. As Fraser explains, living in "households, building communities and sustaining the shared meanings, affective dispositions and horizons of value that underpin social cooperation" ("Contradictions" 101) are not just value-added luxuries but human necessities.[5] Fraser focuses on the gender consequences of this imbalance, whereby women have been called upon to bear the burden of social reproduction, but she demonstrates that it also deeply exacerbates racial and ethnic hierarchies. She also offers a cogent framework for understanding the transformations in the geopolitical economy from the late stages of industrial capitalism to our twenty-first-century crisis.

Fraser outlines three historical phases of the crisis of care beginning with its modern origins in Cultural Turn 2. As we saw emerging in the nineteenth century, the mythical separation of the economic system from social and political values depended on "the idea of 'separate spheres'" (Fraser, "Contradictions" 104): the industrial capital focus on economic production depended on white male authority over economic decisions while women served in the domestic sphere to fulfill all the caretaking activities necessary for life-sustaining forms of social reproduction. In Chapter 8, we saw exactly this racialized, gendered imbalance being reinforced by most of the classical economists (with the exception of John Stuart Mill) at the same time that Marx and Engels offered their critique of imperialist racism and the exploitation of women in the garment factories as well as in their unpaid domestic labor. Of course, huge class inequalities prevented many in the working classes, racial minorities, or the unemployed from ever having the material conditions necessary for successful caregiving. My focus on countermovements during Cultural Turn 2 is crucial because the social reproductive values of cooperation and communality were the main concerns of the early socialists, anarchists, and communists, who offered some of the most vivid alternatives to the exploitation of workers and the antidemocratic nature of corporate hierarchies. But these movements were never sufficient to prevent the escalation of the crisis of care and the cataclysmic effects of endless capital accumulation on the global climate.

Beginning in the nineteenth century, the industrial capital stage of the crisis of care eventually reached a tipping point in the mid-twentieth century. The pressures of the Great Depression and the two world wars led to a significant social transformation resulting in the formation of the modern welfare states following World War II, a period I refer to as Cultural Turn 3. The postwar global economy was orchestrated by the agreements signed by more than seven hundred delegates from the forty-four Allied nations, who in July 1944, toward the end of the war, gathered in Bretton Woods, New Hampshire. The Bretton Woods agreements created the International Financial Institutions (IFI) and established the dollar as a world currency. The World Bank, the International Monetary Fund, and the Marshall Plan (joined later by the GATT, WTO, NAFTA, LAFTA, and other IFI), shaped the newly mapped "Culture of Three Worlds" (Denning) centered on the "Washington Consensus," whereby the United States became the dominant nation in the global economy.

Ironically, the U.S. version of representational democracy depended upon the nondemocratic oligarchies in the Middle East for much of the oil that sustained its economic growth. The European Recovery Program (ERP, or Marshall Plan, 1948–51) also accelerated the growth of U.S. oil companies by paying "for buildings and refineries and installing oil-fired industrial boilers, putting in place the structure needed to convert from coal to oil" (Mitchell 30) so that much of Northern Europe could reorganize itself along the lines of the heavily carbon-dependent U.S. consumerist economy. This ironic reversal of democratic principles was explicitly made part of the new U.S. Cold War policies for enforcing its "strategic interests" internationally. As one of the architects of the Truman Doctrine for the containment of Soviet expansion, George F. Kennan persuasively argued in his famous 1946 "long telegram" from Moscow that "democratic states had to become, in effect, less democratic, and operate more like the state that was said to threaten them" (Mitchell 121). The advocates of strategic vigilance in the face of a "permanent war" never mentioned that it was based on corporate profits orchestrated by "restricting the supply of oil from the Middle East" (122) in order to increase the price of U.S. oil.

But for a while the Cold War policies seemed to work, because Cultural Turn 3 can be divided into two basic phases: the period of expansion, or the "Great Acceleration" (1945–75), characterized by the economic growth of the welfare states; followed by the period of contraction beginning in the late 1970s when, as David Harvey argues, Margaret Thatcher in Great Britain, Deng Xiaoping in China, and Ronald Reagan in the United States became world leaders (See *A Brief History*).[6]

The immediate post–World War II expansionary period of the global economy saw the establishment of what Fraser calls "state-managed capitalism" characteristic of the North Atlantic welfare states and their escalating dependence on remarkably cheap fossil fuels. These modifications of the political economy, based primarily on John Maynard Keynes's version of regulated markets, served to mildly mitigate the crisis by defusing "the contradiction between economic production and social reproduction in a different way—by enlisting state power on the side of reproduction" ("Contradictions" 108) and thus assuming some public responsibility for human resources and providing some limits to financial speculation. Since "the working classes no longer possessed the means to reproduce themselves on their own" (109), the state now had to intervene by providing such basic necessities as social security, schooling, healthcare, childcare, and higher education.

Indeed, in the thirty-five years from 1945–80, university enrollments skyrocketed. Although the primary focus of higher education shifted from teaching to research, and from undergraduate to graduate education, all sectors of higher education were expanding. Beginning with the first GI Bill (formally the Servicemen's Readjustment Act of 1944), followed soon by the Truman Commission on Higher Education's 1947 report, *Higher Education for American Democracy,* the National Defense Education Act (1958), and the Higher Education Act of 1965, this nation invested deeply in higher education—an investment that represents one of the great social experiments of modern times. It produced the most dynamic system of higher education on the face of the earth. Some real care was provided for young adults (at least for me and my generation), because anyone from a middle-class background could dream of attending a university. And we did. Higher education grew exponentially, from less than two million students in 1940 to twelve million in 1980, a rate that far outpaced the growth in population. By 1970, the higher-education system in the United States was the envy of the world for many more reasons than just enrollment and graduation rates, including the vast university investment in pharmaceutical, technological, and military developments. And who could complain when the United States had the highest graduation rates of any nation on the planet?

This all represented "a democratic advance" (Fraser, "Contradictions" 110), but with many caveats and limitations, beginning with the ecological disaster it entailed: the incontrovertible consequence was that the presence of CO_2 in the planet's atmosphere had grown from about 300 parts per million (ppm) in 1950 to more than 400 ppm by 2010. On the ground, the military funding rationales of the Cold War and the Space Race compromised funding for human resources; the new technical languages for managing the "economy" based on national money markets (the GNP was invented in 1944) required expert planning and know-how rather than democratic debate; the expectation that men would work and women stay home legitimated gender hierarchy; racial hierarchies were reinforced by excluding many African Americans from social entitlements; U.S. household debt skyrocketed from nearly zero in 1950 to more than $14 trillion by 2008; and the price of oil also skyrocketed from less than $20 per barrel to more than $100 per barrel by 2008, as the North Atlantic nations gained greater worldwide control of production. "In these respects, social democracy sacrificed emancipation to an alliance of social protection and marketization" (111). In the general terms we have been using, unjust hierarchies were reinforced over more democratic forms of communality.

In the 1970s, however, the Great Acceleration stalled and the global economic contraction that followed was accompanied by a right-wing backlash to the political dissent of the 1960s, a backlash directed against the social movements for social justice (Civil Rights, Women's Rights, Antiwar Protests, etc.) but also emphatically aimed at higher education. For example, two months before his appointment by President Nixon in 1971 as a Supreme Court Justice, Lewis F. Powell wrote his infamous "Powell Memo" (or "Powell Manifesto" as it is sometimes called). It was a remarkably effective rhetorical act. No other document in United States history prior to that time had ever more directly placed higher education under fire as the root cause, "the single most dynamic source" (12), of major American social and economic problems. Powell attacked universities for harboring intellectuals unsympathetic to free-market capitalism, and he called for "faculty balance" in academia. Although it was supposed to be a confidential memo to Eugene Sydnor Jr., the Chairman of the Education Committee of the U.S. Chamber of Commerce, this detailed, lengthy (34-page) memo outlined the reasons that every "major college . . . is graduating scores of bright young men [sic] who . . . despise the American political and economic system" (5). The memo was widely circulated among business organizations, and, rhetorically speaking, served as a trigger for the counterrevolution to the radical and progressive challenges to higher education of the 1960s.

It was remarkably effective. Forty years later, the United States ranked thirty-eighth out of forty-three developed nations in terms of progress in academic attainment (Newfield19). Higher-education costs in the United States are now greater on average than those of any other nation on earth, "with the partial exception of Japan" (133). Tuition in the United States has gone up by nearly 300 percent between 1990 and 2012, "twice the increase seen in health care costs" (24). Student debt in the United States now exceeds 1.4 trillion dollars, greater than any other single source of debt; student loans cannot be liquidated with bankruptcy; there are no statutes of limitations on this form of debt; and such loans have no other form of consumer protection such as are available for credit-card and home-mortgage debt. And in terms of supply and demand, demand has been off the charts: the funding cuts have all happened at the same time that overall U.S. college enrollment rose from twelve million in 1980 to over twenty million students today. During the same period, the proportion of full-time, tenure-track faculty to temporary, non-tenure-track faculty has reversed itself, diminishing from about 70 percent to about 30 percent. Jeffrey Williams accurately describes this transformation from public to private funding for higher education as the shift from the welfare state university to the post-welfare-state university (see "Post–Welfare").

Indeed, it has been a difficult time for people in and out of academia. Neoliberalism collapses the dialectical unity between communality and hierarchy. Everything gets reduced to the market logic of competition, return on investment (ROI), economic metrics—all of which produce hierarchy. These private interests evacuate the public domain. Communal needs for social reproduction, as Fraser points out, disappear from these equations, even though these caretaking activities supply the background support necessary for economic production.

The backlash against the regulations necessary for the welfare state dismantled the accommodations for social reproduction of positive, caregiving activities such as childcare, healthcare, education, and environmental protections. First, the limitations of state-managed capitalism faced ideological critiques emerging out of the social movements of the 1960s that challenged the hierarchies of gender, race, and class (those were the critiques Powell objected to in his influential memo). Second, this ideological critique was accompanied by the widespread decline in global productivity after the 1973 Arab oil embargo. Beginning in the 1970s, most of the welfare-state regulations came undone under the even more extreme version of free-market fundamentalism called "neoliberalism." But the deregulations for the wealthy were accompanied by severe regulations for vulnerable populations. President Nixon's 1972 proclamation of the "War on Drugs" and the regime of "law and order" led to the rapidly increasing practice of mass incarceration: in 1970 the U.S. prison population was about 370,000; in 2018, it is more than 2.3 million. Criminalization was racialized and, in some cases, privatized: although African Americans represent only about 13 percent of the U.S. population, the prison population is 38 percent black;[7] and the Corrections Corporation of America (CCA, founded in 1983, and now called CoreCivic) privatized a significant portion of the incarceration system to make profit off increasing rates of imprisonment. The dynamics of privatization shrank the public domain on all fronts: how could it not affect all students and teachers, for example, when between 1980 and 2010 some states experienced greater than 50 percent decline in inflation-adjusted, per-capita spending on higher education? On the global scale, even though the international financial institutions created after World War II have served the North Atlantic nations, these agreements now have little ability to mitigate the economic and political will of the most powerful corporations, whose operating budgets exceed the GDP of most nations on earth.[8]

In the last forty years, liberal democracies around the world have been rushing to divest themselves of any answerability to basic human needs such as healthcare, childcare, elder care, community care, immigrant care, racial care, gender care, debt care, housing care, prison care, education care, and environmental care. Governments withdraw from these public responsibilities for positive forms of social reproduction under the private market rationales for more austerity, reduced taxes for the wealthiest, and more sacrifices for increased military protection from terror. "The result, amid rising inequality," is the regime of "financialized capitalism" based on "a dualized organization of social reproduction, commodified for those who can pay for it, privatized for those who cannot—all glossed by the even more modern ideal of the 'two-earner family'" (Fraser, "Contradictions" 104). Typical Western ideological dualisms also aided neoliberal arguments that there are no limits to a strictly monetized "economy" freed from the spatial confines of colonial territory and the exhaustion of natural resources. Financial speculations can expand infinitely because, unlike food and fuel, paper money grows endlessly (recall John Law's argument from Chapter 7). Rather than messy democratic debate and egalitarian demands, a wary public could simply rely on the experts to manage the perpetual growth of the GDP through increasingly sophisticated digital technology and big data. In this system, very little is being offered to replace those resources for the basic needs of social reproduction, communal reciprocity, and mutual aid—even though these latter qualities are continually being reproduced somehow, to some degree, in order for life to survive. But unnecessary racial, gender, and ethnic hierarchies continue to sacrifice those citizens with the least resources, mainly those poor and indigenous peoples most vulnerable to the catastrophic effects of climate change. This is not a version of the good life proffered by any advocate of just theory as represented in this book.

From Acceleration to Contraction in English Studies

The specific transformations of English studies since World War II mirror the two-part historical frame for Cultural Turn 3. At the risk of being overly simplistic, the Great Acceleration was primarily dominated by Romantic idealism; responses to the period of contraction have been more akin to radical Romanticism. The Romantic idealism generated in Cultural Turn 2 served during the Great Acceleration as the ideological backbone for the growth of idealist aesthetics and versions of literary formalism such as New Criticism. Their versions of close reading identified their own ahistorical methods with a high spiritual principle located within the formal unities intrinsic to the self-contained texts upon which the methods went to work. For example, in their magisterial *Theory of Literature* (1947), René Wellek and Austin Warren contrast "The Extrinsic Approach to the Study of Literature" to "The Intrinsic Study of Literature." Of course, they privilege the latter over the former by devoting more than half the book to the concluding fourth section on intrinsic methods of "interpretation and analysis of the works of literature themselves" (127). In the same year (1947), Cleanth Brooks published *The Well Wrought Urn,* in which he offered his definition of the "heresy of paraphrase" guaranteeing that the idealized, spiritual meaning of great poetry could not, ultimately, be damaged by the technical, scientific analysis of his own close reading practices. Western metaphysical binarism served the New Critics' purposes well. In fact, Brooks makes it clear in this famous essay that he is concerned with "what the masterpieces had in common," but not at all worried that the idealist aesthetic hierarchies of the canon might also impose some gender, race, or class hierarchies as well: care for the textual object meant the critic did not need to care about social injustice. Brooks adapts Coleridge's notion of organic form, defining literary greatness in terms of "structure" rather than strictly of form because he wants to integrate form and content (thus the organic "structure") of the great poems that demonstrate the "principle of unity . . . an achieved harmony" (*Well Wrought* 195). He does not mean a predetermined form such as a sonnet. Rather, "the achieved harmony" depends on the key "principle of unity" *intrinsic* to the particular poem, ir-respective of any *extrinsic* social or political domains.[9]

Also in the late 1940s, W. K. Wimsatt and Monroe Beardsley published in the *Sewanee Review* their essays "The Intentional Fallacy" (1946), which eliminated from the self-contained text any significant intrusion of authorial intention, and "The Affec-tive Fallacy," (1949), which discredited the subjective emotional experience of the untrained reader. These two essays served as the first two chapters of Wimsatt's influential 1954 text, *The Verbal Icon: Studies in the Meaning of Poetry.* By denying both the writer and the reader any role in the determination of mean-ing, Wimsatt and Beardsley's approach left little space for caring about the reading and writing efforts of students themselves. Acts of producing writing were therefore subordinated to the consumption of literary artifacts so composition courses could be further reduced to a service function carried out by the rapidly increasing cadre of graduate students in English literature. All the technical terms being introduced served a double purpose: liter-ary interpretation could proceed by way of scientifically objective analysis and interpretation of the formal properties of canonical texts ("well wrought urns" and "verbal icons"), thus furthering the professional status of "literature" because it sat on the same bench of reliable objectivity called for by the sciences. But New Critical practitioners could use these hair-splitting devices of formal analysis without ever despoiling the ultimately spiritual encounter of the informed reader's experience of the sublime "text itself." Just as you can't harm the beauty of a living butterfly by putting a dead specimen on the dissecting table, entomology and literary criticism were scientific kin within the modern university.

Given this quick overview of the New Critical retooling of Romantic idealism, we have to admire how effective it was during the period of the "Great Acceleration" (1945–75). For one thing, it gave great power to any professor of literature confronting the huge influx of students attending college on the GI Bill.[10] New Criticism certainly became the dominant theory and practice of what Randall Jarrell called (in his contribution to the first edition of the *Paris Review*) the "Age of Criticism." The literature teacher could demonstrate exactly what the meanings of poems were with as much confidence as any scientist describing the structure of the atom or the coding of DNA. Poems (the New Critics' favored genre) were also short, thus allowing for the instructor to demonstrate his (there were not many women professors in this period) remarkable powers of explicating complex poems in fifty-minute class sessions. Brooks had coauthored with Robert Penn Warren the earlier textbooks *Understanding Poetry* (1938) and *Understanding Fiction* (1943), and these texts worked perfectly in the subsequent Cold War environment because the formal unity of literary texts did not stir political dissent. To use Paulo Freire's famous term, it was the perfect *banking model* of education: an authoritative male professor lecturing to large halls of new students. During the immediate postwar stretch when the economy was accelerating, no leader had to worry that English professors might offer activist critiques of Cold War policy. A harmless humanities wing of the academy could easily be funded along with the more important scientific disciplines.

However, the ostensible "apolitical" work of literary criticism indeed performed significant political work: it was the perfect method for aiding the rise of professionalism after the Second World War, what in 1968 Christopher Jencks and David Riesman called *The Academic Revolution*, and Clark Kerr (in his

1963 *Uses of the University*) called the "multiversity." Higher education moved from a prewar set of relatively elitist institutions enrolling a small coterie of American citizens to a major institution in the formation of contemporary social life. English gained disciplinary status nearly equivalent to that of the sciences because, like the latter, the former now had its specific objects (canonized literature) and its specific methods (close reading). C. P. Snow did not publish his famous book *The Two Cultures* until 1959, when he described the seemingly incommensurable discourses of the hard sciences versus the soft humanities. Yet the New Critics felt that their methods and objects were now nearly as "hard" as those of the sciences. The evidence for their success was eminently clear from the rising numbers all around them: rising enrollments, rising funding, and rising status.

Finally, the apolitical methodology was developed and practiced by many leading New Critics such as Robert Penn Warren, John Crowe Ransom, Allen Tate, and others, who were also notable political conservatives, contributors to the Fugitives movement that arose in the 1920s–30s at Vanderbilt University. For a while (1922–25), they published an influential literary journal, *The Fugitive,* where they first formulated their beliefs that the liberal Northern *industrial* economy was destroying their version of the more "natural" Southern *agrarian* economy. They consolidated their views in a collection of twelve essays, *I'll Take My Stand* (1930), where they defended the stability of their "Southern way of life" (Donaldson xli) as a genteel tradition of white masculinity against the 1920s independent "New Woman" or what Donald Davidson (one of the lead contributors) called the "damned club-women snifflers" (quoted in Donaldson xxiii). That such a "genteel" economy had been based on slavery played no part in their poetics because such extrinsic political concerns had been excluded from their version of close reading: "wholeness of belonging could be found only momentarily within the confines of a poem" (xxv). Warren even published in that volume an essay, "The Briar Patch," where he defended segregation, endorsing the notorious "separate but equal" clause defined by the famous 1896 Supreme Court decision of *Plessy v. Ferguson.* Warren was later embarrassed by this piece, and became a prominent spokesperson for integration after the 1954 *Brown v. Board of*

Education decision. Nevertheless, there was simply nothing in the New Critics' method of literary interpretation that would worry them about these "extrinsic" matters: a white, masculine, Christian "universalism" served to justify their apolitical methodology and to mystify their political ideology. And the depoliticization of higher education of which the New Critics were part worked: during the height of New Critical hegemony in the 1950s, the ties between higher education and the Defense Department led to vastly increased university-based military research.[11] Few literary critics seemed to be worried.

But, as we know, times changed during the 1960s and 1970s, and a period of contraction began with the right-wing backlash signaled in part by the 1970 Powell memo, accompanied by dramatic changes in the geopolitical economy.[12] Within English departments, the changes were incredibly contradictory: the radical Romantic energy for social justice rises while the economic contraction pulls the rug out from under students and faculty.

Indeed, the humanities exploded: a huge interdisciplinary critique of the political economy emerged at the very time that material resources were diminishing. The "Age of Theory" in the 1970s and 1980s fueled dissent because it exposed previously hidden, or ignored, inequalities of gender, race, class, and ethnicity, thus contributing to political and theoretical movements such as feminism, race studies, cultural studies, Marxism, postcolonialism, ecocriticism, and queer theory. The common ground for all these "hermeneutics of suspicion" remains the critique of unjust hierarchies—and that is an ethical, not merely a methodological, ground. The dominant (although not exclusive) model of critique taught in graduate schools was, and still is, depth reading, or symptomatic reading, because Marx, Freud, and Derrida had all promoted this diagnostic model of seeking underlying causes for surface effects, as when the cultural superstructure conceals the economic base; the manifest content of a dream symbolically encodes the deeper, "real" causes located in the unconscious latent content; or when any "text is not a text unless it hides from the first comer . . . the law of its composition and the rules of its game" (Derrida, *Dissemination* 63). With the 1981 publication of his landmark book, *The Political Unconscious,* Fredric Jameson became the most influential theorist of symptomatic reading because he combined the Marxist (*Political*) with the Freudian (*Unconscious*) into a double-barreled advocacy for the hermeneutics of suspicion. Ideological critique requires the powers of a critic to break the mythologized surface to reveal the underlying reality of intersectional hierarchies.[13] No one in my generation or later who sought a job in an English department could avoid these transformations.

The ideological dominance of idealist aesthetics in New Critical clothes certainly retreated or disappeared in most English departments. Yet there still are significant material residues of the idealist discourse that have persisted in the form of institutional hierarchies between literature and criticism, literature and composition, creative writing and literature. The economic contraction intensified market competition for declining jobs in English departments just as the practitioners of these wide-ranging theoretical critiques aimed to expose some of the injustices of the market system. Despite the sometimes competitive sectionality of these diverse "hermeneutics of suspicion," the "sections" just meant that they arose in specific circumstances, a section of the complex and contaminated assemblage of how human beings strive to survive.

In 1989, Kimberlé Crenshaw, the civil rights legal scholar and one of the founders of critical race theory, adopted the term *intersectionality* to emphasize the entanglements of class, race, gender, ethnicity, and other differences ("Demarginalizing"). Her intervention has become a basic assumption in many related disciplines and subdisciplines including rhetoric, literature, composition, linguistics, and cultural studies. Intersectionality is crucial to combat *reductive* forms of binary thinking such as male versus female, white versus black, etc. With two caveats. First, the sectional hierarchies have all been produced in some fundamental ways by the mode of production in any given political economy, and intersectionality should not, therefore, be invoked as a way of evading the material circumstances that produced those injustices. Second, if *all* binary thinking were eliminated, it would be difficult to defend any version of the dialectic, and thus one of the crucial grounds for critical thinking. In the face of complex intersectional forces, the binary needs to move to a higher, more abstract conceptual level that is distinctly not sectional but represented by dialectical unities that affect any theory, method, or paradigm. Sectarian battles for social or institutional legitimacy can disrupt a more common basis for solidarity in nonsectional issues such as social justice and the fundamental dialectical unity between communality and hierarchy.[14]

In recent years, sectional tensions have arisen in debates between "distant reading" and "close reading"[15] and between "surface reading" and "depth reading."[16] These tensions always confront the difficulty of eliminating one pole of a dialectical unity. An ethical commitment to social justice will, however, *always* be adversarial with respect to unjust intersectional hierarchies that show up on the surface or in the depths, via close reading or distant reading. For example, Crystal Bartolovich contrasts symptomatic reading with any version of surface reading that neglects the big picture and forecloses historical and geographical questions of scale. In such instances, "surface reader appeals to the 'text itself' not only mark a pointed withdrawal from politics and theory but also . . . internalize the economic imperative to scale back when we should be asserting the most pressing problems facing our planet" ("Humanities" 116). There is no way to get around Marx's insight that because of the commodity fetishism of consumer culture, the market product often conceals its mode of production. Without attention to depth reading, there is no way to know from any textual surface how the texts themselves were produced, any more than I can tell from the shirt I am wearing what the working conditions were like for those who actually produced it. The rhetorical force of a universalist assertion means that, one way or another, surface/depth, close/distant dynamics affect *any* method or practice. One can, of course, choose to focus on either the surface or the depth, close or distant reading, as often happens, so long as there's no huge conflict from the opposing end of the dialectic that one must suppress. Finally, neither surface versus depth nor close versus distant metaphors can be conceived as rigid, either-or binaries but rather are poles of a spectrum since any individual's actual reading practices can be close to the surface, deep in the depths, or entirely distant from any individual reading experience altogether (see Moretti,

Distant)—these choices depend on the interests of the reader and the nature of the text(s), and, implicitly or explicitly, any of those choices will relate to considerations of social justice.

Just theorists often invoke important historical resources running back to radical Romanticism, and those critics whose recent work has been called "affect theory" have reinvigorated this important dimension of critical theory. Practicing a kind of reparative criticism, these theorists have demonstrated the extended scale of affect: they argue forcefully for reclaiming the "erotics" of reading and thus the emotional, physical, and physiological body in all acts of interpretation and critique. Recall, from Cultural Turn 2, that besides offering a negative critique of the forces of oppression, one form of affirmation among the nineteenth-century radical Romantics was to reclaim from the Neoclassical formalists the health of emotions, feelings, energy, and the body as a necessary correlative to emancipation and freedom. William Blake's vision that "energy is eternal delight" now gets recast in Cultural Turn 3 when "[t]he language of attachment, passion, and inspiration is no longer taboo" (Felski 187). These core energies, joys, and affirmations of care for our lived bodies may seem Romantic, and they are, but together with their suppression and the accompanying pain, they are also the moving force behind righteous anger and struggles against oppression and unjust hierarchies. A materialist critical project calls not just for the hermeneutics of suspicion but also for the hermeneutics of recovery that accounts for a reader's emotional intimacy with the texts and events he or she is responding to even though the intersectional forms and categories for such involvement are not predetermined, as they often are in an idealist aesthetics. Even more, the profoundly metaphysical separation of the mind and the body, the human and the natural, becomes suspect, just as Blake imagined the "contraries" as interdependent, not independent realms.[17] Some alternative strands of the Western tradition invigorated these discourses for the healthy body, for affective resilience, for mutual caring in social reproduction. These universalist aspirations can be crushed by our exhaustion from the relentless hum of demands for economic power for the few. Fundamental commitments to social justice can also recede from the surface and into the depths of our histories of the Western tradition. Recognizing the resources in these movements is part of my justifications for telling this history in *Just Theory*.

The Un-ending of Storytelling

There is no end to this story of just theory. It is all in the past, for sure, but we are everywhere left with the aftereffects of that history. And just theory is present-oriented but future-concerned: How can we live in a more just world? How can we mitigate the crisis of care? "The task," as Donna Haraway says, "is to make kin in lines of inventive connection as a practice of learning to live and die well with each other in a thick present" (1). It is thick because past and future deeply interweave with the present. While no one can predict the future with any certainty, our understanding of history can help us to make informed guesses. We speak of the future mostly in the present subjunctive appropriate for the mood of wish fulfilment: "It *is* important that we *be* fair . . . in any future political system. And it is safest to cast inferences about future endings in the interrogative, as Wolfgang Streeck does in his book, *How Will Capitalism End?* where he explains that we live in a time of "deep indeterminacy" (12). We don't know what will happen, and we face discouragement when contemporary problems seem insurmountable.

What can critical theory possibly do in these circumstances? Well, optimism and hope are among the resources of just theory, although the positive forces will not exactly arrive as a pep talk. As I outlined in the introduction, what Eve Sedgwick calls "reparative criticism" stands in dialectical tension with the important negative critiques based on the hermeneutics of suspicion and the deconstruction of unjust practices of inequality and ethnocentrism. Just theory draws on the dialectical relations between these two strands of critique and affirmation.[18] Despite the importance of both theory and method, the response to the social and political problems we all confront does not depend *exclusively* on a theoretical or methodological answer. But it *always* depends upon our underlying commitment to social justice. During the first two decades of the period of contraction (1970s–80s), many critics indulged in a kind of "theory hope" as if the answers to complex, intersectional injustices depended on just getting the theory correct, clarifying a specific method, or establishing a new revolutionary paradigm so we could all agree.[19] More recently, some humanists have proposed a "New Formalism"[20] that can be helpful so long as it does not uncritically found itself on Romantic idealism, whereby formal unities transcend historical contingencies. The problem with reducing formalism to a method with specific political effects is that it is not the method per se that is political even though a Marxist methodology will clearly lean on political forms of hierarchy and power relations. Heather Dubrow is correct when she argues that even "New Critical procedures can be adapted for a progressive agenda" (xi), although historically speaking that was not often the case. It takes a commitment to envisage social forms of injustice because "form," like content, is pervasive in any methodology. Without ethical commitments, it is at least possible to use formalist methods to justify authoritarian forms of social hierarchy.

"Just theory" is, therefore, not a single theory or method: it names a loose assemblage of related theories, methods, and stories with different strategic aims even if they share some common ground. Indeed, the word *just* appears first in the title of this book to indicate that the ethical choices precede methodological procedures and tactical decisions. At their best, all instances of just theory share commitments to social justice through the transformation of unjust hierarchies. Even as I have sometimes highlighted methodological difficulties, the response to the social and political problems we all confront in our new geological epoch does not depend *exclusively* on a new theory, a new method, or a new paradigm. Theories, methods, paradigms (as normal practices) are invaluable tools that can be put to quite varied uses depending on the motives and commitments of the user.

The communality/hierarchy dialectic is not a method, even though it certainly has methodological implications, because it operates at such a hierarchically abstract level that it necessarily affects *all* specific theories and methods. When we call something a dialectical unity (such as appearance and reality) we *are* asserting a universal claim, so we take a risk and must be prepared to argue that such a claim is not what Wallerstein called an anti-universal universal. That is why I can bring the communality/hierarchy dialectical relationship to bear on New Criticism as well as on Marxism, on formalism as well as on materialism, with their vastly different methodological assumptions and procedures. In short, attention to the relations between communality and hierarchy lends itself to revealing injustices across a wide range of social, political, theoretical, and methodological terrains. As Aristotle told us long ago, ethos precedes logos. Yet often as academics we feel that we must place a fig leaf of method over our ethical and political commitments—as if a commitment to justice were not also a commitment to truth, accuracy, and the common good. Grand as it sounds, all forms of knowledge in all disciplines have an implicit ethical commitment, or should have, to increase the possibilities for human flourishing for all people, even in times of epochal climate change, and even though such commitments are always contaminated, never pure and absolute. Indeed, that is a vested interest for just theorists. In Chapter 6, we saw how Immanuel Kant very carefully specified that what he called the "disinterested" pursuit of knowledge was actually based on deep human *interests,* from simple curiosity to complex ways to improve human life.[21] But, unfortunately, its frequent correlative, "knowledge for its own sake," is a close cousin of idealist aesthetics, and can be terribly misleading, sort of on the same axis as our current mantra, "profit for its own sake."[22] Knowledge does not have a personified, self-centered, and idealized "sake" that human beings must satisfy regardless of the needs of real people (nor does profit). Curiosity, imagination, and the desire to seek knowledge often function best in nonmarket networks that cannot be easily measured or counted. To this extent, broad-ranging terms such as Western metaphysics, radical Romanticism, materialist aesthetics, and environmental science, for example, are not theories we can simply adopt: they are names for diverse traditions that we can draw on from the historical archive and reformulate in our own interests, for our own historical moment. Some of these resources can aid our efforts to survive the Sixth Extinction, resist the rise of authoritarianism around the world, and resolve the crisis of care.

In contrast, the crisis of care depletes these resources through the economic calibration of all values: deceptively "objective" mathematical models for decision making promote standardized assessment practices across all social and educational domains. It as if John Law's notoriously destructive "economic idealism" had returned with a vengeance (see Chapter 7). But as Stefan Collini succinctly puts it, "Not everything that counts can be counted" (120). We can certainly evaluate and judge things, and for that we need narratives, qualitative descriptions, and discursive modes rather than only statistical objectivity and quantitative norms. Such qualitative evaluation calls for time, effort, and resources— the very things that market control tries to minimize. As the radical Romantics knew long ago, most of the positive, nonmarket values for communality and social reproduction do not end up on a balance sheet: how do you count the social bonds of care, reciprocity, intimacy, nurture, love?

But reliable data still speak volumes. Those of us in the humanities untrained in quantitative methodology still need to get our hands dirty with data. After the past forty years, the evidence is now in and the bill has come due. As Thomas Piketty has now documented, Karl Polanyi's basic point was correct: the fundamental law of capitalism is not increasing convergence on human freedom but increasing divergence, increasing inequality, and increasing hierarchy. Piketty expresses this law in the simple formula, r > g: the rate of return on investments is always greater than the rate of growth in the economy. Like many of the participants in the nineteenth-century countermovements (Chapter 8), Karl Marx also understood both sides: the dynamism of the capitalist world economy has produced enormous growth in overall global wealth, but the costs in terms of violence, war, and genocide have also been quite extreme. In short, capital grows capital, but not always jobs for workers. In his radical Romantic phases, Wordsworth's insistence on the healing capacities of human beings in the natural world provide a powerful backdrop to the contemporary environmental movement even if we need to resist his occasional slide toward an idealized "nature" over there, in the daffodils. Like others from this tradition, he would be outraged if he were alive today to witness the extinction of so many natural wonders like the coral reefs. The overwhelming evidence supporting Piketty's law completely contradicts the belief that there ever was or could be some kind of "free market." And, on closer inspection, that truth was insisted upon long ago, not only by many of the alternative theories, but even by the leading classical economists. Markets do not, by themselves, achieve equilibrium by virtue of some magical "invisible hand," as Adam Smith explained, even though many people used his term but did not read his book (see Chapter 8). As Smith himself persistently argued, markets fail. Indeed, climate change now registers as the most disastrous case of market failure in history.

Nevertheless, it is certainly true that what we mean by class struggle in the geopolitical economy now comes under intense pressure to modify the terms of analysis to accommodate the radical changes that have taken place. Literature, art, and culture are not just superstructural add-ons to the economic base—all cultural, social, and political domains are interrelated and interdependent: dynamic geopolitical networks of intersecting hierarchies and commonalities. New theories require new histories of the past that provide us with the resources that have often been omitted from the dominant discourse of critique in the Western tradition. The mobile, diffuse, and geographically vast reach of oil production has shattered the older, localized production of coal that allowed for collective action by workers to develop (see Mitchell), just as it has created a larger, technically sophisticated managerial class to make decisions when the labor demands for oil are considerably smaller than for coal. These vast geopolitical entanglements might seem far removed from the academic world, but they are not, if only because a kind of chiasma has taken place in terms of organized labor: in 1975, nearly 40 percent of the American labor force was organized into unions and collective bargaining agreements, whereas higher education was the least unionized segment of the workforce. But by the early twenty-first century, it was the reverse: the nonacademic unionized labor force had diminished to about 9 percent whereas the rise of the academic labor movement meant that nearly 40 percent of faculty in public higher education worked under collective bargaining agreements (see Bousquet). Until recently, English professors were not called upon to understand local collective bargaining agreements or global climate change, but times have indeed changed.

Virtually every bit of the information we have about climate change or inequality reflects our dependence on others for reliable knowledge about the world where reciprocity, shared understandings, and collective social life can, even in fragmented and contaminated ways, produce some versions of an interactive knowledge commons. We have to be able to translate between our fields: as Anna Tsing puts it, "it is useful to consider science a translation machine" (217), even as we recognize that translation itself can be messy, open-ended, and sometimes incommensurable across disciplines, languages, cultures, and nations. Nevertheless, what we translate can become a public good "whose benefit continues to increase as it approaches universal access" (Newfield 312). The absence of these benefits leads to a "post-truth," "fake news" world of tyranny and authoritarianism because the latter suppress the freedoms required for all human beings to enjoy the resources of health, longevity, education, and the possibilities for human flourishing.[23] There is no surprise here: "Neoliberal policies have always been intended to weaken democratic and egalitarian politics by moving control from public representatives to the private forces of the market" (Mitchell 224). After World War II, when many nations struggled to gain independence from colonial rule, "the number of democracies in the world expanded from thirty to roughly a hundred" (Remnick 20). But since 2000, this process has reversed itself.[24] When "the citizens of 94 countries suffer under nondemocratic regimes" (Kasparov and Halvorssen D-1), this means that nearly four billion people, more than half the world's population, have virtually no rights to alter their own terrible living standards, especially if climate change continues to accelerate.

To counter these powerful forces of political authoritarianism and economic privatization, we still need a strong and vibrant public sphere supportive of higher education, yet those spaces are going extinct about as fast as the earth's flora and fauna. As Klein puts it, "we are all in the sacrifice zone now" (*This Changes* 315). Defund life-sustaining forms of social reproduction and you defund the truth about climate change, mass extinction, and global authoritarianism. That's a cultural, political, and economic situation we all have to confront with the most persuasive rhetoric we can muster if we hope to survive the Sixth Extinction. The familiar refrain that because we are in perpetual economic crisis there is no money for these things is simply false, and it is a logic that has never affected the funding for any bank bailout plan nor any global military venture we have deemed necessary. Besides, the system is never totalizing: there are cracks in it everywhere, and stories to be told about those cracks that we should listen to, just as we must hear the stories of the countermovements from CT2—they too located some fractures in the dominant system.

The possibilities for human flourishing are always potentialities for the future, never fully actualized in the present or the past, even though such potentialities must to some degree be experienced within the material realities of contemporary life. The Western tradition has given rise to many potential visions of a better future: such foundational terms as *democracy, freedom, emancipation, universalism, transcendence, justice, liberty*—these contested terms all rest on different premises, for sure, but they all draw us toward a future that is imperfectly rendered in the present. Nothing we can point to in our actual worlds, past or present, can fully exemplify or fulfill our wishes for a better world: there has never been in any of our recorded history a material manifestation of our limitless desires. As Fraser puts it, "We know it means something deeper and more robust and egalitarian than social democracy" but we also have to "frankly admit that we don't know exactly what that means . . . we have a hard time defining the positive program" ("Capitalism's Crisis" 35). Yet many works of art, literature, ethnography, and theory offer us imaginatively vivid renderings of new possibilities (not just utopian "nowheres") that can aid our efforts at "defining a positive program." As we have seen in this book, momentary pockets of possibilities also materialized to varying degrees in specific social movements and alternative communities in the past, such as in ancient Greece; in the French Revolution; in the Haitian Revolution; and in the Paris Commune. And today there is evidence of such desires in many environmentalist and social justice movements around the world.

It is important that we include these moments in our histories of the Western tradition because they directly and indirectly affect everything we do in English departments and the humanities. *Just Theory* has tried to situate theoretical ideas, literary texts, and philosophical debates within geopolitical struggles over the foundational terms. What's common about the advocates of just theory is that they all stand against unfettered hierarchy and the rise of authoritarianism, both of which deeply threaten human well-being on this planet. No matter how different from the present our unimaginable future contexts may be, we can't simply avoid asking these foundational questions as they enter the political imaginary.

But we have to be careful as well as caring. Communality and reciprocity do not emerge from romantic ideals that neglect human action in the material world. There is no social justice without reparations for the material injustices of the past for which all privileged citizens share some obligations.[25] In our plutocratic age, history has, indeed, produced such powerful geographical inequalities as those between the North and the South, gated communities and shantytowns, the affluent suburbs and the impoverished inner cities.[26] So there's nothing "common" about the racialized geographies of contemporary social life. To no one's surprise, violent crime rates have escalated in impoverished and racialized neighborhoods, so that any theory about reciprocity and communality has to include tangible reparations for the injustices of the past. The geographical hierarchies are also reproduced within our educational institutions when a depleted core of tenure-track faculty are replaced by contingent faculty who are financially vulnerable and lack any genuine kind of academic freedom. No one in higher education should forget that many of our colleagues are suffering from that structural readjustment. Our wish lists for the future cannot just be idle dreams about a common social life that has never existed.

In Cultural Turn 3, escalating inequality and devastating forms of climate change go hand in hand with the crisis of care. Despite remarkable socioeconomic divergences, every human being is vulnerable. As the reign of cheap energy disappears into a carbon-based ecological collapse, Judith Butler puts it quite well: "Our shared exposure to precarity is but one ground of our potential equality and our reciprocal obligations to produce together conditions of livable life" (*Notes* 218). This positive project for the commons must complement the negative critique of injustice. We must rebuild the crucial domains of social reproduction, a task commonly shared by the many movements struggling for more equality.[27] Some strands of the Western tradition also shared those commitments, and we may need to make that history of engagement accessible to many more people if we hope to work for a livable future for all human beings. Social reproduction includes basic human needs for art, literature, theory, and criticism, so the liberal arts and humanities are fundamental to the *Arts of Living on a Damaged Planet* (Tsing et al.), not just a peripheral add-on to the market economy. The Sixth Extinction is no longer a vision of a diminishing future but a reality of our present planetary life in the Anthropocene. Perhaps we can even imagine ways to divest from the short-term language of crisis to envision the long-term care for our future lives on the planet. This book has been devoted to that hope.

For that kind of imagination, this book's focus on the Western traditions of just theory needs to be in conversation with other traditions. Part of the skills we learn in the humanities as practitioners of close reading is the ability to see distant connections in the proximate details. Those of us acculturated in the West have considerable social obligations to pay attention to indigenous and non-Western voices who are vulnerable to the hierarchies of our geopolitical systems.

With that hope in mind, I will end with the words of the anthropologist Anna Tsing, because her kind of storytelling resonates with our work in the humanities. We don't abandon our disciplinary heritage in English studies when we reach out to other disciplines like anthropology, but rather we enrich our abilities to read and write about our cultures just as we combat provincialism and rigid ethnocentrisms. We have to work locally with those commitments even though the contribution of such actions to larger social movements will be uncertain, hit-or-miss, and unpredictable. Tsing's exploration of the many indigenous groups of matsutake mushroom pickers takes her from Oregon to Asia and all over the world, into the deep recesses of our global economy where privatization, commodification, and exploitation (as well as local respect and enjoyment) of one of nature's resources, a mushroom, becomes an uncannily representative story of our planetary ecology and the symbiotic relations between the human and the natural worlds. As an anthropologist, Tsing exemplifies the dialectic between local and global, and thus between close reading and distant reading: "Cosmopolitan knowledge develops out of historical mergings" (239), she says, even as she imagines "the challenge of living without" (2) the assured comforts of modernization and progress. We live in a time of widespread insecurity: "everyone depends on capitalism but almost no one has what we used to call a 'regular job'" (3). Perhaps those of us in the humanities can learn from the matsutake and the mostly indigenous foragers who make a living from them, since many of her chapters can be taught in writing classes or graduate seminars in English departments. Both the mushrooms and the pickers demonstrate a remarkable ability to survive in what might otherwise seem to be precarious circumstances, the "blasted landscapes" wrought by ecological disasters. The spores of this unusual fungi bear only one set of chromosomes, rather than the usual paired units, so it can propagate in multiple ways, because its "genetic apparatus . . . is open-ended, able to add new material . . . to adapt to environmental shifts and to mend internal damage," surviving because of its "Mosaic bodies! Chemical sensing that creates communal effects!" (238). In her concluding chapter, "Further Adventures of a Mushroom," Tsing asks, "What kind of book is this that refuses to end?" Her answer is simple: "In this kind of storytelling, stories should never end, but rather lead to further stories" (287). Our hopes for a livable future may depend on our attentiveness to such stories. We must listen carefully to the "non-Western and non-civilizational storytellers, to remind us of the lively activities of all beings, human and not human" (vii). And she concludes: "We can still explore the overgrown verges of our blasted landscapes—the edges of capitalist discipline, scalability, and abandoned resource plantations. We can still catch the scent of the latent commons—and the elusive autumn aroma" (282).

Such poetic storytelling seems like a good example of just theory.

NOTES

Preface

1. I have been using the term *cultural turns* in my graduate seminars since 1988, and in 1995 I published an essay describing the three cultural turns, "From Ancient to Moderns." In 2009, Fredric Jameson published *The Cultural Turn: Selected Writings on the Postmodern, 1983–1988*, in which his sense of the "cultural turn" toward postmodernism matches what I have been calling Cultural Turn 3, although Jameson himself never uses the term *cultural turn* in the book (other than the title).

2. In the preface to *An Aesthetic Education in the Era of Globalization*, Gayatri Spivak has had to explain to her undergraduate students "why I cannot teach a regular survey" (xv) of the "History of Literary Criticism." I share this inability to teach a "regular survey" with my graduate students.

3. There are several single-volume overviews that survey the Western critical tradition. In my mind, the best of these is M. A. R. Habib's massive (nearly 800-page) *History of Literary Criticism and Theory: From Plato to the Present* (2008). See also Pelagia Goulimari; Richard Harland; and Anthony Cascardi. Anne H. Stevens touches on all major figures but in ways compatible with the materialist view of *Just Theory*.

4. See for instance Isaiah Berlin, who in *The Roots of Romanticism* acknowledges the importance of the movement, but criticizes its naïve emotionalism and irrationalism. Unfortunately, that book is deeply flawed by reducing "romanticism" to its least common denominator.

5. Even though he was a friend of Wordsworth, Arnold also thought the latter was not critical enough in his poetry, "so wanting in completeness and variety"; and he had even harsher words to say about "Shelley so incoherent" (*Function* 16). Arnold had more conflictual views of the French Revolution. He attacked Edmund Burke's conservative views of the Revolution, recognizing it as "an event of much more powerful and world-wide interest" than the English revolt against Charles I, even though he judged it to be "practically less successful" (22) as a political

transformation. Indeed, Arnold criticized the Revolution as the "grand error" whereby everyone was "quitting the intellectual sphere and rushing furiously into the political sphere" (28).

6. Arnold exemplified the aesthetic idealist view that the appreciation of great poems must be based on "the object in itself as it really is" (13), a view that will later be adapted by the mid-twentieth-century New Critics. The term "philistine" is taken from his famous 1859 book, *Culture and Anarchy*.

7. For example, the academic/political figure Michael Ignatieff (a one-time Canadian leader of the opposition Liberal Party) is quoted as saying, in an article appropriately titled "The Would-Be Philosopher King," that "Political life can make you extremely contemptuous of the world of books. . . . That's all *just theory*" (Goldstein, my italics).

8. See Chapter 4 of Sedgwick's *Touching Feeling*. Following Ricoeur, Sedgwick describes the "hermeneutics of suspicion" as a fundamentally paranoid style of theorizing, and, in contrast, suggests that "the desire of a reparative impulse . . . is additive and accretive" (149).

9. The French philosopher Alain Badiou speaks of "just ideas," resonating with very much the same meaning I am attaching to "just theory" ("The Idea of Communism" 8–9, 12). See also his *Saint Paul: The Foundation of Universalism*.

10. See Wendy Brown (81), where she cites Timothy Mitchell's *Rule of Experts*. See also Mitchell, *Carbon Democracy*, 124–27.

11. See an expanded version of this argument in Neil Larsen's essay "Literature, Immanent Critique, and the Problem of Standpoint" in Nilges and Sauri.

Chapter 1: Introduction

1. One of the most frequently cited lines of the French psychoanalyst, Jacques Lacan, was his pronouncement in *Écrits* that "there is no meta-language" (311).

2. Or, more recently, George Yancy has pointed out that such philosophy only "masquerades as universal. Philosophy is always already performed by bodies that are sexed, gendered, and culturally coded in some fashion" (1).

3. In this context, see Siep Stuurman's monumental study of the rise of the discourse of equality and commonality. Remarkably, he does not

even mention the alternative movements of socialism, anarchism, and communism.

4. See Immanuel Wallerstein's *European Universalism*. Wallerstein demonstrates that European universalism is really a kind of anti-universal universalism. He advocates for a truly "universal universalism."

5. Spivak also argued in this 1980 essay that the subaltern was "irretrievably heterogeneous." Terry Eagleton criticized her belief that "all universalism is reactionary" ("In the Gaudy Supermarket"). Spivak has modified her own views in her later work, especially *An Aesthetic Education*, where she speaks of "planetary readers," clearly a move toward considering geological and planetary history. Spivak herself came to regret her use of the term *strategic essentialism* (see Chapter 3, Note 14).

6. The philosophical distinction between immanence and transcendence has a long-standing tradition of debates. They all run the risk of racism, however, since "Whiteness is true transcendence, an ecstatic mode of being; blackness, however, in its ontological structure is true immanence, a thing unable to be other than what it was born to be" (Yancy 12).

7. See, for example, the conclusion to *The Political Unconscious*, where Fredric Jameson quotes Paul Ricoeur in championing "the dual nature of the hermeneutic process" (284).

8. Timothy Morton argues that our contemporary encounters with overwhelmingly large "hyperobjects" "end the possibility of transcendental leaps 'outside' physical reality" (*Hyperobjects* 2).

9. For example, Seyla Benhabib speaks of the "transnational migrations" (10) and "context-transcending appeal" (19) of the discourse of human rights, but for her, "context-transcending" means broader in scope, both spatially and temporally, rather than outside or above *all* contexts. See also Chakrabarty (5) on the universalism in postcolonialism.

10. As Swanson et al., argue: "The rigid separation of the humanities and natural sciences was an ideology for modern Man's conquest, but it is a poor tool for collaborative survival" (M7–8).

11. The conservative critic Arthur Herman devotes his book, *The Cave and the Light*, to this stereotypical vision of the division between Plato and Aristotle. He ends up admiring the work of the ultimate free-market guru, Ayn Rand. Needless to say, I do not arrive at those conclusions.

12. As Susan Buck-Morss explains, we are offered "the contemporary slogan, Think Global–Act Local" but such a project "requires modifica-

tion. We need first to ask what it means to Think Global, because we do not yet know how" (x).

13. Jodi Dean articulates this point quite well: "division is common to communication" (121). She therefore cautions those on the political left not to eschew all forms of hierarchy.

14. For instance, differences with respect to the meaning of *community* have triggered many complex debates such as Benedict Anderson's analysis of the birth of nations as "imagined communities" based on illusory ethnic and linguistic commonalities. Or, in the 1970s, Stanley Fish introduced into literary criticism the influential term *interpretive communities*.

15. Graeber uses the term *communism* in the sense that I use *communality,* and my sense is that he runs into the historical problems I mention.

16. The first, and so far only, woman to win the Nobel Prize in Economics (2009), Elinor Ostrom, has pioneered a vision of the commons based on local resources and community needs. While often cited by the political left for her advocacy of the "commons" and socioecological systems managed by communities, she has also been championed by the right for her resistance to government control and her advocacy for the nonregulation of markets. See especially *The Future of the Commons* (2012), and her landmark book, *Governing the Commons* (1990).

17. Abraham Maslow's famous "hierarchy of needs" provided a model of individual psychological health based on a progressive series of human needs rising all the way up to emotional and spiritual forms of self-actualization. This psychological hierarchy was supposedly common to all humans.

18. To this extent, these terms are often related to a similar dialectical contradiction between freedom and domination (see Harvey, *Seventeen,* Chapter 14). See also Chandra Talpade Mohanty on "commonalities," "differences," and "universal concerns" (226).

19. As she puts it, the hermeneutics of suspicion can, in its reductive versions, come to "rely on the prestige of a single, overarching narrative: exposing and problematizing hidden violence in the genealogy of the modern liberal subject" (139).

20. See Bartolovich ("Organizing"). Eagleton argues that "[t]hose radicals who instinctively mistrust the notion of hierarchy should ask themselves whether they really believe aesthetics to be as important as

apartheid. . . . Most political radicals . . . are committed to some notion of hierarchical determination" (*Ideology* 331).

21. See Bartolovich ("Organizing" 97–98).

22. Recent campus disturbances over controversial speakers become inflamed when First Amendment rights for free speech cannot be distinguished from academic freedom. See, for instance, Joan Scott's essay "How the Right Weaponized Free Speech."

23. Naomi Klein reports the findings of a Yale research study providing empirical evidence "that people with strong 'egalitarian' and 'communitarian' worldviews . . . overwhelmingly accept the scientific consensus on climate change. Conversely, those with strong 'hierarchical' and 'individualistic' worldviews . . . overwhelmingly reject the scientific consensus" (*This Changes* 36).

24. Morris notes that "the historian Norman Davies has found no fewer than twelve ways that academics define the West, united only by what he calls their 'elastic geography'" (41).

25. See especially Samir Amin's *Eurocentrism*, and Dipesh Chakrabarty's *Provincializing Europe*.

26. Actually, in 1865 the date was recognized as about 10,000 BCE. The date of 9,700 BCE as the shift from the Pleistocene to the Holocene was only officially ratified (in 2008) by an International Commission on Stratigraphy. The ICS has not officially approved the division of the Holocene into three ages, but there is a working group of the organization considering this proposal, as it is supported by many stratigraphers. See Davies, 188–92.

27. See Chris Harman's account (3–31) of the emergence after 10,000 BCE of "civilizations" based on extreme hierarchy, slavery, sexism, and class divisions that often crushed the "primitive communism" of the foraging peoples.

28. Morris and his team of researchers have developed a mathematical model of social development based on the combination of four key factors: energy capture, urbanism, information processing, and the capacities to make war.

29. See also Jared Diamond's expanded analysis of the climatic and geographical advantages of the Fertile Crescent that allowed for unprecedented growth of both agricultural crops and domesticated animals (169–205).

30. As an example of this gap, Morris points out that "China's first proper writing system [appeared] (around 1250 BCE) . . . and the first proper writing in Mesopotamia (around 3300 BCE)" (123).

31. As Eric Cline cautions, based on archeological evidence it remains unanswered "whether the Hebrew Exodus from Egypt was an actual event or merely part of myth and legend" (95).

32. As Eagleton sums it up, "The universal, then, is not some realm of abstract duty set sternly against the particular; it is just every individual's equal right to have his or her difference respected, and to participate in the common process whereby that can be achieved" (*Ideology* 414–15). See also Jean-Luc Nancy.

Chapter 2: Why Is Plato So Upset at the Poets, and What Is Western Metaphysics?

1. Most of these conjectures about Socrates's drinking abilities derive at least partly from the account in Plato's *Symposium,* where by early morning Socrates is left drinking with only Aristophanes, Agathon, and Aristodemus (who was "only half awake"). No one was able to follow his arguments about tragedy and comedy, as they were "sleepy," until "first of all Aristophanes dropped, and then, when the day was already dawning, Agathon. Socrates, when he had put them to sleep, rose to depart" (*Republic* 365). At the beginning of the dialogue, Socrates is said by Eryximachus to be "an exceptional being, and able either to drink or to abstain" (323).

2. As Graeber puts it: "Axial Age spirituality, then, is built on a bedrock of materialism" (244).

3. See Havelock's *The Greek Concept of Justice.*

4. Wood acknowledges that "[t]here is, however, one sense in which Plato can be read as an expression of democratic ideals—and that is, paradoxically, precisely in his adoption of the ethic of craftsmanship as a means of attacking democracy" (*Peasant-Citizen* 145). In her later work, *Citizens to Lords,* she also acknowledges that with the overthrow of the Thirty Tyrants in 403 BCE "Plato praised the moderation of the returning democrats" (65).

5. See Wood, *Peasant-Citizen* 148.

6. Recent evidence suggests that when the Parthenon was completed in 438 BCE as a kind of memorial to the devastating attack, burning, and looting of Athens by the Persians in 480 BCE, it actually served

as a site for human sacrifices, a reminder that our image of the Golden Age of Classical Greece might be significantly more idealized than the realities now indicate.

7. Graeber refers to it as the "military-coinage-slavery" complex (229).

8. Ironically, Pericles gained consensus as a leader by convincing other citizens of his wealth and nobility even as he himself was often seen as a radical populist of the day, trying to extend enfranchisement to more citizens. He was the General or Strategos for Athens from 461 to 429 BCE.

9. In *Peasant-Citizen and Slave,* Wood convincingly demonstrates that while it was clearly a "slave society," ancient Athens also "had as its corollary a citizen population of working peasants and craftsmen" (1) in which "the majority of citizens labored for a livelihood" (2). Nevertheless, Wood also admits that slavery did exist on a "massive scale," particularly in the mines. In 431 BCE, of a total population of about 310,000, more than one-third, about 110,000 appear to have been slaves (Wood, *Peasant-Citizen* 43).

10. In the *Apology,* Socrates points out that even those who think they are wise really are not wise at all, but since Socrates claimed not to possess any wisdom, he became, paradoxically, the wisest.

11. In Book 3 of the *Republic,* Plato condemns the poet, but he does not offer another criterion for that judgment. He also discusses poetry in a number of his dialogues, especially the *Ion,* the *Apology,* the *Protagoras,* the *Symposium,* the *Cratylus,* and the *Laws.* However, the *Republic* is by far his most rigorous critique of the poet.

12. Significantly, in the image I have chosen, the prisoners appear as if they might be women (although it is hard to tell). Yet in Plato's allegory all the prisoners are expressly men (all the pronoun references are masculine, and he several times refers to "men").

13. Plato's allegory owes a great deal to the pre-Socratic philosopher, Parmenides, and Plato acknowledges as much, especially in his dialogue of that name, *Parmenides.* Parmenides, however, never wrote what we would call philosophy; the only remaining source we have from him is a poem of about 160 lines called "On Nature."

14. See Havelock, *Preface* 208–9.

15. "Therefore, if there is no one, the others neither are, nor can be imagined to be, one or many. . . . if there is no one, there is nothing at

all" (Plato, *Collected* 956). The implication is that since there clearly is something, there must be the original Forms, or the "one."

16. See the epilogue, where I address the efforts of Stephen Best and Sharon Marcus to try to shift away from the interpretative power of depth reading to what they call "surface reading."

17. Book 5 of the *Republic* is where Plato deals most fully with the issue of sex and gender. Wood also documents a strange irony: "[I]t remains a remarkable feature of Greek history that the position of women seems to have declined as the democracy evolved" (*Peasant-Citizen* 115).

18. Raj Patel offers some compelling qualifications about the commonly held belief that philosophy emerged from the elite classes who had time to contemplate the world of abstractions and thought, whereas slaves performed the labor and thus had literally no time to think or use the dialectic. As Wood argues, "it was because of the democratic engagement of Athenian peasants that slavery was not *more* widespread" (*Peasant-Citizen* 186n9).

19. Habib does refer to Havelock in an endnote, and he several times mentions the educational function of poetry (*History* 11), as well as mentioning the oral nature of poetry as "a pre-existing multitude of local traditions in oral song" (15), but he never investigates poetry in an oral culture.

Chapter 3: Reframing the *Republic*

1. Parry also worked with the famous French philologist Georges Dumézil, who had also been deeply influenced by Meillet. Dumézil also became one of the mentors for Michel Foucault.

2. Together with his assistant, Albert Lord, and later through the editorial work of his son, Adam Parry, Parry formulated what has been called the Oral Formulaic Hypothesis, which maintains that the formulaic structure of the Homeric epics is due to the oral process of composing them through memorization and repetition. See Lord's *The Singer of Tales*; and Parry's *The Making of Homeric Verse*. Adam Parry acknowledged that there was at least one precedent for the belief that there was no single man called Homer: "A vain and irascible Frenchman of the seventeenth century, the Abbé d'Aubignac, has the best claim to the originator of the Homeric Question. . . . the poems handed down to us in his name are no more than a collection of earlier rhapsodies" (Introduction xii). Adam Parry adumbrates the long line of questions about Homer that preceded his father's work, and he acknowledges that the latter was a synthesizer: "It could fairly be said that each of the

specific tenets which make up Parry's view of Homer had been held by some former scholar. . . . Parry's achievement was to see the connection between these disparate contentions and observations" (xxii). Robert Wood (c. 1717–1770) actually seems to have conjectured that Homer was an oral poet, as Milman Parry indeed proved; others had conjectured that the Homeric epics were stitched together out of fragments rather than composed as a linear narrative by one author. See also, Ong, *Orality*, 17–30. More recently the work of Barry Powell also confirms that Homer was "the certainly illiterate oral singer" who composed in "a perfect hexameter" (237).

3. An important qualification is necessary: the shift from oral to literate culture has often been unfortunately conceived (at times even by Havelock and Ong) as an inevitable improvement in consciousness or cognition, a "great leap" from a lower form of oral bondage to a higher form of literate thinking. As Beth Daniell and others have argued, this is a terrible mistake, primarily because it ethnocentrically elevates literate moderns over illiterate primitives. For that reason, I treat all aspects of orality and literacy as social changes, changes in technologies of communication, opening new possibilities for imperialistic as well as beneficial forms of social and political life. As Daniell argues, "literacy is multiple, contextual, and ideological" (403) because "writing is woven into a society's structures of power" (405), and "literacy can oppress or resist or liberate" (406), depending upon circumstances. Literacy in ancient Greece was not some sudden, remarkable increase in mental abilities. I differ from Daniell in her paradoxical valorizing of *all* "postmodern little narratives" and condemning *all* grand narratives: for her, we should be universally opposed to *any* "universal principles" (406). For good ethical reasons (see p. 407), nonetheless, Daniell argues against *all* forms of ethnocentric injustice, and I share that desire for a universal even if it is so hard to achieve.

4. Ellen Meiksins Wood argues that "coinage was a later invention than was traditionally assumed" (*Peasant-Citizen* 94). Perhaps, but there is clear evidence, as Marc Shell documents, that the first coins were produced around 600 BCE, and he includes in the appendix an image of the first known inscribed coin, the Stater of Ephesus from 600 BCE. David Graeber also confirms that "the first coins were minted around 600 BC in the kingdom of Lydia" (244).

5. It is important to draw some contextual qualifications of the claims about blind memorization primarily because oral performance allowed for flexibility and variation. See Ong (*Orality* 21).

6. For Havelock and Ong, primary orality refers to those cultures that are exclusively oral, to the extent that they have not even heard of or

experienced literacy. Even the knowledge that others do the tasks of reading and writing affects the conditions of an oral culture.

7. Some scholars have indeed found it hard to believe that people could memorize so much material. See Nicholas Evans (189–90).

8. There have been extended debates, especially in the past forty years, making sharp distinctions between the Platonists and the sophists, (foundationalist versus pragmatic, modern versus postmodern), but my intention is to at least qualify that binary situation. See, for instance, Susan Jarratt.

9. Barry Powell notes that the early protocuneiform writing systems consisted of about twelve hundred signs, but by 2800 BCE these were reduced to six hundred, "a number that remained average for the next 2,500 years in standard cuneiform script" (77).

10. As Morris explains: "In Greece the palaces destroyed after 1200 BCE were not reoccupied and the old bureaucracy disappeared. . . . Population, craftsmanship, and life expectancy all declined; a dark age set in" (219). Incidentally, the Biblical story of Moses probably refers to these years.

11. As Powell elaborates, "The Greek alphabet was a single invention that took place at a single time. All writing systems, as far as we know, were invented by single men, never by groups or committees" (231).

12. The most notable exception is the fifteenth-century creation of the Korean alphabet, which was accomplished, quite amazingly, in three years following the decree by King Sejong. This alphabet was resisted by many at the time, and only gained wider acceptance within the last century (Ong 92).

13. It is almost impossible to determine the extent of literacy across the population. Powell speculates that it could seem minuscule in fifth-century Athens: "how many Athenians, say, could read and write a longer text of average complexity in the fifth century BC—5 percent?—but by any measure an ocean of people by comparison to the minuscule social, political, and religious elites of the old Eastern societies" (244). Nevertheless, it is most likely the case, following Ong, that the extent of literacy dramatically rose in Plato's lifetime.

14. Spivak later came to regret the way this term came to be misused by many to simply justify general forms of essentialism, and thus perpetuate the forms of epistemic violence she set out to critique. As she puts it in a 1993 *boundary* 2 interview: "I said that I no longer want to use it.

... [M]y notion just simply became the union ticket for essentialism" (Darius and Jonsson 35).

15. As a simple example, consider Gustav Freytag's 1863 model of what came to be called the Freytag pyramid: adapting Aristotle's three-part sequence of beginning, middle, and end, Freytag mapped out the five phases of the quintessential dramatic plot: the exposition, the rising action, the climax, the falling action, and the denouement.

16. Interestingly, everything that we know about the pre-Socratic philosophers might well have been filtered through Aristotelian translators, particularly Aristotle's student Theophrastus. As a result, they are seen to speak in the voice of being, the copula, but they make what might seem like simple-minded statements, as for example Thales's claim that "The world is water." But these early thinkers might have been working in a much different oral mode.

17. They could have, for instance, followed Isocrates, who in his *Areopagiticus* envisions a society in which there was harmony between social classes because the rich would share their wealth with all citizens. Likewise, the sophist Protagoras, who was often rendered in quite positive terms in the Platonic dialogues, offered more pragmatist orientations to knowledge and politics.

18. Havelock also spoke of the "Homeric state of mind" (*Preface*, Chapter 8, 134–44).

19. With respect to acculturation and childrearing it should be noted that Plato offers some astonishing ideas. For example, in Book 5, Plato's basic model for childrearing can only be conceived of as communal, communist, or socialist.

Chapter 4: Finding Love (and Writing) in All the Wrong Places

1. The serious part about these jokes is that the basic structure of authority has been embedded in the prepositional phrase "in the name of . . .". Derrida, for example, lists such possibilities as "in the name of truth; that is, in the name of knowledge of truth" (*Dissemination* 69). Other examples include: in the name of God, in the name of the father, in the name of the state, etc.

2. The ancient Greeks simply do not have our terms such as *gay, lesbian, homosexual, transgender, queer*, etc. (see Foucault, *History*). Their absence signals very different attitudes in ancient Greece about normative sexuality.

3. The racist overtones of these white and black images are hard to ignore, especially the black one: "The other horse, however, is huge, but crooked, a great jumble of a creature, with a short thick neck, a flat nose, dark color, grey bloodshot eyes" (*Phaedrus* 38).

4. It seems rather remarkable, but so far as I can determine, Derrida never refers to Havelock.

5. As Judith Butler argues, "There will be no metalanguage. . . . It will be the labour of transaction and . . . an opening towards alternative versions of universality that are wrought from the work of translation itself" ("Competing" 179).

6. In Plato's day, his arguments were against the relativism of the sophists. But the picture is more complex than might appear, because Plato is himself full of irony. As Derrida puts it: "And in that way isn't he the spitting image of a sophist? a pharmakeus? a magician? a sorcerer? even a poisoner? and even one of those impostors denounced by Gorgias?" (*Dissemination* 117).

Chapter 5: Aristotle's Natural Classification of Things

1. See especially the work of Luciano Canfora and Kelly Trumble.

2. As the classical scholar Anthony Kenny explains, Aristotle's "own papers were vast in size and scope—those that survive today total around a million words, and it is said that we possess only one-fifth of his output" (90).

3. Aristotle himself distinguished between *exoteric* and *esoteric* texts: exoteric being the ones intended for a broader public audience; the esoteric texts being designed more for in-house specialists—his students—and of a more technical nature. Most of what has been saved appears to be of the esoteric version, but as Edward Corbett explains, "the *Rhetoric* was addressed to an Athenian audience . . . during Aristotle's first residence in Athens (367–343) or during his second residence (335–322)" (ix).

4. As Edward Corbett explains, "it was more likely that a literate slave enscribed the copy of a text than that the author laboriously wrote out the words. Very often, the students themselves made copies of the lectures delivered in the schools" (ix).

5. As Anthony Kenny puts it, "In his major works Aristotle's style is very different from that of Plato or any of his other philosophical predecessors. . . . It may be that the texts we have are the notes from

which he lectured; perhaps even, in some cases, notes taken at lectures by students present" (74).

6. In the *Metaphysics*, Aristotle comes back and repeats this same assertion: "In the *Phaedo* the case is stated in this way—that the Forms are causes both of being and of becoming" (205).

7. Anthony Kenny agrees (as do many others) with this basic assessment: Aristotle "took a large part of his philosophical agenda from Plato, and his teaching is more often a modification than a repudiation of Plato's doctrines. The philosophical ideas that are common to the two philosophers are more important than the issues that divide them" (68).

8. The *Rhetoric* draws almost word for word from Aristotle's previous analysis of the syllogism in both the *Prior Analytics* and the *Posterior Analytics*.

9. As a good general example, see Northrop Frye's magisterial 1957 book, *Anatomy of Criticism:* his "anatomy" adopts Aristotle's three basic categories as his starting point.

10. This is true even in the *Gorgias*, a text generally considered Plato's critique of sophistry, but itself full of irony, humor, play, and rhetoric—signs of Socrates's own verbal performance.

11. Curtis White makes the same point in different terms: "Whether or not we as a culture ever learn to think metaphysically, we are thought metaphysically every day. Aristotle's hylomorphic theory of composition—the division of matter and form, body and mind—thinks through us as the most commonsensical set of assumptions. Every day we think in Aristotle, whether we know it or not" (*Middle Mind* 172).

12. Aristotle's supposedly universal character typologies are redolent with ethnocentric biases. Consider, for instance, this passage: "In the Characters there are four points to aim at. . . . Such goodness is possible in every type of personage, even in a woman or a slave, though the one is perhaps an inferior, and the other a wholly worthless being" (*Rhetoric* 242).

13. As Anthony Kenny explains, "Productive sciences are, naturally enough, sciences that have a product. . . . Theoretical sciences are those that have no product and no practical goal, but in which information and understanding is sought for its own sake" (75).

14. Again, as mentioned in Chapter 2 on the *Republic*, Plato is later, in the *Laws*, much more dogmatic and polemical in his presentation of the

imaginary state, where he clearly favors aristocratic rule by the educated few rather than democratic participation by all citizens.

Chapter 6: Rewriting Western Metaphysics for a Revolutionary Age

1. There are, indeed, ongoing debates among geologists and stratigraphers, who chart the epochs, periods, eras, and eons of geological deep time. The best summary of these debates can be found in Chapter 2 (41–68) of Jeremy Davies's *Birth of the Anthropocene*. As he explains, there is a subsidiary of the International Commission on Stratigraphy, called the Anthropocene Working Group, that is working to formally adjudicate the various dates proposed for the official beginning of the epoch. Crutzen, John McNeil, and their colleagues maintain that the changes beginning around 1800 constitute "Stage 1" with the rise of the fossil fuel industries; "Stage 2" is called the "Great Acceleration" after 1945 (Davies 45). Davies himself prefers to think of Stage 1 as the "end-Holocene event" (194) because he argues for the advantages of a strictly stratigraphic definition that could be determined, as all geological time periods have been, by empirical evidence in the earth's layers. Such stratigraphic evidence does not really begin to show up until "Stage 2," particularly because of the beginning of the thermonuclear age at the end of World War II. In any case, Cultural Turn 2 focuses on the geopolitical transition into the Carbon Age that will eventually produce the "Great Acceleration."

2. The first crude steam engines were invented around 1705–12 by Thomas Newcomen, but they were highly inefficient, and Watt's two-chamber cooling condenser model with a rotary motion made all the difference. Then, with the double-action piston (yielding power on both push and pull strokes), Watt patented this improved invention in 1782. Watt himself invented the term "horse-power" to measure the output of such engines. But we must keep in mind a huge qualification with respect to our focus on Watt: as Bonneuil and Fressoz argue, "the Anthropocene did not arise fully armed from the brain of James Watt, . . . but rather from a long historical process of economic exploitation of human beings and the world" (229).

3. Chris Harman documents this growth of coal output in England: "from 500,000 tons in 1650 to five million tons in 1750 and 15 million in 1800" (234). Since 1983, China has been the world's largest coal producer, and China was also the pioneer in early uses of coal, using it to smelt copper as early as 1000 BCE, long before it had any significance in Europe.

4. In 1795, the Speenhamland system in Great Britain aimed to provide some way of tying wages to the price of bread. In practice, however, it

often meant that the parishes picked up the differences in wages, which often remained below subsistence level (see Raj Patel).

5. See especially Ellen Meiksins Wood, *The Origin of Capitalism*.

6. See Wendy Brown, *Undoing the Demos*, which both explicates and updates Foucault's analysis.

7. For Foucault, the new form of governmental reason "marks the birth of this dissymmetrical bipolarity of politics and the economy" (*Birth*, 20). His point is that the separation of these domains is an "illusion," or an "error," yet it gains real political force when it becomes embedded as a discursive actuality in the discourse of the age.

8. M. H. Abrams's celebrated distinction between the Enlightenment version of art as a representational "mirror" of the world and the revolutionary Romantic view of art as a kind of "lamp" lighting up the beauty of the world is another description of the social transformation of the period. However, Abrams does not distinguish the radical and liberal strains of Romanticism.

9. When academic disciplines formed during that latter half of the nineteenth century, aesthetics would first be seen as a subdiscipline of the general discipline of philosophy. But as Jacques Rancière makes eminently clear in *Aesthetics and Its Discontents,* aesthetics is not merely an academic discipline, nor is it just an idealistic escape from the material world.

10. The great Romantic theorist, Morse Peckham, found Blake's stylistic effects "bizarre" (14). As he put it, "it is not difficult at all to assume a position towards the Romantics from which 'sickness' is the nicest thing one can say about them" (15).

11. Peckham articulated the radical intentions of the poets this way: "They began . . . a process of undermining the ideological superstructure of Western culture, and of culture itself, an undermining which, it may be, is the only human hope" (14).

12. The ideological connection between literary critics and priesthood will have a long carryover in the twentieth century. For example, T. S. Eliot maintained that the literary elite were a necessary cultural priesthood. In *Notes Towards the Definition of Culture* (1948), he describes the work of literary critics as functionally similar to the role of priests. F. R. Leavis modified Eliot's formulation to account more fully for the richness of literary experience, but in *The Great Tradition* (also published in 1948), Leavis described the role of the critic as being to develop the

cultural "discrimination" that would ensure the preservation of literary greatness. Leavis acknowledged right from the beginning of his career, in the 1932 publication of *New Bearings in English Poetry,* that only a small, elite coterie were likely to fully appreciate the literary masterpieces.

13. Peckham views what he calls "cultural transcendence" as the great achievement of the Romantic poets. However, like Abrams, he does not distinguish between the radical and idealist strains of Romanticism.

14. Blake intended the title to be an ironic play on Emmanuel Swedenborg's work, *Heaven and Hell,* which represents the more typical Manichean view of good and evil, heaven and hell.

15. Blake abhorred the eighteenth-century British sexual laws against sodomy, the restrictive marriage laws, and the cult of virginity that circulated in the emerging mass-market presses serving the dominant culture of "virtue."

16. In the context of these exclamatory cries for freedom we can see, in retrospect, some of the ethnocentrism of his day, as Blake says in this final section of the poem, "O Jew, leave counting gold!" and "black African! (Go, winged thought, widen his forehead). . . ."

17. The first, 1798, volume included four poems by Coleridge, including "The Rime of the Ancient Mariner," and the rest were poems by Wordsworth. Wordsworth arranged for the publication of the second edition under his own name, and this was followed by a third version in 1802, and final version in 1805. Wordsworth continued to revise the "Preface" until 1840.

18. John Clare seems to be the primary exception to that point, and, indeed his poetry offered a unique and alternative vision to that of the dominant Romantics. See Schragel.

19. Many critics have noted Wordsworth's more conservative turn later in his life. As Thomas Pfau puts it, after about 1808, Wordsworth "adopts traditional poetic forms" and "endorses an unmistakably nationalist and conservative tone" (147).

20. See especially Timothy Morton's *Ecology without Nature.* Also see ecofeminist theorists such as Greta Gaard; Maria Mies and Vandana Shiva; Val Plumwood; Noël Sturgeon; Karen J. Warren; and Anna Tsing.

21. Listen to a couple of passages in the *Preface* where Wordsworth elaborates in gendered terms: "He is a man speaking to men: a man,

it is true, endowed with more lively sensibility, more enthusiasm and tenderness" (437).

22. Oren Bracha provides a brief articulation of this process.

23. Mark Rose explains this process quite well in his article: "Nine-Tenths of the Law."

24. As Corynne McSherry explains, "Language . . . gave substance to the idea, or what would later be called the 'tangible means of expression.' . . . This object could be copied, of course, and the ideas within it circulated, but the author's expression remained as 'personal' as her very self. . . ." (40).

25. David Simpson offers a materialist reading of the poem's configuration of the commodity form: "The daffodils are planted in the soil of the commodity" (172). I agree, although Simpson never addresses the key gender difference that is also part of the commodity form.

26. Actually, as J. Shawcross explains, much of the influence of the German philosophers on Coleridge took place over the years immediately following his return to England, where he had arranged to have many of the philosophical books shipped back home, and it appears that the real depth of his indebtedness to Kant occurred when he had the time to read those books in England.

27. As Marcus Weigelt explains, the second, 1787, edition, has proved to be the standard. The first edition appeared in 1781, but Kant did not take great care in proofing the manuscript, and it appeared with many errors. Unfortunately, the 1787 edition did not resolve all these issues, and Kant revised some sections so much that there are semantic inconsistencies. Weigelt bases his translation on that by Max Muller in 1881 (revised in 1896), and there have been several other translations. (See Weigelt, "Introduction," in Kant, *The Critique of Pure Reason*.)

28. To be fair, Kant did not abandon the analysis of the soul, as he wrote an entire section of the *Critique of Practical Reason* (1788) explaining, "The immortality of the Soul as a Postulate of Pure Practical Reason" (130–32); but more often he developed a vast technical vocabulary to counter the older diction.

29. The complex structure of the first *Critique* can easily lead one to get lost in the sections, parts, chapters, and subsections, but in Kant's mind the organizational structure was the key to the entire systematic metaphysics.

30. In the *Critique of Pure Reason* Kant goes on to explicate one of the most complex sets of categories, axioms, principles, judgments, and concepts ever developed. Kant outlines twelve categories, fundamental concepts, as it were, of objectively knowing and classifying the world. Recall from Chapter 5 that Aristotle had delineated ten categories by which we apprehend the world. Kant's categories are completely different from Aristotle's, but this reworking of the fundamental categories still reflects Aristotelian formalism, by which the first category, "whatness" or substance, provides the basis for all the other categories.

31. As Derrida puts it, "no one can any longer separate knowledge from power, reason from performativity, metaphysics from technical mastery" (*Eyes* 95). Kant clearly meant to separate out the constative truth of philosophy from the performative commands of state powers. But his work can be seen as a contractual intervention intending to limit the powers of the state and the church.

32. For Readings, Kant's idealism meant that the "University is a *fictional* institution. Reason can only be instituted if the institution remains a fiction, functions only 'as if' it were not an institution. If the institution becomes real, then reason departs" (6). Readings misses the real powers Kant is negotiating in the "conflict of faculties."

33. "On the Common Saying: 'This May be True in Theory, but It Does Not Apply in Practice,'" in *Kant: Political Writings*, 61–92.

34. This quotation comes from "Reviews of Herder's Ideas on the Philosophy of the History of Mankind" (*Kant: Political Writings*, 201–20).

35. This quotation comes from "The Metaphysics of Morals" (*Kant: Political Writings*, 132–75).

36. The quotation is taken from Kant's 1764 book *Observations on the Feeling of the Beautiful and Sublime*. In this text Kant not only classifies what for him are the four basic races (White, Negro, Chinese, and Indian), but also distinguishes traits of different nationalities, so it is perhaps not surprising that the Germans are those who have the greatest capacity to participate in the experience "of the sublime and . . . of the beautiful" (54) whereas the Negroes have the lowest capacity because they "have by nature no feeling that rises above the trifling" (55).

37. Wordsworth also adopted the basic Kantian aesthetics whereby poetry allows access to the "subjective universal," as in the following passage from the "Preface" where he claims to have had "a deep impression of certain inherent and indestructible qualities of the human mind" (435), an echo of the Kantian transcendental unity of apperception.

38. Quoted by Shawcross in "Supplementary Note" to his 1907 edition of the *Biographia*, xcii.

39. In Chapter 9 of the *Biographia* Coleridge briefly but directly addresses the influence of Kant on his thinking: "After fifteen years' familiarity with them [Kant's many works], I still read these and all his other productions with undiminished delight and increasing admiration" (84).

Chapter 7: The *Prelude* to the Revolution

1. As Robert Heilbroner explains, Smith's "book took hold slowly. It was eight years before it was quoted in Parliament. . . . It was not until 1800 that the book achieved full recognition" (67).

2. A year before the publication of Spivak's famous essay, a similar charge of political idealism was registered by Carl Schmitt in *Political Romanticism* (1986). Despite these critiques, Kir Kuiken argues that most of the Romantics' texts "are never straightforwardly progressive or conservative; instead, they are sites of contestation, often between more than one conflicting tendency" (17). Simpson links Derrida, Marx, and Wordsworth in a powerful reading of the radical Romantic side of Wordsworth. He would see Spivak's reading as part of a historically dated tendency from the 1980s that loses "the deep bite of Wordsworth's self-critique" (2). But Spivak is less concerned with the individual virtues of Wordsworth than with the discursive strain of Romantic idealism that did, indeed, transcend the political economy. Simpson never refers to Spivak's essay on Wordsworth, although he does cite her several times, including references to other essays in the same well-known book, *In Other Worlds*.

3. Kuiken also contends that "Coleridge and Wordsworth tended to revert to positions late in life that restored much of the political theology they had spent their early careers challenging" (4).

4. This section owes a great deal to the extensive scholarship in the field of composition studies about the origins of the field. My cursory summary cannot possibly do justice to the invaluable historical work done by, among others, James Berlin, Patricia Bizzell and Bruce Herzberg, John Brereton, Robert Connors, Sharon Crowley, Susan Miller, Thomas Miller, James Murphy, Stephen North, and W. Ross Winterowd.

5. Actually, it was Blair's book that had an elaborate title: *Lectures on Rhetoric and Belles Lettres, to Which Are Added, Copious Questions: And an Analysis of Each Lecture by Abraham Mills, Teacher of Rhetoric and Belles-Lettres.*

6. The institutional importance of rhetoric as a service function was, however, combined with its devaluation as an imaginative art or social practice. Moreover, rhetoric slid out of view of the canons of literary theory, as we can see in any theory anthology compiled in recent years. I have addressed these issues before in *The Knowledge Contract*, Chapter 7.

7. For practical reasons, Spivak contrasts the 1805 and 1850 versions, but as Simpson reminds us it is not so dualistic: what we really have is "the immensely complex manuscript history of Wordsworth's mid-career drafts of his autobiographical epic" (146).

8. Spivak's first point is much more psychoanalytically framed and works at a much more conjectural level than the more sociohistorical points 2 and 3.

9. See also Mark Poster's essay, "Furet and the Deconstruction of 1989" from his book *Cultural History and Postmodernity: Disciplinary Readings and Challenges*. (François Furet is the author of the influential 1978 text *Interpreting the French Revolution*, a text central to these arguments.)

10. Simpson articulates Wordsworth's admission of interpretive wavering amidst the rush of social changes: "The radical uncertainty of Wordsworth's poetry oscillates between claims for pure aesthetic pleasure and the experience of pure bewilderment" (183).

11. The Estates General consisted of roughly three hundred representatives from the First Estate, three hundred representatives from the Second Estate, and six hundred representatives from the Third Estate. In 1789, when the First and Second Estates tried to exclude the Third Estate from their joint meeting in Versailles, the nearly six hundred members of Third Estate met outside the palace on a tennis court to jointly sign what came to be called the "Tennis Court Oath," which led to the formation of the National Assembly as the Third Estate vowed to take over political power.

12. See Giovanni Arrighi and Beverly J. Silver's essay, "Capitalism and World (Dis)order." Arrighi and Silver provide a succinct overview of the four periods of capitalist expansion.

13. See Albert O. Hirschman, *The Passions and the Interests: Political Arguments for Capitalism before Its Triumph*. (Thanks to Ralph Cintrón for suggesting this source.)

Notes

Chapter 8: Women's Rights, Class Wars, and the Master-Slave Dialectic

1. The full title is actually *A Vindication of the Rights of Men, in a Letter to the Right Honourable Edmund Burke; Occasioned by His Reflections on the Revolution in France* (1790).

2. This is true even as women in the eighteenth century found many outlets for writing about and satirizing the restrictive codes for masculinity and femininity in the dominant culture.

3. The term *laissez-faire,* which literally translates as "let it be" or "let do" has a much longer history going back to the late seventeenth century, but it has come to be a shorthand for an economic system free from state intervention, or even a nickname for capitalism itself. Ironically, none of the nineteenth-century classical economists used the term to describe their own theories.

4. Curtis White goes so far as to say: "Smith's work is not a how-to or a moral justification of capitalism; it is a plan for mitigating the inevitable destructive effects on the people most vulnerable to it" (*Barbaric* 109). See also Giovanni Arrighi's *Adam Smith in Beijing.*

5. As he puts it: "though the wear and tear of a free servant be equally at the expence of his master, it generally costs him much less than that of a slave. . . . [T]he work done by freemen comes cheaper in the end than that performed by slaves" (*Wealth* 113).

6. Arrighi argues "that there is no notion in [Smith's] work of self-regulating markets as in the neoliberal creed. . . . Substantively, the action of the government in Smith is pro-labour, not pro-capital. . . . Current conceptions turn him completely upside-down" ("Winding" 84).

7. The first census of the British population took place in 1801.

8. As Robert Heilbroner elaborates: "When Malthus published his *Principles of Political Economy* in 1820, Ricardo went to the trouble of taking some 220-odd pages of notes to point out the flaws in the Reverend's arguments, and Malthus positively went out of his way in his book to expose the fallacies he was sure were inherent in Ricardo's point of view" (85).

9. As Heilbroner puts it: "What is important is that the dire implications of rent envisioned by Ricardo never came to pass. For the industrialists finally did break the power of the landlords and they did finally secure the importation of cheap food" (99).

10. Heilbroner affirms that "at a basic level the vision of both Malthus and Ricardo is not fundamentally at odds with that of Smith" (102).

11. Graeber also claims that "many of Adam Smith's most famous arguments appear to have been cribbed from the works of free-market theorists from medieval Persia" (19).

12. As Karatani argues, "Proudhon was the first to raise a fundamental objection to this statist form of socialism" (*Structure* 235). Marx found objectionable Proudhon's absolute rejection of any historical role for the state.

13. The debates among the many versions of anarchism have led to such subcategories as individualist vs. social anarchism; mutualist anarchism; syndicalist anarchism; anarcho-anarchism; collective anarchism, etc.

14. Although he was a young man at the time of the Paris Commune in 1871 (he joined the International Workingmen's Association in 1872), the Russian Peter Kropotkin will go on in the early twentieth century to develop some of the most radical forms of anarchism based on mutual aid.

15. The original title of this book is *Phänomenologie des Geistes,* and it has long been a difficulty for translators to render the German term *geist,* which is literally translated as "spirit" but which in German also carries the sense of "mind," which has a much more analytic, modern inflection. As Walter Kaufmann explains: "A few of his terms create special difficulties; for example, *Geist.* To be perfectly idiomatic, one would have to render it now as spirit, now as mind, now as intellect, now as wit" (*The Portable Nietzsche* 3).

16. The best source for Hegel's theories of art can be found in his post-humously published volume, *Lectures on Aesthetics.*

17. Significantly, the final chapter of the *Logic* is entitled "The Doctrine of the Notion."

18. In the twenty-first century, John McMurtry has written extensively about the importance of "universal life-values." See also Fredric Jameson, "Marxist Criticism and Hegel."

19. Andrew Cole has argued that Hegel's actual terms, *lord* and *bonds-man,* referred more to the feudal relations that characterized economic and political life in Germany at the beginning of the nineteenth century. For Hegel, the French Revolution meant freedom from feudalism much more than the rise of industrial capitalism. (See Cole 65–85.)

20. As Buck-Morss argues: "Since the 1840s, with the early writings of Karl Marx, the struggle between the master and slave has been abstracted from literal reference and read once again as a metaphor—this time for the class struggle" (56).

21. See Habib, *A History* (384). Habib argues that although some philosophers such as Bertrand Russell made fun of Hegel for this remark, Hegel was recognizing the amazing world-historical significance of Napoleon in the course of world-historical process.

22. As Karatani explains, despite their growing theoretical differences, "Marx made common cause with the Proudhonists up until the Paris Commune" (*Structure* 250).

23. The psychodynamics of fetishism became especially significant in Freud's famous 1927 article on fetishism, in which he analyzed why some men chose odd objects for sexual gratification (yet Freud never considered fetishism in women).

24. The postcolonial critic E. San Juan Jr. offers a critique of those who would celebrate "the cult of the hybrid and heterogeneous, the indeterminate and the fragmented" (71) when such celebrations can cover up the underlying need of some oppressed groups for solidarity. See also Harvey, *Condition* 82.

25. The discourse of "innovation" gained considerable appeal with the 1997 publication of Clayton M. Christensen's *Innovator's Dilemma* (and his subsequent books). See Jill Lepore's essay "The Disruption Machine" for a critique of the rallying cry for constant "disruption" as a business practice. See also Jeffrey J. Williams, "Innovation for What?"

26. Harvey calls this process of rapid adaptation of production to shifting market trends "flexible forms of accumulation" (*Condition*); or, as Jameson put it, the postmodern valorizing of differences has become "the cultural logic of late capitalism" (*Postmodernism*). Both of these writers offer powerful critiques of Jean-François Lyotard's famous pronouncement of the "end of grand narratives" and the valorizing of dissensus over consensus.

27. As Alan Sinfield explains, "It is the project of ideology to represent such relations . . . as harmonious and coherent, so effacing contradiction and conflict; and the project of cultural materialists to draw attention to this" (9). The terms "dominant, residual, and emergent" were first proposed by Raymond Williams in *Marxism and Literature*.

28. On the personal circumstances of Marx's relationship with his wife, see Mary Gabriel's *Love and Capital*. In *Gender Work*, Robin Truth Goodman documents Marx's linking of gender and labor, but she is also one of the few materialist feminists to also acknowledge Marx's troublesome personal actions.

29. Karatani argues that "rather than criticize Marx for this, we should devote ourselves to the task of extending the work Marx carried out in *Capital* into the domains of state and nation" (*Structure* 16). See also Benedict Anderson, who raises similar questions in the introduction to *Imagined Communities*.

Chapter 9: The Struggle between Communality and Hierarchy

1. As Engels put it in his 1891 introduction to Marx's book: "The massacre of defenceless men, women and children, which had been raging all through the week on an increasing scale, reached its zenith. . . . The 'Wall of the Federals' at the Père Lachaise cemetery, where the final mass murder was consummated, is still standing today, a mute but eloquent testimony to the savagery of which the ruling class is capable as soon as the working class dares to come out for its rights" (Marx, *Civil War* 17). There have been ongoing debates over the exact number of Communards murdered, ranging from the conservative 25,000 (which I have adopted) to as many as 40,000.

2. As Karatani explains, Marx "foresaw that the Commune would immediately encounter interference and obstruction from foreign states. It is impossible to abolish the state in one country while leaving it intact elsewhere" (*Structure* 251). Marx believed that "[r]ather than usurp state power . . . socialists should first devote themselves to rebuilding Paris and France from the chaos of defeat in war" (250). Marx's initial objections to the Proudhonist/Bakuninist plans for the revolution in Paris have not been well known because he did not publish them, expressing them primarily in private correspondence.

3. As Kristin Ross argues, one of the enduring legacies of the Commune was "the way hierarchy came to be contested in the realm of the social imagination of the Communards before it was attacked on the political and economic level" (*Emergence* 4).

4. See, for instance, Jodi Dean's critique of the familiar ahistorical sense of a fixed essence shared by communism, the Soviet Union, and Stalinism.

5. Of course, the fact of industrial growth in the nineteenth century here marks the most obvious contrast with the contemporary situation.

Prior to our current crisis, it was not industrial production but financial manipulation that was expanding at a record pace.

6. Change the name of the war, and those last two sentences sound hauntingly familiar to the contemporary situation in the United States and other parts of the world such as the European Union.

7. See Hobsbawm's qualifications of the image of the "nutty" Saint-Simonians and the contradictions between socialist universal justice and technological versions of capitalism (*Age of Capital* 57).

8. As Donny Gluckstein puts it: "Haussmann's central Paris became a haven for the rich, a 'Babylon,' a nineteenth-century theme park known 'for its carnival flash, a crazy tinsel circus of all fleshly pleasures and all earthly magnificence'" (52).

9. On this point, a common misinterpretation of Marx is that he held the belief that capitalism would eventually self-destruct under its own corrosive contradictions. But as David Harvey argues, "I cannot actually find where Marx said this, and from my own reading of him I think it extremely unlikely that he would ever have said such a thing" (*Seventeen* 220). Moreover, as Thomas Piketty has now documented, capital has developed many alternative ways of adjusting and recovering from cyclical periods of diminished profits (see *Capital* 52–55).

10. Under the Second Empire, as Alistair Horne explains, "Political meetings were virtually banned, and censorship of the Press was complete. . . . On Louis-Napoleon's coming to power a large number of Socialist deputies had been proscribed and expelled from France" (28). But with the new freedom of press act, as David Harvey explains, "The means of representation and communication were multiplying rapidly. . . . By the late 1860s, newspapers and journals were opening up every month" (*Paris* 263).

11. Prosper Olivier Lissagaray related a remarkable tale of trying to use balloons to carry manifestos to the surrounding peasants (182).

12. The full text of the document called the "Programme" can be found in William Pembroke Fetridge's personal account of the Paris Commune, published in August of 1871. Fetridge's narrative stands as one of the most hostile representations of the Commune, and he throughout accuses the Communards of "stupid arrogance" (132) and ridicules the "absurdity" of their claims and the "insane terms" represented in the "Programme" (153). Fetridge was an American editor at Harper's, producing among other texts such popular ones as *Harper's Guide-Book*

to Europe and the East, and no doubt the Parisian experiment put a damper on American tourists in France.

13. See Tom Hayden, who provides a useful critical analysis of the significance of the Port Huron Statement to the contemporary Occupy Movement.

14. Similarly, the Port Huron Statement empowered "the individual as autonomous but interdependent with other individuals, and the community as a civic society" (Hayden 14).

15. In 1872, Marx and Engels wrote a preface to the second edition of the *Communist Manifesto,* explaining how recent events in world history, most explicitly the Paris Commune, required them to amend their earlier argument that the proletariat alone could assume control of the state.

16. David Harvey puts it in the context of the struggle over urban control (*Rebel* 128).

17. In Harvey's assessment, the Commune "pitted ideals of centralized hierarchical control (the Jacobin current) against decentralized anarchist visions of popular control (led by the Proudhonists)" (*Rebel* 8). See also *Paris: Capital of Modernity,* where he explains that "the politics of the Commune were hardly coherent . . . " (325).

18. Michael Hardt and Antonio Negri's work on the "multitude" tries to negotiate broad solidarity despite remarkable local differences (see *Multitude*). See also Victor Wallis, "Capitalism Unhinged."

19. Ross offers a wise caution about highlighting the Marx/Bakunin conflict, but she arrives at a similar assessment of key strategic tensions: "The intricacies and drama of the Marx/Bakunin split have dominated our perception of the politics of the period immediately after the Commune and led to an often reductive and overdrawn opposition—still bitterly and tiresomely rehearsed today—between an anarchist focus on political domination on the one hand and a Marxist focus on economic exploitation on the other" (*Communal* 108).

20. Harrington argues throughout for the virtues of socialism: As he explains, "under capitalism, there is a trend toward a growing centralization and planning that is eventually global, but it takes place *from the top down;* under socialism, that process is *subjected to democratic control from below by the people and their communities*" (9).

21. In his subsequent 1873 publication of *Statism and Anarchy,* Bakunin had made clear his objections to any effort to take over the state

bureaucracy, and, in particular, he worried deeply over the rise of the German Empire. As Harvey puts it, "In 1872 . . . there occurred the radical political break between the Marxists and the anarchists that, to this day, still unfortunately divides so much of the left opposition to capitalism" (*Paris* 8).

22. Karatani likewise argues that in this period, for Marx, "issues of nation and ethnicity became increasingly important, taking their place alongside issues of class" (*Structure* 258).

23. Unfortunately, it appears that, according to William Henderson, Marx also, in a letter to Engels, made some very racially derogatory comments about Lassalle's complexion and hair, suggesting that he was "niggerlike" (71).

24. Of course, Marx and Engels gave Kautsky much to go on with re-spect to seizing and holding state power. As they explain in *Critique of the Gotha Programme,* "the proletariat will, from the beginning, have to seize into its hands organized political State power and with its help smash the resistance of the capitalist class and reorganize society" (58).

25. Lenin devoted a book to the topic: *The Proletarian Revolution and the Renegade Kautsky.*

26. As Harrington elaborates, for Lenin: "There would be no 'state' above the people, no parliament that, once elected, would acquire a life of its own. The masses in their workplaces and villages would be the executive and the legislature all in one. The model was Marx's idealized version of the actual practice of the Paris Commune of 1870–71" (65).

27. Particularly significant in this context is the recent work by Jodi Dean; Bruno Bosteels; and Costas Douzinas and Slavoj Žižek.

28. Marx also quickly recognized the significance of Darwin's evolu-tionary history for his own version of materialist history. As Timothy Morton argues, "Marx thought that Darwin was helpful to materialism" (*Ecological Thought* 45).

Chapter 10: From God's Great Chain to Nature's Slow-Motion Evolution

1. On this point, Gould follows the work of the science historian Frank Sulloway, who wrote two essays in 1982 that revealed Darwin's confu-sions over the evidence regarding species and varieties. With respect to the evolutionary significance of the different tortoise carapaces from tortoises living on different islands, Darwin recognized no such signifi-

cance because his creationist assumptions led him to believe that such differences in varieties were not important. As Sulloway puts it, during their long voyage across the Pacific Ocean "Darwin and the other crew members gradually ate their way through the evidence that eventually, in the form of hearsay, was to revolutionize the biological sciences. Regrettably, not one of the thirty Chatham Island carapaces reached England, having all been thrown overboard with the other inedible remains" (quoted in Gould, "Darwin at Sea" 575).

2. Just a bit later yet, he still remarks that "[c]ertainly no clear line of demarcation has as yet been drawn between species and sub-species" (*On the Origin* 482).

3. Darwin sums up his survey of the evidence: "The races differ also in constitution, in acclimatisation, and in liability to certain diseases. Their mental characteristics are likewise very distinct" (*Descent* 900). Geography demonstrates these differences: "the different races of man are distributed over the world in the same zoological provinces, as those inhabited by undoubtedly distinct species and genera of mammals" (901).

4. In short, to treat Nietzsche as if he had a lifelong, consistent vision is simply ahistorical, and that is a strange irony for Eagleton, given his otherwise constant attention to history.

5. In the "Preface to the First Edition," Schopenhauer speaks of "the school of the divine Plato," and he surmises that "the influence of Sanskrit literature will penetrate no less deeply than did the revival of Greek literature in the fifteenth century" (*World* xv).

6. Nietzsche was certainly not alone in his growing antagonism toward Schopenhauer. Indeed, many people found Schopenhauer to be an extremely difficult man in his personal life. For instance, Bertrand Russell described Schopenhauer as "exceedingly quarrelsome and unusually avaricious" and added, "It is hard to find in his life evidences of any virtue other than kindness to animals. . . . In all other respects he was completely selfish" (758).

7. In his introduction, Raymond Guess puts this even more forcefully: "Nietzsche thinks . . . that Socrates is a deeply abnormal, unhealthy man, a man of stunted and perverted instincts and a diseased intellect that has run wild" (in Nietzsche, *Birth* xxi).

Epilogue

1. According to Jeremy Davies, the reality is that only about one percent "of all species are thought to have been altogether exterminated in

recent times" (36). But given the current *rate* of extinctions and species population crashes, humans are still on course to accelerate the Sixth Extinction "within a geologically brief spell" (37).

2. Today that ideological split has become deeply magnified. In *How Will Capitalism End?*, Wolfgang Streeck concludes by asking what is left for any kind of just theory "if the social is separated from the economic—and often from the political as well" (243).

3. The feminist discourse of the "crisis of care" has emerged in recent decades in both academic and nonacademic discourse. An example in a more public venue is Ruth Rosen's article "The Care Crisis" in the *Nation* (2007). Other contributors to this discourse include Daniel Boffey; Cynthia Hess; Johanna Brenner and Barbara Laslett; and Robin Truth Goodman.

4. See also Bourdieu and Passeron's influential book, *Reproduction in Education, Society, and Culture;* and Bourdieu, "Cultural Reproduction and Social Reproduction."

5. Caroline Levine also counters the tendency in the humanities to particularize local difference as an exclusively disruptive value: "[I]f we set our aesthetic and political sights on exception and disruption, it will always be difficult to celebrate the reproduction and maintenance of daily life, which in practice is so often women's work" ("Model" 645).

6. Historians argue about different pivotal years. Besides Harvey's focus on the global leadership transformations in 1978–1980, others choose the political impact of turmoil in 1968; others choose the economic impact of the OPEC oil embargo in 1973. But no one doubts that the unprecedented acceleration in capitalist expansion diminished after the 1970s.

7. See the Federal Prison Bureau report, "Inmate Race" (United States, Dept. of Justice).

8. See also Jane Mayer's and Nancy MacLean's historical studies of the radical right and their influence on the destruction of the welfare state.

9. Of course, Romantic idealism was not confined solely to English departments. A good example of how it affected the art world can be found in Roland Barthes's wonderful book *Mythologies,* especially the chapter "The Great Family of Man," where he examines the ideological implications of Edward Steichen's famous photographic show in the 1950s, together with the book of the same title. As Barthes argues, the

self-evident universal fact of human birth and death provides an ideal-ized formal unity for the "ambiguous myth of the human 'community'" (100). Sociopolitical, racial, and gender hierarchies disappear into the universal frame: "[B]ut in the whole mass of the human problem, what does the 'essence' of this process matter to us, compared to its modes which, as for them, are perfectly historical? . . . It is this entirely historified work which we should be told about, instead of an eternal aesthetics of laborious gestures" (102). "Eternal aesthetics" is another name for Romantic idealism.

10. New Criticism was not the only game in town: in 1953 Stanley Hy-man described in *The Armed Vision: A Study in the Method of Literary Criticism* ten different approaches (such as psychoanalysis, Marxism, archetypal criticism, etc.). Yet most English professors professionalized their work as guardians of the great Western tradition of canonized literature normalized by the New Critics.

11. For example, in 1956 C. Wright Mills exposed the depolitical myth on the grounds that "the economic and the military have become struc-turally and deeply interrelated, as the economy has become a seemingly permanent war economy; and military men and policies have increasingly penetrated the corporate economy" (215). The reality was the opposite of the apolitical myth sustained by the New Critics because higher education contributed deeply to that mission. As Mills argues: "Some universities, in fact, are financial branches of the military establishment, receiving three or four times as much money from military as from all other sources combined" (217).

12. Of the many helpful overviews of the last forty years in the his-tory of literary criticism and theory, I recommend Jeffrey J. Williams's "Criticism Live." Williams's story recognizes the fractal splintering and increasing formation of new subdisciplines while acknowledging the forces of academic professionalism under a neoliberal political economy.

13. Christopher Nealon offers an important qualification about the paradigmatic status of symptomatic reading: "almost none of the 'symptomatic reading' in the United States has had anything to do with Marxism" (22). In the United States, a lot of what has counted for symptomatic reading has followed psychoanalytic, deconstructive, or poststructuralist models of allegorical deep reading, rather than the Marxist base-superstructure model.

14. As Paolo Freire argued long ago: "Sectarianism is an obstacle to the emancipation of mankind. . . . Not infrequently, revolutionaries them-selves become reactionary by falling into sectarianism in the process of responding to the sectarianism of the Right" (37).

15. The dialectical unity between distant and close reading broaches the subject of the huge impact of digital humanities, but that really calls for another book. Briefly speaking, the advocates for distant reading such as Franco Moretti and his former student, Matthew Jockers, begin by making absolutist claims attacking close reading in "*all* of its incarnations, from the new criticism to deconstruction" (Moretti, *Distant* 48, my italics) or suggesting that close reading is "impractical" and "*totally* inappropriate as a method of studying literary history" (Jockers 7, my italics). They then back off those absolutist claims when they seek "a balance between the abstraction of model-building and the vividness of individual examples" (Moretti, *Distant* 1–2); or hope that "close reading . . . will continue to reveal nuggets" (Jockers 9). Moretti claims that distant reading provides knowledge because "distance is a condition of knowledge," but that closeness to individual texts and care about details is not a condition of knowledge? Caring about both distance and closeness is a dialectical unity for anyone concerned about knowledge whether one chooses to focus on distance or closeness. Besides, digital environments and multimedia have also opened new possibilities for close reading, deep learning, and vivid experiences by intensifying graphic and auditory dimensions suitable for interactive classrooms and networking collaborations. Even with these digital wonders, we should also be wary of indulging any too idealistic slide into cyberutopianism given the troubling dimensions of what has been called "platform capitalism" (Srnicek) or "surveillance capitalism" (Zuboff). The advocates for distant reading have more appropriately referred to their methodology as "computational criticism," "quantitative formalism" (Moretti, *Canon/Archive* ix), or "quantitative hermeneutics" (304–5)—in practice, these methods can be used on individual texts (such as Moretti does with *Hamlet*) as well as on big data from thousands of texts.

16. In 2009 the journal *Representations* published a special volume, "The Way We Read Now," in which editors Stephen Best and Sharon Marcus advocated "surface reading" as opposed to "depth reading," thus favoring one side of a dialectical unity and, in their minds, correcting the dominant, symptomatic reading model that favors depth. But as they eventually acknowledge toward the end of their essay, you can't have one without the other, any more than you can have the surface of the ocean without the depths. You cannot invent a metaphor of the textual surface that either encompasses or denies the deep traces of intersectional differences not otherwise visible on the surface, whether economic, historical, psychological, or geological, for that matter: the two terms dialectically define each other. For these reasons, Best and Marcus's efforts to pare away from the two-dimensional text any three-dimensional sense of thickness or hidden depth often seem torturous. By the end of their introduction, however, they arrive at a more conciliatory view: "the desire for a more complete view of reality are also aims of

both schools of thought" (19). In a recent interview, Marcus does point to the dangers of valorizing the depth in a stereotypical, phallocratic way: "Traditionally, depth tends to be associated more with masculine seriousness, whereas surfaces are dismissed as superficial, associated with a kind of deceptive, cosmetic, or trivial femininity" (91). Dialectical unities will always be perverted when combined with sexist, racist, or any other kind of bias.

17. As one of the most notable proponents of affect theory, Lauran Berlant, explains: "Bodies were elevated as, in a sense, smarter and more knowing than minds, although ultimately the distinction heads toward exhaustion" (124).

18. See especially Rita Felski's *Limits of Critique,* where she argues that the "hermeneutics of suspicion" can be limiting when it neglects the "hermeneutics of recovery," or, citing Sedgwick, the positive force of "reparative criticism." See also *PMLA,* vol. 132, no. 2, March 2017 for the section "On Rita Felski's *The Limits of Critique*" (331–91).

19. I argued in *The Knowledge Contract* that, contrary to many left-wing hopes, paradigm changes are not revolutionary, at least in terms of political revolutions. Thomas Kuhn's version of paradigms was fundamentally conservative. His main point was that disciplinarity works by having a normal practice, shifting, and then reestablishing a new normal practice. Joseph North's argument for a new paradigm for literary studies as a revolutionary turn seems to completely miss Kuhn's point about the fundamentally conservative nature of paradigms.

20. *New Formalism* (or *neo-formalism*) is a term that comes primarily from a movement in poetry beginning in the 1980s and 1990s (see Jarman and Mason, and, for an overview, Robert McPhillips). More recently, see *New Literary History,* vol. 48, no. 2, Spring 2017 with its special section on "Aesthetics Now." See also Marjorie Levinson's "What Is New Formalism?" and Verena Theile and Linda Tredennick's collection, *New Formalisms and Literary Theory.* These all represent sophisticated efforts to prevent formalism from being reduced to New Critical versions of aesthetic idealism. See also Caroline Levine's *Forms: Whole, Rhythm, Hierarchy, Network* (2015), because she so clearly has ethical commitments to critique social forms that radiate with unjust hierarchies.

21. On this point, see, for instance, Jürgen Habermas's book, *Knowledge and Human Interests.*

22. As Collini puts it: to believe that "knowledge is pursued 'for its own sake' . . . may mis-describe the variety of purposes for which different kinds of understanding may be sought" (55).

23. In her 1951 classic *The Origins of Totalitarianism,* Hannah Arendt insists that "[t]he ideal subject of totalitarian rule is not the convinced Nazi or the dedicated communist, but people for whom the distinction between fact and fiction, true and false, no longer exists" (474).

24. As David Remnick reports, "since 2000, nation-states of major consequence . . . have gone in the opposite, authoritarian direction" (20).

25. As Naomi Klein puts it, we need to become "unafraid of powerful words such as *redistribution* and *reparation,* and intent on challenging Western culture's" global dominance (*No,* 262).

26. See Matthew Desmond's landmark book, *Evicted: Poverty and Profit in the American City.*

27. See Judith Butler's recent book *Notes toward a Performative Theory of Assembly.*

WORKS CITED

Abrams, M. H. *The Mirror and the Lamp: Romantic Theory and the Critical Tradition*. Oxford UP, 1953.

Adams, Hazard, editor. *Critical Theory since Plato*. Harcourt Brace Jovanovich, 1971.

Adorno, Theodor. *Minima Moralia: Reflections from Damaged Life*. Translated by E. F. N. Jephcott, Verso, 2006.

Amin, Samir. *Eurocentrism: Modernity, Religion, and Democracy: A Critique of Eurocentrism and Culturalism*. Translated by Russell Moore and James Membrez, 2nd ed., Monthly Review Press, 2009.

Anderson, Benedict. *Imagined Communities: Reflections on the Origin and Spread of Nationalism*. Verso, 1993.

Anderson, Kevin B. *Marx at the Margins: On Nationalism, Ethnicity, and Non-Western Societies*. U of Chicago P, 2010.

———. "Marx's Capital After 150 Years: Revolutionary Reflections." *Socialism and Democracy*, vol. 31, no. 3, Nov. 2017, pp. 1–10.

Arendt, Hannah. *The Origins of Totalitarianism*. Harcourt, Brace, Jovanovich, 1973.

Aristotle. *The Basic Works of Aristotle*. Edited by Richard McKeon, Modern Library, 2001.

———. *The Metaphysics*. Translated by W. D. Ross, RBJones.com, 2012.

———. *Politics*. Translated by Benjamin Jowett, Dover Publications, 2000.

———. *The Rhetoric and the Poetics of Aristotle*. Translated by W. Rhys Roberts and Ingram Bywater, Modern Library, 1984.

Arnold, Matthew. *Culture and Anarchy and Other Writings*. Cambridge UP, 1993.

——. *The Function of Criticism at the Present Time.* With *An Essay on Style,* by Walter Pater. Macmillan, 1895.

Arrighi, Giovanni. *Adam Smith in Beijing: Lineages of the Twenty-First Century.* Verso, 2007.

——. "The Winding Paths of Capital: Interview by David Harvey." *New Left Review*, no. 56, Mar.–Apr. 2009, pp. 61–94.

Arrighi, Giovanni, and Beverly J. Silver. "Capitalism and World (Dis) order." *Review of International Studies*, vol. 27, no. 5, Dec. 2001, pp. 257–79.

Badiou, Alain. "The Idea of Communism." Douzinas and Žižek, pp. 1–14.

——. *Saint Paul: The Foundation of Universalism.* Stanford UP, 2003.

Baillie, J. B. Translator's introduction. Hegel, *Phenomenology*, pp. xiii–xliii.

Bakunin, Mikhail. "The Paris Commune and the Idea of the State." Marx, Bakunin, and Kropotkin, pp. 75–87.

——. *Statism and Anarchy.* Translated and edited by Marshall S. Shatz, Cambridge UP, 1999.

Barthes, Roland. *Mythologies.* Translated by Annette Lavers, Hill and Wang, 1972.

Bartolovich, Crystal. "Humanities of Scale: Marxism, Surface Reading—and Milton." *PMLA*, vol. 127, no. 1, Jan. 2012, pp. 115–21.

——. "Organizing the (Un)Common." *Angelaki: Journal of Theoretical Humanities*, vol. 12, no. 3, 2007, pp. 81–104.

Barzun, Jacques. *Classic, Romantic, and Modern.* U of Chicago P, 1975.

——. *Romanticism and the Modern Ego.* Little, Brown, 1943.

Benhabib, Seyla. *The Rights of Others: Aliens, Residents and Citizens.* Cambridge UP, 2004.

Bentham, Jeremy. *An Introduction to the Principles of Morals and Legislation.* Dover Publications, 2007.

Berlant, Lauren. *Cruel Optimism.* Duke UP, 2011.

Berlin, Isaiah. *The Roots of Romanticism.* Edited by Henry Hardy, Princeton UP, 1999.

Best, Stephen, and Sharon Marcus, editors. *The Way We Read Now.* Spec. issue of *Representations,* no. 108, Fall 2009.

Blair, Hugh. *Lectures on Rhetoric and Belles Lettres.* Edited by Linda Ferreira-Buckley and S. Michael Halloran, Southern Illinois UP, 2005.

Bonneuil, Christophe, and Jean-Baptiste Fressoz. *The Shock of the Anthropocene: The Earth, History and Us.* Translated by David Fernbach, Verso, 2017.

Bosteels, Bruno. *The Actuality of Communism.* Verso, 2011.

Bourdieu, Pierre. "Cultural Reproduction and Social Reproduction." *Power and Ideology in Education,* edited by Jerome Karabel and A. H. Halsey, Oxford UP, 1977, pp. 487–511.

———. *Distinction: A Social Critique of the Judgement of Taste.* Translated by Richard Nice, Harvard UP, 1984.

Bourdieu, Pierre, and Jean Claude Passeron. *Reproduction in Education, Society, and Culture.* Translated by Richard Nice, Sage, 1977.

Bousquet, Marc. *How the University Works: Higher Education and the Low-Wage Nation.* New York UP, 2008.

Bracha, Oren. "The Ideology of Authorship Revisited: Authors, Markets, and Liberal Values in Early American Copyright." *Yale Law Journal,* vol. 118, no. 2, Nov. 2008, pp. 186–271.

Brooks, Cleanth. *The Well Wrought Urn.* Harcourt, Brace, 1947.

Brown, Wendy. *Undoing the Demos: Neoliberalism's Stealth Revolution.* Zone Books, 2015.

Bryson, Bill. *A Short History of Nearly Everything.* Broadway Books, 2003.

Buck-Morss, Susan. *Hegel, Haiti, and Universal History.* U of Pittsburgh P, 2009.

Butler, Judith. "Competing Universalities." Butler, Laclau, and Žižek, pp. 136–81.

———. *Notes toward a Performative Theory of Assembly.* Harvard UP, 2015.

———. "Restaging the Universal: Hegemony and the Limits of Formalism." Butler, Laclau, and Žižek, pp. 11–43.

Butler, Judith, Ernesto Laclau, and Slavoj Žižek. *Contingency, Hegemony, Universality: Contemporary Dialogues on the Left*. Verso, 2000.

Canfora, Luciano. *The Vanished Library: A Wonder of the Ancient World*. Translated by Martin Ryle, U of California P, 1989.

Cascardi, Anthony J. *The Cambridge Introduction to Literature and Philosophy*. Cambridge UP, 2014.

Chakrabarty, Dipesh. *Provincializing Europe: Postcolonial Thought and Historical Difference*. Princeton UP, 2000.

Cintrón, Ralph. "Abandon All Hope Ye Who Enter Here: Democracy and Climate Change." *Works and Days*, nos. 70/71, 2018, pp. 189–211.

Cline, Eric H. *1177 B.C.: The Year Civilization Collapsed*. Princeton UP, 2014.

Cole, Andrew. *The Birth of Theory*. U of Chicago P, 2014.

Coleridge, Samuel Taylor. *Biographia Literaria, or Biographical Sketches of My Literary Life and Opinions*. Edited by George Watson, J. M. Dent & Sons, 1965.

———. *Lay Sermons*. Edited by R. J. White, Princeton UP and Routledge & Kegan Paul, 1972. Vol. 6 of *The Collected Works of Samuel Taylor Coleridge*.

———. *On the Constitution of the Church and State*. Edited by John Colmer, Princeton UP and Routledge & Kegan Paul, 1976. Vol. 10 of *The Collected Works of Samuel Taylor Coleridge*.

———. *Poetical Works*. Edited by J. C. C. Mays, Princeton UP and Routledge & Kegan Paul, 2001. Vol. 16 of *The Collected Works of Samuel Taylor Coleridge*.

———. "Shakespeare's Judgment Equal to His Genius." Adams, pp. 460–62.

Collini, Stefan. *What Are Universities For?* Penguin Books, 2012.

The Compact Edition of the Oxford English Dictionary. 2 vols. Oxford UP, 1971.

Connors, Robert J. *Composition-Rhetoric: Backgrounds, Theory, and Pedagogy*. U of Pittsburgh P, 1997.

Corbett, Edward P. J. Introduction. Aristotle, *The Rhetoric*, pp. v–xxvi.

Crenshaw, Kimberlé. "Demarginalizing the Intersection of Race and Sex: A Black Feminist Critique of Antidiscrimination Doctrine, Feminist Theory and Antiracist Politics." *The University of Chicago Legal Forum*. Spec. issue, *Feminism in the Law: Theory, Practice and Criticism*, 1989, pp. 139–68.

Crutzen, Paul J., and Eugene F. Stoermer. "The 'Anthropocene.'" *Global Change Newsletter*, no. 41, May 2000, pp. 17–18.

Daniell, Beth. "Narratives of Literacy: Connecting Composition to Culture." *College Composition and Communication*, vol. 50, no. 3, Feb. 1999, pp. 393–410.

Danius, Sara, and Stefan Jonsson. "An Interview with Gayatri Chakravorty Spivak." *Boundary 2*, vol. 20, no. 2, Summer 1993, pp. 24–50.

Darwin, Charles. *The Descent of Man, and Selection in Relation to Sex.* Wilson, pp. 767–1248.

———. *On the Origin of Species*. Wilson, pp. 441–760.

Davies, Jeremy. *The Birth of the Anthropocene*. U of California P, 2016.

Dean, Jodi. *The Communist Horizon*. Verso, 2012.

Debord, Guy. *The Society of the Spectacle*. Translated by Donald Nicholson-Smith, Zone Books, 1995.

Denning, Michael. *Culture in the Age of Three Worlds*. Verso, 2004.

Derrida, Jacques. *Dissemination*. Translated by Barbara Johnson, U of Chicago P, 1981.

———. *Ethics, Institutions, and the Right to Philosophy*. Translated by Peter Pericles Trifonas, Rowman and Littlefield Publishers, 2002.

———. *Eyes of the University: Right to Philosophy 2*. Translated by Jan Plug and others, Stanford UP, 2004.

———. "White Mythology: Metaphor in the Text of Philosophy." Translated by F. C. T. Moore, *New Literary History*, vol. 6, no. 1, Autumn 1974, pp. 5–74.

Desmond, Adrian, and James Moore. *Darwin: The Life of a Tormented Evolutionist*. Warner, 1992.

Desmond, Matthew. *Evicted: Poverty and Profit in the American City.* Crown Publishers, 2016.

Dewey, John. *The Influence of Darwin on Philosophy and Other Essays in Contemporary Thought.* Indiana UP, 1965.

———. *The Quest for Certainty: A Study of the Relation of Knowledge and Action.* Capricorn, 1960.

Diamond, Jared M. *Guns, Germs, and Steel: The Fates of Human Societies.* W. W. Norton, 1999.

Donaldson, Susan V. "Introduction: The Southern Agrarians and Their Cultural Wars." *I'll Take My Stand: The South and the Agrarian Tradition,* by "twelve Southerners." 75th anniversary ed., Louisiana State UP, 2006, pp. ix–xl.

Douglass, Frederick. "[What to the Slave Is the Fourth of July?]" Untitled speech delivered 5 July 1852, Rochester, NY. http://www.mass humanities.org/files/programs/douglass/speech_abridged_med.pdf

Douzinas, Costas, and Slavoj Žižek, editors. *The Idea of Communism.* Verso, 2010.

Downing, David B. "Ancients and Moderns: Literary Theory and the History of Criticism." *Teaching Contemporary Theory to Undergraduates.* Edited by Dianne F. Sadoff and William E. Cain, MLA, 1994, pp. 31–44.

———. *The Knowledge Contract: Politics and Paradigms in the Academic Workplace.* U of Nebraska P, 2005.

Dubrow, Heather. Foreword. Theile and Tredennick, pp. vii–xviii.

Eagleton, Terry. *The Ideology of the Aesthetic.* Basil Blackwell, 1990.

———. "In the Gaudy Supermarket." *London Review of Books,* vol. 21, no. 10, 13 May 1999, pp. 3–6.

———. *Literary Theory: An Introduction.* U of Minnesota P, 1983.

Eliot, T. S. *Notes towards the Definition of Culture.* Faber and Faber, 1973.

Erdman, David V., editor. *The Poetry and Prose of William Blake.* Doubleday, 1970.

Evans, Nicholas. *Dying Words: Endangered Languages and What They Have to Tell Us.* Wiley-Blackwell, 2010.

Eze, Emmanuel Chukwudi. *Race and the Enlightenment: A Reader.* Blackwell, 1997.

Felski, Rita. *The Limits of Critique*. U of Chicago P, 2015.

Ferguson, Niall. *The Ascent of Money: A Financial History of the World*. Penguin Books, 2008.

Fetridge, W. Pembroke. *The Rise and Fall of the Paris Commune in 1871: With a Full Account of the Bombardment, Capture, and Burning of the City*. Harper & Brothers, 1871.

Forbes, Duncan. Introduction. Hegel, *Lectures*, pp. vii–xxxv.

Foucault, Michel. *The Birth of Biopolitics: Lectures at the Collège de France, 1978–79*. Ed. Michel Senellart, Palgrave Macmillan, 2004.

———. *The History of Sexuality: An Introduction*. Translated by Robert Hurley, Vintage, 1990.

———. "What Is an Author?" *Language, Counter-Memory, Practice: Selected Essays and Interviews*. Edited by Donald F. Bouchard, translated by Donald F. Bouchard and Sherry Simon, Cornell UP, 1977, pp. 113–38.

Fraser, Nancy. "Contradictions of Capital and Care." *New Left Review*, no. 100, July/Aug 2016, pp. 99–117.

Fraser, Nancy, and Sarah Leonard. "Capitalism's Crisis of Care: A Conversation with Nancy Fraser." *Dissent*, Fall 2016, pp. 30–37.

Freire, Paulo. *Pedagogy of the Oppressed*. Translated by Myra Bergman Ramos, 30th anniversary ed., Continuum, 2000.

Freud, Sigmund. "Fetishism." *Miscellaneous Papers, 1888–1938*. Hogarth Press and Institute of Psycho-Analysis, 1927, pp. 198–204. Vol. 5 of *Collected Papers of Sigmund Freud*, edited by James Strachey.

Frye, Northrop. *Anatomy of Criticism: Four Essays*. Princeton UP, 2000.

Furet, François. *Interpreting the French Revolution*. Translated by Elborg Forster, Cambridge UP, 1981.

Gabriel, Mary. *Love and Capital: Karl and Jenny Marx and the Birth of a Revolution*. Little, Brown, 2011.

Gilbert, Scott F. "Holobiont by Birth: Multilineage Individuals as the Concretion of Cooperative Processes." Tsing et al. M73–M89.

Global Language Monitor. https://www.languagemonitor.com/global-english/no-of-words/

Gluckstein, Donny. *The Paris Commune: A Revolution in Democracy.* Haymarket Books, 2011.

Godwin, William. *Enquiry Concerning Political Justice, and Its Influence on Morals and Happiness.* Forgotten Books, 2015.

Goldstein, Evan R. "The Would-Be Philosopher-King." *Chronicle of Higher Education,* 4 Nov. 2013.

Goodman, Robin Truth. *Gender Work: Feminism after Neoliberalism.* Palgrave Macmillan, 2013.

Gould, Stephen Jay. "Darwin at Sea." *The McGraw-Hill Reader.* Edited by Gilbert H. Muller, 2nd ed., McGraw-Hill, 1985, pp. 570–80.

Goulimari, Pelagia. *Literary Criticism and Theory: From Plato to Post-colonialism.* Routledge, 2015.

Graeber, David. *Debt: The First 5,000 Years.* Melville House, 2011.

Green, Peter. *Alexander of Macedon, 356–323 B.C.: A Historical Biography.* U of California P, 1991.

Gregor, Mary J. Translator's introduction. Kant, *Conflict,* pp. vii–xxxiv.

Gregory, John. *A Father's Legacy to His Daughters.* Garland, 1974.

Habermas, Jürgen. *Knowledge and Human Interests.* Translated by Jeremy J. Shapiro, Beacon Press, 1972.

Habib, M. A. R. *A History of Literary Criticism and Theory: From Plato to the Present.* Blackwell, 2008.

———. *Literary Criticism from Plato to the Present: An Introduction.* Wiley-Blackwell, 2011.

Haraway, Donna J. *Staying with the Trouble: Making Kin in the Chthulucene.* Duke UP, 2016.

Hardt, Michael, and Antonio Negri. *Assembly.* Oxford UP, 2017.

———. *Multitude: War and Democracy in the Age of Empire.* Penguin Books, 2004.

Harland, Richard. *Literary Theory from Plato to Barthes: An Introductory History.* St. Martin's Press, 1999.

Harman, Chris. *A People's History of the World.* Verso, 2017.

Harrington, Michael. *Socialism: Past and Future.* Arcade, 2011.

Harvey, David. *A Brief History of Neoliberalism*. Oxford UP, 2007.

———. *A Companion to Marx's* Capital. Verso, 2010.

———. *The Condition of Postmodernity: An Enquiry into the Origins of Cultural Change*. Blackwell, 1990.

———. *The Limits to Capital*. Verso, 1999.

———. *Paris, Capital of Modernity*. Routledge, 2005.

———. *Rebel Cities: From the Right to the City to the Urban Revolution*. Verso, 2012.

———. *Seventeen Contradictions and the End of Capitalism*. Oxford UP, 2014.

Havelock, Eric A. *The Greek Concept of Justice: From Its Shadow in Homer to Its Substance in Plato*. Harvard UP, 1978.

———. *The Origins of Western Literacy: Four Lectures Delivered at the Ontario Institute for Studies in Education, Toronto, March 25, 26, 27, 28, 1974*. Ontario Institute for Studies in Education, 1976.

———. *Preface to Plato*. Harvard UP, 1963.

Hawthorne, Nathaniel. *The Blithedale Romance*. W. W. Norton, 1958.

Hayden, Tom. "Participatory Democracy: From the Port Huron Statement to Occupy Wall Street." *The Nation*, 16 Apr. 2012, pp. 11–23.

Hegel, Georg Wilhelm Friedrich. *Hegel's Philosophy of Right*. Translated by T. M. Knox, Oxford UP, 1981.

———. *Lectures on the Philosophy of World History. Introduction: Reason in History*. Translated by H. B. Nisbet, Cambridge UP, 1975.

———. *The Phenomenology of Mind*. Translated by J. B. Baillie, 2nd rev. ed., Dover Publications, 2003.

———. *The Science of Logic*. Translated by William Wallace, Hythloday Press, 2014.

Heilbroner, Robert L. *The Worldly Philosophers: The Lives, Times, and Ideas of the Great Economic Thinkers*. Rev. 7th ed., Simon & Schuster, 1999.

Henderson, William Otto. *Marx and Engels and the English Workers and Other Essays*. Cass, 1989.

Herman, Arthur. *The Cave and the Light: Plato versus Aristotle, and the Struggle for the Soul of Western Civilization*. Random House, 2014.

Hesiod. *Theogony*. Translated by Norman O. Brown. Prentice Hall, 1953.

Hirschman, Albert O. *The Passions and the Interests: Political Arguments for Capitalism before Its Triumph*. 20th anniversary ed., Princeton UP, 1997.

Hobsbawm, Eric J. *The Age of Capital, 1848–1875*. Random House, 1996.

———. *The Age of Revolution, 1789–1848*. Vintage, 1996.

———. *Industry and Empire: From 1750 to the Present Day*. Penguin Books, 1969.

Horne, Alistair. *The Fall of Paris: The Siege and the Commune 1870–71*. Rev. ed., Penguin Books, 2007.

Hyman, Stanley Edgar. *The Armed Vision: A Study in the Methods of Modern Literary Criticism*. Rev. ed., Vintage, 1955.

Jameson, Fredric. *The Cultural Turn: Selected Writings on the Postmodern, 1983–1988*. Verso, 2009.

———. "Marxist Criticism and Hegel." *PMLA*, vol. 131, no. 2, Mar. 2016, pp. 430–38.

———. *The Political Unconscious: Narrative as a Socially Symbolic Act*. Cornell UP, 1981.

———. *Postmodernism, or, the Cultural Logic of Late Capitalism*. Duke UP, 1992.

Jarman, Mark, and David Mason, editors. *Rebel Angels: 25 Poets of the New Formalism*. Story Line Press, 1996.

Jarratt, Susan C. *Rereading the Sophists: Classical Rhetoric Refigured*. Southern Illinois UP, 1998.

Jarrell, Randall. "The Age of Criticism." *Poetry and the Age*. Knopf, 1953, pp. 70–95.

Jaspers, Karl. *The Origin and Goal of History*. Routledge, 2010.

Jaszi, Peter, and Martha Woodmansee. Introduction. Woodmansee and Jaszi, pp. 1–13.

Jencks, Christopher, and David Riesman. *The Academic Revolution.* Doubleday, 1968.

Jockers, Matthew L. *Macroanalysis: Digital Methods and Literary History.* U of Illinois P, 2013.

Kant, Immanuel. *The Conflict of the Faculties.* Translated by Mary J. Gregor, U of Nebraska P, 1992.

———. *Critique of Judgment.* Translated by J. H. Bernard, Dover Publications, 2005.

———. *Critique of Practical Reason.* Translated by Thomas Kingsmill Abbott, Dover Publications, 2004.

———. *Critique of Pure Reason.* Translated by Marcus Weigelt, Penguin Books, 2007.

———. *Kant: Political Writings.* Edited by Hans Reiss, translated by H. B. Nisbet, 2nd ed., Cambridge UP, 1991.

———. *Observations on the Feeling of the Beautiful and Sublime.* Translated by John T. Goldthwait, U of California P, 2004.

———. *Prolegomena to Any Future Metaphysics.* Translated by James W. Ellington, Hackett Publishing, 2001.

Karatani, Kojin. *The Structure of World History: From Modes of Production to Modes of Exchange.* Translated by Michael K. Bourdaghs, Duke UP, 2014.

Kasparov, Garry, and Thor Halvorssen. "The Rise of Authoritarianism Is a Global Catastrophe." *Pittsburgh Post-Gazette*, 19 Feb. 2017, pp. D-1+.

Kaufmann, Walter, editor and translator. *The Portable Nietzsche.* Penguin Books, 1982.

Kenny, Anthony. *Ancient Philosophy.* Oxford UP, 2004. Vol. 1 of *A New History of Western Philosophy.*

Kerr, Clark. *The Uses of the University.* Harper, 1963.

Klein, Naomi. *No Is Not Enough: Resisting Trump's Shock Politics and Winning the World We Need.* Haymarket Books, 2017.

———. *This Changes Everything: Capitalism vs. the Climate.* Simon & Schuster, 2015.

Kolbert, Elizabeth. *The Sixth Extinction: An Unnatural History*. Picador, 2014.

Kuhn, Thomas S. *The Structure of Scientific Revolutions*. 2nd ed., U of Chicago P, 1970.

Kuiken, Kir. *Imagined Sovereignties: Toward a New Political Romanticism*. Fordham UP, 2014.

Lacan, Jacques. *Écrits: The First Complete Edition in English*. Translated by Bruce Fink, W. W. Norton, 2007.

Larsen, Neil. "Literature, Immanent Critique, and the Problem of Standpoint." Nilges and Sauri, pp. 63–78.

Latour, Bruno. *Reassembling the Social: An Introduction to Actor-Network-Theory*. Oxford UP, 2007.

Leavis, F. R. *The Great Tradition: George Eliot, Henry James, Joseph Conrad*. Penguin Books, 1972.

———. *New Bearings in English Poetry*. Faber and Faber, 2008.

Lenin, V. I. *The Proletarian Revolution and the Renegade Kautsky*. Communist Press, 1918.

———. *State and Revolution*. 2nd ed., International Publishers, 1943.

Lepore, Jill. "The Disruption Machine: What the Gospel of Innovation Gets Wrong." *The New Yorker*, 23 June 2014.

Levine, Caroline. *Forms: Whole, Rhythm, Hierarchy, Network*. Princeton UP, 2015.

———. "Model Thinking: Generalization, Political Form, and the Common Good." *New Literary History*, vol. 48, no. 4, Autumn 2017, pp. 633–53.

Levinson, Marjorie. "What Is New Formalism?" *PMLA*, vol. 122, no. 2, Mar. 2007, pp. 558–69.

Lissagaray, Prosper Olivier. *History of the Paris Commune of 1871*. Translated by Eleanor Marx, Red and Black Publishers, 2007.

Loewen, James W. *Lies My Teacher Told Me: Everything Your American History Textbook Got Wrong*. Simon & Schuster, 1996.

Lord, Albert B. *The Singer of Tales*. Edited by David F. Elmer, 3rd ed., Center for Hellenic Studies, Harvard University, 2019.

Lyotard, Jean-François. *The Postmodern Condition: A Report on Knowledge*. Translated by Geoff Bennington and Brian Massumi, U of Minnesota P, 1984.

MacLean, Nancy. *Democracy in Chains: The Deep History of the Radical Right's Stealth Plan for America*. Scribe Publications, 2017.

Malthus, Thomas. *An Essay on the Principle of Population*. Edited by Geoffrey Gilbert, Oxford UP, 2008.

Marx, Karl. *Capital*. Edited by David McLellan, abridged ed., Oxford UP, 2008.

———. *The Civil War in France: The Paris Commune*. 2nd ed., International Publishers, 1988.

———. *Critique of the Gotha Programme*. Martin Lawrence, 1933.

———. *Critique of Hegel's "Philosophy of Right."* Translated by Annette Jolin and Joseph O'Malley, Cambridge UP, 1970.

———. *The Poverty of Philosophy*. https://www.marxists.org/archive/marx/works/1847/poverty-philosophy

Marx, Karl, Mikhail Bakunin, and Peter Kropotkin. *Writings on the Paris Commune*. Red and Black Publishers, 2008.

Mayer, Jane. *Dark Money: The Hidden History of the Billionaires behind the Rise of the Radical Right*. Anchor, 2017.

McLellan, David. *Karl Marx: Selected Writings*. 2nd ed., Oxford UP, 2000.

McMurtry, John. *The Cancer Stage of Capitalism: From Crisis to Cure*. 2nd ed., Pluto Press, 2013.

McPhillips, Robert. *The New Formalism: A Critical Introduction*. Expanded ed., Textos Books, 2005.

McSherry, Corynne. *Who Owns Academic Work? Battling for Control of Intellectual Property*. Harvard UP, 2001.

Mill, John Stuart. *Autobiography*. Penguin Books, 1989.

———. *On Liberty*. Edited by David Spitz, a Norton Critical Edition, W. W. Norton, 1975.

———. *Principles of Political Economy and Chapters on Socialism*. Oxford UP, 2008.

———. *The Subjection of Women.* MIT P, 1970.

Mills, C. Wright. *The Power Elite.* Oxford UP, 1999.

Mitchell, Timothy. *Carbon Democracy: Political Power in the Age of Oil.* Verso, 2013.

Mohanty, Chandra Talpade. *Feminism without Borders: Decolonizing Theory, Practicing Solidarity.* Duke UP, 2003.

Moretti, Franco, editor. *Canon/Archive: Studies in Quantitative Formalism from the Stanford Literary Lab.* n+1 Foundation, 2017.

———. *Distant Reading.* Verso, 2013.

———. "Fog." *New Left Review,* no. 81, May 2013, pp. 59–92.

Morris, Ian. *Why the West Rules—For Now: The Patterns of History, and What They Reveal about the Future.* Picador, 2010.

Morton, Timothy. *The Ecological Thought.* Harvard UP, 2010.

———. *Ecology without Nature: Rethinking Environmental Aesthetics.* Harvard UP, 2009.

———. *Hyperobjects: Philosophy and Ecology after the End of the World.* Minnesota UP, 2013.

Murphy, James J., editor. *A Short History of Writing Instruction from Ancient Greece to Modern America.* 2nd ed., Routledge, 2001.

Nancy, Jean-Luc. *Being Singular Plural.* Translated by Robert D. Richardson and Anne E. O'Byrne, Stanford UP, 2000.

Nealon, Christopher. "Reading on the Left." Best and Marcus, pp. 22–50.

Newfield, Christopher. *The Great Mistake: How We Wrecked Public Universities and How We Can Fix Them.* Johns Hopkins UP, 2016.

Nietzsche, Friedrich. *The Birth of Tragedy and Other Writings.* Edited by Raymond Geuss and Ronald Speirs, translated by Speirs, Cambridge UP, 1999.

———. *The Gay Science, with a Prelude in Rhymes and an Appendix of Songs.* Translated by Walter Kaufmann, Vintage, 1974.

———. *Human, All Too Human.* Translated by R. J. Hollingdale, Cambridge UP, 1996.

———. "On Truth and Lying in a Non-Moral Sense." Nietzsche, *Birth*, pp. 139–53.

———. *Thus Spoke Zarathustra: A Book for All and None*. Translated by Walter Kaufmann, Modern Library, 1995.

Nilges, Mathias, and Emilio Sauri, editors. *Literary Materialisms*. Palgrave Macmillan, 2013.

North, Joseph. *Literary Criticism: A Concise Political History*. Harvard UP, 2017.

Nye, John V. C. "Political Economy of Anglo-French Trade, 1689–1899: Agricultural Trade Policies, Alcohol Taxes, and War." AAWE Working Paper no. 38. American Association of Wine Economists, 2009.

Ong, Walter J. *Orality and Literacy: The Technologizing of the Word*. With additional chapters by John Hartley, 30th anniversary ed., Routledge, 2012.

Oreskes, Naomi, and Erik M. Conway. *Merchants of Doubt: How a Handful of Scientists Obscured the Truth on Issues from Tobacco Smoke to Global Warming*. Bloomsbury Press, 2010.

Ostrom, Elinor. *The Future of the Commons: Beyond Market Failure and Government Regulation*. Institute of Economic Affairs, 2012.

———. *Governing the Commons: The Evolution of Institutions for Collective Action*. Cambridge UP, 1990.

Owen, Robert. *A New View of Society: Essays on the Principle of the Formation of the Human Character, and the Application of the Principle to Practice*. Prism Key Press, 2013.

Oxford English Dictionary Online. OED.com.

Palumbo-Liu, David, Bruce Robbins, and Nirvana Tanoukhi, editors. *Immanuel Wallerstein and the Problem of the World: System, Scale, Culture*. Duke UP, 2011.

Parry, Adam, editor. *The Making of Homeric Verse: The Collected Papers of Milman Parry*. Oxford UP, 1987.

Patel, Raj. *The Value of Nothing: How to Reshape Market Society and Redesign Democracy*. Picador, 2010.

Peckham, Morse. *Romanticism and Ideology*. Wesleyan UP, 1995.

Pfau, Thomas. "The Pragmatics of Genre: Moral Theory and Lyric Authorship in Hegel and Wordsworth." Woodmansee and Jaszi, pp. 133–58.

Piketty, Thomas. *Capital in the Twenty-first Century*. Translated by Arthur Goldhammer, Harvard UP, 2014.

Pinkard, Terry. *Hegel: A Biography*. Cambridge UP, 2000.

Plato. *The Collected Dialogues of Plato, including the Letters*. Edited by Edith Hamilton and Huntington Cairns, Princeton UP, 1961.

———. *Phaedrus*. Translated by W. C. Helmbold and W. G. Rabinowitz, Bobbs-Merrill, 1956.

———. *The Republic and Other Works*. Translated by Benjamin Jowett, Anchor Books, 1973.

Polanyi, Karl. *The Great Transformation: The Political and Economic Origins of Our Time*. 2nd ed., Beacon Press, 2001.

Pope, Alexander. "An Essay on Criticism." Blackmask Online, 2003. http://www.searchengine.org.uk/ebooks/33/23.pdf

Poster, Mark. *Cultural History and Postmodernity: Disciplinary Readings and Challenges*. Columbia UP, 1997.

Powell, Barry B. *Writing: Theory and History of the Technology of Civilization*. Wiley-Blackwell, 2012.

Price, Munro. *The Road from Versailles: Louis XVI, Marie Antoinette, and the Fall of the French Monarchy*. St. Martin's Press, 2003.

Proudhon, Pierre-Joseph. *What Is Property? An Inquiry into the Principle of Right and of Government*. Forgotten Books, 2008.

Rajagopalachari, C. *Mahabharata*. P. V. Sankarankutty Dy. Registrar for Bharatiya Vidya Bhavan, 2005.

Rancière, Jacques. *Aesthetics and Its Discontents*. Polity, 2009.

Rand, Richard, editor. *Logomachia: The Conflict of the Faculties Today*. U of Nebraska P, 1992.

Readings, Bill. *The University in Ruins*. Harvard UP, 1996.

Reeve, C. D. C. Introduction. Aristotle, *Basic Works*, pp. xv–xxi.

Remnick, David. "One Hundred Days." *The New Yorker*, 1 May 2017, pp. 17–21.

Ricardo, David. *The Principles of Political Economy and Taxation.* Dover Publications, 2004.

Ricoeur, Paul. *Freud and Philosophy: An Essay on Interpretation.* Translated by Denis Savage, Yale UP, 1970.

Robbins, Bruce. *Perpetual War: Cosmopolitanism from the Viewpoint of Violence.* Duke: UP, 2012.

Romano, Carlin. *America the Philosophical.* Vintage, 2013.

Rose, Mark. *Authors and Owners: The Invention of Copyright.* Harvard UP, 1995.

———. "Nine-Tenths of the Law: The English Copyright Debates and the Rhetoric of the Public Domain." *Law and Contemporary Problems,* vol. 66, no. 1/2, Winter–Spring 2003, pp. 75–87.

Rosen, Ruth. "The Care Crisis." *The Nation,* 12 March 2007.

Ross, Kristin. *Communal Luxury: The Political Imaginary of the Paris Commune.* Verso, 2015.

———. *The Emergence of Social Space: Rimbaud and the Paris Commune.* Verso, 2008.

Russell, Bertrand. *A History of Western Philosophy.* Simon & Schuster, 1972.

Said, Edward. *Orientalism.* Vintage, 1979.

Saint-Simon, Claude Henri. *Lettres d'un habitant de Genève.* Hachette Livre, 2012.

San Juan, E., Jr. *Beyond Postcolonial Theory.* Palgrave Macmillan, 1997.

Say, Jean Baptiste. *A Treatise on Political Economy, or, the Production, Distribution, and Consumption of Wealth.* Translated by C. R. Prinsep, Longman, Hurst, Rees, Orme and Brown, 1821.

Schmitt, Carl. *Political Romanticism.* Translated by Guy Oakes, MIT P, 1986.

Schopenhauer, Arthur. *The World as Will and Representation.* Translated by E. F. J. Payne, vol. 1, Dover Publications, 1969.

Schragel, Jeffrey. *An Ecocritical Examination of British Romantic Natural History Writing.* 2010. Indiana U of Pennsylvania, PhD dissertation.

Scott, Joan W. "How the Right Weaponized Free Speech." *Chronicle of Higher Education.* 7 Jan. 2018, pp. B9–11.

Sedgwick, Eve Kosofsky. *Touching Feeling: Affect, Pedagogy, Performativity.* Duke UP, 2003.

Shawcross, J. Introduction. *Biographia Literaria,* by Samuel Taylor Coleridge, edited by Shawcross, Oxford UP, 1965, pp. xi–lxxxix.

Shell, Marc. *The Economy of Literature.* Johns Hopkins UP, 1993.

Shelley, Percy Bysshe. *A Defence of Poetry.* Adams, pp. 498–513.

Simpson, David. *Wordsworth, Commodification and Social Concern: The Poetics of Modernity.* Cambridge UP, 2009.

Sinfield, Alan. *Faultlines: Cultural Materialism and the Politics of Dissident Reading.* California UP, 1992.

Smith, Adam. *Lectures on Rhetoric and Belles Lettres.* Edited by J. C. Bryce, Oxford UP, 1976. Vol. 4 of *The Glasgow Edition of the Works and Correspondence of Adam Smith,* general editor, A. S. Skinner.

———. *The Wealth of Nations.* Bantam Books, 2003.

Snow, C. P. *The Two Cultures and the Scientific Revolution.* Martino Fine Books, 2013.

Spivak, Gayatri Chakravorty. *An Aesthetic Education in the Era of Globalization.* Harvard UP, 2013.

———. "Can the Subaltern Speak?" *Marxism and the Interpretation of Culture.* Edited by Cary Nelson and Lawrence Grossberg, U of Illinois P, 1988, pp. 271–313.

———. *In Other Worlds: Essays in Cultural Politics.* Routledge, 2006.

Srnicek, Nick. *Platform Capitalism.* Polity Press, 2017.

Steffen, Will, Paul J. Crutzen, and John R. McNeill. "The Anthropocene: Are Humans Now Overwhelming the Great Forces of Nature?" *Ambio,* vol. 36, no. 8, Dec. 2007, pp. 614–21.

Stevens, Anne H. *Literary Theory and Criticism: An Introduction.* Broadview Press, 2015.

Streeck, Wolfgang. *How Will Capitalism End? Essays on a Failing System.* Verso, 2016.

Strunk, William, Jr., and E. B. White. *The Elements of Style*. 4th ed., Pearson, 1999.

Stuurman, Siep. *The Invention of Humanity: Equality and Cultural Difference in World History*. Harvard UP, 2017.

Swanson, Heather, Anna Tsing, Nils Bubandt, and Elaine Gan. "Introduction: Bodies Tumbled into Bodies." Tsing et al., pp. M1–M12.

Theile, Verena, and Linda Tredennick. *New Formalisms and Literary Theory*. Palgrave Macmillan, 2013.

Trumble, Kelly. *The Library of Alexandria*. Illustrated by Robina M. Marshall, Clarion Books, 2003.

Tsing, Anna Lowenhaupt. *The Mushroom at the End of the World: On the Possibility of Life in Capitalist Ruins*. Princeton UP, 2015.

Tsing, Anna, Heather Swanson, Elaine Gan, and Nils Bubandt, editors. *Arts of Living on a Damaged Planet*. 2 vols., U of Minnesota P, 2017.

United States, Dept. of Justice, Federal Bureau of Prisons. "Inmate Race." https://www.bop.gov/about/statistics/statistics_inmate_race.jsp

Universal Declaration of Human Rights. United Nations. http://www.un.org/en/universal-declaration-human-rights/

Wallerstein, Immanuel. *European Universalism: The Rhetoric of Power*. New Press, 2006.

———. *World-Systems Analysis: An Introduction*. Duke UP, 2004.

Wallis, Victor. "Capitalism Unhinged: Crisis of Legitimacy in the United States." *Socialism and Democracy*, vol. 31, no. 3, Nov. 2017, pp. 11–23.

Watson, George. Introduction. Coleridge, *Biographia Literaria,* pp. ix–xxii.

Weigelt, Marcus. Introduction. Kant, *Critique of Pure Reason*, pp. xv–lxix.

White, Curtis. *The Barbaric Heart: Faith, Money, and the Crisis of Nature*. PoliPointPress, 2009.

———. *The Middle Mind: Why Americans Don't Think for Themselves*. Harper One, 2004.

White, R. J. Editor's introduction. Coleridge, *Lay Sermons*, pp. xxix–xlvii.

Williams, Jeffrey J. "Criticism Live: The History and Practice of the Critical Interview." Spec. issue on Literary Interviews. *Biography*, vol. 41, no.2, 2018, pp. 235–55.

———. "Innovation for What? The Politics of Inequality in Higher Education." *Dissent*, Winter 2016.

———. "The Post–Welfare State University." *American Literary History*, vol. 18, no. 1, Spring 2006, pp. 190–216.

Williams, Raymond. *Keywords: A Vocabulary of Culture and Society*. Oxford UP, 1976.

———. *The Long Revolution*. Broadview Press, 2001.

———. *Marxism and Literature*. Oxford UP, 1978.

Wilson, Edward O., editor. *From So Simple a Beginning: The Four Great Books of Charles Darwin*. W. W. Norton, 2006.

Wolff, Richard. *Democracy at Work: A Cure for Capitalism*. Haymarket Books, 2012.

Wollstonecraft, Mary. *An Historical and Moral View of the Origin and Progress of the French Revolution and the Effect It Has Produced in Europe*. Scholars' Facsimiles and Reprints, 1975.

———. *A Vindication of the Rights of Woman*. Edited by Carol Poston, a Norton Critical Edition, 2nd ed., W. W. Norton, 1988.

Wood, Ellen Meiksins. *Citizens to Lords: A Social History of Western Political Thought from Antiquity to the Late Middle Ages*. Verso, 2011.

———. *The Origin of Capitalism: A Longer View*. Rev. ed., Verso, 2017.

———. *Peasant-Citizen and Slave: The Foundations of Athenian Democracy*. Verso, 1989.

Woodmansee, Martha. *The Author, Art, and the Market: Rereading the History of Aesthetics*. Columbia UP, 1994.

Woodmansee, Martha, and Peter Jaszi, editors. *The Construction of Authorship: Textual Appropriation in Law and Literature*. Duke UP, 1994.

Wordsworth, Dorothy. *Journals of Dorothy Wordsworth.* http://www
.archive.org/stream/journalsofdoroth027709mbp/journalsofdoro-
th027709mbp_djvu.txt

Wordsworth, William. *The Collected Poems of William Wordsworth.*
Wordsworth Poetry Library, 1998.

————. "Preface to the Second Edition of *Lyrical Ballads.*" Adams,
pp. 432–43.

————. *The Prelude; Or, Growth of a Poet's Mind.* Wordsworth, *Collected,* pp. 750–893.

World Wide Words. http://www.worldwidewords.org/articles/how
many.htm.

Yancy, George. *What White Looks Like: African American Philosophers
on the* Whiteness *Question.* Routledge, 2004.

Zuboff, Shoshana. "Big Other: Surveillance Capitalism and the Prospects
of an Information Civilization." *Journal of Information Technology,*
vol. 30, no. 1, Mar. 2015, pp. 75–89.

INDEX

Note: A "t" following a page number indicates a table; an "f" indicates a figure.

on Marx, 406n2
on Paris Commune, 294
on political economy of Holo-
    cene, 16
on Proudhon, 264
on Romanticism, 7
on state ownership and capital-
    ism, 313
Kasparov, Garry, 378
Kaufmann, Walter, 337, 347,
    348, 349, 350
Kautsky, Karl, 315–17
Kerr, Clark, 367–68
Keynes, John Maynard, 360
Klein, Naomi, xxii, 352, 378,
    387n23
Kolbert, Elizabeth, 355
Kropotkin, Peter, 264
"Kubla Khan" (Coleridge), 199
Kuhn, Thomas, 414n19
Kuiken, Kir, 202

Labor theory of value, 286
Labor unions. *See* Workers'
    unions
Lacan, Jacques, 384n1
Laclau, Ernesto, 4
Laissez-faire, 153, 244, 282,
    403n3
Lassalle, Ferdinand, 315
Law, John, 220–21, 230, 232–36
The Laws (Plato), 33
Leavis, F. R., 397–98n12
*Lectures on the Philosophy of
    World History* (Hegel),
    277–79
Lenin, Vladimir, 316–17, 409n26
Levine, Caroline, 5
Liberalism
    and capitalism, 152
    formation of, 152
    and hierarchy vs. communal-
        ity, 13, 14
    and Romantic idealism, 154
Linguistic transparency, 92

Literacy
    and abstract concepts, 73–75
    and cognitive development,
        72–73
    and copula verb form, 73–74
    emergence of, in ancient
        Greece, 68–76
    extent of, in ancient Greece,
        392n13
    invention of alphabets, 68–69
Literary critics, 397–98n12. *See
    also* New Critics
Literature. *See also* Poetry and
    drama
    vs. composition, in English de-
        partments, 8, 22, 209–10,
        214–15, 217
    as divorced from sociohistori-
        cal context, 255, 366–69
    multiple meanings of, 155–56
    Romantic meaning of, 208
Logic, laws of, 111
Lord, Albert, 390n2
Louis XVI, 227, 228
Louverture, Toussaint, 267
Low culture, 156, 210
Lyell, Charles, 324, 328
Lyotard, François, 6

Mahabharata, 4, 338–39
Malthus, Thomas, 247, 326
Marcus, Sharon, 413–14n16
*Maria, or The Wrongs of
    Woman* (Wollstonecraft),
    243–44
Market economy, 152–53. *See
    also* Capitalism
"The Marriage of Heaven and
    Hell" (Blake)
    and brutality of capitalism,
        157–59
    cave in, vs. Plato's cave al-
        legory, 157–58
    as critique of Western meta-
        physical formalism,
        156–57

257–59
virtues of, 408n20
Social justice and equality
and communality, 12
and "just theory," xix–xx,
373–74
and Paris Commune, 319
Social reproduction, 357–59,
363–65, 381
Sociohistorical context
economics as divorced from,
246, 254–55
of irony, 86–87
necessity of, 92–93
and orality/literacy shift, 81
of Platonic view of poetry,
53–57
poetry as freed from, in *Poetics* (Aristotle), 121, 126,
128–29
of *The Republic* (Plato), 79
transcendence of, and Romantic idealism, 208
Solon, 60
"A Song of Liberty" (Blake), 164
Sophocles, 122, 125–26
Southey, Robert, 193
Spencer, Herbert, 331
Spivak, Gayatri
and aesthetics vs. politics,
208–9
on "epistemic violence," 5
reading of *The Prelude* (Wordsworth), 216–19, 401n2,
402nn7–8
on "strategic essentialism," 74,
385n5, 392–93n14
The Statesman's Manual
(Coleridge), 194–95
Steffen, Will, 147
Stoermer, Eugene, 147
Strauss, David, 269
Streeck, Wolfgang, 373, 411n2
The Subjection of Women (Mill),
253

Substance, as concept, 107–10,
180–81
Subsumption, 288
Sulloway, Frank, 409–10n1
Surplus value, 286–88, 318
Swanson, Heather, 6
Syllogism, 110–11

Theory. *See* "Just theory"
Third Estate, 228–29, 402n11
Thus Spoke Zarathustra
(Nietzsche), 344–45
Trade unions. *See* Workers'
unions
Transcendence
discourses of, 4
Kant's view of, 181
nature as Romantic goal,
160–61
and Plato's forms, 48
and racism, 385n6
and universalism, 5–6
variable meanings of, 7
and Western metaphysical
metaphors of rising, 49–51
in Wordsworth's *Prelude*,
223–26
Tsing, Anna, xiv, 11, 378,
381–82

Übermensch, 347, 350–51
Unions. *See* Workers' unions
United Nations Universal
Declaration of Human
Rights (1948), 306
Universalism. *See also* Western
metaphysics
and Aristotelian view of poetry, 123
and binary split of subject vs.
object, 78–79
and climate change, 9–10
and Coleridge, 197–98
and discourse of aesthetics,
183

Women
  Aristotle on role of, 132–33
  capitalist exploitation of, 289
  education of, 238–39, 241–43
  and evolutionary theory, 334
  Mill on role of, 253
  and Paris Commune, 306–7
  Plato on role of, 51
  Wood on role of, 390n17
Women's Union, 306–7
Wood, Ellen Meiksins
  on Aristotle, 28
  on coinage, 391n4
  on Greek alphabet, 70
  on Homeric poetry, 60
  on inequality, 52
  on market economy, 153
  on Plato, 45–46, 51
  and Platonic irony, 33
  on similarities of Plato and
    Aristotle, 112
  on slavery, 389n9
  on sociohistorical context, 93
  on women's role, 390n17
Woodhull, Victoria, 289
Woodmansee, Martha, 176
Wordsworth, Dorothy, 170–72,
  175–76
Wordsworth, William. *See also*
  specific works
  adaptation of sister's prose,
  171–72

aesthetic theory, 220–21
and Coleridge, 193–94
concerns about authorship,
  176
and French Revolution, 207
and Mill, 252
on poetic genius, 201
shift of, from Romantic radical
  to idealist, 217–18, 236
works:
  "I Wandered Lonely as a
    Cloud," 170–71, 175–76
  "Preface" to *Lyrical Bal-
    lads*, 164–70
  The Prelude, 209–10,
    216–26
  "A Slumber Did My Spirit
    Seal," 160
Workers' unions, 262, 299
Writing. *See also* Authorship
  "arche-writing," 101
  as collaborative vs. individual
    process, 173–74
  and meaning, 100–101
  Plato's ambivalence toward,
    85–86, 97, 99, 101–2

Yancy, George, 384n2, 385n6

Žižek, Slavoj, 4

AUTHOR

David B. Downing is Distinguished University Professor of English at Indiana University of Pennsylvania where he has been teaching for thirty years. His scholarship over the past two decades has contributed to what many have called Critical University Studies. As editor of the journal *Works and Days*, his recent special volumes have included, among others, "Information University: Rise of the Education Management Organization" (2003); "Education as Revolution" (2013); "Scholactivism: Reflections on Transforming Praxis Inside and Outside the Classroom" (2016); and "Capitalism, Climate Change, and Rhetoric" (2018). Downing is the author of *The Knowledge Contract: Politics and Paradigms in the Academic Workplace* (2010) and the editor or coeditor of *Academic Freedom in the Post-9/11 Era* (2010), *Beyond English, Inc.: Curricular Reform in a Global Economy* (2002), and several other books.

This book was typeset in Sabon by Barbara Frazier.
Typefaces used on the cover include Trajan Pro and Cochin.
The book was printed on 50-lb. White Offset paper
by Seaway Printing Company.